Leisure and Death

Leisure and Death

An Anthropological Tour of Risk, Death, and Dying

Edited by
ADAM KAUL AND JONATHAN SKINNER

UNIVERSITY PRESS OF COLORADO
Louisville

© 2018 by University Press of Colorado

Published by University Press of Colorado
245 Century Circle, Suite 202
Louisville, Colorado 80027

All rights reserved

 The University Press of Colorado is a proud member of the Association of University Presses.

The University Press of Colorado is a cooperative publishing enterprise supported, in part, by Adams State University, Colorado State University, Fort Lewis College, Metropolitan State University of Denver, Regis University, University of Colorado, University of Northern Colorado, Utah State University, and Western State Colorado University.

ISBN: 978-1-60732-788-2 (hardcover)
ISBN: 978-1-60732-728-8 (paperback)
ISBN: 978-1-60732-729-5 (ebook)
doi: https://doi.org/10.5876/9781607327295

Library of Congress Cataloging-in-Publication Data

Names: Kaul, Adam R., editor. | Skinner, Jonathan, 1970– editor.
Title: Leisure and death : an anthropological tour of risk, death, and dying / edited by Adam Kaul, Jonathan Skinner.
Description: Boulder, Colorado : University Press of Colorado, [2018] | Includes bibliographical references and index.
Identifiers: LCCN 2017041388| ISBN 9781607327882 (cloth) | ISBN 9781607327288 (pbk.) | ISBN 9781607327295 (ebook)
Subjects: LCSH: Dark tourism. | Death—Social aspects.
Classification: LCC G155.A1 L424 2018 | DDC 338.4/791—dc23
LC record available at https://lccn.loc.gov/2017041388

Cover illustration: Postcard of the Cliffs at Moher, County Clare, Ireland, ca. 1890–1900, from the Library of Congress Prints and Photographs Division, Washington, D.C. 20540. Digital ID: ppmsc 09847.

In memory of Cyril Schäfer

Contents

Leisurely Death and Dying? Body, Place, and the Limits to Leisure—a Prologue
  Jane C. Desmond   ix

Leisure and Death: An Introduction
  Adam Kaul and Jonathan Skinner   3

PART 1: LEISURE AND DEATH ON THE MOVE

1. Dying in a Strange Land: Tourism, Hospitality, and Promises to the Dead
   Maribeth Erb   41

2. Days of Wine and Walking: Leisure, Excess, and Authenticity on the Camino
   Keith Egan   58

3. Johan Huizinga Goes Tombstoning with the Devil
   Patrick Laviolette   77

PART 2: TOURIST ENCOUNTERS WITH THE DEAD

4. Leisure in the "Land of the Walking Dead": Western Mortuary Tourism, the Internet, and Zombie Pop Culture in Toraja, Indonesia
   Kathleen M. Adams   97

5. That "Awful Margin": Tourism, Risk, and Death at the Cliffs of Moher
   Adam Kaul   122

6. Tourism of Darkness and Light: Japanese Commemorative Tourism to Paradise
   Shingo Iitaka   141

Part 3: Life, Decay, and the Sensual Experience of Death

7. Memento Mori and Tourist Encounters with Authentic Death in European Ossuaries
   Cyril Schäfer with Ruth McManus   163

8. Parading through the Storm: Risk, Death, and Parades in Northern Ireland
   Ray Casserly   190

9. How to Eat an Endangered Species: Gastronomic Tourism and Cinta Senese Pigs
   Rachel A. Horner Brackett   206

Part 4: Afterlife and After-Leisure

10. The Social Life of the Dead and the Leisured Life of the Living Online
    Tamara Kohn, Michael Arnold, Martin Gibbs, James Meese, and Bjorn Nansen   227

11. Rumor Has It: Leisure, Gossip, and Distortion at Funerals in Central Greece
    Stavroula Pipyrou   246

12. "If You Go Down in the Woods": British Woodland Burial, Leisurely Funerals, and Recreational Burial Grounds
    Hannah Rumble   261

   Epilogue: Obituary Preparing Activity
   James Fernandez   281

   List of Contributors   295

   Index   301

Leisurely Death and Dying?

Body, Place, and the Limits to Leisure—a Prologue

JANE C. DESMOND

In a world of few universals, death is one. Yet the meanings crafted through engagements with death are, as every anthropologist knows, specific to times, places, and communities. From the anguished to the ghoulish and on to the death-defying risk taking that seems to laugh at inevitability, ethnographic studies of death-related practices reveal a wide variety of engagements, some of which fall into the category of "leisure." Yet even within that range, death itself is rarely regarded as a leisure practice, at least for the one dying. In this book, the nexus of death and leisure—uncovered, speculated on, and even embraced as play—is an illuminating node, a confluence of the unexpected that helps us see anew both ends of the knot: "death" and "leisure."

What happens, the authors and editors of this volume ask, when individuals or groups insert the practices of leisure into the realm of death, so often associated with fear and grief (e.g., by taking photographic "selfies" with the deceased at a funeral), and vice versa—when people insert death or death-defying risk into the realm of leisure, so often associated with carefree pleasure, joy, play, and recreation, perhaps by searching for "zombies" while on holiday in Indonesia? By focusing on this leisure-death pairing, can we understand more deeply either of those terms and the associated social practices they refer to? What conceptual frames might we use?

In the last two decades, academic discussions of "dark tourism" have, as Kaul and Skinner note in their robust introduction to this book, been a key avenue to explore the nexus of death and leisure practices. Tours to sites of carnage, like those

DOI: 10.5876/9781607327295.c000a

associated with the Holocaust, or to sites of murder, like the Texas Book Depository in Dallas, from which President John F. Kennedy's fateful assassination shot was taken, have generated a growing sector of contemporary tourism focused on trauma.

The concepts associated with "dark tourism" and the debates surrounding it have generated insights about how tourists use their leisure time to, as some have argued, "enliven" their daily lives through an encounter with the dead. But this book demonstrates that, as fecund as those investigations may have been, they do not go far enough in helping us understand the contours and limits of leisurely encounters with death. Those contours, Kaul and Skinner argue, extend far beyond the tourist realm. They write: "Through the lens of leisure we are intentionally attaching the study of death to a new, burgeoning set of sub-disciplines in anthropology that cross over into adjacent fields, including the anthropologies of tourism, food, sport, heritage, and religion" (19). At times, they note, these arenas slip over into dark tourism, but they also diverge strongly from it. Therefore, we see that death is not always "dark," and leisurely engagement with death and sites associated with it—as spectator—is not always tourism.

As the reader plumbs the four parts of this book for their shared themes and resonances and then reads across those divisions for bulges and ragged catches of productive mismatch and nonalignment, the very category of "leisure" itself comes under pressure.

CONSIDERING "LEISURE"

Kaul and Skinner point toward the limitations of earlier Marxist interpretations of leisure as nonproductive bourgeois privilege and linger instead on Huizinga's leisurely notion of "play" as an arena of potential imaginings. The book's chapters show that "leisure" can range from death-defying cliff dives ("tombstoning" at the Devil's Frying Pan in Cornwall, UK) to picnicking in a forested field of graves. It can mean inserting remembrance of past death and violence into the sensual pleasures of beach strolling in Palau or the musical mayhem of parades in Northern Ireland. It can mean the disciplined daily walking of pilgrimage (whether in the religious or secularly spiritual sense) traversing the nearly 800 kilometer Camino de Santiago in northwestern Spain to its ending point at the sepulcher of Saint James in Santiago de Compostela, where solemn commitment mixes with the hedonistic pleasures of end-of-day tongue-satisfying wines.

What this range of practices has in common is that somewhere in each experience is an encounter with the dead or with the notion of dying. This can come imaginatively, through historical resonance of the place or through encountering the material presence of the dead—for example, standing among the clean and artfully arranged skulls and bones of 20,000 long dead on a tour to a centuries' old ossuary in Oppenheim, Germany, seeking what many tourists there call "transcendence."

What can we gain by calling all of these disparate practices "leisure?" Is this term serviceable just because we lack another category? The implicit (residual) dividing line here is still between "work" and non-work, it seems, or "required" and "optional" behaviors. Immediately, exceptions flood in to smudge those divisions, as recent discussions of leisure reveal. We can understand walking the Camino toward the relics of a dead saint as "working" on our spirituality, deepening our capacity for self-knowledge. Should we reconfigure the nexus? What if we turn the focus onto the questions "what is gained, by whom, and why" from these practices?

One of the questions the book pushes us to consider is this: if the designation "postmodern" is, in fact, a useful marker of (and moniker for) a substantial historical shift, does it also point to a rezoning of how we categorize aspects of our lives? What are the hallmarks of "leisure" in various communities across the globe today? If a wealthy New York stock broker is making deals on the phone while sitting on a beach in Phuket, is she on "vacation"? If a father is kicking a soccer ball with his five-year-old son on the local pitch in his neighborhood in San Salvador, is he "playing" or "parenting"? Or does this questioning of the category "leisure" simply underline the polysemic nature of so many categories of sociality, a proliferation of possible meanings that our very acts of conceptual categorization—"leisure," "mourning," "play," and so on—by the very act of naming, necessarily tamp down and mask?

In closing their introduction, Kaul and Skinner hint at the challenges of rethinking "leisure" as a category. They note that for some theorists like Simon Coleman and Tamara Kohn (2007), Mihalyi Csikszentmihalyi (1981), and Victor Turner (1982), respectively, leisure is a form of disciplined freedom, a state of psychological flow, or a liminal period. For Kaul and Skinner, while any of these aspects may be present, the unexpected union of leisure and death is especially powerful because it is "when self and sociality are remade, reproduced, remarked upon" (30). Extending the implications of this book farther, we can take this idea of analyzing the unexpected interpenetrations of seemingly distinct zones (in this case, death and leisure) as a model. In what other arenas of social practice do we find unexpected mixes of behaviors and desires?

Taken together, these chapters challenge us to ask whether and how the term *leisure* itself still has analytical purchase or—to redeploy Kaul and Skinner's evocative phrase—whether our concepts of "leisure" now also need to be remade, reproduced, and remarked upon. If leisure as a category is still useful in denoting a special zone of behavior, actions, and meanings in specific communities, what are its limits? Its defining characteristics? What does the constitution of such an imagined zone enable, permit, or foreclose; and how does that contribute to or articulate changes in social relations? Ray Casserley's chapter in this book, on parading in Northern Ireland, is a great example of how an event might simply be categorized as "public leisure," but that it in fact is "leisure and" and "leisure as"—as the performance of politics, rioting, remembrance, urban geographic reinscription, and of masculinity and working-class status along with religious affiliation, all rendered with the sonic and gustatory pleasures of marching bands and festive foods. What are the limits of "leisure" as an analytic? How does it relate to other analytics, like "place" and "kinesthesia"?

CONSIDERING PLACE AND KINESTHESIA

If this book convincingly demonstrates that even "leisure" embraces aspects of death and the dead, then we must reconfigure our notions of leisure into a more complex realm of joyful or grief-stricken, playful or solemn, enjoyable or excruciating sought-after *experiences*. The gossiping funeral attendees in Greece, the gastronomic tourists eating heritage hogs in Italy, the hikers on the Camino, the beach-strolling Japanese commemorative tourists in war-marked Palau, the rambling walkers in a UK "green" cemetery . . . each of these is moving through land turned to landscape and space turned to place by the inscription of memories and meanings over time, by multiple communities. Reading across the grain of the chapters in this book, we find that a key analytic is the kinesthetic—the actions of embodied participants in specific places.

"Space" becomes a socially significant "place" when it is inscribed with meanings, and motion becomes action when it is purposefully enacted in those places. A jump into the air is just a leap off the ground, unless that jump is performed cliffside, as Kaul describes in his chapter, at the Irish Cliffs of Moher, site of numerous suicides. That leap is staged by young visitors, ironically and for the camera, to supposedly show the last moment of levitation before the inevitable hand of gravity pulls the body over the cliffs and into eternity. A playful wink at the performance of suicide, this action unites kinesthetic rendition with implied affective commentary— "Ha ha! I'm not jumping, but it looks like I am. Here's me—not dying!" A playful staging of one's own death, a simulacrum of suicide suitable for posting on social media, has to be carefully calibrated on the cliffs—too close to the edge and it could become real, too far away and it doesn't look like it could be suicidal. In that act of calibration—the stepping near and away, the "how does this look" interaction with the cameraman—is the "edgework" Kaul analyzes. It is the delight of simulated risk, crafted through the union of movement, body, place, and affect.

If "affect" refers to the physical experiences of emotion—the rushing of blood, the tightness in our chests, the shortness of breath, or its long, slow escape in a sigh—then we see the importance of keeping the body center stage in so many of these analyses. All but one of these chapters (which discusses the Web) involve the physical presence of the actant in a specific place and time. The detailed ethnographies that give us such rich, particular, empathic renderings of these experiences make clear the absolute centrality of that physical presence to how meanings emerge. The experiences under analysis here are deeply embodied and sharply felt—uniting body and emotion in moments of heightened experiential awareness.

Authors gesture toward this experiential realm and how it yields meaning by drawing on several different analytic frames—from the notion of the dead as the "ultimate other" that marks the "real" as an antidote for the mundanity of daily life, to the idea of "fantastic realism," invoked by Kathleen Adams in this volume, following Jørgen Ole Bærenholdt and Michael Haldrup (2004, 86) to suggest that "physically encountered reality" reinforces "imaginative geography," enabling tourists to make these experiences "part of their lives and identities."

Each of these ideas leads us toward an understanding of how meaning making proceeds through action and embodied presence in specific places already inscribed with sediments of meaning, ready to be activated through new overlays with each encounter. The literal re-sculpting of muscles by the act of walking for days, weeks, along the Camino in Spain corresponds with the spiritual remodeling so many seek through this act of making a pilgrimage. The "doing" counts and is central to how meaning emerges.

The one chapter in this book that turns away from physical presence as a ground of meaning takes us into the virtual reality of Facebook, where bodily materiality evaporates and can be masked through avatars. Here the physical body of the Facebook person/persona can be decoupled by death, with the persona living on through continued interaction by the deceased's "friends." In what ways is this a new genre of memory and memorialization and in what ways simply the digital version of remembering through reminiscence face to face, among members of a community who knew the deceased? The key word is "deceased"—the ceasing to function of the person's physical body—"death" if not "social death."

ON "DEATH" WITHOUT "DYING"

If "death" permeates our leisure practices, dying does not. That consistent omission is as crucial as what is contained in the book's case studies. What none of these chapters nor the specific practices they analyze focus on are actual leisure encounters with dead bodies or with the often messy, unaesthetic, sometimes excruciating *process* of dying. Clean remnants of the dead (ancient, un-individuated piles of ossuary bones, for example); sites where people died in the past; imagined and desired but never seen "walking dead" or "zombies"; and encounters with happy heritage pigs, once admired grunting on the hoof, now magically transformed (offsite) to meat on the plate—all of these do not foster experiences that confront the facticity of dead bodies, their materiality in flesh and blood, in scent and substance. We encounter death without dying.

The one chapter in the book that does link tourism and an actual dead body is about the death of a tourist on holiday in Indonesia and sensitively explores the local community's complex response to this death of an outsider and its logistical, ethical, and social demands. But that chapter is about the aftermath of an unexpected death while on a leisure vacation, not about seeking leisurely encounters with the dead. The other counterexample, examining the enjoyment of gossiping at a Greek funeral with the recently deceased in place, reconfigures "mourning" to include a range of behaviors, including the subtly gleeful, under the imprimatur of funereal customs. But even here the body is "clean," prepared for display to insiders, community members, and family and not subject to inspection by casual leisure seekers or observed dying or putrefying. This type of display might fall in the realm of what Kathleen Adams calls in her chapter the "pornography of the macabre."

Let's push the entanglements of death and leisure farther. Can we imagine leisure practices inserted not only into the invocation of "death" but also into the process of dying? Can we imagine, for example, tours to the hospice-sponsored hospital rooms of the "authentically dying?" Perhaps as a way to raise expenses for end-of-life care? Unthinkable? Or perhaps we can imagine the development of niche tourism, focusing on tourism for the terminally ill. We are all dying, but only some of us know it is imminent. Does this knowledge create a new community with new leisure needs? New desires?

Pushing further still, is the suffering that is so often part of dying something that could conceivably be commodified and sold as a leisurely spectatorial experience, like going to the theater? Can we imagine an artist arranging to have put on display his or her own un-embalmed, un-plastinated, "natural" bodily remains so that people can observe decay—a public rendition of the FBI's forensic training site in North Carolina of decomposing bodies in situ called the Body Farm? These forms of leisure are unthinkable or nearly so. They are even hard to bring into the realm of the imagination because they cross, for many contemporary communities, an un-crossable line into an unseemly actual "pornography of death," to repurpose sociologist Geoffrey Gorer's still resonant term from more than half a century ago (Gorer 1955). They link up with unbearable spectacles (like snuff films, ISIS videos of beheadings, or earlier public executions). Perhaps there are communities where a witnessing of the dying process is a socially sanctioned public leisure zone—but for many communities around the world, the process of death is sutured to the medical and religious/spiritual realms. Based on the evidence in this book, we can say that at the intersection of leisure and death, adrenalin is in, putrefaction is out. Remembering the historical dead is in, but actually seeing the dying is out.

Ultimately, the chapters in this book pose a challenge for us. Crafted with careful attention to cultural specificity; rendered with closely observed, empathic, and thoughtfully analyzed detail, the observations here provide us with numerous comparative opportunities. As capacious as it is, this book makes no claims to being "global" or all-comprehensive. No responsible ethnography could or would do so. Yet the variety here is substantial, in terms of locales and communities and events and practices under consideration. Given that variety, what is missing is striking and just as important as what is present.

If, as this volume suggests, death is everywhere in many people's leisure practices, the realm of leisure, however we understand it in this book, does not encompass the dying or the decaying bodies of the newly dead. This remains—even in "postmodernity" with its CSI televisual embrace of postmortem visuals and even in the age of "selfies" at funerals—a sanctified realm, a physically intimate one, as yet off limits to the types of public practices investigated here. Ultimately "dying," not "death," may mark the limits of contemporary leisure.

REFERENCES

Bærenholdt, Jørgen Ole, and Michael Haldrup. 2004. "On the Tracks of the Vikings." In *Tourism Mobilities: Places to Play, Places in Play*, ed. Mimi Sheller and John Urry. London: Routledge.

Coleman, Simon, and Tamara Kohn. 2007. "The Discipline of Leisure: Taking Play Seriously." In *The Discipline of Leisure: Embodying Cultures of Recreation*, ed. Simon Coleman and Tamara Kohn, 1–22. Oxford: Berghan.

Csikszentmihalyi, Mihalyi. 1981. "Leisure and Socialization." *Social Forces* 60 (2): 332–40. https://doi.org/10.2307/2578438.

Gorer, Geoffrey. 1955. "The Pornography of Death." In *Death, Grief, and Mourning*, ed. Geoffrey Gorer, 192–99. New York: Doubleday.

Turner, Victor. 1982. *From Ritual to Theatre*. New York: PAJ.

Leisure and Death

Leisure and Death

An Introduction

ADAM KAUL AND JONATHAN SKINNER

> How many ways has death to surprise us!
> —Montaigne (1957, 58)
>
> The problem of the dead . . . is also that of travellers.
> —Jean Didier Urbain (in Doquet and Evrard 2008, 176)

JONATHAN, NOVEMBER 18, 2013:

I sit in my rental car. I have a choice to make. I'm following Interstate 74 through Illinois from Urbana-Champaign, where I am a resident scholar, to Rock Island to meet Adam and to give a talk at Augustana College. I can take a brief detour north, or I can continue my journey. To the north is the town of Washington, an urban debris field with a bruised population following the touch-down of a tornado. I had seen the ominous clouds hurtling across the skies and heard the spotters with their radio warning system as it crossed the state. It has laid waste to this town, and I was curious from the landmark-less photos to see the place firsthand. Was this ghoulish and voyeuristic? How would I be received? Could I drive up to the destruction and then reverse back? Would I be welcomed or be in the way?

For many, a denial of death is the only way to live. And yet, there are some who find that the careful but idle rumination about dying makes living all the richer.

Should we fear death and even deny its existence altogether or drive headlong and confront death head-on in all its horrors and ironies? This collection of essays looks at the awkward and unsettling, perhaps even macabre, relationship between leisure and death—as though death (the final frontier) and the dead (the final Other) are the new postmodern exotic. At first cold blush, this might seem odd. What has leisure got to do with death? Are they not polar opposites of light and dark, the extremes of a continuum of activity? In this volume we are examining the connection between leisure and death that has deep historical roots, in terms of both social behavior and a more philosophical contemplation of death. Further, there is a serious and persistent, though too-often ignored, engagement with death in our leisure practices. We are defined by death and use our mortalities to meditate and mediate—even to bring us—life. This thesis is apparent in the chapters in this book—each a careful ethnographic case of death in leisure and leisure in death.

We also hope to set the stage for this connection in this introduction where we first look to define contemporary relations with death, especially in "The West" an archaeology of social mores from spectacles of public execution to death in popular culture. We then look to the shift from industrial-scale death in the twentieth century, so characterized by the two world wars, to the industry of death in the twenty-first century—and as Rumble describes in the final chapter in this volume, its deindustrialization more recently—with the cultural moment of the corpse on display across film and television screens, in global exhibitions, and permeating our personal heartlands. Post 9/11, we are all now potential terrorist victims and, as such, death invites itself as an unwelcome guest while we travel on holiday, while we linger at restaurants with friends, while we attend sporting events.

The third section of this introduction is where we review the anthropology of death literature. Here, the first and second deaths explained by Robert Hertz have a leisure space between them: the body is laid to rest, quite literally. It is during that time that the deceased becomes a tourist attraction for Adams in her chapter on selfies with modern "zombies" in Indonesia. Finally, we connect leisure and death through the prism of obsidian. Several authors in the following pages use dark tourism and dark leisure just like Renaissance astrologer John Dee's shewstone, an Aztec "smoke mirror," for scrying. This form of niche tourism is an unholy alliance, an "odd conjunction" according to Tony Seaton (2012, 521). It uses "death" as an adjective and tourism as a prefix. It is leisure with an edge to advance Stephen Lyng's (1990) "edge*work*": leisure practices that give us an opportunity to connect and feel alive through imaginative glimpses into the dead of the past. This is a complex and contentious form of tourism that needs critiquing, but with more than just a spade and bucket[list].

In this volume, we think it is useful to couch "dark tourism" in a much larger critical discussion about death and leisure more generally. Both leisure and death are a timeout, an absence from society. French anthropologist Didier Urbain (1978) drew this equivalence in his study of graveyards in the 1970s, resting places in the departed's voyage to the afterlife, a metaphor he extends to those taking their rest in the holiday resort, symbolically dead. Absent from society, the tourist disappears ritually and temporarily but not completely. Theirs is "an anti-suicide or anti-exodus treatment" (Urbain in Doquet and Evrard 2008, 176): the tourist is immortal. From this position, tourists are drawn to the spectacular.

LEISURE AND DEATH SPECTACULAR

ADAM, OCTOBER 2014:
The door of the four-seater Cessna airplane opened with a roar, and I focused all of my mental energy on trying (but failing) to remember the shockingly brief instructions about skydiving we were given before leaving the ground. My "instructor" smiled impatiently as I squatted, paralyzed, next to the open door. He gave me the thumbs-up sign to confirm that I still wanted to go through with my first tandem jump. As the plane circled at 11,000 feet over the landing site, I continued to stare blankly at him until, impatient, he screamed in my ear "are you good to go?" Despite myself, I nodded and slowly put one foot out onto the supports of the tiny wing, the landscape below looking like cartography. Then suddenly the pair of us, like Gabreel and Saladin in Rushdie's The Satanic Verses, *plummeted toward the ground at terminal velocity. I had never known a sensation like it. My eyes rolled back into my head, and I slipped into a brief but powerful altered state of consciousness as we spun head over heels. I was disembodied, edging on some sort of event horizon, unmoored and unearthed. Was this fun, or was this what dying feels like?*

In the contemporary Western imaginary, we are often fixated upon the death of others, even while attempting to deny our own (Becker 1973). Popular public executions have served the twin purpose of disciplining and entertaining wider society in Enlightened Europe (Foucault 1975). The consumption of death practices has been the focus of entertainment and the locus of a macabre humor across the centuries, well beyond nineteenth-century American and British broadside ballads about them (Saltzman 1995, 103). These twin tensions of attraction and repulsion in relation to the death of others versus the death of the self persist with folksongs about the execution of Ted Bundy in 1989 circulating as pithy social warnings in similar fashion to the social

FIGURE 0.1. Photo by SkyDiveTwinCities, purchased by Adam Kaul, used with permission, 2014.

media postings and re-postings of Saddam Hussein's gruesome execution in 2006 (Foltyn 2008, 157). We may no longer attend executions ourselves, but professional and amateur reporters act as our proxies and bring them into our homes.

Placed in this historical context, modern forms of death-centered entertainments are not significantly different. In other words, if we now recognize that "death has become a fascinating and macabre tourist site" (Phipps 1999, 83), then it is also time to acknowledge that death has long been a fascinating and macabre playground where a multitude of leisure activities occur. The *CSI* television series and the plethora of contemporary "slasher" movies and vampire series are gruesome episodes of what Geoffrey Gorer, examining the Western denial of death, labeled the "pornography of death" in 1955. It is during times of prudery about death, he argued, that the subject becomes taboo and simultaneously the subject of fantasy.

Travel to sites of death is not new either: tourists on the Grand Tour have taken in the wondrous ruins of Pompeii since its uncovering in 1599; and as highlighted in Egan's contribution in this volume, for a thousand years pilgrims have crisscrossed Christendom to worship the bones of saints and martyrs, and members of the aristocratic leisured classes have trod the battlefields of Waterloo for souvenirs ever since the evening of June 18, 1815, with the stench of death not yet stale (Seaton 1999). Gazing at live battles continues to be a leisurely practice: summer 2014, Israeli citizens lined up sofas along the hills of Sderot to watch and cheer the bombing of Gaza (Mackey 2014). In the West, the viewing of corpses has a long—and sometimes criminal—history (Penfold-Mounce 2010), from Mark Twain's fascination with the Paris Morgue (MacCannell 1989) to the contemporary globally touring *Body Worlds* exhibition of Gunther von Hagen's plastinated "citizen corpses" (Desmond 2011) and the long history of "lifelike" displays of dead animals via taxidermy (Desmond 2002). In this epoch, posthumous stars now go on world tours, although, like the dead on television, they are dehumanized and robbed of personality. Animal taxidermy is not so different from the plastinated human corpses in the end. The spectacle of death figures on the television sofa as well as in the bedroom. It is no longer restricted to the deathbed or death row.

Everyday deaths have had a long history of public ritual in the West. In his classic treatment on the subject, *Western Attitudes towards Death*, Philippe Ariès explained that a century ago "death was a ritual organized by the dying person himself, who presided over it and knew its protocol . . . It was also a public ceremony. The dying man's bedchamber became a public place to be entered freely" (Ariès 1974, 11–12). However, in the twentieth century a contradictory culture of death began to emerge in Europe and America: one's own death became an intensely personal and private affair (Ariès 1974, 55–56) and even a sort of embarrassing, unnatural transgression that should take place alone, out of sight from others. Post–World War II, we entered into an era of death denial. "Once tame and familiar," the philosopher Vincent Barry writes, "death has become alarmingly strange" (Barry 2007, 33). Simultaneously, the death of others was sometimes exalted and glamorized (Ariès 1974, 55–56). These two socio-psychological maneuvers, while contradictory, also go hand in hand. For example, Gorer claims that the taboo of death itself turned dying and any acknowledgment of it into a kind of secretive and furtive obsession. "In the 20th century," he argues, "there seems to have been a remarkable shift in prudery; whereas copulation has become more 'mentionable,' particularly in what [Gorer] labels Anglo-Saxon societies, death has become more and more 'unmentionable'" (Gorer 1955, 195). Sex and death, Freud's eros and thanatos, have a lot in common.

In our attempt to unravel the often contradictory relationship with leisure and death, it will help to step back first and ask what death is in the first place. As it turns out, defining it is not easy. Conceptualizing it through anthropology is even more difficult. Can one assume that, like pregnancy, a person cannot be "sort of" dead and that birth and death are two of life's universals? On the surface, it would seem like a binary: one is alive, and then, like a switch being turned off, one is dead.

Or so runs out the domineering, spiritless, Western biomedical death model. But as anthropologist Nigel Barley explains: "Death is like every other category. It works well in a rough-and-ready way but attempts to define it lead to a sort of internal collapse" (Barley 2006 [1995], 52; see also Barry 2007, 15–30). The suggestion is that death (or conception for that matter) is less an event than a process. As some of the contributions to this volume point out, online social media allows for the possibility that the original—in the sense of death before believed reincarnation or resurrection—passing of the individual no longer necessitates the passing of the person. In an age of high-tech medicine that can sustain some aspects of a person's body but not others, what of patients whose bodies are kept alive but most or all brain function is gone? Dying is perceived by some to be a biomechanical process in which the medical industry attempts to find a soulless "cure" for each stage in the incurable process of dying. The final frontier, death, is being fractured by the bold.

During the course of the twentieth century, the social spaces of death became the domain of teams of institutional "professionals"—not of the family or even the dying person themselves. Medical professionals objectify the body and control the process of dying. This impinges upon the dying person's opportunities to subjectively author his or her own death. Institutionalization and sanitization—both literally and figuratively—accelerated rapidly across the late twentieth century as the hospital became the locus of the dying and the dead. The very idea of dying at a hospital, a place where one ostensibly goes to be *restored* to health, has placed death in the category of an illness to be cured rather than an inevitable fate to be endured by us all (Ariès 1974, 87–88). This "curative resistance" to death at all costs has played out forcefully in the modern medical industry, opening up a range of contentious bioethical questions about brain death, organ transplants, and the right to die (Barry 2007, 15–30).

In *Symbolic Exchange and Death*, postmodern theorist Jean Baudrillard (1993) attempts to explain this continental shift when he argues that a modern, capitalist orientation creates a linear sense of time in which death is no longer connected intimately with the living but instead is rendered the opposite of—and anathema to—life. He goes so far as to claim that it is an increasing condition of late modernity that we exile the dead "further and further away from the group of the living" (Baudrillard 1993, 126). This thesis of Western "death denial" nearly became a foregone conclusion in the second half of the twentieth century, not just for Baudrillard but also among sociologists, psychologists, and social scientists (Feifel 1959; Kübler-Ross 1969; Becker 1973; Ariès 1974). More recently, it has been suggested that Americans and Europeans are coming around to face death more honestly and more authentically as part of a death "revival" (cf. Walter 1994; Árnason and Hafsteinsson 2003).[1] Still, in the mid-twentieth century Gorer (1955, 197) noted that while "natural death became more and more smothered in prudery, violent death has played an ever-growing part in the fantasies offered to mass audiences." Whatever our cultural feelings and understandings about our own deaths, writing from our US/UK vantage point, in this postmodern era we would appear to have increased our appetite for consuming the death of others as part of an ironic, consumable, postmortem entertainment.

THE CULTURAL MOMENT OF THE CORPSE

It is interesting and controversial that death in modernity is so associated with entertainment. The appearance of violence and death in our leisurely consumption of popular culture is not new, but there have been notable shifts during the last decade or more that reflect a growing concern with death and dying. "Whether flesh, fantasy, or some hybridized version of the two, this is the corpse's cultural moment" (Foltyn 2008, 155). Foltyn argues that there is a growing ambivalence about death that fuels a post-disaster, post-millennial, post-9/11, post-self, and postmodern voyeurism. Its expression is widespread and varied but includes television shows about forensic anthropology like the *CSI* franchise *Bones* (Kruse 2010) and a seemingly endless number of movies and television shows about "undead," "living dead," and post-human versions of ourselves. Modern death-as-entertainment is mediated and flattened into two dimensions for easy digestion, a symbolic cannibalism. In addition, a leisurely consumption of books, television shows, and movies set in dystopian post-apocalyptic scenarios is now widespread, pointing to a concern with the death of culture itself.[2] But the commodification of death as a source of entertainment, leisure, and enjoyment edges into grisly territory that we think is worthy of serious and somber analysis even when it is reported as "just in good clean fun." Far from it, so the contributors to this volume argue.

Before television, before photography even, public executions were staged and consumed as theatrical performances (Schuyler 2008, 16). Ruth Penfold-Mounce points to an important moment in the Western obsession with the bodies of the dead and the criminal corpse: an ideal case in point is the execution and public dissection of William Burke, the infamous Scottish body snatcher and murderer who supplied Edinburgh Medical College with a steady inventory of cadavers between 1827 and 1828 (Penfold-Mounce 2010, 256). The public dissection of Burke's lifeless body captured the public's voyeuristic imagination to such an extent that thousands of people shuffled past Burke's corpse. Subsequently, body parts from the dissection, such as his skeleton and "a book bound in his skin upon which was printed 'Burke's Skin, 1829,'" were displayed as museum exhibits at Edinburgh University (Penfold-Mounce 2010, 256–57). His skeleton, death mask, and the book are still on display at Surgeon's Hall, Edinburgh.

We have always had a "morbid fascination." We continue to be curious about, threatened by, and attracted to gore, to death, to the incomprehensible that we try to make explicable by recourse to magic, religion, and now science. We have an unhealthy and insatiable lust for these tales of grave robbers and stories from beyond the grave. The "entertainments" surrounding the executions of Ted Bundy and Saddam Hussein, described above, lead us to ask if things are really so different today. To give another contemporary example, following the videotaped execution of American Israeli journalist Daniel Pearl by Pakistani militants in 2002 and the beheading of American freelance radio-tower repairman Evan "Nick" Berg two years later by Islamic extremists in Iraq, downloads of execution videos began to spike every time they were released by terrorist organizations, sparking heated debates about ethics, freedom of the press, and viewers' motives (Larson 2014, 78–82). A number of "shock sites" (Larson 2014, 82) posted the footage as entertainment so we can consume others' deaths in the private and leisurely spaces of our own homes.

While this post-emotional (cf. Mestrovic 1999) consumption of death deserves our condemnation, it is ironic that an increasing consumption of the fictionalized dead—and the increasingly detailed depictions of death and dying—on television is deemed perfectly acceptable. The focus on the corpse as the product of criminality in particular suits a neoliberal, post-9/11 period. In today's death-centered crime dramas, such as the *CSI* franchise, the corpse is the only "true" evidence that can be trusted. Witness testimonies and circumstantial evidence are literally unbelievable (Kruse 2010, 81). In this sense, the use of the corpse-as-truth fits into our increasingly technocratic era as the dehumanized body rather than the self is the only thing that is measureable, real, and empirically assessable. It also befits an epoch that is increasingly comfortable with violence in general. A neoliberal consumption of the dead is not just fiction, though. As Nancy Scheper-Hughes documents in unsettling detail, the global transplant market in human organs operates under medical bioethics that "bring it into alignment with neoliberal conceptions of the human, the body, labor, value, rights, and economics" and has therefore "capitulated to the dominant market ethos" (Scheper-Hughes 2004, 61). In entertainment and in day-to-day life, death is increasingly a product to be cataloged, measured, and consumed. In this volume, we intend to write against this zeitgeist in an effort to re-humanize the dead.

HONORING THE DEAD

When drawing connections between leisure and death, we want to point out that it is not our intention to make light of the dark geography we are considering. Sensationalism is not the goal of the work we do. We follow Kathleen Adams's thoughtful warning in her contribution to this volume. As Adams points out, an uncritical and sometimes leisurely voyeurism of risk, death, and dying can lead to what she terms "pornographies of the macabre." Instead, we intend to rather seriously consider what happens when what we might heuristically qualify as the lightness of leisure and the darkness of death collide. However, as this project has come to fruition, we have noted a somewhat disturbing but unsurprising reaction to the topic from friends and colleagues that might be summarized by a recent two-word reaction from a respected scholar who asked what the book was about: he simply said "cool topic." That was the end of the conversation. Of course, the reality of death is often horrible, heart-wrenchingly sad, terrifying, and tragic.

We have faced the very real tragedy of death with one of our own contributors to this book. The emails from Cyril Schäfer suddenly stopped during the summer of 2015. His Facebook page was frozen and, upon investigation, we learned from friends and colleagues that he had suddenly passed away. Although we only knew Cyril through this project, we found ourselves drawn into a personal tragedy playing out from New Zealand right across the globe. It led us to once again reflect on death and its coldness-turned-"cool." The painful irony of Cyril's passing brought the seriousness of the volume's topic into sharp "relief." We were temporarily paralyzed by the news but, after consulting with Cyril's family and colleagues, we decided that the best way to honor his memory was to proceed with the publication of his chapter. We take a moment here to ask the reader to honor Cyril Schäfer's memory as well and to reflect on the motivations that led you to pick up this book and open its pages. If death, as Montaigne proposed, has many ways to surprise us, this volume is one attempt to go beyond the disturbing, surface "cool factor" and to deepen and humanize our understanding of the multifaceted ways people encounter, experience, and ascribe meaning to risk, death, and dying.

THE ANTHROPOLOGY OF DEATH: FOUR FRAMES

ADAM, JANUARY 3, 2016
We begin to see the connections between leisure and death everywhere. Friends and family all seem to have anecdotes. It is in the news, too: a story in the Associated Press about "mock funerals" in Seoul, South Korea, during which customers pay to "die" and are enclosed in a casket for a brief meditative period. The invented ritual, meant to alleviate stress, is a fast-growing business for funeral homes (Kim 2015). Another story leaps out at me as I leisurely sip coffee and read the morning paper. It is about a woman who plays the harp and sings for terminal patients as they slip away into death. She calls herself a music thanatologist (Hollis 2016). Later, scanning my Facebook and Twitter feeds, I run across a

story about a Lithuanian designer who has invented a "euthanasia rollercoaster" with the sole intent to kill its riders in one last euphoric death-fall (Hunter 2016).

Both leisure studies and death studies are interdisciplinary fields, each extensive and complex in its own right. While reaching out to adjacent disciplinary arenas, this volume intentionally grounds itself in anthropology. We are not the first to point out that the topic of death and dying was of interest to early anthropologists as they attempted to systematically catalog the world's beliefs about death and funerary customs into hierarchies and networks of cultural diffusion. Well into the twentieth century, as many anthropologists reoriented the discipline toward a scientific search for cultural patterns, death was often approached with "coolness and remoteness . . . at a safe distance from one's own society" (Palgi and Abramovitch 1984, 385). Since the postmodern turn, there has been a humanizing of the topic of death and dying and a more complicated understanding of it as a messy and contradictory process instead of a neat set of categories. We hope the present volume adds to this trend. Simultaneously, the burgeoning sub-discipline of medical anthropology over the last few decades has led to an investigation of the meanings surrounding death in relation to the body itself. In our view, a contemporary anthropology of death allows us to open, unpack, and problematize it. In our analysis of the collision of leisure and death, ethnographic specificity and the comparative method prompt us to approach death as socially constructed, processual, diverse, and meaningful and to contemplate diverse social worlds of death, life and afterlife, the post-dead, the twice-dead (Lock 2002), the Mexican Day of the Dead, and so on.

Here, it might be most useful to highlight several prominent thematic waypoints on the map that can help guide our way through the territory of anthropological theorizing about death and dying rather than attempt to provide a comprehensive review as others before us have done (cf. Palgi and Abramovitch 1984; Barley 2006 [1995]; Kaufman and Morgan 2005; Robben 2011, among others). We fully recognize that there are many other ways to dissect the literature on the anthropology of death and dying, but for our purposes we confront it topically instead of chronologically and divide the literature into several themes useful to us: death and the objectifying impulse, death up close, death as dis/embodied, and our own approach in this volume, leisure and death.

Frame 1: The Objectifying Impulse

We begin by recognizing that death was on the minds of the founding fathers and mothers of anthropology, for instance, Edward B. Tylor, whose theory about the animistic origins of religion in his classic *Primitive Culture* (Tylor 1871) hinged on the idea that the spirit or soul lives beyond the death of the body. According to Godfrey Lienhardt, "Tylor's theory of the basis of religion . . . arose, he thought, when primitive peoples had reflected upon their experience of immaterial forms in dreams, or considered the difference between a living man and his corpse" (Lienhardt 1966, 116). And one of the founding texts in the social sciences, Émile Durkheim's (1897) *Le Suicide*, suggested that taking one's own life is at least in part the result of wider social and religious patterns rather than simply a moral or psychological failing of the individual. Even though today it may seem obvious, one of the primary goals of *Le Suicide* was to prove empirically that social structures and social forces exist at all, thereby elevating the discipline of sociology to the status that psychology and the biological sciences held in his day (Pope 1976, 155). It was novel and contentious for Durkheim to conclude that "collective tendencies have an existence of their own" (Durkheim 1951 [1897], 311).

Using the complementary methods of in-depth ethnographic inquiry and cross-cultural comparison, anthropologists also focused on death in relation to social and ritual structures well into the twentieth century. As we describe below, the ultimate goal of this kind of work was to uncover the underlying logic and structure of individual societies or to theorize about hidden structural patterns of various sorts—for example, psychological (e.g., Benedict 1959 [1934]), symbolic (e.g., Turner 1969), mythic, and neurological (e.g., Levi-Strauss 1992 [1955]). In relation to the anthropological study of death in particular, there was a focus on normative beliefs and behaviors within single societies and how they fit within the social structure (Kaufman and Morgan 2005, 318–19). At the same time, cross-cultural comparisons between societies in regard to death and dying were used to further theoretical arguments about the nature of humanity and society. In the sense that many twentieth-century anthropologists were searching for universal scientific laws of human behavior, their theories about death and dying were not so much a break from earlier nineteenth-century ideas as they were extensions of them.

To give an illustration: despite the fact that Bronislaw Malinowski's Functionalist paradigm was a radical departure from the Evolutionist and Diffusionist theories of the previous generation, he, too, concluded that among other root causes, death lay at the root of religious belief. This is apparent when he wrote: "the physiological phases of human life, and, above all, its crises, such as conception, pregnancy, birth, puberty, marriage, and death, form the nuclei of various rites and beliefs" (Malinowski 1948, 20). Malinowksi's long-term fieldwork methods are foundational in anthropology and provided his discussions with sustained ethnographic specificity about the Trobriand Islanders with whom he lived. However, his Functionalist theory was as universalist as the theories of Tylor or Morgan before him, who claimed that all cultures were evolving along a single path toward civilization.

On the American side of the Atlantic around the same 1930s period, Ruth Benedict "used" the anthropology of death to prop up her theoretical arguments as well. Benedict (1959 [1934]) discusses death in her *Patterns of Culture* but does so in service to her concepts of the "configuration" and "integration" of cultures (cf. 243–44). She makes use of detailed ethnographic data about the Zuni, the Dobu, and the Kwakiutl in three extensive chapters, but this is all to get at her larger arguments, and only the material about the Zuni was collected by herself. According to Benedict, in a well-integrated culture, beliefs, behaviors, and rites concerning dying, death, and the afterlife should naturally conform to the overarching pattern of the culture, its "personality writ large." "A culture, like an individual, is a more or less consistent pattern of thought and action," she writes (1959 [1934], 46).

Mid-century, Claude Levi-Strauss published the book *Tristes Tropiques*, transforming his career from anthropologist into public intellectual. He writes about life and death warmly and with careful attention to the ethnographic context (cf. Levi-Strauss 1992 [1955], 230–46), but in that regard, this is an unusual book for Levi-Strauss because he typically uses the subject of death as a means for advancing his theories about the binary symbolic structures of human nature and the human mind. More typical examples of his breezy cross-cultural method can be found in works like *The Savage Mind* (Levi-Strauss 1966 [1962], 79–80, 191–200). Complex beliefs, emotions, and behaviors are reduced to formulaic binaries or triads of single words or phrases strewn across schematic illustrations. In a classic example he pairs "dream," "life," "death" with "historical rites," "rites of control," "mourning rites" in a schema devoid of the human experience (Levi-Strauss 1966 [1962], 237).

During the second half of the twentieth century, the symbolic interpretive work of Mary Douglas (2003) illustrated how societies overcome the "pollution" of death. Victor Turner's (1969) ideas about liminality in *The Ritual Process* greatly expanded on the idea of death as a rite of passage (and also rites of passage as symbolic death and rebirth), influencing a generation of scholars in anthropology and beyond. But again, his exposition of liminal states, forests of symbolism, and planes of classification was in the end a detailed description of the ritual *structure* (and anti-structure) rather than the lived experience of ritual supplicants.

While some of these approaches address or at least mention what Renato Rosaldo calls "the *emotional force* of a death" (Rosaldo 1989, 2, original italics), most anthropological writing about the topic used a far more cold and objectivist tone. This is true for works right up into the 1980s like *Death and the Regeneration of Life*, edited by Maurice Bloch and Jonathan Parry, in which they attempt to synthesize a "sociological analysis" of death and the "organizational aspects of society in which it occurs" with an analysis of the cultural and symbolic logic of funerals

(Bloch and Parry 1982, 6). Reaching further back, a classic example roundly criticized by Rosaldo (1989) is Jack Goody's (1962) *Death, Property, and the Ancestors*. Throughout the book, Goody describes mourning and ritual behavior of the LoDaaga people of West Africa in great detail but with the cool and distanced tone of a laboratory scientist; the book is even peppered with lists, formulas, and charts that reduce mourning and bereavement to a kind of "periodical chart" in tabular form (cf. 87–88, 164–65, 267). "One can only wonder," Rosaldo writes scathingly, "at the objectifying impulse" (Rosaldo 1989, 57). But Goody is not the only one Rosaldo singles out: "Most ethnographic descriptions of death stand at a peculiar distance from the obviously intense emotions expressed, and they turn what for the bereaved are unique and devastating losses into routine happenings" (Rosaldo 1989, 57). For Rosaldo, the lived experience of death became all too real after his wife, Michelle's, tragic early death in the field in 1981 when she slipped into a gorge. Following Rosaldo's critiques, we hope to avoid the "objectifying impulse" in our coverage of risk, death, and dying in the following pages. Ours is, we hope, a far more human approach to the topic grounded in ethnographic detail.

Frame 2: Death up Close

It was a Durkheimian disciple and colleague of Marcel Mauss, Robert Hertz, who is often cited for laying the groundwork for most key twentieth-century notions in anthropology about death. Hertz used a broader, cross-cultural framework than Durkheim, who had kept his focus on France and neighboring Western nations. Hertz made less of a lasting impact on the social sciences than did Mauss or Durkheim, though, in part because his own death occurred so early in his career. He was killed at thirty-three in 1915 during World War I. However, he had already published a series of articles on death and mourning (Evans-Pritchard 1960, 10).[3] One of Hertz's goals was to prove that what one believes about death, how survivors deal with the body, and how they mourn the loss are all what Peter Berger and Thomas Luckmann (1989 [1966]) would later call "social constructions." Hertz wrote that "death has a specific meaning for the social consciousness; it is the object of collective representation" (Hertz 1960 [1907], 28). In this way, his work extended Durkheim's in that it made the case for collective social meaning and social forces. In his analysis of secondary funeral practices in which the dead are mourned not just at the time of death but a year or more later as well, Hertz outlined some of the main themes discussed today in the anthropology of death: death as a process rather than an event, the idea of a social death that does not necessarily coincide with biological death, death as a ritual rebirth, and death as a person's entrée into the realm of the ancestors (Hertz 1960 [1907]). He also starts with what seems like a very modern discussion about the elusive nature of death and how it defies definition. "We all believe we know what death is," he begins, "yet questions arise... Even for the biologist death is not a simple and obvious fact" (Hertz 1960 [1907], 27).

Ideas about death as a process, or distinguishing between a biological and a social death, might seem novel or exotic to a European or North American public, but they are common cross-culturally. In the volume *The Meaning of Death*, anthropologist David G. Mandelbaum (1959) describes the beliefs and rituals of the Kota people of South India who have two funerary rituals: the "green funeral" and the "dry funeral." One aspect of their beliefs about death and dying is striking in this regard: it illustrates well the processual nature of death and the distinctions between the biological self and the social person, ideas outlined by Hertz decades earlier. "The dead man," Mandelbaum explains, "continues to have certain attributes of social personality until his second funeral. Most importantly, a widow is still her husband's wife up to the conclusion of the Dry Funeral. If she becomes pregnant after his physical death but before his second funeral, the child is his, shares his name, clan, and property... Hence the faithful widow of a man who has died without a son will conscientiously try to become pregnant before the end of his Dry Funeral" (Mandelbaum 1959, 191–92).

On the one hand, Hertz's theoretical ideas were ahead of his time, but, on the other, Hertz has much in common with other early thinkers on the subject because of his cool objectivism and his armchair methodology. Edward E. Evans-Pritchard makes note of it in the introduction to the 1960 English translation: "One feels sometime[s] in reading these essays a remoteness from the realities of primitive life," and he goes on to explain that neither Durkheim nor any of his pupils "had ever seen a primitive people" in person (Evans-Pritchard 1960, 23). What we hope to accomplish in the present volume is to echo Hertz's attention to process and the social construction of meaning while avoiding his "remoteness" and lack of ethnographic specificity. Death is a part of being human, not apart from being human.

Instead, we follow Renato Rosaldo (1989), whose succinct critical summary of "classical" ethnographic analysis in his important essay "Grief and the Headhunter's Rage" marked a key turning point not only for death studies but for the discipline as a whole. Rosaldo turned our attention away from the ways death fits into the social or symbolic structure of societies and toward the emotional and lived experience of death and mourning. This is a decidedly cultural rather than sociological approach to the subject, since we focus in this volume on the affective experience of the event(s) instead of the formulas by which societies structure their rituals and beliefs about that event. Moreover, a key argument for Rosaldo is that we need to position ourselves in relation to the subject at hand, as he himself does in his essay about his own wife's death. For Rosaldo, this is no mere theoretical exercise. He describes how he never fully understood the Ilongot peoples' explanation for why they practice headhunting until his wife's tragic slip. It was only then that he understood the links between the heavy emotions of mourning the dead and the release the Ilongot feel in the rage of headhunting. "Either you understand it or you don't," he writes about the headhunting. "And, in fact, for the longest time I simply did not" (Rosaldo 1989, 1–2). Suddenly, though, in that moment the combined feelings of grief and rage in the face of death the Ilongot had described to him came crashing down on him, too. For Rosaldo, it was a terrible way to discover that positionality shapes our ethnographic interpretations. Since then, instead of following the impulse to objectify death and dying, he implored ethnographers to approach the lived experience of our subjects with sensitivity, a respect for a sense of humanity, and a closeness to the scene. In the collection that follows, we present case studies that take this advice to heart.

FRAME 3: DEATH AS DIS/EMBODIMENT

By the 1980s, several threads had come together out of the feminist critique and the broader postmodern turn that had a profound impact on how anthropologists analyzed the unborn, the living, and the dead as they exist within the wider social milieu. Hertz had acknowledged the differences between "the self" versus "the person" as early as 1907 (Hertz 1960 [1907], 77), and Marcel Mauss had initiated a more forceful discussion about those differences as a total social phenomenon in a 1938 lecture. It was not until the 1980s, however, that the "category of the person" (Carrithers, Collins, and Lukes 1985), which is socially produced (Strathern 1988) and which is quite different from the idea of a sovereign, atomized individual, found fertile ground in which to grow. With the idea of the "social person" more firmly in place, much more could be said about how a biological death does not necessarily correspond with an individual's social death. Personhood relies on social relations, and, as such, one's social death need not correspond to the (in)exact moment of biological death. In fact, in the chapters that follow this introduction, the secondary funerary customs described by Adams in Tana Toraja and the "living" personhood of the dead in social media described by Kohn and colleagues illustrate this distinction.

Another prominent thread focusing on death and the body emerged with the combination of feminist studies, Foucault's influential ideas about biopolitics, the burgeoning field of medical anthropology (Kaufman and Morgan 2005, 327–28), and a sharpened focus outside of academia on bioethics in an age when end-of-life decisions are increasingly complex (Kaufman and Morgan 2005, 319). Biomedical technology has presented us with numerous moral and practical problems. One challenge is to (re)define death itself. As mentioned earlier, Hertz cogently illustrated in 1907 that biological death is not coterminous with one's social death, that death is a process rather than an event. So, these are not new ideas. However, in an age of high-tech interventions, organ transplants, and the ability to artificially support a patient's body even after "brain death," biological death has turned into a series of excruciating "mini-deaths" as organs slowly shut down despite the efforts of medical professionals. Ariès describes what he calls "these little silent deaths": "Death is a technical phenomenon obtained by a cessation of care, a cessation determined in a more or less avowed way by a decision of the doctor and a hospital team... Death has been dissected, cut to bits by a series of little steps, which finally makes it impossible to know which step was the real death" (Ariès 1974, 88). Exactly how doctors ought to designate the official "declaration of death" is highly contested now in the medical profession as well as in the public and the courts (Barry 2007, 15–30).

If the body does not die all at once, then the dying individual may come to occupy liminal spaces between life and death. Popular science writer Nick Lane (2005) considers death apoptosis writ large as our mitochondria commit programmed cell death. At a more macro social level, octogenarian anthropologist Ed Bruner, for example, sometimes feels he is "partially dead" when overlooked at academic conferences he once used to headline (Bruner 2014, 30). More forthrightly, Nancy Scheper-Hughes takes this distinction further, describing the deceased as "very dead" while the brain dead are "dead/not quite dead" (Scheper-Hughes 2004, 31). Scheper-Hughes's recent work on the global commodification of human organs (cf. Scheper-Hughes 2000, 2004) illustrates how the body—at least in part(s)—lives on after the individual occupying it has long since died. Her recent exploration of human organs trafficking is a disturbing example of the moral dilemmas that arise when biotechnology and capitalism collide with the material afterlife of human remains. Given the loose oversight of the organ transplant "industrial complex" and the exploitation of the global poor, Scheper-Hughes's work on death and the "afterlife" of human organs raises questions about the (im)moral terrain at the intersection of globalized medicine and neoliberal economics and culture.

At the same time, even supporters of her work recognize the controversy surrounding the ethics of her own methodological exploration of that "uncanny" territory (Suarez-Orozco 2000, 217). While Scheper-Hughes argues that her work is driven by a politicized and laudable desire to advocate for the most powerless, ironically, her self-described "militant" approach and her breathless writing—which can sometimes feel like she is going for shock value as much as a sense of social justice—lack the kind of sensitivity we hope to achieve here. She goes so far as to describe her work as "muckracking" and "enraged ethnography" (Scheper-Hughes

2004, 35); others consider it "desecrating" (Egan and Murphy 2015, 138). Moreover, she conducts globally oriented multi-site fieldwork at 10,000 feet in elevation that by her own admission resembles undercover investigative journalism as much as it does ethnography (Scheper-Hughes 2004). By contrast, this volume attempts to ground our discussions of risk, death, and dying in specific social contexts, close to our subjects, hearing and "keening" their lament.

Frame 4: Death as Leisure

Scheper-Hughes uses the framework of tourism to discuss the mobility of people and organs across the globe. Specifically, she calls it "transplant tourism" (Scheper-Hughes 2004, 36). In a similar framework, others discuss "suicide tourism" when people travel to destinations that allow medically assisted suicide (see below; for a small sample of recent analyses, see Gross et al. 2007; Higgenbotham 2011; Huxtable 2009). This raises an important distinction about the present volume. Here, we explore leisurely activities—tourism included—that intersect with risk, death, and dying. But we argue that "dark tourism" and other forms of "dark leisure"—for want of better expressions—are distinct from examples of travel such as transplant tourism or suicide tourism because the latter are mobilities unfocused on leisure. What we seek here is to explore how risk, death, and dying intersect with a wide range of leisure-oriented pursuits, from tourism to social media and from dining to bird watching.

There would seem to be a range of new avenues to explore in the anthropology of death and dying, and, once again, it seems that anthropologists have turned their attention more fully toward the subject. In the introduction to *Death, Mourning, and Burial* (2011), Antonius C.G.M. Robben calls for six new directions in the anthropological study of death: (1) a more developed anthropological critique of other fields such as biomedicine, (2) a bolder commitment to cross-cultural comparison, (3) more self-reflective analysis à la Rosaldo, (4) more focus on the material culture of death, (5) analyses that are much more death-centered as opposed to using death to actually study the living, and (6) studying death through the various sub-disciplines in anthropology (Robben 2011, 12–14). No single work can hope to cover all of these areas, but the present volume addresses at least three of these concerns. First, although many authors in the volume focus on European geographic contexts, most chapters examine death and dying cross-culturally. With this connection between leisure and death in place, we hope the present volume prompts even more cross-cultural examinations from all over the world. Second, our intention is to take a "death-centered approach," which Robben suggests. Finally, through the lens of leisure, we are intentionally attaching the study of death to a new, burgeoning set of sub-disciplines in anthropology that cross over into adjacent fields, including the anthropologies of tourism, food, sport, heritage, and religion. One fast-emerging cross-disciplinary area the present volume intersects with but also significantly diverges from is the study of "dark tourism" where leisure studies engages with sites of death, dying, and atrocity (cf. Lennon and Foley 2000). As anthropologists, our preoccupation here, though, is with the living at these sites.

MOVEMENT, ENCOUNTER, EXPERIENCE, AND AFTERLIFE

JONATHAN, AUGUST 10, 2015
We are on a summer day trip to the coast, to Beachy Head, an infamous beauty spot and notorious death spot—a site for suicide. It is a wry trip: part break, part research curiosity while editing Adam Kaul's chapter in this volume about the Cliffs of Moher and that awful margin between life and death glooming large across the landscape. Here lies another such site (see figure 0.2). We see the crosses lining a misty cliff edge. I feel vertigo, and senses slide and spin from proximity to the 500-ft chalk wall. A male tourist tries to point down the side of the cliff, mentioning "a man," "a body" in broken English. We leave flustered and later return along the path among more visiting tourists. A family is talking to one of the chaplains who patrol the edge, a Christian crisis and suicide prevention team I want to research. They are concerned for a man they saw pacing around, jacketless, half an hour ago. I mention a tourist trying to point out a body. We return to the spot: "Seven o'clock." He looks. I don't. He calls his headquarters, the police, the coast guard. I take a photograph.

Let us now take you through the contributions to this collection. Leisure and Death on the Move is the first section in the volume, beginning with Maribeth Erb considering the death of the tourist in Indonesia in instances where violence and pleasure collide. Faced with the occasional violent death of a tourist, tourist locations such as Labuan Bajo, on the island of Flores in eastern Indonesia, can take on different meanings and become threshold settings between paradise and Hell, where actors and agents have different changing responsibilities associated with them. With death, the onus on hospitality shifts to one of responsibility. Should the locals engage in traditional death rituals of guarding the corpse, the mete, for tourists such as the ill-fated Bob from New Zealand, a lost traveler who lost his life? Erb raises challenging issues surrounding the changing value of the tourist—alive and dead—and their impact on the moral as well as financial economy of the host community.

The moral dimension surrounding lives lost continues in the second chapter in this section, where Keith Egan looks at how the modern-day pilgrimage to Santiago—the Camino de Santiago—serves as "a moral anchor." Quite literally,

FIGURE 0.2. Calling in a suicide at Beachy Head. Photo by Jonathan Skinner, 2015

the walk, a self-imposed route march, puts the tourist/pilgrim back on track in life. The re-creation of this medieval physical purgatory allows walkers to self-author, to re-script, to gain traction over their life narratives that they feel have run out of control, ahead of them, a-kilter. This jilting takes place at a pace they are comfortable with and represents for many a symbolic death as they traverse this liminal ground. There is an authenticity about the participants' time-out or time-in-between: both the physicality of the process—involving the "natural" body, unmediated by technological modernity, and the link to the past, to medieval pilgrimage across Europe and the intimate spirituality of a personal presence with the remains of Saint James. The contrast between tourism and spirituality is evinced here, between making a life as a tourist living life to the fullest potential and engaging with the taking of a life that can be referring back to Christian religion—a death cult if ever there was one (see the Dark Tourism, Leisure, and the Subjunctive section below)—or to the burdens of the deceased or one's mortality, all of which precipitate the pilgrim's peregrinations. In other words, the dead Other can move the Self.

In the third and final chapter in this section, Patrick Laviolette introduces us to free climbing and "tombstoning," hazardous activities involving either traversing a cliff face or throwing oneself off an overhang into water. This is facing death or, rather, playing with the potential for death. The risky behavior turns a landscape into an adventure-scape or a play-scape, frightening with a frisson. Laviolette suggests that this form of play is marginal and subversive for thrill seekers who want to jump a leap of faith rather than carry out their death wish. Mashing up art theory (Andy Warhol's aesthetics in anticipating danger) and anthropology (Johan Huizinga's theory of play as simultaneously emancipatory and ordering), Laviolette gives us a framework for how he and others experience the rush of the fall, the clarity and sense of purpose felt in the aftershock of the moment with its uncertainties. This is in contrast to the inevitability of the suicide jumper and so anticipates, and provides an antithesis to, Kaul's chapter later on. Like the pilgrims, these recreational thrill seekers reject industrial modernity and seek a return to elemental living. They are in their element in the extreme. Unlike the pilgrim, however, this is a feeling they return to again and again. They do not tire from their pilgrimage. In each chapter in this section, death for the mobile tourist, pilgrim, and thrill seeker is a marginalizing experience with, respectively, ritual, symbolic, and ludic qualities.

Part 2 of this volume looks at Tourist Encounters with the Dead. In the first chapter in this section we return to Indonesia, to Tana Toraja, where the rituals of cleansing and re-dressing the corpses of ancestors have led to Western mortuary tourism. Kathleen Adams examines leisure in the "Land of the Walking Dead" as westerners search out the "Torajan zombies" on the internet and in their physical travels. They have been attracted by the (social) media photographs of so-called zombies, first imaged as selfies with deceased relatives but subsequently decontextualized as the images go viral. This tourist practice reanimates, for Adams, the debate on mortality that holds out for the possibility of interaction with the (un)dead. The tourists are perhaps playing with the nature of death, theirs and the others. This is a more comfortable engagement with a fraught issue that is often buried away: here, though, the normative Western order of life and death can be met, inverted, and re-imagined. It is not so much a metaphor about enslavement or the violence of society as an attraction to the spectacular in society that we mentioned earlier. This is extreme ethnic tourism exploiting the ultimate Other. Or even in the non-West where one is more inured to violence and death and its many forms of immolation (cf. Scheper-Hughes 1992).

The prevention of death is the subject of the next chapter, with Adam Kaul looking at the awful margin, the edge between land and sea, between life and death, between Ireland and the Atlantic that dramatically cuts the environment at the Cliffs of Moher. This tourist site is a known suicide destination and a place where patrons play with the boundaries of life and death. As such, it can be a transformative and restorative space where the great majority of people reject imminent death and so affirm life. For those who die by suicide over the cliffs, there is the Catholic stigma of committing a mortal sin. In a less religious time, the experience of the Cliffs of Moher is more about risk and entertainment, a family-friendly version of Laviolette's thrill seekers who take selfies at angles to give the impression of their imminent suicide or watch high-tech trailers in the new Interpretive Centre of a bird plummeting down the cliff face into the sea—an anthropomorphic or shamanistic non-suicide. As with Adams's zombie hunters, the tourist mocks the risk of death, as well as evincing an ambivalent push-pull, repulsion-attraction with the cliff face. Is laughing in the face of our fate our mechanism for processing and coming to terms with it? Perhaps this lies at the heart of the macabre and the spectacular that we find at steep cliffs all across the world, from Ireland's Moher to England's Beachy Head and Brazil's Pedra do Telégrafo. Furthermore, for Kaul, tourists' visit to the Cliffs of Moher is a natural confrontation with death as opposed to the unnatural state of the living dead zombie. Akin to Egan's pilgrim, the tourist narrates or imagines his or her potential fate. This seldom comes to pass, and so the experience comforts the tourists and quickens their spirit for life when they turn their backs on the cliffs. For those who do not return, Kaul makes the point that the site of their suicide extends their social world, as the memory of the person comes to be inextricably connected to the locale. In effect, the cliff side becomes a romantic prosthetic of death.

Tourists' encounter with death continues in the final chapter in this section. Here, Shingo Iitaka explores the interconnections between war memory and tourism on the Palau Islands of Micronesia, the setting of vicious land and sea battles between the Japanese and Americans during World War II. Thousands of soldiers, sailors, and civilians on both sides of the conflict lost their lives during the Pacific War. The islands are still pockmarked with bomb craters, and the leftover detritus of war can still be viewed on this landscape and in its surrounding waters. Iitaka chronicles the development of memorial tours (*ireidan*) to Palau that have grown in popularity since the late 1960s as Japanese veterans/tourists/pilgrims mourn the dead in paradise. This juxtaposition of warscape and South Seas paradise, of dark tourism with light tourism so Iitaka suggests, is a tourism of counterpoint, one that is complementary rather than opposing as days are spent variously diving for warships, strolling through gardens, laying memorial wreaths, sunbathing on beaches. Sometimes the blending is more immediate, such as a recreational dive trip passing the ruined body of a Japanese Zero fighter plane for photos. We should beware the essentialization, then, of death from leisure and the notion that death and leisure are mutually exclusive. Traveling for leisure and touring to sites of death can be integrated activities in tourists' itineraries. These entanglements become more apparent in the third section in this volume: Life, Decay, and the Sensual Experience of Death.

The war tourists to the Palau Islands are attracted to the authenticity of their tourist gaze. Authenticity in the tourist endeavor features in many of the chapters in this volume. In the next chapter, European ossuaries, vestiges of the medieval *memento mori*—memorials to the living, reminders that they, too, will soon die—are seen as exhibit spaces of the authentic death. We respectfully include here, next, our colleague Cyril Schäfer's chapter that was a work in progress when he himself suddenly died. It has been completed by his close friend and colleague Ruth McManus, also from New Zealand. It is a dramatic piece about how death, a phenomenon increasingly sequestered and tabooed in twentieth-century Western societies, is becoming more and more transparent in the twenty-first. But this is not a new phenomenon: a number of repositories for the remains of the dead, such as charnel houses and ossuaries, have long been sites for the aesthetic display of exhumed bodies, the skulls and bones set in spectacular mass displays. This "second 'burial'" is a confrontation with death that has become a tourist attraction in many European countries. Schäfer toured a number of these contemporary dark tourism sites in Germany and Czechoslovakia. He found "real" undomesticated death sought out but commodified, Disneyified, and made banal by the selfie. Ironically, the dead had to be protected from the nonchalance of the living. These tangible instances of the disappeared were too rearranged and too polished and bleached for visitors to feel a transcendence or supra-natural spirituality or to get a waft of the stench of death. They thus came away from them numb—unlike the reactions of the (suicide) tourist, pilgrim, veteran, or thrill seeker.

The last two chapters in this section of the volume consider narratives of heritage and their violent present. Ray Casserly looks at the contentious sounds of the parading tradition in Northern Ireland where traditional music is associated with a politicized past, and Rachel Horner Brackett looks at nostalgia for a simpler past through specialist breeding in Tuscany, a practice attracting gastro-tourists from around the world. In very different ways, both chapters are about a sensual heritage in people's traditional living that is perceived to be under threat. In both research practices, the anthropologists are also deeply engaged with their study groups: Casserly as a musician and drum instructor, Horner Brackett as volunteer farmworker and butchering assistant. In Northern Ireland, Casserly notes that music has political meaning. It is more than leisure entertainment. It divides the communities, symbolizes the differences, and serves as a boundary marker: traditional Irish music with songs of famine and political struggle for Roman Catholics, military marching music for Protestants parading in defense of their rights and memorializing their dead. Annually, the July 12 parades, Unionist parades commemorating the Battle of the Boyne in 1692, lead to casual rioting on the streets and a standoff between members of the two communities. This rioting expresses a discontent with the political status quo in the country. It is also casual, leisurely for all its dangerousness, a rite of passage for youths growing up in a "just" post-conflict environment. For them, Casserly suggests, the rioting and the risk of death it creates becomes a badge of honor as the conflict years are reenacted for a few days each year. Recreational violence spills out of the commemoration of the July–November

1916 Battle of the Somme when Ulstermen spilled blood for their country. The historical narrative of survival is sustained through what Republicans—those who want to absorb Northern Ireland into the Republic of Ireland—see as a taunting triumphalist display of traditional authority.

Sensual heritage practices and traditional ways have been extended in a different way as we swap songs of famine for gastro-tourism on an estate in Tuscany. There, tourists pay for a food experience with the endangered Cinta Senese pig, savoring its leisurely pastoral life and paradoxically relishing its culinary death. Horner Brackett found that, for a number of tourists, the visceral and deadly transformation of the pigs into pork products is a part of their tourist experience: they want to experience the "full cycle" of meat production on the farm rather than the invisible death and butchery they get from supermarket chains. Furthermore, the taste of the meat is better after the animal's "leisurely" death, according to the farm manager. These bloodthirsty tourists are modern subjects pursuing a traditional cultural capital and manmade leisure capital by buying and biting into a "slow" sensory experience with a particular food. This chapter introduces an important link that is often missed in the literature on dark tourism: a leisurely tourist engagement with *animal* death.

The final section in this volume is titled Afterlife and After-Leisure. Here, we have three chapters that look at leisure and social relations with the dead. Beginning with the virtual, Tamara Kohn, Michael Arnold, Martin Gibbs, James Meese, and Bjorn Nansen look at the social life of the dead on Facebook, where over 30 million virtual personas linger in longevity on social media far beyond their physical years. Kohn and colleagues examine how these dead maintain a presence in these leisure spaces for the living. In their Facebook memorialization they are "the lively dead"— our colleague Cyril Schäfer would be included in this. These sites are suspended, repurposed, tended, and maintained by friends and followers, trawled for data and trolled for kicks such that Kohn and colleagues contend there is an ongoing diachronic relationship with the dead. This is more than an online wake. In addition to memorialization, Kohn and colleagues look at networked images on Facebook that circulate as selfies taken at funerals and selfies taken before dying. The former is a transgressive act to gain ironic currency on social media and so has a different meaning than the selfies with zombies Adams writes about. The latter is a subjunctive referent to our future engagement with death insofar as an "it could have been me" and our imagination of the forthcoming pain. Here, the infra-ordinary of our lives with mundane social media leisure practice is recontextualized into the extraordinary social spectacle on social media. These are digital *memento mori*.

The second chapter in this section presents a fine-grained analysis of the spread of rumors and gossip at a funeral in traditional Greece. This imaginative narration of death, Stavroula Pipyrou argues, is part of the subject's social death. She gives the detailed example of Panos, a wealthy businessman, part-outsider, who died suddenly of cardiac arrest. The gossip about his lives and loves creates an individual and collective history of the person—the dividual—as he dissolves into the gossipers' memories. Death again precipitates leisure in the sense of the leisurely comments made about Panos. The silence and re-fabrication are coping mechanisms as a trace of the now absent person. For Pipyrou, death invites these speculations, and they pass through the community as a form of entertainment. These narrative and narrated additions to Panos become a verbal prosthesis that re-creates and multiplies him. In death, leisure practice extends Panos and makes him "legion."

Linking with Pipyrou, fecundity and decomposition as concepts are also apparent, literally, in the last chapter in the volume, as Hannah Rumble looks at the changing British "deathscape" of the burial space. She looks at how the recreational woodlands or pastoral fields are becoming "natural" burial grounds. From Adams to Horner Brackett, time factors into the transitions between life and death. A non-sequestered, "slow" approach to burial in recreational space brings the living and the dead more informally together, Rumble finds. Reading a book, eating a picnic, walking a dog, "lingering" through open-air burial services are all more natural, rounded ways of engaging with one's grief. In these hallowed willowed grounds, leisure, life, and death become entangled. As Rumble opines, "natural" becomes the capacity for these burial places to bring the living and the dead more informally together. A meadow or woodland as a "natural burial ground" is an example of minimal memorialization but is "theme parking" all the same and the focus for the visitor—typically, a local or a family member more so than a tourist. For each, it is seen as life-affirming. Thus, we end the book with a hopeful counterpoint to the common assumption that we live in denial of death. Perhaps we are finally coming around to embracing our mortality once again.

DARK TOURISM, LEISURE, AND THE SUBJUNCTIVE

JONATHAN, DECEMBER 13, 2014
I'm taking field notes during a tango class and an evening of dancing in London. Graham is sitting near the entrance to a Sunday night milonga in the center of London. He's scanning the room for his usual dance partners while making witty conversation with those passing into the venue. He's not dancing yet, instead cursing the music that does not suit his Sunday mood:
"I hate this tango lift music. I want to feel wrist-slashing music. To get to my soul. I was brought up on rock and roll. At my time of life, I want a teacher to give me moves I can actually do. I don't have much time left. It's not as though I started dancing in my twenties or thirties."

Leisure specifically meets death in dark tourism, that new niche or intersection between tourism and trauma. The term emerged from a special issue of the *International Journal of Heritage Studies* (1996) edited by John Lennon and Malcolm Foley. It was subsequently elaborated upon in their 2000 book *Dark Tourism* and has led to the rise of an Institute for Dark Tourism Research at the University of Lancashire under the directorship of Philip Stone. Lennon and Foley suggest that the concept is a symptom of our postmodern age. It is a desire to view the commoditized remains of the industrial-level atrocity around us. It has spawned a range of studies on this topic, from slavery and contested heritage sites in the Deep South (Dann and Seaton 2001; Seaton 2012) and the former Nazi Germany (Macdonald 2009) to analyses of new forms of commemoration and memorialization at Ground Zero (Sather-Wagstaff 2011; see also Phipps 1999; Edkins 2004; Sharpley and Stone 2009; Skinner 2010; Stone 2011; Sturken 2007). Advocates suggest that dark tourism is an opportunity for the living to reflect on their living. They contend that these deathscapes have become leisure spaces for meditation on mortality and, as such, mediation points for the temporary visitor. As Stone (2013, 308) writes, "Visiting sites of mortality can reveal ontological anxieties about the past as well as the future." In our volume we suggest that these sites are lodestones that are Janus-faced, *pointing out* the past and, by doing so, also *pointing to* our inevitable future. For Anthony Seaton, the *memento mori* associate dark tourism with a wider and more established Romancing with death. Mass dark tourism is for him an upscaling of thanatourism—an obsessive "Christian fatality" (Seaton 2012, 528) that has burgeoned for centuries.

The chapters in this volume coalesce around this leisure, tourism, and death nexus while also expanding the range of leisurely encounters with death beyond tourism. They seek to avoid some of the more marked criticisms associated with "dark tourism" research: whether distinctions of gradations of "dark, darker, darkest tourism" (Stone 2006; Sharpley 2009; Hepburn 2012); whether politically incorrect and racially color biased (Bowman and Pezzullo 2009); whether fragmenting or reductionist, establishing a "periodic table of dark matter" (Dale and Robinson 2011, 215). As anthropologists, ours has been an emic take on the relationship between leisure and death: rather than strip out the human subject and dehumanize the experience of death and dying, we retain the complexity and particularism of lived experiences and press for the tactile and tactical humanism suggested by Abu-Lughod (1993). This is apparent in the characterization of Bob from New Zealand (Erb), Kerry from the United States (Egan), Panos the Vlach (Pipyrou), Facebook Jim (Kohn and colleagues), the administrator (Rumble), and the tourist center staff members who double as suicide counselors (Kaul), as well as in the various involved positions of the researching anthropologists who jump (Laviolette), butcher (Horner Brackett), and walk (Egan). Both authors and subjects spell out their hopes, fears, desires, worries, imaginations. By so doing, they too—like the sites described, or "attractions" rather—face backward as well as forward.

It would be too easy to characterize this book as a compendium of "dark leisure" and so fall foul of the criticisms of dark tourism above. Instead, our slant is more temporal, toward a subjunctive approach to death and leisure. The subjunctive is an apt way of approaching these topics because it expresses a state of unreality, one typically positioned ahead in something imagined or wished, such as a vacation experience. It also allows us to position ourselves as the tourist and to think about what was. Chris Rojek (1993) makes a related point in his classic *Ways of Escape*. Visiting the Texas Book Depository, Rojek (1993, 138) points out that "one is asked to project oneself into the past." For Rojek, leisure is commonly understood as an "arena of 'freedom,' 'choice' and 'self-development'" (1993, 4), as a cultural practice "in a state of voluntarism" (2010, 1). It is an experience akin to an escape from modern life by the alienated worker who has been seduced into emulating a form of bourgeois culture. Echoing Dean MacCannell (1989, 6) on modern mass leisure ("the alienation of the worker stops where the alienation of the sightseer begins"), Rojek holds to an understanding of leisure filtered through a Marxist lens as the prerogative of the bourgeois leisured-class-turned-leisure-society (cf. Seabrook 1995). Leisure is traditionally "the reward for work" (Rojek 2010, 1). As leisure subjunctive, it is an aspirational false consciousness that keeps us to the treadmill while we tramp toward "a future near at hand but elsewhere" (Rojek 1993, 214). Thus, Rojek develops Baudrillard (1981) to describe late twentieth-century leisure in a postindustrial era—postmodern leisure—as empty, depthless, and more sensational than meaningful. It is almost as if notions of leisure have indeed turned full circle, back to the indolence and quiescence criticized as an understanding of leisure by Thorstein Veblen at the cusp of the twentieth century.

Where Veblen (1994 [1897], 28) saw leisure as the "non-productive consumption of time," leisure is no longer about self-improvement or self-actualization, struggle or transformation. We (re)make our destinations and fashion our own authenticities. Boundaries are ever blurred in this hyper-real, post-leisure, and post-tourism condition. To give an example, in the period October 2015 through March 2016, the Bristol Museum "staged" the exhibition *Death: The Human Experience* (Bristol Museum and Art Gallery 2016b). This was a public space fashioning a set of contemporary exhibitions, installations, and public discussions around the subject of death. Part education, part leisure, part provocation, part advertisement, the events were supported by the independent global charitable foundation the Wellcome Trust and

FIGURE 0.3. Listening to "suicide tourist" testimony in re-created Dignitas room, Bristol Museum. Photo by Hannah Rumble, 2016.

sponsored by the Co-operative Funeralcare, with a range of Dying Matters leaflets running seamlessly from instruction in "Talking to Children about Dying" (Dying Matters n.d.) to booking one's own funeral with the cooperative with "My Funeral Wishes" (Dying Matters n.d.). The latter is the trade name of Funeral Services Limited, a subsidiary of the Co-operative Group, one of the United Kingdom's largest food retailers—which, incidentally, also has a joint-venture travel business with the high-street travel agent Thomas Cook (Co-Operative Group 2016). This is an example of a leisure-and-death-business simultaneously running over 900 funeral homes and more than 1,200 high-street travel shops.

Part of the exhibition consisted of an installation, a re-creation of a room in the Dignitas flat in Zurich where members come for assisted dying. Some would argue that these visitors are "suicide tourists" (Gauthier et al. 2015), though what constitutes leisure and tourism is up for debate—particularly if the visitor does not return alive, and his or her preoccupations during the journey are more about death and dying than recreational. In figure 0.3, contributor Hannah Rumble has taken a photo of Jonathan Skinner listening to the voice of someone who has died by assisted suicide at Dignitas. On the wall to his right, out of frame, is a photo of the real room this room has been made to resemble, only in that room there are no voices or testimonies. This hyper-real room has been enhanced for ostensible educational purposes, as noted by the presumed curator: "The space will allow visitors to explore their own feelings about the debate through a sensory as well as an intellectual experience guided by medical, ethical, philosophical and emotive elements" (Bristol Museum and Art Gallery 2016a).

CONCLUSIONS: A POSTMODERN POSTMORTEM

In play, anthropologists see (re)creation. In the global playground, we use tourism as a ritual practice in which to imagine anew, to perform and enact and reexamine our place in the natural order. Play is a part of leisure. It is also what makes us human: *homo ludens* for Johan Huizinga (1950). It is an opportune time in which to test, dissolve, and revolt against the norms and conventions of social structure. It is the time of anti-structure, to invoke the late anthropologist Victor Turner (1982), the liminoid experience in contemporary secular society such as the rave or a football match (St. John 2008): "Just as when tribesmen make masks, disguise themselves as monsters, heap up disparate ritual symbols, invert or parody profane reality in myths and folk-tales, so do the genres of industrial leisure, the theatre, poetry, novel, ballet, film, sport, rock music, classical music, art, pop art, etc., *play* with the factors of culture, sometimes assembling them in random, grotesque, improbable, surprising, shocking, usually experimental combinations" (Turner 1982, 40, original italics). In this light, the seemingly improbable connections between leisure and death are made entirely probable, perhaps even expected.

These structured, theatrical playtimes on an industrial scale are the times when we are "permitted" to perform differently and work on establishing our proto-narratives of what could have been and still can be fashioned out of what was (cf. Appadurai 1996). Taken to the extreme, this is "serious leisure" when the practice becomes "core" and the practitioner becomes "committed" to his or her activity (Stebbins 2007), whether body building, studying, hunting, walking, praying, making a pilgrimage, dancing. This systematic release is a form of disciplined freedom for anthropologists Coleman and Kohn (2007), a state of "flow" for psychologist Csikszentmihalyi (1981). To take a leaf out of Coleman and Kohn's *The Discipline of Leisure* (cf. 2007, 2), what we are certain of in this volume is that leisure and death are the times when self and sociality are remade, reproduced, remarked upon.

The confrontation between death, dying, and leisure may be nothing new, as we have illustrated in this introductory chapter, but we have also argued that the nature of our current leisurely consumption of death reflects our particular moment. After all, as Talcott Parsons wrote, death "has needed to be redefined and newly analyzed, virtually with every generation" (1978, 255). In this late-capitalist, neoliberal era, when everything is a commodity, even death is for sale. In the postmodern world in which everything is ironic, even death is a joke, a subject for casual and festive entertainments. And in a cultural moment of hyper-individuation and digital cybernetic life-worlds in which the selfie has become the symbolic avatar of the self, the expiration of one's life no longer means the end of one's personhood. Refracting the subject of risk, death, and dying through the lens of leisure, it seems that indeed death still has many ways to surprise us.

NOTES

1. Not everyone is so convinced. Some have questioned the thesis of death denial (cf. Parsons 1978; Barry 2007).

2. The commodified consumption of death is found not only in the abstract in pop culture; it is also quite literal. Death in the West is a mortuary-industrial complex (for an early journalistic critique of the US mortuary industry, see Mitford 1963). America, for Ariès, has a "very characteristic mixture of commerce and idealism [where burials] are the object of showy publicity, like any other consumer's item, be it soap or religion" (Ariès 1974, 101).

3. Hertz's essays were compiled by Mauss into a single volume in 1928 and later translated by Needham and Needham and republished as *Death and the Right Hand* in 1960.

REFERENCES

Abu-Lughod, Lila. 1993. *Writing Women's Worlds: Bedouin Stories*. Berkeley: University of California Press.

Appadurai, Arjun. 1996. *Modernity at Large: Cultural Dimensions of Globalization*. Minneapolis: University of Minnesota Press.

Ariès, Philippe. 1974. *Western Attitudes towards Death*. Baltimore: Johns Hopkins University Press.

Árnason, Arnar, and Sigurjón Baldur Hafsteinsson. 2003. "The Revival of Death: Expression, Expertise, and Governmentality." *British Journal of Sociology* 54 (1): 43–62. https://doi.org/10.1080/0007131032000045897.

Barley, Nigel. 2006 [1995]. *Grave Matters: Encounters with Death around the World*. Long Grove, IL: Waveland.

Barry, Vincent. 2007. *Philosophical Thinking about Death and Dying*. Belmont, CA: Thompson Wadsworth.

Baudrillard, Jean. 1981. *For a Critique of the Political Economy of the Sign*. St. Louis, MO: Telos.

Baudrillard, Jean. 1993 [1976]. *Symbolic Exchange and Death*. London: Sage.

Becker, Ernest. 1973. *The Denial of Death*. New York: Free Press.
Benedict, Ruth. 1959 [1934]. *Patterns of Culture*. Geneva, IL: Houghton Mifflin.
Berger, Peter, and Thomas Luckmann. 1989 [1966]. *The Social Construction of Reality: A Treatise in the Sociology of Knowledge*. New York: Doubleday.
Bloch, Maurice, and Jonathan Parry, eds. 1982. *Death and the Regeneration of Life*. Cambridge: Cambridge University Press.
Bowman, Michael S., and Phaedra C. Pezzullo. 2009. "What's So 'Dark' about 'Dark Tourism'? Death, Tours, and Performance." *Tourist Studies* 9 (3): 187–202. https://doi.org/10.1177/1468797610382699.
Bristol Museum and Art Gallery. 2016a. "Death: Is It Your Right to Choose?" Accessed March 7, 2016. https://www.bristolmuseums.org.uk/bristol-museum-and-art-gallery/whats-on/death-is-it-your-right-to-choose/.
Bristol Museum and Art Gallery. 2016b. *Death: The Human Experience*. Exhibition, October 24, 2015–March 13, 2016. Accessed March 6, 2016. https://www.bristolmuseums.org.uk/bristol-museum-and-art-gallery/whats-on/death-human-experience.
Bruner, Edward. 2014. "The Aging Anthropology." *Anthropology and Humanism* 39 (1): 27–31. https://doi.org/10.1111/anhu.12034.
Carrithers, Michael, Steven Collins, and Steven Lukes. 1985. *The Category of the Person: Anthropology, Philosophy, History*. Cambridge: Cambridge University Press.
Coleman, Simon, and Tamara Kohn. 2007. "The Discipline of Leisure: Taking Play Seriously." In *The Discipline of Leisure: Embodying Cultures of Recreation*, ed. Simon Coleman and Tamara Kohn, 1–22. Oxford: Berhahn.
The Co-Operative Group. 2016. "Who We Are." Accessed March 6, 2016. https://www.co-operative.coop/corporate/aboutus/an-introduction/.
Csikszentmihalyi, Mihalyi. 1981. "Leisure and Socialization." *Social Forces* 60 (2): 332–40. https://doi.org/10.2307/2578438.
Dale, Crispin, and Neil Robinson. 2011. "Dark Tourism." In *Research Themes for Tourism*, ed. Peter Robinson, Sue Heitmann, and Peter U.C. Deike, 205–17. Wallingford: CABI.
Dann, Graham M.S., and Anthony V. Seaton, eds. 2001. *Slavery, Contested Heritage, and Thanatourism*. New York: Haworth Hospitality Press.
Desmond, Jane. 2002. "Displaying Death, Animating Life: Changing Fictions of 'Liveness' Taxidermy to Animatronics." In *Representing Animals*, ed. Nigel Rothfels, 159–79. Bloomington: University of Indiana Press.
Desmond, Jane. 2011. "Touring the Dead: Imagination, Embodiment, and Affect in Gunter Von Hagen's Body Worlds Exhibitions." In *Great Expectations: Imagination and Anticipation in Tourism*, ed. Jonathan Skinner and Theodossopoulos Dimitrios, 174–219. London: Berghahn Books.

Doquet, Anne, and Olivier Evrard. 2008. "An Interview with Jean Didier Urbain—Tourism beyond the Grave: A Semiology of Culture." *Tourist Studies* 8 (2): 175–91. https://doi.org/10.1177/1468797608099247.

Douglas, Mary. 2003 [1966]. *Purity and Danger: An Analysis of Concepts of Pollution and Taboo*. London: Psychology Press.

Durkheim, Émile. 1897. *Le Suicide: Étude de Sociologie*. Paris: Felix Alcan.

Durkheim, Émile. 1951 [1897]. *Suicide: A Study in Sociology*, trans. John A. Spaulding and George Simpson. Glencoe, IL: Free Press.

Dying Matters. n.d. "Talking to Children about Dying." Let's Talk about It leaflet. Accessed November 11, 2016. www.dyingmatters.org.

Dying Matters. n.d. "My Funeral Wishes." Let's Talk about It leaflet. Accessed November 11, 2016. www.dyingmatters.org.

Edkins, Jenny. 2004. "Ground Zero: Reflections on Trauma, In/Distinction and Response." *Journal for Cultural Research* 8 (3): 247–70. https://doi.org/10.1080/1479758042000264939.

Egan, Keith, and Fiona Murphy. 2015. "Honored Ancestors, Difficult Legacies: The Stability, Decline, and Re-Emergence of Anthropologies in and of Ireland." *American Anthropologist* 117 (1): 134–41. https://doi.org/10.1111/aman.12174.

Evans-Pritchard, Edward E. 1960. "Introduction." In *Death and the Right Hand*, ed. Robert Hertz, trans. Rodney Needham and Claudia Needham, 9–24. Glencoe, IL: Free Press.

Feifel, Herman. 1959. "Introduction." In *The Meaning of Death*, ed. Herman Feifel, xi–xvi. New York: McGraw-Hill.

Foley, Malcolm, and John Lennon. 1996. "Editorial: Heart of Darkness." *International Journal of Heritage Studies* 2 (4): 195–97. https://doi.org/10.1080/13527259608722174.

Foltyn, Jacque Lyn. 2008. "Dead Famous and Dead Sexy: Popular Culture, Forensics, and the Rise of the Corpse." *Mortality* 13 (2): 153–73. https://doi.org/10.1080/13576270801954468.

Foucault, Michel. 1975. *Discipline and Punish: The Birth of the Prison*. New York: Random House.

Gauthier, Saskia, Julian Mausbach, Thomas Reisch, and Christine Bartsch. 2015. "Suicide Tourism: A Pilot Study on the Swiss Phenomenon." *Journal of Medical Ethics* 41 (8): 611–17. https://doi.org/10.1136/medethics-2014-102091.

Goody, Jack. 1962. *Death, Property, and the Ancestors: A Study of the Mortuary Customs of the Lodagaa of West Africa*. Stanford, CA: Stanford University Press.

Gorer, Geoffery. 1955. "The Pornography of Death." In *Death, Grief, and Mourning*, ed. Geoffery Gorer, 192–99. New York: Doubleday.

Gross, Charles, Tinka Markham Pipe, Angela Bucciarelli, Kenneth Tardiff, David Vlahov, and Sandro Galea. 2007. "Suicide Tourism in Manhattan, New York City, 1990–2004."

Journal of Urban Health: Bulletin of the New York Academy of Medicine 84 (6): 755–65. https://doi.org/10.1007/s11524-007-9224-0.

Hepburn, Sharon. 2012. "Shades of Darkness: Silence, Risk, and Fear among Tourists and Nepalis during Nepal's Civil War." In *Writing the Dark Side of Travel*, ed. Jonathan Skinner, 122–42. Oxford: Berghahn.

Hertz, Robert. 1960 [1907]. *Death and the Right Hand*, trans. Rodney Needham and Claudia Needham. Glencoe, IL: Free Press.

Higgenbotham, Gregory. 2011. "Assisted Suicide Tourism: Is It Tourism?" *Tourismos: An International Multidisciplinary Journal of Tourism* 6 (2): 177–85.

Hollis, Jennifer L. 2016. "Songs of Transition." *New York Times Sunday Review*, January 3, 2016, 9.

Huizinga, Johan. 1950 [1938]. *Homo Ludens: A Study of the Play-Element in Culture*. New York: Roy.

Hunter, Isabel. 2016. "The White-Knuckle Ride to Your Death: Euthanasia Rollercoaster Will Be the Last Thrill You Ever Get—Although Experts Warn You May Spend Your Final Moments Feeling Sick." *Daily Mail*, January 16. Accessed March 10, 2016. http://www.dailymail.co.uk/news/article-3402836/The-white-knuckle-ride-death-Euthanasia-rollercoaster-thrill-experts-warn-spend-final-moments-feeling-SICK.html.

Huxtable, Richard. 2009. "The Suicide Tourist Trap: Compromise across Boundaries." *Bioethical Inquiry* 6 (3): 327–36. https://doi.org/10.1007/s11673-009-9170-5.

Kaufman, Sharon R., and Lyn M. Morgan. 2005. "The Anthropology of the Beginnings and Ends of Life." *Annual Review of Anthropology* 34 (1): 317–41. https://doi.org/10.1146/annurev.anthro.34.081804.120452.

Kim, Hyung-Jim. 2015. "South Korean 'Mock Funerals' Seek to Ease Life's Stresses." *Associated Press*, December 22. Accessed January 1, 2016. https://bigstory.ap.org/article/ca51585586894fd7808a1e282d17ae27/skorean-mock-funerals-seek-ease-lifes-stresses.

Kruse, Corinna. 2010. "Producing Absolute Truth: *CSI* Science as Wishful Thinking." *American Anthropologist* 112 (1): 79–91. https://doi.org/10.1111/j.1548-1433.2009.01198.x.

Kübler-Ross, Elisabeth. 1969. *On Death and Dying*. New York: Collier.

Lane, Nick. 2005. *Power, Sex, Suicide: Mitochondria and the Meaning of Life*. Oxford: Oxford University Press.

Larson, Frances. 2014. *Severed: A History of Heads Lost and Heads Found*. New York: Liveright.

Lennon, John, and Malcolm Foley. 2000. *Dark Tourism: The Attraction of Death and Disaster*. London: Continuum.

Levi-Strauss, Claude. 1966 [1962]. *The Savage Mind*. Chicago: University of Chicago Press.

Levi-Strauss, Claude. 1992 [1955]. *Tristes Tropiques*. New York: Penguin Books.

Lienhardt, Godfrey. 1966. *Social Anthropology*. London: Oxford University Press.

Lock, Margaret. 2002. *Twice Dead: Organ Transplants and the Reinvention of Death*. Berkeley: University of California Press.

Lyng, Stephen. 1990. "Edgework: A Social Psychological Analysis of Voluntary Risk Taking." *American Journal of Sociology* 95 (4): 851–86. https://doi.org/10.1086/229379.

MacCannell, Dean. 1989. *The Tourist: A New Theory of the Leisure Class*. New York: Schocken Books.

Macdonald, Sharon. 2009. *Difficult Heritage: Negotiating the Nazi Past in Nuremberg and Beyond*. London: Routledge.

Mackey, Robert. 2014. "Israelis Watch Bombs Drop on Gaza from Front Row Seats." *New York Times*, July 14. Accessed December 1, 2017. https://www.nytimes.com/2014/07/15/world/middleeast/israelis-watch-bombs-drop-on-gaza-from-front-row-seats.html?_r=0.

Malinowski, Bronislaw. 1948. *Magic, Science and Religion, and Other Essays, Selected by Robert Redfield*. Boston: Beacon.

Mandelbaum, David G. 1959. "Social Uses of Funeral Rites." In *The Meaning of Death*, ed. Herman Feifel, 189–217. New York: McGraw-Hill.

Mestrovic, Stjepan. 1999. *Postemotional Society*. London: Sage.

Mitford, Jessica. 1963. *The American Way of Death*. New York: Simon and Schuster.

Montaigne, Michel de. 1957. *The Complete Works of Montaigne: Essays, Travel Journals, Letters*, trans. Donald M. Frame. Palo Alto, CA: Stanford University Press.

Palgi, Phyllis, and Henry Abramovitch. 1984. "Death: A Cross-Cultural Perspective." *Annual Review of Anthropology* 13 (1): 385–417. https://doi.org/10.1146/annurev.an.13.100184.002125.

Parsons, Talcott. 1978. "Death in the Western World." In *Encyclopedia of Bioethics*, vol. 1, ed. Warren T. Reich, 255–61. New York: Free Press.

Penfold-Mounce, Ruth. 2010. "Consuming Criminal Corpses: Fascination with the Dead Criminal Body." *Mortality* 15 (3): 250–65. https://doi.org/10.1080/13576275.2010.496618.

Phipps, Peter. 1999. "Tourists, Terrorists, Death, and Value." In *Travel Worlds: Journeys in Contemporary Cultural Politics*, ed. Raminder Kaur and John Hutnyk, 74–93. London: Zed Books.

Pope, Whitney. 1976. *Durkheim's Suicide: A Classic Analyzed*. Chicago: University of Chicago Press.

Robben, Antonius C.G.M. 2011. *Death, Mourning, and Burial: A Cross-Cultural Reader*. Malden, MA: Blackwell.

Rojek, Chris. 1993. *Ways of Escape: Modern Transformations in Leisure and Travel*. Macmillan. https://doi.org/10.1057/9780230373402.

Rojek, Chris. 2010. *The Labour of Leisure*. London: Sage.

Rosaldo, Renato. 1989. "Grief and the Headhunter's Rage." In *Culture and Truth*, 1–21. Boston: Beacon.

Saltzman, Rachelle H. 1995. "'This Buzz Is for You': Popular Responses to the Ted Bundy Execution." *Journal of Folklore Research* 32 (2): 101–19.

Sather-Wagstaff, Joy. 2011. *Heritage That Hurts: Tourists in the Memoryscapes of September 11*. Walnut Creek, CA: Left Coast.

Scheper-Hughes, Nancy. 1992. *Death without Weeping: The Violence of Everyday Life in Brazil*. Berkeley: University of California Press.

Scheper-Hughes, Nancy. 2000. "The Global Traffic in Human Organs." *Current Anthropology* 41 (2): 191–224. https://doi.org/10.1086/300123.

Scheper-Hughes, Nancy. 2004. "Parts Unknown: Undercover Ethnography of the Organs-Trafficking Underworld." *Ethnography* 5 (1): 29–73. https://doi.org/10.1177/1466138104041588.

Schuyler, Susan. 2008. "Gallows Drama: Public Execution, Crowds, and Victorian Theater." *Nineteenth Century Studies* 22: 15–29.

Seabrook, Jeremy. 1995. "From Leisure Class to Leisure Society." In *The Sociology of Leisure: A Reader*, ed. Chas Critcher, Peter Bramham, and Alan Tomlinson, 97–104. London: Chapman and Hall.

Seaton, Anthony. 1996. "Guided by the Dark: From Thanatopsis to Thanatourism." *International Journal of Heritage Studies* 2 (4): 234–44. https://doi.org/10.1080/13527259608722178.

Seaton, Anthony. 1999. "War and Thanatourism: Waterloo 1815–1914." *Annals of Tourism Research* 26 (1): 130–158. https://doi.org/10.1016/S0160-7383(98)00057-7.

Seaton, Anthony. 2012. "Thanatourism and Its Discontents: An Appraisal of a Decade's Work with Some Future Issues and Directions." In *The SAGE Handbook of Tourism Studies*, ed. Tazim Jamal and Mike Robinson, 521–42. London: Sage.

Sharpley, Richard. 2009. "Shedding Light on Dark Tourism: An Introduction." In *The Darker Side of Travel: The Theory and Practice of Dark Tourism*, ed. Richard Sharpley and Phillip Stone, 3–22. Bristol: Channel View.

Sharpley, Richard, and Phillip R. Stone, eds. 2009. *The Darker Side of Travel: The Theory and Practice of Dark Tourism*. Buffalo, NY: Channel View.

Skinner, Jonathan. 2010. "Introduction: Writings on the Dark Side of Travel." *Journeys* 11 (1): 1–28. https://doi.org/10.3167/jys.2010.110101.

St. John, Chris. 2008. "Victor Turner and Contemporary Cultural Performance: An Introduction." In *Victor Turner and Contemporary Cultural Performance*, ed. Chris St. John, 1–40. Oxford: Berghahn.

Stebbins, Robert. 2007. *Serious Leisure*. New Brunswick, NJ: Transaction.

Stone, Philip. 2006. "A Dark Tourism Spectrum: Towards a Typology of Death and Macabre Related Tourist Sites, Attractions, and Exhibitions." *Tourism: An Interdisciplinary International Journal* 54 (2): 145–60.

Stone, Philip. 2011. "Dark Tourism: Towards a New Post-Disciplinary Research Agenda." *International Journal of Tourism Anthropology* 1 (3–4): 318–32. https://doi.org/10.1504/IJTA.2011.043713.

Stone, Philip. 2013. "Dark Tourism Scholarship: A Critical Review." *International Journal of Culture, Tourism, and Hospitality Research* 7 (3): 307–18. https://doi.org/10.1108/IJCTHR-06-2013-0039.

Strathern, Marilyn. 1988. *The Gender of the Gift: Problems with Women and Problems with Society in Melanesia*. Berkeley: University of California Press. https://doi.org/10.1525/california/9780520064232.001.0001.

Sturken, Marita. 2007. *Tourists of History: Memory, Kitsch, and Consumerism from Oklahoma City to Ground Zero*. Durham, NC: Duke University Press. https://doi.org/10.1215/9780822390510.

Suarez-Orozco, Marcelo M. 2000. "The Global Traffic in Human Organs: Commentary." *Current Anthropology* 41 (2): 217–18.

Turner, Victor. 1982. *From Ritual to Theatre*. New York: PAJ.

Turner, Victor. 1969. *The Ritual Process: Structure and Anti-Structure*. Chicago: Aldine.

Tylor, Edward B. 1871. *Primitive Culture: Researches into the Development of Mythology, Religion, Philosophy, Art, and Custom*, vols. 1–2. London: John Murray.

Urbain, Didier. 1978. *La Société de Conservation: Etude sémiologique des cimetières d'Occident*. Paris: Payot.

Veblen, Thorstein. 1994 [1897]. *The Theory of the Leisure Class*. Mineoloa, NY: Dover Thrift Editions.

Walter, Tony. 1994. *The Revival of Death*. London: Routledge.

PART I

Leisure and Death on the Move

1

Dying in a Strange Land

Tourism, Hospitality, and Promises to the Dead

MARIBETH ERB

THINKING ABOUT TOURISM, DEATH, AND VIOLENCE: WHAT IS THE VALUE OF A DEAD TOURIST?

> We say goodbye as we depart and some even cry a little, as at a funeral, for we are dying symbolically (Graburn 1989, 27).

Death, a classic topic in anthropology (cf. Hertz 1960 [1907]; Bloch and Parry 1982; Cederroth, Lindstrom, and Bloch 1988), has engaged considerable interest in tourism studies with the recent surge in attention to thano-, or "dark," tourism (Lennon and Foley 2000; Sharpley and Stone 2009; Stone and Sharpley 2008)—leisure visits to places of death and disaster (such as sites of assassinations, death camps, battlefields).[1] Moreover, some academic attention has been paid to a variety of "dark" tourism that is not just memorializing the dead but also glamorizing the visitors' own brush with death, something Kathleen Adams has termed "danger zone tourism," suggesting that apparent threats to loss of life make the tourist experience more "authentic" (Adams 2001, 274–75; see also Phipps 1999, 81–83; Kaul's interesting discussion of that "awful margin," this volume). To my knowledge, however, few have looked at actual tourist deaths, with the exceptions of Erik Cohen (2008, 2009), who discussed tourist deaths in Thailand as a result of the 2004 Indian Ocean tsunami, and Susan Frohlick (2010), who examined the murders of two American exchange students in Costa Rica in an area noted for visits by young Western women often referred to as a form of "sex tourist."[2] In fact, Cohen suggests that social scientists' analysis of tourist deaths is practically nonexistent. The possibility of dying while away is not something either the tourist or the travel industry wants to call attention to, and Cohen comments that "in the popular imagination, death and tourism belong to utterly different spheres of life" (Cohen 2009, 184).

Despite this clearly true observation, writings on topics central to tourism often obliquely raise the question of death. Nelson Graburn (quoted above), in one of the earliest publications on the anthropology of tourism, calls tourism a "sacred journey"; like a "rite of passage," which moves an individual through a symbolic death (Turner 1967), tourism symbolically represents a death of the "ordinary self" and an absence from normal life. Photographs and souvenirs have also inspired scholars to think about the relationship of travel with death since, as Susan Sontag suggests, photographs are always *memento mori*; "To take a photograph is to participate in another person's (or thing's) mortality, vulnerability, mutability... all photographs testify to time's relentless melt" (Sontag 1977, 15; see also the interesting discussion of online photographs of the dead and selfies at funerals in Kohn et al., this volume, as well as Adams, this volume). In a similar way, Jon Goss reflects on the souvenir as a remembrance that "consumed under conditions of socio-spatial estrangement... embodies a material and spiritual trace... and so works simultaneously to embody both absence and loss and presence or restoration" (Goss 2004, 329). Thus, although the tourist experience may not normally be thought of as a contemplation of death, the separations and memories that are an intrinsic part of the tourist journey open reflections on the mortality of the traveler and the possibility that a return may not take place.

Experiencing violent death as a pleasure-seeking tourist is considered the most tragic of ends, but Peter Phipps (1999) queries both the innocence and the "value" of the "dead tourist" in his examination of the interrelationship between tourists and terrorists. Terrorists place a certain value on the innocence encoded in the image of a tourist, which may allow them to manipulate and negotiate in political exchanges. Although they are often seen to be associated with opposing spheres, Phipps suggests that a sustained consideration is needed of the relationship between tourism and violence more generally (Phipps 1999, 74). Tourists' strident expression of their "right" to access all corners of the earth is a kind of militancy, and the increasing security concerns at airports and border crossings have also become a "naturalized artefact of the tenuous relationship between travel and violence" (Phipps 1999, 75). Sally Ann Ness (2005) also queries the "innocence" of the tourist paradise, suggesting that tourism indeed begets violence; the beatific landscapes of paradise suppress a violent underside of displacement and exclusion of locals, producing resentment that may bubble into various forms of retaliation—something she refers to as the "darker side of place" (an idea that resonates with the idea of a "geography of death," discussed in chapters by Kaul and Pipyrou, this volume).

One can argue, therefore, that the "hospitality" encoded in the tourism encounter is always a fundamentally "aporetic" one, as Jacques Derrida argues for hospitality in general (Derrida 1999, 2000a, 2000b; Erb 2013). Hospitality, he suggests, is best articulated as "hostipitality," hostility and hospitality combined. In tourism locales this is especially evident, as poignantly voiced by Jamaica Kincaid in her book *A Small Place*, in which she chides tourists for never pausing to consider how much people in places they visit "cannot stand you," calling the tourist "an ugly thing" (Kincaid 1988, 17). Tourism violence, therefore, may not always erupt into actual violence but consists of the tense encounter between "host" and "guest." This suppressed violence is especially strong at the "threshold," Derrida suggests, where the host is asserting mastery over the home "at the very moment of welcoming" (Derrida 2000b, 7) but at the same time becomes "the hostage of the one he receives, the one who keeps him at home" (Derrida 2000b, 9). The "host," therefore, becomes limited in what he or she is able to do because of the presence of the "guest." This suppressed violence makes thinking about the death of tourists an interesting issue in regard to the paradox of hospitality (see Erb 2013).

Death in tourism locales has been interestingly analyzed by Erik Cohen in regard to tourist deaths in Thai resorts in the wake of the 2004 Indian Ocean tsunami. For Cohen, one of the interesting questions is whether the "hierarchy of the living" (Cohen 2009, 185) is reflected in dealing with the dead. While tourists "may be treated, under normal conditions, with much pomp and circumstance as (paying) guests," Cohen argues, "they are also strangers, who do not belong to the host community, and towards whom the hosts have no overarching obligations" (Cohen 2009, 185). Does a disaster change the treatment of tourists from one of privileged "guests" to strangers who deserve little attention or who are even a nuisance to locals trying to deal with mass death? In the Thai case, Cohen's investigation showed that the "hierarchy" of the living was indeed reproduced in the treatment of the bodies of the dead, but his examination opens the more general question of how tourists' deaths are treated by local communities. Does the peculiarity of tourism's social space and dynamics make the way a tourist's death is treated something different than the ordinary for local communities?

The social space of tourism may be analyzed as a "contact zone," which Mary Louise Pratt defines as "social spaces where disparate cultures meet, clash, and grapple with each other, often in highly asymmetrical relations of domination and subordination" (Pratt 2008, 7). How does the context of tourism, with the expectation of pleasure but the possibility of tragedy, affect the incidence of death? How does the contrast in cultural expectations that exists between foreign tourists and a local community play out when a tourist dies? How do the shifting meanings of "hospitality" and "responsibility" that tourism brings intersect with the contrast between life and death in tourism spaces?

I address these questions not in the context of a major disaster, as did Cohen, but in the context of the rare incidence of ordinary tourist death in a place where, until recently, tourism developments have been very incipient. My examination focuses on a town, Labuan Bajo, on the island of Flores in eastern Indonesia where I have been observing tourism developments since the mid-1990s. Unlike the resorts of Thailand examined by Cohen, the western part of the island of Flores and its main town, Labuan Bajo, have only recently turned into popular tourism destinations as a result of the growing interest in visiting the unique and endangered giant lizards, the Komodo "dragons" (*Varanus komodensis*), found on some islands off the coast of western Flores, and the increasing popularity of Komodo National Park as a site of marine tourism.

I started to ask questions about the deaths of tourists in 2009 when I began examining changing attitudes toward foreigners and hospitality with the growth of tourism. In Indonesia, a number of dramatic events have resulted in major losses of life in tourism areas, most notably in Bali in 2002 and 2005 with the Legian and Jimbaran bombings and in Jakarta in 2003 and 2009 with the Marriot and Ritz Carlton hotel bombings, all instigated by radical Islamic groups targeting sites frequented by Western tourists. The numbers of tourist deaths in western Flores, however, have been very small. The Government Tourism Board of Western Manggarai Regency, in fact, could only tell me of three deaths it had helped handle: one in the late 1990s, one in 2001, and one in 2014. Several other cases of tourist deaths on Komodo Island were related to me by tour guides, but since their bodies were not brought back to Flores but went directly to Bali by boat, the tourism board was apparently not aware of the deaths and did not mention them. Though the number of incidents is extremely small and gives no definitive answer as to to how tourist deaths will be handled in western Flores, the incidents themselves were very notable to local residents and those who deal with tourists. I examine how tourists' deaths create a puzzle for the living community, how the responsibility for the deaths is managed, and what value tourist deaths might hold. Given the idea of suppressed violence in the hospitality encounter suggested earlier, I also consider whether living and dead tourists are treated differently. I suggest that examining the way these few tourist deaths were dealt with will give insights into the meaning of death, as well as the contradictions, miscommunications, and shifts in social relations and the expectations of responsibility and hospitality that are found in tourism spaces; through this I hope to open new ways of contemplating death and dying in a strange land.

DEATH IN A STRANGE LAND: TOURISM, HOSPITALITY, AND RESPONSIBILITY IN WESTERN FLORES

> The question of the foreigner concerns what happens at death and when the traveller is laid to rest in a foreign land (Derrida 2000a, 87)

In 2001, I was present when a "tourist" died in Labuan Bajo. He was a New Zealander named Bob (a pseudonym), an apparent refugee from the Australian Army who had gone AWOL, so I heard, because of the trauma he had experienced the previous several years in East Timor. As a "tourist" he was perhaps not typical, since his stay in the area was not as temporary as most or, obviously, for the purpose of leisure. However, from the point of view of the local community, he was a "turis," a kind of ethnic category that includes reference to foreigners who apparently have lots of money but often unclear purposes for being on Flores and who hold no real connection to the local community (Erb 2000). Bob had arrived in western Flores a full-bodied, healthy young man, confident of his ability to survive in the toughest conditions. People told how Bob had been teaching the police to do Kung Fu, and everyone was in awe of his prowess. He had ordered a small sailing boat at one of the fishing communities along the coast south of Labuan Bajo through a local guide at the hotel where he had first stayed. The guide had taken a huge commission from the transaction, almost as much money as the boat maker himself. When Bob found out how much the boat maker had actually been paid for the boat, he confronted the guide and demanded that he return some of the money. The guide, who had already spent the money, refused to pay him back and disappeared from Labuan Bajo, returning only after the New Zealander had died.

Although Bob did not know how to sail, he set out to learn, and his plan had been to sail the boat to Sulawesi and Kalimantan, though locals had warned him that the boat was much too small for that kind of journey. His first trip to a nearby island had taken him two days (only an hour from the town by motor boat). He had subsequently set out to sail to Bima on Sumbawa Island (a journey that takes ten to twelve hours by ferry and bus), where apparently he had planned to fly to Bali and then on to Singapore to renew his passport and visa. Information that emerged later, in the form of a postcard sent to Bob by his family, seemed to indicate that he had hoped to receive money in Bali from his family to make the trip to Singapore. An English woman, one of the very few foreigners resident in Labuan Bajo at that time, told me she had seen the postcard, which the postman brought to her about two weeks after Bob's death. Although she had not known Bob, the postman did not know where else to deliver it; since she was a resident foreigner in the town, she was a logical choice. The postcard had given her chills because the family wrote that they were arranging to get the money and it would be coming soon, but they had no concerns that he would manage in the interim since he always maintained control over everything and would never be beaten by anything.

As it turned out, however, Bob had been beaten; he returned to Labuan Bajo a week and a half later, according to one local hotel owner, a totally changed person. He was thin and weak and appeared very ill. A boy who worked in one of the restaurants found him collapsed on a table and told him to go to the hospital, but Bob responded that he had no money. The boy gave him 50,000 rupiah (at the time about 5 USD) so he could go. Staff at the hospital related later that it had been too late; he was very sick with malaria and had no red blood cells left. He needed a blood transfusion, but it was beyond their capabilities at the local clinic to give him one, and the hospital was five–six hours away by car. He died within hours of arrival at the hospital.

The day after he died, I visited his corpse where it lay in a room in the hospital. Although I had heard stories about him after my arrival the previous week, I had not met him. The nurse stated that the hospital was awaiting instructions as to what to do with him. News circulated that a helicopter would come to take away his body, but no one came and I heard that he was eventually buried in the graveyard next to the hospital. I was told that local guides had "guarded" the corpse every night before his burial, a practice known as "mete" that is done at the deaths of local people. During mete, typically the family will provide cigarettes and refreshments for the young people who stay up all night guarding the corpse, but Bob had no family in Labuan Bajo, and no money was ultimately provided by his family to arrange for his death and burial expenses.

The story of this man's death intrigued me because he had been the only tourist who had ever been buried in Labuan Bajo. Although another tourist had died in Labuan Bajo a few years earlier, the circumstances of that death were different. The similarities and differences in how the two deaths were handled raise interesting questions about the dynamics of tourism encounters in Labuan Bajo and about the value of life and death. The first tourist, a Dutchman, had been staying at a local homestay run by a Manggaraian family. He was a more typical tourist and had been snorkeling near a small island not far from Labuan Bajo when he had a heart attack and drowned. The man's family had been easily contacted and had promised to provide all the money to buy a coffin and transport the corpse to Bali and on to the Netherlands. The arrangements were made by the owners of the hotel where the man had stayed, and they were subsequently reimbursed through the Dutch Embassy.

A local woman, who herself once ran a homestay, commented to me about what she saw as the irresponsibility of those hotel owners who, according to her, had profited from the tourist's death. They and the police who helped arrange for the body transfer doubled all the costs associated with providing the coffin and transporting the corpse so they could capitalize on the family's offer of reimbursement. The woman who told me the story was incensed because, as was the case for the New Zealander, local guides had done mete for the corpse yet saw none of the money sent to reimburse "services" provided for the dead Dutchman. The guides had paid out of their own pockets for cigarettes and food as they sat up and watched the corpse while waiting for its transport. This money should have been sponsored by the owner of the hotel where the man had stayed, my friend said. In fact, regarding the death of the New Zealander, there had also been a breach of social duty, she said, by the man who owned the hotel where Bob had initially stayed. This owner's cousin had been the one who mediated the boat transaction and cheated Bob out of his money. Again, since the New Zealander had been a guest at his hotel, the hotel owner should have sponsored the food and drink for the young people who guarded the corpse. She was particularly incensed because, although she had met the hotel owner in the hospital where she saw him visiting Bob's corpse, he had not admitted having a connection with the man. She had asked him to lead prayers for Bob (since he was a prayer leader in the local Catholic Church), but he said no one knew the man's religion. She had suggested that the hotel association of Labuan Bajo, of which he was a member, contribute money to the mete, but no money was forthcoming. Later, she felt it was a further disgrace when she found out that the New Zealander had stayed at this church leader's hotel.

These stories open up the question of what kind of responsibility people have toward both the living and the dead within the Florenese world of social relations. The young men who regularly become "guides" in Labuan Bajo often try to take advantage of a "hospitality" encounter in the tourism sphere by offering services to tourists and then overcharging them, as the one guide (the cousin of the hotel owner) did with Bob. Getting as much "good fortune" from these encounters as possible is one of the dynamics of Labuan Bajo tourism (Erb 2000, 2004, 2005, 2013) and it often happens in tourist spaces, especially in the Global South. It is more normal for these types of interactions to take place where prices are flexible and not fixed, such as when guides mediate in the renting of transportation or get a commission on various kinds of sales. It is less likely for a hotel owner to ask for a high price, since room prices tend to be more fixed and stable. It is interesting, therefore, to see how the hotel owners, in the context of tourist deaths, were the ones accused of "cheating" the dead, whereas the guides who guarded the corpse, who more commonly take advantage of the living, were seen to be serving the dead with less thought of profit and sometimes no recompense at all. This raises questions as to the nature of the relationship between the living and the dead (discussed in the chapters by Kohn et al. and Pipyrou, this volume) and why guides would be willing to sacrifice for dead tourists but not living ones. What is the value of death in the Florenese social world?

DIFFERING VALUES OF LIFE AND DEATH IN THE CONTACT ZONE

One of the Europeans who opened a dive shop in Labuan Bajo in the late 1990s ran into a number of difficulties with locals because of different ideas about "value" and "worth" (see also Erb 2013). Among a number of other matters, one staff member who worked for him mentioned that the owner and his wife kept a freezer full of food just for their dog—which even had its own bedroom. With no children, the dog was seen as a member of the family, not uncommon among affluent people in the West. However, the Labuan Bajo staff, most of whom were from Flores, were annoyed by this, feeling that the dog was treated far better than they were—a belief that led to considerable envy among the employees. Dogs in Flores are not typically pampered as pets but are kept for hunting or as a source of food. A very different kind of value is placed on their lives and deaths among Florinese in comparison to the ideals and practices of westerners who live in Labuan Bajo.

The competing difference in attitudes is also strongly felt in regard to human life and death. European missionaries who have worked for a long time in the Manggarai regency (the district of western Flores) were often frustrated by and angry about the value Manggaraian people placed on the dead. One priest related his aggravation when a man he had sponsored to enter the hospital to be cured from tuberculosis used the money instead to stage an elaborate ritual for his dead wife. The man, so the priest said, did not believe he would be able to heal if this ritual were not done for his dead wife "on the other side," since she would continue to send illness to him if he did not attend to her needs in the world of the spirits.

The great value and respect paid to the dead has not gone without criticism by Manggaraians themselves. One friend in Labuan Bajo criticized the death practices in his village, saying people were becoming irresponsible with their money, not recognizing the importance of saving it and using it wisely. A number of his relatives were trying to convince him to go to his natal village and help support an elaborate ritual to build new gravestones for their ancestors. Gravestones, apparently, were becoming the newest consumption item and the way people tried to show off their newfound wealth to others.

This kind of criticism has recently been voiced very strongly in a Manggaraian internet forum where offshore Manggaraian people who live and work elsewhere have come to question the way they and other people in eastern Indonesia appear to value the dead more than the living. One of the internet posters, who works with non-government organizations (NGOs) on maternal and infant health, had been concerned about the rate of maternal and infant mortality in the province of Nusa Tenggara Timur (NTT) where Flores is located. He visited various officials from the Ministry of Health in Jakarta, as well as the World Bank, the World Health Organization (WHO), and the United States Agency for International

Development (USAID), trying to get advice and assessments about the serious maternal health situation in his province. Many different factors were mentioned, but one struck him most forcefully: "The people in Nusa Tenggara Timur province have more respect and concern for the dead than for the living," one commentator said. Various respondents who shared their experiences in other parts of the world, where infant births were well prepared for and pregnant mothers carefully tended, confirmed that NTT was distinctive and perhaps negligent in this regard. Their experiences in various "contact zones" had fueled criticism of their own traditional practices and beliefs.

RESPECTING THE DEAD

> "My mother told me that she is happy that I work with ata pe'le'sina [people from the other side]."
> —A TOURIST GUIDE, WORKING IN LABUAN BAJO, AUGUST 2000

Rituals for the dead in parts of western Flores, as elsewhere in eastern Indonesia, can be rather elaborate. These rituals have several stages that mirror the stages people go through in life, particularly through marriage (Erb 1993). The expense of these rituals is a way of continuing to keep social ties with a vast network of relatives; those who refuse to perform the rituals or contribute to the ritual labor of kin are considered asocial individuals. Looking at rituals from an economic perspective, which is increasingly the case in the contemporary world, makes some community members reluctant to continue them, but others argue that they are important for maintaining a socio-religious identity and maintaining a certain order in one's life. There is thus a struggle between the ideas of the excessive wastefulness of ritual, both marriage and death rituals—for many years a view held by European missionaries—and the revitalization of cultural identity, which is particularly apparent in urban areas and in the "reform" era emerging after the fall of long-term New Order president Suharto (Davidson and Henley 2007).

Labuan Bajo, like many towns on Flores Island, has a strong village feel; but unlike some other towns on Flores, it is highly culturally/ethnically diverse. It is not only the recent increasing numbers of Europeans who have begun to set up businesses and reside in Labuan Bajo or the increasing flows of tourists through the town that make the place multi-cultural. At its core, Labuan Bajo has always had a mixed population, since it was a congregation of villages of fishing folk from various surrounding islands in earlier centuries. These people from different ethnic groups, as well as more recent immigrants from other islands, have come to participate in the dominant Manggaraian ethnic group's ritual life as contributors. Rituals to gather money to send children off to school, rituals to gather funds for bride-wealth payments, rituals to make arrangements for the dead all have the potential to encompass people into networks of relations in the contemporary Florinese world, even if those people are not kin or members of the same cultural group.

The encompassing of the unrelated into ritual responsibilities is clearly articulated in the care for the immediate dead. *Tobo*, a dead body, must be wrapped—*mbakung*—and guarded prior to burial. The waiting for burial is done so that various kin and acquaintances can pay their respects to the dead, presenting them with their "tears"—*wae luqu*—in the form of a small amount of money. Tear money is given out of respect but also out of fear of the dead. Any passerby who becomes aware of a death must give some *wae luqu*; otherwise the spirit will wreak havoc upon that individual. Between towns, one often sees a sign on the road that a wake is in progress. The drivers of buses and cars will stop and get out to give the family a small bit of money. This money is essential so the spirit will not cause problems for the travelers. When one goes to visit a corpse, one is not allowed to "leave," that is, one cannot say "goodbye" or the spirit of the dead will follow that person home. People who have visited a corpse need to wash themselves, at least a token wash of the face, before entering their own homes so as not to bring any lingering spirits of the dead into the house with them.

The danger of death is not just about the spirit but also about the dead body. It is important that someone is always present to guard the corpse, an activity referred to above as mete. This is done to guard against the possibility that the corpse might be wakened. If at least one person stays awake to watch the body, it will never reanimate. This is done for all the dead, as mentioned, even tourists who lie in the hospital waiting for burial or removal. There is, then, a social duty to watch over the body of every human being, even if that person has no relation to the watchers. In Labuan Bajo, it is usually male tour guides who take turns guarding the corpse. The reason they do it, I was told, is not so much because they are afraid of the spirit of the dead but because the person, even if he or she is a stranger, is a fellow human being, and the body must be guarded so it will not waken. This is what they would do for all people, and it is perhaps especially necessary for dead tourists who may have no family there to do it for them. So guides, who come from all over Manggarai and even further east on Flores looking for work in Labuan Bajo and are thus away from home, out and about like tourists, are considered the appropriate ones to do the job of guarding the corpse.

The changing social responsibility in this regard and a more complete picture of the meaning of mete became clear to me recently when I heard about another tourist death in Labuan Bajo in 2014—a Spanish woman who had died from lung complications after diving. Her family had specifically given instructions that her body not be preserved with formaldehyde; therefore, the government tourism board had arranged that her body be kept on ice and stored in the only air-conditioned room available, that is, in the tourist information center—a macabre conflation, one might say, of tourism and death.[3] Government security officials guarded the body and regularly refreshed the ice to keep the body cold. When I asked whether this guarding was mete, a friend vigorously denied it. Mete, it seems, is not simply the guarding of the body but is a social task associated with receiving, it might be said, the spirits of the dead who have come to take the newly dead to the "other side." Since this woman would not be buried in Labuan Bajo, there was no need to "receive" the spirits of the dead. However, the Dutch tourist mentioned earlier, who died in 1999, was also not buried in Labuan Bajo and yet the guides did mete for him. Further consideration of the differences between these two deaths helps illuminate the changing social landscape of Labuan Bajo that has been affected by tourism, as well as ideas of social responsibility alluded to above. The Dutch tourist stayed in a local hotel and was accompanied by local guides. The Spanish diver was a customer of a more recently opened dive shop owned by an American and staffed by a mix of locals and foreigners. Unaware of local ideas about death, the social responsibility associated with death was not considered by those who "hosted" this woman; they were only concerned that they had no legal responsibility for her death. Since the family had clearly shown that it would take over the responsibility for repatriating the body, the tourism board officials also saw no need to arrange for anything more than the technical aspects of preserving it.

A particularly interesting thing about tourists is their close association with the world of the spirits, not a surprising connection since they are people who were at one time considered unknowable and unclassifiable. In fact, tourists have been known to be referred to as *ata pe le sina*, "people from the other side"—the "other side" being where the spirits dwell and everything is done opposite from the world of the living. Spirits move around at night instead of during the daytime, so "receiving" them is logically done at night. Many myths relate other logics associated with interacting with spirits; offerings to them are always "a little," small bits of rice and sacrificial meat, since what is a little to us is actually a lot to them (Erb 1993, 1996, 2000). This association between spirit and foreigner, between deceased and tourist, was made in subtle ways with the reception of tourists in some of the first village communities tourists visited in a semi-commercial way. There, tourists were greeted as honored guests, given the appropriate types of offerings made to honor all kinds of visitors, including the spirits, but also treated with the logic that "we give you a little, in exchange you give us a lot." A little bit of money would be offered to them in hope that in return they would give a lot more (Erb 2000). The logic of taking from tourists, therefore, and trying to get as much "good fortune" as possible is not necessarily an exploitative logic but instead a logic of dealing with people from the "other side."

PROMISES TO THE DEAD

In 2009, wanting to find out more about the dead New Zealander and what people thought of him years after his death, I went to the government tourism board; indeed, officials there remembered him. In fact, one of them, an old acquaintance named Charles (a pseudonym), had been the one who made most of the arrangements associated with Bob's wake and burial. "His burial was delayed," Charles told me, "because the New Zealand Embassy could not locate his family; after three days, the doctor would no longer allow the removal of the body." So Charles contacted the embassy to help arrange procedures to bury the body of a foreigner on Indonesian soil. Eventually, Charles also contacted Bob's family, who gave permission via fax to bury the body in Labuan Bajo. They also sent a letter they asked him to read at the burial, done according to Manggaraian culture and with a Protestant service, since the family told Charles that Bob was Protestant.

"No money was given by the family for the hospital bills or the burial," Charles related; neither the family nor those who had profited from Bob's visit in Labuan Bajo took any responsibility for these matters. Although the tourism board and the hospital director asked the sub-district head for money to cover these expenses, the head stated that no funds were available in the government coffers for such an occurrence. Hence, the hospital director waived the hospital fees, and the tourism board chipped in money to pay for the cement to make the gravesite. "We asked for money to mete as well," Charles said, who was among those who guarded the body, but the government refused to contribute funds to pay for cigarettes, coffee, cakes, and cards. Charles also mentioned the New Zealander's shoes, fantastic boots from the Australian Army that the police in Labuan Bajo wanted to take, but Charles insisted on his right to have them "since I have arranged his burial." So he took the shoes and buried them with Bob along with all of his other things; in this way, Charles underscored his respect for the body and its burial and his willingness to sacrifice materially on behalf of the dead.

After he had related the story of Bob's burial, I asked Charles if I could see the gravesite. On the way, we bought candles to burn at his grave, and Charles related that at the burial ceremony, even though he had never met Bob when he was alive, "I promised to be his 'brother,' " since Bob had no other family in Labuan Bajo. Charles was therefore very glad that I had shown up and asked about this New Zealander, since it reminded him of his duty to visit the grave, pray for Bob's soul, and put a name on the gravestone. Charles's promise to the dead, to his brother, would be fulfilled. Charles, who had never known him, represented the Manggaraian willingness to sacrifice for a dead tourist, a dead stranger.

CONCLUSION: DEATH, RESPONSIBILITY, AND HOSPITALITY IN A TOURIST CONTACT ZONE

It appears that tourists, despite their lack of social place in the community and the different ways they are treated in life, will be absorbed into the usual obligatory relations associated with death. Their bodies will be guarded as a social obligation that is morally placed on those who had connections with them, that is, those who guided them or gave them a place to stay in their hotels/homestays. Although people seem to have no compunction about taking advantage of tourists in life, doing so in death becomes the object of considerable criticism and hesitation. The dead must be respected no matter who they were. In Manggaraian terms, a dead tourist is a doubly important object of respect, since these tourists are not only dead as human beings but are seen as already having a connection with those on "the other side" prior to their demise. Their spiritual qualities in life make them potentially more potent in death.

What is the value, then, of a tourist death? Phipps suggests that live tourist hostages may have more value as dead tourists depending upon the particular political situation. This points to the fact that tourism cannot be considered in a vacuum and must be understood within a political context. The politics of tourism in Labuan Bajo has predominantly been one of local politics, however. People negotiate and struggle with one another for ways to make money and profit both within tourism and from tourists. The value of dead tourists, in situations like this, is in some ways the same as that of live tourists. Some see the opportunity to raise prices, double costs, and profit from their deaths. But the work of death, done most frequently by young males who have the stamina to watch all night for the safety of the corpse and the community, is a value that cannot readily be capitalized; though people may complain about the expense, they do not expect to be paid for the service even when it is done for a tourist. People in the world of the dead have a different value than those in the world of the living, and this is an important underpinning of Manggaraian socio-religious understandings. The violence toward tourists, therefore, which breaks out and encompasses tourist locales elsewhere and therefore creates a value for dead tourists, is not something that has been prevalent in the context of Labuan Bajo. A subliminal hostility, because of struggles over services and prices, exists in the tourism encounter, but it is not usually strongly expressed and has almost never resulted in physical violence.

However, I suggest that the "darker side of place," as Ness (2005) argues, as a result of the displacement and marginalization of locals, is not ever far away within a tourism context. Some people in Labuan Bajo profit from tourists and tourism, but there are those who have been more marginalized. Fishing communities who were traditionally the majority population in this coastal area and throughout neighboring islands have lost some of their livelihood options with the creation of Komodo National Park and the international concern for conservation (Erb 2012), which limited their fishing grounds and strictly clamped down on fish bombing and the use of cyanide in fishing. These people, especially those from neighboring islands who entered the park to fish illegally or to poach animals, have periodically been the targets of violence as those who have stood in the way of conservation. They have also periodically been the instigators of violence.

In July 2013 several violent incidents, aimed particularly at tourism developments, occurred in the vicinity of Labuan Bajo. The first was a massive bombing of the coral reefs that, as attractions of the diving industry, have become one of the mainstays of the tourism focus in Labuan Bajo and Komodo National Park. Staffs at the dive shops in Labuan Bajo were horrified and many expressed disgust and anger toward the fishermen, originating from a neighboring island, who had vented their rage apparently at the industry and the "product" of which it was so proud. The second was an incident of attempted rape of a white Canadian woman on a beach very close to the town, which took place among a number of newly built luxurious hotels just after sunset. The woman, who had been sitting on the beach enjoying the sunset view, was attacked by a number of men, also from the more marginalized fishing communities on another island. They were drunk, and it appeared that their intention was not so much sexual as to show humiliation and anger toward her as a tourist. At least this is the interpretation many in the tourism industry gave of the event. Her clothes were partially ripped and her body viciously scratched, but apparently sexual assault was not attempted. This incident sent a chill through the tourism community, although most tourists were not aware that it had occurred. As Frohlick suggests about the murder of the two female tourists in Costa Rica, violence toward tourists is a suggestion of deeper social problems coming to the surface (Frohlick 2010, 67).[4] The intended audience appears to have been the local tourism community itself, and the assault on the woman was a symbol of the anger of those who have been left out of the developments and to whom tourists represent no benefit. The politics of this violence begins to suggest broader acts of terrorism toward tourists, where their innocence might be questioned; and their value, living or dead, needs to be understood against a background that is national or global instead of local. Incidents like this in which the value of the "dead" tourist shifts to a different plane, one in which the violence toward people and places in the tourism arena is directed toward a different audience than a purely local one, are still infrequent in Labuan Bajo. With further tourism developments, however, the incidents of tourist deaths and their meaning to the local community are likely to change in the coming years.

NOTES

1. An early version of this chapter was presented at the IUAES conference in Manchester, August 5–10, 2013. I thank Douglas Farrer for including me in the panel he organized on death and the Department of Sociology at the National University of Singapore for providing funding so I could attend this conference.

2. Frohlick was disturbed that much of the media coverage of these murders seemed to "blame the victims" as foolish girls looking for sexual escapades with Costa Rican men, despite there being no evidence that the two students had any interest in forming sexual relationships or that they had been raped (Frohlick 2010, 60–66).

3. This information center is not very close to the main tourism stretch and does not get many visitors, which is why they could readily use one of the rooms to store the body without alarming passing tourists.

4. Though in the case of the Canadian woman, the attack was not used by the media to make any insinuations against her possible sexual liaisons with local men.

REFERENCES

Adams, Kathleen. 2001. "Danger-Zone Tourism: Prospects and Problems for Tourism in Tumultuous Times." In *Interconnected Worlds: Tourism in Southeast Asia*, ed. Peggy Teo, T. C. Chang, and K. C. Ho, 265–81. Oxford: Pergamon. https://doi.org/10.1016/B978-0-08-043695-1.50020-0.

Bloch, Maurice, and Jonathan Parry, eds. 1982. *Death and the Regeneration of Life*. Cambridge: Cambridge University Press. https://doi.org/10.1017/CBO9780511607646.

Cederroth, Sven, J. Lindstrom, and Maurice Bloch, eds. 1988. *On the Meaning of Death*. Upsala: Acta Universitatis Upsaliensis.

Cohen, Erik. 2008. "Death of a Backpacker: Incidental but Not Random." *Journal of Tourism and Cultural Change* 6 (3): 209–26. https://doi.org/10.1080/14766820802647624.

Cohen, Erik. 2009. "Death in Paradise: Tourist Fatalities in the Tsunami Disaster in Thailand." *Current Issues in Tourism* 12 (2): 183–99. https://doi.org/10.1080/13683500802531141.

Davidson, Jamie S., and David Henley, eds. 2007. *The Revival of Tradition in Indonesian Politics: The Deployment of Adat from Colonialism to Indigenism*. London: Routledge.

Derrida, Jacques. 1999. "Hospitality, Justice, and Responsibility: A Dialogue with Jacques Derrida." In *Questioning Ethics: Contemporary Debates in Philosophy*, ed. Richard Kearney and Mark Dooley, 65–83. London: Routledge.

Derrida, Jacques. 2000a. *Of Hospitality: Anne Dufourmantelle Invites Jacques Derrida to Respond*. Trans. Rachel Bowlby. Stanford, CA: Stanford University Press.

Derrida, Jacques. 2000b. "Hostipitality." *Angelaki* 5 (3): 3–18. https://doi.org/10.1080/09697250020034706.

Erb, Maribeth. 1993. "Becoming Complete among the Rembong: This Life and the Next." *Southeast Asian Journal of Social Science* 21 (2): 10–36. https://doi.org/10.1163/030382493X00099.

Erb, Maribeth. 1996. "Talking and Eating: Sacrificial Ritual among the Rembong." In *For the Sake of Our Futures: Sacrificing in Eastern Indonesia*, ed. Signe Howell, 27–42. Leiden, Netherlands: Leiden University.

Erb, Maribeth. 2000. "Understanding Tourists: Interpretations from Indonesia." *Annals of Tourism Research* 27 (3): 709–36. https://doi.org/10.1016/S0160-7383(99)00102-4.

Erb, Maribeth. 2004. "Miscommunication and Cultural Values in Conflict: Reflections on Morality and Tourism in Labuan Bajo, Flores, Indonesia." *Tourism: An Interdisciplinary International Journal* 52: 75–89.

Erb, Maribeth. 2005. "Limiting Tourism and the Limits of Tourism: The Production and Consumption of Tourist Attractions in Western Flores." In *Indigenous Tourism: The Commodification and Management of Culture*, ed. Chris Ryan and Michelle Aicken, 155–89. London: Elsevier. https://doi.org/10.1016/B978-0-08-044620-2.50017-1.

Erb, Maribeth. 2012. "The Dissonance of Conservation: Environmentalities and the Environmentalisms of the Poor in Eastern Indonesia." *Raffles Bulletin of Zoology* 25: 3–15.

Erb, Maribeth. 2013. "Gifts from the Other Side: Thresholds of Hospitality and Morality in an Eastern Indonesian Town." *Oceania* 83 (3): 295–315. https://doi.org/10.1002/ocea.5026.

Frohlick, Susan. 2010. "The Sex of Tourism: Bodies under Suspicion in Paradise." In *Thinking through Tourism*, ed. Julie Scott and Tom Selwyn, 51–70. Oxford: Berg.

Goss, Jon. 2004. "The Souvenir: Conceptualizing the Object(s) of Tourist Consumption." In *A Companion to Tourism*, ed. Alan A. Lew, C. Michael Hall, and Allan M. Williams, 327–36. Malden, MA: Blackwell. https://doi.org/10.1002/9780470752272.ch26.

Graburn, Nelson. 1989. "Tourism: A Sacred Journey." In *Hosts and Guests: The Anthropology of Tourism*, 2nd ed., ed. Valene L. Smith, 21–36. Philadelphia: University of Pennsylvania Press.

Hertz, Robert. 1960 [1907]. "A Contribution to the Study of Death." In *Death and the Right Hand*, trans. Rodney Needham, 29–88. Oxford: Clarendon.

Kincaid, Jamaica. 1988. *A Small Place*. New York: Farrar, Straus, Giroux.

Lennon, John, and Malcolm Foley, eds. 2000. *Dark Tourism: The Attraction of Death and Disaster*. London: Continuum.

Ness, Sally Ann. 2005. "Tourism-Terrorism: The Landscaping of Consumption and the Darker Side of Place." *American Ethnologist* 32 (1): 118–40. https://doi.org/10.1525/ae.2005.32.1.118.

Phipps, Peter. 1999. "Tourists, Terrorists, Death, and Value." In *Travel Worlds: Journeys in Contemporary Cultural Politics*, ed. Raminder Kaur and John Hutnyk, 74–93. London: Zed Books.

Pratt, Mary Louise. 2008. *Imperial Eyes: Travel Writing and Transculturation*, 2nd ed. London: Routledge.

Sharpley, Richard, and Phillip R. Stone, eds. 2009. *The Darker Side of Travel: The Theory and Practice of Dark Tourism*. Bristol: Channel View Publications.

Sontag, Susan. 1977. *On Photography*. New York: Farrar, Straus and Giroux.

Stone, Philip, and Richard Sharpley. 2008. "Consuming Dark Tourism: A Thanatological Perspective." *Annals of Tourism Research* 35 (2): 574–95. https://doi.org/10.1016/j.annals.2008.02.003.

Turner, Victor. 1967. "Betwixt and Between: The Liminal Period in Rites de Passage." In *The Forest of Symbols: Aspects of Ndembu Ritual*, 93–111. Ithaca, NY: Cornell University Press.

2

Days of Wine and Walking

Leisure, Excess, and Authenticity on the Camino

KEITH EGAN

The medieval Camino de Santiago pilgrimage, which flows west across Europe to the northwest Spanish city Santiago de Compostela, is a remarkable example of European heritage tourism. The full Spanish leg of the most popular route, the French Way, takes a month to walk the nearly 800 kilometers from Roncesvalles at the foot of the Pyrenees to Santiago de Compostela in Galicia, Spain. Contemporary pilgrims walk to travel "authentically"—in the footsteps of medieval pilgrims long since passed who carved the original path by walking—while they follow leisurely itineraries of Spanish culture and European history. Authenticity is a key resource in securing for today's pedestrian pilgrim a sense of doing something worthwhile. Across a range of domains—historical, cultural, spiritual, religious, social, and biographical—penumbral, leisure activities outside the "settled area of the self" (Jackson 2009, xii, 117) authenticate experiences of self-authoring and sociality, in this case by walking Spain to Saint James the Greater, supposedly resting in the chancel in Compostela's cathedral, pilgrim to his own remains (see figure 2.1).[1] Searching for articulations of the authentic, whether the real or the religious, pilgrims experience productive ambivalences—leisure without luxury, tourist-trap memorials, "abundant histories" (Orsi 2008), and the resources to generate some much-needed wherewithal for life. Whether pausing by roadside monuments to deceased pilgrims or visiting the tombs of medieval royalty, leisure and death converge uncertainly on this pilgrimage in a variety of fascinating ways, in the tension between tourism that embraces life and spirituality that acknowledges death, between healing and recreating, and between

DOI: 10.5876/9781607327295.c002

FIGURE 2.1. The sepulchre of Saint James in the cathedral in Santiago de Compostela

walking and words written or read. Along the way, all the pleasures and delights of the northern Iberian Peninsula await discovery.

In this chapter I chart some of these tensions, how leisure and spirituality mutually reinforce pedestrian pilgrims' projects of taking time to reconsider their lives and their encounters with mortality through bodies and memorials past and present. I sketch pilgrims' hesitant discarding of abundance for "leisure without luxury" and how the Camino, as an increasingly leisurely pursuit, nevertheless facilitates therapeutic tourism. I argue that these ambivalent axes are not antagonistic; pilgrims are liberated as they pursue experiences of coping and joy, experiences that remain incomplete projects of becoming. The journey tests and gladdens, but the destination is the harshest lesson, I conclude, as pilgrim identities fostered over many weeks experience a sudden demise when these newly minted selves are abruptly absorbed into James's shrine, leaving pilgrims feeling bereft when indistinguishable from surrounding holidaymakers in Santiago.

JANUS IN JULY: THE TWO FACES OF SAINT JAMES

The Camino de Santiago represents the ambivalence of contemporary pilgrimage as both an authentic spiritual endeavor and a leisurely exercise with a darker past.

Saint James the pilgrim (Peregrino) is depicted with a cloak, a wide-brimmed hat, walking stick, and wine gourd walking to his own shrine, an iconic condensation of the virtues of humility, simplicity, and resilience for pilgrims to assume and tourists to consume. The scallop shell, worn with pride by pilgrims, is the symbol of Saint James. His feast day, July 25, can attract millions to the city; many pilgrims aim to arrive on that day if possible, at which time much of this material culture of the Camino—the hats, sticks, shells, and gourds—is purchased in great quantities by pilgrims and tourists alike.

Saint James has another face, though: Santiago Matamoros, slayer of Moors, defender of Iberia against Islam. Matamoros first appeared at the (fictional) battle of Clavijo near Logroño in 844, depicted on a white horse with sword held high, riding through a field of slain Muslims.[2] This sword is the basis of the cross of Santiago, the emblem of the medieval military knights of the Order of Santiago, whose motto was *"Rubet ensis sanguine Arabum"* (my sword is red with the blood of Arabs). This portrayal of Santiago, drawn from similar representations of El Cid, is often found alongside the Peregrino imagery. Over the entrance to the Iglesia de Santiago de Real in Logroño, for instance, only days into the pilgrimage, walking pilgrims pass the two sculpted images, with Matamoros dominating the Peregrino below. Matamoros's sword is often as prevalent as the Peregrino's scallop shell.[3] At journey's end in Santiago, pilgrims enjoy the local delicacy, *tarte Santiago*, a dry cake with the cross of Santiago adorned on it.

While Rome and Jerusalem have continually been central sites in Judeao-Christian sacred geography, Santiago de Compostela became a focus for sectarian nationalism from the ninth century, a lightning rod for Spain's own crusade. Templars, Hospitallers, and other warrior knights took up residence along the route to protect pilgrims. Powerful promoters appeared, such as King Alfonso III (1210–79) and Archbishop Diego Gelmirez (1069–1149), who traveled across Europe to disseminate news of the pilgrimage. The pilgrimage remained popular throughout the medieval era in part because of its greater accessibility as the Jerusalem of the West, but later its ability to confer a complete remission of sins in Holy Years kept numbers flowing in. Once the third-most-popular destination for medieval Christian pilgrims, the route's popularity dwindled in the wake of European Reformations, the onset of the Enlightenment, and the rise of secular modernity. In the late twentieth century the pilgrimage experienced a renaissance as a worldwide tourist phenomenon.

In its twentieth-century reanimation, the Camino shed these religious and sectarian roots in favor of a global market. The city of Santiago became a United Nations Educational, Scientific, and Cultural Organization (UNESCO) World Heritage Site in 1985 (the pilgrimage was included in this designation in 1993), and the pilgrimage was promoted as the European Union's (EU's) first European Premier Cultural Itinerary, offering history, culture, the "real" Spain, and evidence of a European pedigree. The pilgrimage itself draws hundreds of thousands of pilgrims along its well-serviced hostel network. Indeed, building on the success of the French Way, the dominant route that flows through Navarre and Castile y Leon, other regions are developing "rediscovered" routes.

The Catholic pilgrimage is greatly attenuated these days as its branding expands. The marketed European secular itinerary has stifled the reanimation of the medieval Spanish Catholic pilgrimage in favor of the walk itself as a journey of exploration. Churches, for instance, mark out rhetorical nodes that recall the journey's Catholic roots, but with messages coded for medieval minds. The heart of the walk today is the bucolic idyll between refuges and the serendipity of being with other pilgrims. The many eldritch, empty churches along the way lack the heat of everyday use. Because of this absence of consistent use, the churches are increasingly kitschy hybrids of tourist attractions and monuments to the Camino's authentic past and defiant sectarian glory. In contrast, modern marketing stresses journeying, culture, and history above religion.

The erosion of this Catholic interpretation, then, is not ad hoc. Santiago's 1995 bid to become the 2000 European City of Culture, for instance, highlighted a complex articulation of "culture" as the most persuasive reason to choose Santiago. The city is deliberately situated as a place of "cultural pluralism and transformation" and "solidarity and tolerance" (Roseman 2004, 79), "a green city" (Roseman 2004, 80), and a center of European, rather than Spanish, culture (Roseman 2004, 78). These representations, which bring funding for promotion, coincided with the pilgrimage being promoted as an itinerary of "European, rather than Christian, identity and comradeship" (Roseman 2004, 78). The pilgrimage has promoted representations of the route and the city as more "cultural" and less "religious" (Reader 2013, 177). Thus, the modern Camino is losing its medieval legacy as pilgrims and promoters alike embrace contemporary tourist patterns of movement, rest, and recreation along the Camino. Ironically, as the Camino becomes more accessible, pilgrims report a loss of aura, its authentic feel; and walkers especially can worry more about what sets them apart from "mere" tourists.

An extended leisure activity such as walking the Camino is also suffused in grand narratives such as Europe's genesis—Goethe believed the idea of Europe was born on the Road to Santiago—and the clash of Christian and Islamic civilizations. The route also retains the capacity to host more personal projects of being, such as recreation, and becoming, such as the "re-creation of the self" (Coleman and Kohn 2007, 2) that draws so many pilgrims to the Camino. It is perhaps then in part as a result of the loss of the religious narrative of the contemplative journey of the suffering soul that death has been linked by pilgrims as another axis of authenticity on this heritage pilgrimage (see Margry 2007, 24–25).

DAYS OF WINE AND WALKING: ENCOUNTERS WITH AUTHENTIC PILGRIMS

For Camino pilgrims, there are rules: start early, walk every day (cycle if you must, though cyclists only approximate the rules and the route), carry everything you need on your back, and follow the yellow arrows that mark the route west. These rules highlight the importance of simplicity and discipline. Pilgrims do not tour about; although they deviate to visit important religious sites within walking distance, they must progress west every day. Pilgrims shed the excess speed of contemporary life to walk west at "human speed" (Frey 1998, 18), through a slower, more meditative backspace, having to reduce their material world to the contents of a backpack.

It can be hard for refuge and shrine operators anywhere to gauge which religious pilgrims are authentic. For many promoters, keeping such a query in abeyance represents a compromise between maintaining a shrine's or refuge's profit margin and having hordes of sightseers arrive to consume the site in satisfying ways. Dress codes, calls to silence and reverence, and certifications of genuine motive issued by one's bishop have been some of the measures instituted at such places at various points in time. Too much bare flesh, too much noise, and too many reasons for coming are unwelcome indicators of excess, implying an enduring flippancy. Yet shrine operators value tourist money and must offer an experience of the "really real" (Geertz 1973) that inspires equal measures of awe and delight for visitors, who will vote for favorite shrines "with their feet and with their wallets" (Reader 2013, 116). Thus, while Camino pilgrims continue to need a pilgrim's passport, stamped each day to access cheap hostels, church authorities in Santiago now offer a secular version of the coveted "certificate of completion" for those not declaring a pious motive to travel.

Various motives drive pilgrims, though the more popular the pilgrimage becomes, the less religion figures as a factor. Pilgrims need not finish in one effort, either; some walk stages to reach Santiago over successive years to fit the Camino into their lives. Many, however, leave careers and lives to walk a full Camino, often discarding the debilitating staleness of their lives, jobs, even marriages to explore new directions. The Camino regularly acts as a cipher and moral anchor, capable of containing and grounding the significant toll of lives adrift (Egan 2011). The fact that the Camino also offers a range of sensuous engagements with the land and the people who populate the walk is not a matter of authenticity per se ("there are many authenticities" [Frey 1998, 136]). Pilgrims instead cultivate a poetics of peregrination, a practice and a performance of coping, healing, and recovering selves, experiencing pleasure and joy. Many pilgrims reflecting on their journey recall the photos and small memorials left by other pilgrims on the Camino, which, in turn, recalls those who have passed away to those who pass by. One internet site displays two instances:

> A picture of someone's son just on a post. When I read it he was the same age as me. I don't know why but it really touched me. There was no mention of why it was there or what had happened, only that he had died in 1997. I've often wondered what his story was and why his parents chose that spot. Stuartm (https://www.caminodesantiago.me/community/threads/stautues-and-monuments-along-the-camino.24203/)

> A marker acknowledging a couple's Camino. They had lost both their sons, one to a motorcycle accident at the age of 20 (2008), and the other to a snowmobile accident at the age of 25 (2012). They were walking to honor the memory of their boys. It was truly heartbreaking and moving. Nreyn12

The Camino is a shared, public forum for the presentation of selves under reconstruction through leisurely walking. Such discoveries are vital for affirming the journey and one's personal motives. The pilgrimage, a symbolic death in itself, grounds liminal selves (see Csordas 1994; Dubisch 1995, 218). The dead are in this context a scarce resource; the dead, or, more properly, traces of them acting as *momenti mori*, can secure the walk as a worthy endeavor for pilgrims. The 150 pilgrims who have died along the way and are memorialized are stark reminders that this itinerary can exact its own price. Memorials can be both effervescent, evoking solidarity, and sobering, evoking sorrow, for passers-by; it is not unusual to pass a memorial and find a pilgrim there in quiet contemplation.[4] The pilgrim memorials represent a more individual sense of the Camino, the tragedy of a single pilgrim's death clearly marked. The monuments of those who have fallen while undertaking the Camino add to the allure of the pilgrimage; some monuments are more aesthetic, such as the artwork of a bicycle representing a German cycling pilgrim's death outside El Acebo (figure 2.2), while others are less ostentatious and more descriptive, such as the simple monument to a Dutch pilgrim outside Melide (figure 2.3).

Leisure has become a difficult activity to defend when it is easily conceived as an unproductive waste of time. As a different kind of time and a different experience of time, traveling by foot slows down every rhythm—of movement, of rest, of consumption; breathing, distance, and stretch—attenuating body and mind in productive unproductivity. Time becomes distance, and while Camino entrepreneurs commodify part of this time as a leisure walk filled with productive and consumptive pleasure, the walk itself stretches beyond that interpretation, too. Even though there have been relatively few pilgrim deaths en route, pilgrims who have since passed are also brought back to the Camino—sometimes figuratively through the kinds of

FIGURE 2.2. Monument marking the death of a German pilgrim in El Acebo (León). Note the stones left on the monument by passing pilgrims.

markers the pilgrims above stumble across, but former pilgrims have also requested that family members walk with their ashes. Even though death is rare, then, those deaths seem to "carry a great deal of symbolic weight," as Kaul (this volume) argues, though condensing not so much *ironic* entanglements with death here as *subjunctive* ones, openings into newer aspirational territories for peripatetic pilgrims.[5]

FIGURE 2.3. A simple memorial to a Dutch pilgrim who died en route to Santiago in Melide (Galicia)

How do pilgrims authenticate unfolding Caminos? First, pilgrims follow in Saint James's steps as he walks, uniquely, to his own resting place, traveling to assume into themselves their own ragged and confusing transitions through life. They also follow in Jesus's footsteps as an iconic pilgrim (Webb 2002, 159), passing monuments to others who died in their attempts to travel to Santiago. This creates ambivalence for contemporary pilgrims, few of whom have uncomplicatedly religious motives for being there but who know that to die on pilgrimage is, in Christian terms, to die in a state of grace. Many travel as walking monuments to loved ones who have passed or been gravely ill. These pilgrims have been a great solace to others who find evidence of the Camino's worthiness in having come across such individuals. John, who marked his sister's passing while walking the previous year by following her route, inspired a musician to compose a violin piece that he performed in the cathedral in Santiago, serving as a powerful affirmation affecting all those present who knew John's difficult story (see Egan 2012).

When writing this moribund list of motivations, though, it can be easy to forget the joy and serendipity of travel through Spain at human speed.[6] Mortality and leisure converge on the Camino, in the mezzanines of what pilgrims come to know as everyday life and what Victor Turner described as part-tourist, part-pilgrim (Turner 1978, 20, 11). There is no purity for these travelers, however, only exquisite mixtures of piety, play, and promotion. The Camino is replete with values: self-reliance, endurance, discipline, tenacity, completion. In the physicality of the walking pilgrimage, pilgrims are exemplars of the success of overcoming the ambivalence of mixing recreation with the re-creation of the self (Coleman and Kohn 2007, 2).

"THE JOURNEY ITSELF IS HOME" (MATSUO BASHO)

The Camino pilgrim's day typically begins before sunrise—dressing and packing quietly in a torch-lit dormitory, sleepily stretching outside while surveying potential companions. Pilgrims walk, alone at first, until gradually ad hoc groupings become forged in the morning heat, the effort of the day's journey, and the evening's revelry, where walking companions become dinner companions. The daily walk lasts up to seven hours, with habitual breaks for breakfast, brunch, early lunch with beer (San Miguel) or wine (Rioja). In these days the pilgrim's muscles tighten, tans form, and the body grows, pushing out through the skin to meet the ground beneath (regularly, it must be said, involving huge blisters). Pilgrims routinely survey companions' bodies, offering support, advice, and occasionally erotic encounters; care takes many forms. When pain and blisters appear, great attention is given; pilgrims lance each others' blisters and massage each others' sore legs at day's end. Each afternoon a hostel is secured for ritual washing, laundry, and napping. Having marched purposefully through the back places of a rustic Spanish morning, previously dusty, tired pilgrims are no less Janus-faced than their patron saint, transforming through rituals of ablution into discerning tourists to partake in a more sensuous Spain through local sites—village bars and churches, city shopping districts, cathedrals, and museums—sampling wines, tapas, and other local delicacies. The camera documents and authenticates, the phone relays the day's news and events, and pilgrims break bread with new friends, reliving the day over a cheap and cheerful *Menu del Peregrino*.

Only when a busload of tourists stops by resting pilgrims during a day's walk can tension lines rupture the rhythms of this idyll. Tourists consume pilgrim backspaces through photographs as part of the authentic pilgrimage landscape being sought. They recognize pilgrims as authenticating Santiago, their destination, while pilgrims see tourists as confirming the authenticity of their choice to walk. Some pilgrims grimace, but others are good sports and join in group photos. Tourists are roundly denounced later, though, for their choice of transport. The important rules have been broken, and the difference between the two types of travelers is clearly evoked.

The month or more of a Camino is not spare time; it is a time in-between, which opens out into a world in-between. As a world-making act, this walk is as much political as contemplative, "thinking made concrete" (Solnit 2002, 6). Pilgrimage time is not wholly productive in a capitalist sense; it is temporally and spatially between experiences of pilgrims' discarded regimes. Equally, though, it engenders its own form of discipline.[7] Effort brings results, if not freedom. The resources are life-giving; life is re-experienced as never a simple choice between being and nothingness but as one of "more or less" liveliness, lesser or greater mortality (Hage, in Jackson 2005, x). The lives of long-term pilgrims are experienced as lives endured transforming into lives enjoyed in the presence of pilgrims who populated the route for a thousand years. Pilgrimage can offer a different excess, based on spirituality and the miraculous on a road that draws the imagination beyond the bounds of the body, abundant alternatives to a world experienced as too rationalized, too centered on economic instrumentality (Reader 2007, 12).

PILGRIMS' REPRESENTATIONS OF THE CAMINO

The reemergence of Santiago as an important destination for Catholics worldwide has been greatly supported by two papal visits in 1982 and 1989, as well as the granting of plenary indulgences during Holy Years. The Camino as a modern route, however, has been cultivated by local promoters who in the mid-twentieth century recovered and reanimated a largely forgotten walkway. The Camino's renewed popularity has also been aided by pilgrim-promoters, such as Paulo Coehlo (1992), Cees Nooteboom (1997), and Shirley MacLaine (2001), who piqued the interest of a global readership. For both Coehlo and MacLaine, the Camino was a repository of the transcendent, a store of personal renewal through contact with an authentic spirituality leeching from modernity. Coehlo sought out the chalice of Jesus Christ and the mythic remnants of the Crusader ethos, while MacLaine imaginatively explored the transcendent wildernesses of Lemuria and Atlantis on the road.[8]

Authors writing about their Caminos are an interesting group; their experiences, their willingness to "return to the scene of the crime" (Taussig 2011, 22) in their writings reveal the power of the Camino as a kind of palimpsest, a mystic writing pad of a pilgrimage inscribed and reentered, ambivalently searching for clues and meanings that had previously arisen or eluded them. Writing as (re-)walking exposes a curious source of authenticity for writers and readers alike. Writing about walking moves constantly between staking a claim for authorship (authority) and being a source of authority itself (mimetic credibility [see Bruner 1994, 399]). The production of a written memoir helpfully complicates the question of the primacy of the act of walking over the act of writing.[9] Further, it allows for the examination of the relationship of movement to being, of the requirement to move in order to reinvigorate a life endured in the company of literary-imaginative ghosts; "the ghost is not simply a dead or a missing person but a social figure, and investigating it can lead to that dense site where history and subjectivity make social life" (Gordon 1997, 8).

The model of the authentic Camino is in evidence in Walter Starkie's classic account of his Camino travels in the 1950s, as a religious pilgrim immersed in the medieval pilgrimage on a "quest of healing solitude" (Starkie 1957, 83), seeking out the Camino's churches and myths, Saint James's miracles and likenesses along the way. Fluent in Spanish and Italian, Starkie engaged and conversed easily; he read the land and medieval architecture as he moved, on foot and by bus. He rarely encountered other pilgrims on a largely unused route, but he followed the route as described in the world's first travel brochure, the twelfth-century *Codex Calixtinus*. Yet even Starkie found himself confounded by a pilgrim "who was so much the embodiment of the medieval pilgrim with his habit, his broad hat, his long staff and bare feet that I felt ashamed of my modern clothes and my well-shod feet" (Starkie 1957, 231). Nevertheless, he lamented an emerging form of "robot-like" peregrination relying on modern transport as a "'pilgrimage without tears' for the millions" and called for a return to older ways, to slower "unsupervised" pilgrimage as a more authentic inner journey akin to Bunyan's *Pilgrim's Progress* (Starkie 1957, 323–24).

Kerry Egan (no relation), an American pilgrim who described her pilgrimage in the aftermath of her father's passing, exemplifies the more common existential pilgrimage today, where the tension is with how to resolve the motives for peregrinating rather than justifying one's presence. For Egan, laughter among strangers evoked her last purely happy time before her father's passing: "I realized I'd been numb for months" (Egan 2004, 47). Her walk to Saint James's relics suggested "a refutation of the victory of death" (Egan 2004, 53); life spilled over as she neared the apostle's bones: "But first, you have to get through death" (Egan 2004, 87). Camino rituals—walking, unburdening, bringing a stone to leave at the Cruz de Ferro—allow a larger story to impinge on the personal tragedy, to take charge of it and ease the moment.[10] For Egan, her grief had finally begun. Her moratorium had ended, as "the feeling I came away [with] from the Cruz de Ferro was not that I handed over my heaviness to God but rather that I could bear it . . . the heaviness of grief is like blood—it's built into our bodies, gushing from time to time through wounds that remind us of how vulnerable we are" (Egan 2004, 180). In Egan's account at least, peace was possible when burdens were relinquished. Grief became the "deepest form of prayer" (Egan 2004, 210), and the Camino succeeded in giving her an answer "by walking, by breathing, by beauty, by anger, by joy, by love . . . I needed to be cracked open to grieve" (Egan 2004, 207). Her grief was interleaved with lighter moments, too—sharing cherries bought by the roadside with her boyfriend, being chased by a cow, walking with an eccentric pilgrim. By the time she arrived in Santiago, Egan was overtaken with fits of giggling and released great peals of laughter, no longer a pilgrim but no longer the woman who had set out earlier, either (Egan 2004, 218–20). Such accounts are solid sellers, setting potential pilgrim imaginations alight; these accounts are both testaments and itineraries for those who come after.

PILGRIMAGE IN THE VALLEY OF THORNS

Different mortal remains articulate different meanings around the Camino. The tombs and sarcophagi of medieval kings and queens remain on display in the cathedrals, and larger churches are available as spectacles of the past majesty of European royalty, enshrined in great architectural beauty and delight, high gothic ceilings reaching to the infinite. The supposed remains of Saint James in Santiago reach further back, to antiquity and the age of martyrs, the body acting as provenance for the destination, an emanatory source of pilgrims' mimesis that witnesses to the real and their plodding toward the Jerusalem of the West.

The Spanish memorial to the Civil War (1936–39) dead that makes its appearance on Montes de Oca is more raw, as many bodies of those who disappeared are imagined to be buried in unmarked graves by the roadsides. The inscription "*No fue inútil su muerte, fue inútil su fusilamiento*" (their deaths were not in vain, only their executions [by firing squad]), is more poignant, especially given that travel guides describe the memorial as commemorating the nearby dumpsites of dozens of Civil War rebels.

Conversely, local moral entrepreneurs who dedicated their lives to popularizing the forgotten Camino are honored, notably Don Elías Valiña Sampedro in O Cebrero (Dunn and Davidson 1996, xlvii, notes 24, 26), who marked the forgotten path in Galicia with the iconic yellow arrows with the help of Picaud's Codex Calixtinus.

The Camino's many pasts are a cornucopia of solutions available to make sense of longings, needs, and insufficiencies felt keenly in a present that easily leaves us disoriented and overwhelmed (see Jackson 2007, 59). The overlapping Catholic, European, and Spanish pasts of the Camino are wells of conclusions to be tapped—the Camino's historical continuity provides a ground for less permanent pilgrim biographies. Equally, the retreat into nature is a "profoundly ambivalent [relationship]" (Jackson 2007, 139) with intra-psychic and inter-subjective forces that retain the power to both end us and renew us (Jackson 2007, 141). To the extent that pilgrims answer the need to act, those actions are at the beginning of the mystery beyond ordinary language (see Jackson 2007, 152).

The need to become something else—pilgrims, El Peregrino himself—to assume a "life-in-death stillness" through sympathetic magic, to become a dead pilgrim and travel to his resting place, is an attempt to break with the "catastrophic spell of things" (Taussig 2011, 129). A line of pilgrims and tourists becomes one dead pilgrim, reanimated and dying again in the cathedral's charnel. Pilgrims emerge as tourists surrounded by the reified pilgrimage, the kitsch of iconic and fetishized shards of the pilgrimage, more easily transportable. The stuff of walking becomes badges of witness: Santiago effigies, shells, gourds, and staffs. Whether this is a triumph of consumerism over experience is hardly the point. The two feed off of and into each other. This new pilgrim-tourist authenticates the material but does not complete the process of authentication. Between the world of the ossuary in the cathedral and the worldly markets for souvenirs outside, "the experience that shatters experience ... the astonishment of enchantment in a disenchanted world ... a 'dialectic at a standstill'" (Taussig 2011, 129–30) throws pilgrims into the everyday swirl of the old city of Santiago. No longer pilgrims, as the rule to walk no longer applies, one may still feel changed, fractally reproduced in shop windows filled with kitsch and by tourists wearing affordable pilgrim costumes.[11] Such unspeakable urban encounters are relegated to ordinary quotidian occurrences—there are no more extraordinary events, encounters that have taken place "while someone else is eating or opening a window or just walking/dully along" (Auden, cited in Taussig 2011, 130).

All of these realizations occur in the midst of the "invisible crowd of the dead" (Taussig 2011, 131), a millennium of visitors to the cathedral. Have pilgrims succeeded in authenticating their lives, in participating in life, and found it desirable, (re-)enchanted, mystified, consecrated? It is difficult to know if any pilgrim's experience has led to an authentication of life through an escape from one habitus into another. Pilgrims are left with shards and fragments, all that can be grasped of life—awkward glances sideways in the midst of life flowing by anyway, lives lived joyfully by chance, amateurish and improvised for the most part. But to be an amateur means to do something for the love of it. Pilgrims buy their souvenirs, the campier the better, to wink knowingly at the material excess and diminished authenticity of their pilgrimage. My favorite souvenir is a bright red T-shirt with an alien dressed as Saint James saying ¿*Quién dice que no soy peregrino*? (Who says I am not a pilgrim?).

ALL CHANGED, CHANGED UTTERLY: ARRIVING AS ENDING

A difficult lesson the Camino can impose upon pilgrims is that the journey begins before the pilgrim is prepared. One can be, in existential terms, "thrown" into the decision to walk. Another difficult lesson is that, after habituating oneself to the daily rituals of progress and care, the walk ends. The last days' walking paradoxically resembles the medieval pilgrimage with its noise and bustle, even with youth groups and package tourists in iconographic paraphernalia. Arriving in Santiago is often anticlimactic; modern excess reclaims one's imagination, and the simple life of the last weeks—the pain, tears, laughter, and camaraderie—is washed away. Before one is ready to finish, the pilgrim in Santiago becomes just another tourist. There is nowhere else to go; the pilgrim's liminoid state is absorbed, leaving the pilgrim to tour the city, surrounded by artifacts manufactured as far away as China (see Roseman and Fife 2008, 113). Walkers who had surrendered/suspended modernity for this mediated medieval sensibility are abruptly thrown again, this time out of the Camino. After witnessing the final resting place of Saint James the pilgrim in a dark, cramped, and busy chamber under the cathedral, the embodied landscape of the journey yields to a new visual landscape of tourism and kitsch for pilgrims, one that refracts the Camino's iconic status when the cheap shells, wine gourd, staff, and cloak are worn to emulate those arriving on foot, who in turn emulate the Peregrino. As a Spanish priest told Nancy Frey (1998, 163), it is "like being kicked out of Eden."

Pilgrims congregate for midday mass at the cathedral in Santiago, in part to meet each other but also in the hope of seeing the impressive *botafumeiro* (the thurible that dispenses incense), which takes seven men to swing, a formidable tourist attraction in itself (tour groups can donate money to ensure the thurible's operation on a given day). Following my first fieldtrip along the Camino in 2000, I spent three days meeting pilgrims I knew who arrived at the cathedral after I did. I realized that I knew fewer people each day and anxiety set in; the evidence of my incredible first pilgrimage was fading. Later that evening I happened upon Fernanda and her boyfriend, Miguel, and we bought a bottle of wine to share in the shelter of the portico of the Casa del Cabildo, behind the cathedral. We reminisced about the last month, comparing the differences in our journeys, hostels, other pilgrims, and local characters we had met; and we drank to friends who had left for home. Our conversation covered much of the loneliness we were already feeling. Fernanda told me: "What I miss most is waking up and starting to walk every day like a routine . . . Every day was a new learning about my limits . . . from body to soul . . . every day a different place to know . . . a different face to meet . . . more knowledge . . . so . . . I miss everything . . ."

Thus has the route to Finisterre, a small coastal village 75 kilometers farther west (Herrero 2008), emerged as a pilgrim afterlife, three days' more walking or two hours by bus. Although church authorities disapprove of this nature-oriented end to the Camino, the route and destination are becoming popular. In 2004, at the edge of the Atlantic Ocean, my fellow pilgrims and I selected an item of our pilgrim's clothing. On the beach, following the ritual we had heard about from others, we made a pile and burned the clothes. When we turned away, taking the bus to Santiago among tourists whom we imagined had not walked a single day, we found ourselves lost, in the crowd and in our own thoughts.

CONCLUSION

The Camino represents weeks of effort along hundreds of kilometers of pathways, roadsides, country tracts, and city streets—providing time and space but crucially also supplying the metaphor of the road, the sense of progress west, moving "at a human pace" (Frey 1998), and becoming an extended act that envelops the walker. The constant freshness of the territory means every day is relentless; staying still is not an option, not if one wishes to sleep that night or to get food or continue the journey as a pilgrim. The Camino thus offers itself as an extended process of methodically forgetting the urgency of grief or inadequacy through punctuated moments of emotional intensity and physical difficulty.

The allure of pilgrimage is in part the serendipity of the encounter with the itinerary and rules of the road (its arrows, backpacks, and blisters), as each day affords its own opportunities for petrification and enchantment. Pilgrims can equally be enchanted by the dead, enlisted as encounters with authentication and authorship, for instance, through pilgrim memorials. Rather than imparting a "macabre meaning" on the Camino landscape as Kaul (this volume) shows occurring in Doolin, there is a different cultural geography at play on a pilgrimage. The actuality of death actually affirms the genius loci of a memorial in a pilgrim topography and authenticates the mode of travel that finds such spaces and validates the range of otherwise contradictory practices of playful tourist-pilgrims on a medieval pilgrimage. These memorials do not evoke horror; they invoke a more comfortable margin by which to navigate life on the Camino.

The body's flexibility and the collection of souvenirs produce a kind of dialectic, meanings pushed together—corporeal recreation and mechanical reproduction. Walking enchants; material culture petrifies. Books, backpacks, and boots; scallop shells, wine gourds, and Santiago cakes all circulate in an adventure toward the mythologized bones of Saint James, the pilgrim slayer of Moors. Nothing prepares the pilgrim for the quotidian analogue of the walk. After the pilgrimage, walking, reading, and writing often fold into each other, modes of moving a body, feet first, then gaze, then hands, through a landscape of contact, memory, imagination, and communication. One can divine a site for anticipation from this inescapable parataxis of the text, for discerning one's own prospects on such a journey. The text remains to be read, dreamed by the reader; the journey creates the condition of being possessed without realizing it (see Taussig 2011, 56).

Ultimately, in Santiago Cathedral it is not that the pilgrimage has no more pilgrims but rather that walking pilgrims are becoming indistinguishable from tourist-pilgrims as they come face to face with the remains of Saint James the pilgrim. The two types of visitors mingle, blurring distinctions. Tourists and pilgrims do not greet each other with mild disdain because they are so different but because they are not different enough. The fluid, amorphous walking pilgrimage that had enveloped pilgrims becomes suddenly different and less attractive. Both groups of visitors shift uneasily in each other's company, the pilgrims unhappy to have to wait in line with adulterating tourists and the day-trippers somewhat disconcerted by the odor emanating from such scruffy visitors; the chief differences between them are the pilgrims' dishevelment and mild olfactory repulsion. Pilgrims' accretions of aspects of Santiago Peregrino are reabsorbed in the charnel under his cathedral and pilgrims reemerge—having attended the bones—with no more arrows to follow.

Pilgrims who embrace a simpler period of existence seek the "wherewithal of life" (Jackson 2013) in anticipation of a hoped-for abundance. Days of wine and walking create meaning and fellow-feeling while moving between excesses. The pilgrimage is powerful when walked and written into being. It is in some respects another form of excess, not leaving the Camino behind but dragging it into an afterlife toward Finisterre or at home. But in other respects, accounts testify to the Camino's power as a tourist route that permits and facilitates something that feels and reads like healing: the pilgrimage as a salve if not salvation. If one can admit that pilgrimage is leisure with authentic purpose in the presence of the dead who lend symbolic weight to the choice to walk, then the total experience is one of being a pilgrim *and* a tourist; mixing endurance and enjoyment creates a fertile escape into life within manageable limits.

NOTES

1. Walking has a long pedigree in Christian thinking, one that underscores the virtue of shedding worldly excesses to travel to a holy place (Sumption 1975, 180). These categories are untidy, though; walking is authentic, cycling less so. Traveling by horse is difficult to categorize and thus treated with polite disregard. Those who travel by car are seen as utterly inauthentic (see Frey 1998, 18). One pilgrim completed the pilgrimage on a unicycle and was refused a certificate of completion, even though bikes are formally recognized—an Orwellian instance of two wheels good, one wheel bad.

2. Pilgrims assume the likeness of Santiago Peregrino, who is also Matamoros, the patron of ethnic cleansing on two continents, during Christian resistance to Islamic expansion in Europe and the Reconquista of Iberia (711–1492) and subsequently as patron of the South American conquistadors from the fifteenth to seventeenth centuries.

3. The scallop shell became a powerful talisman, worn by pilgrims returning from James's remains. The shell could be bought only in Santiago; under a decree by Pope Clement VI in 1262, anyone caught selling the shell outside the archdiocese of Santiago was excommunicated.

4. Memorials are monitored on the internet, where pilgrims pass messages through blogs to locals to ensure memorials are maintained after difficult weather.

5. The Camino is inescapably an itinerary into an imagination of the other, and I would argue that it counts as much for Spanish pilgrims as for those from other countries. Spain is still in the making, as yet unhealed from the scars of the Franco regime and its procrustean insistence on national unity. What I have argued here may apply *a fortiori* to pilgrims visiting Spain, but it cannot be discounted for Spanish pilgrims traveling to explore the north of their country. The quickly silent faces of Basque pilgrims when policemen walk within earshot are just one sign of the significant differences between regions.

6. The present, the here-and-now for many people, seems to be insufficient and excessive, both existentially shallow and terrifyingly real. Lacking the "wherewithal of life" (Jackson 2013), people seek clearings to sense some ephemeral solidarity, investing themselves in a lively itinerary into mortality, where they can alternate between the *spiritu divino* and the "*spirito de vino*" (although San Miguel beer is the unofficial beverage of the Camino).

7. Pilgrims often leave their jobs to walk the Camino, a decision that interrupts their job prospects and affects their earnings potential for the rest of their lives. The disciplined leisure of the Camino, then, can be seen to be productively damaging over the course of the pilgrim's life, but it potentially offers new trajectories for that life course, too. Camino leisure is a creative attempt to push back against "productive" leisure.

8. The actor Martin Sheen (2011) recently starred in a successful film as well about a father grieving his son's passing on pilgrimage, subsequently donning his son's backpack to finish the son's Camino. Jenna Bush, the daughter of former US president George W. Bush, brought a Secret Service detachment and the global media with her when she walked in 2004.

9. For an excellent fictional account of such a quandary, see Lodge 2011.

10. The Cruz de Ferro marks the boundary into Galicia, dedicated originally to Mercury, Roman god of boundaries. Pilgrims leave a stone, picture, or memento behind to prepare for the final leg of the journey. The ritual of bringing a stone here is reputed to have been a practice Bishop Diego Gelmirez initiated, asking pilgrims to Santiago to bring stone to rebuild the cathedral following its destruction by the Muslim general Almanzor in 1007.

11. This space that remakes the pilgrim-tourist is periodically even crueler: during a Holy Year, the Puerta de Perdón is opened and tourist numbers spike. Just walking through the door grants a full indulgence. Pilgrims who have walked for a month receive only one-third indulgence (Gitlitz and Davidson 2000, 346). While few pilgrims are so religious or sinful that they have traveled the Camino for the indulgence, the fact that tourists have not earned this dispensation through "authentic" effort dismays many walkers. For many pilgrims, it is a step too far.

REFERENCES

Bruner, E. 1994. "Abraham Lincoln as Authentic Reproduction: A Critique of Postmodernism." *American Anthropologist* 96 (2): 397–415. https://doi.org/10.1525/aa.1994.96.2.02a00070.

Coehlo, P. 1992. *The Pilgrimage*. Trans. A. Clarke. New York: Harper Perennial.

Coleman, S., and T. Kohn. 2007. "The Discipline of Leisure: Taking Play Seriously." In *The Discipline of Leisure: Embodying Cultures of Recreation*, ed. S. Coleman and T. Kohn, 1–22. New York: Berghahn Books.

Csordas, T., ed. 1994. *Embodiment and Experience: The Existential Ground of Culture and Self*. Cambridge: Cambridge University Press.

Dubisch, J. 1995. *In a Different Place*. Princeton, NJ: Princeton University Press. https://doi.org/10.1515/9781400884414.

Dunn, M., and L. Davidson. 1996. "Bibliography of the Pilgrimage: State of the Art." In *The Pilgrimage to Compostela in the Middle Ages*, ed. M. Dunn and L. Davidson, xxiii–xlviii. New York: Routledge.

Egan, Keith. 2011. "'I Want to Feel the Camino in My Legs': Trajectories of Walking on the Camino de Santiago." In *Encounters of Body and Soul in Contemporary Religious Practices: Anthropological Reflections*, ed. A. Fedele and R. Blanes, 3–22. New York: Berghahn Books.

Egan, Keith. 2012. "Walking Back to Happiness? Modern Pilgrimage and the Expression of Suffering on Spain's Camino de Santiago." In *Writing the Dark Side of Travel*, ed. J. Skinner, 99–121. New York: Berghahn Books.

Egan, Kerry. 2004. *Fumbling: A Pilgrimage Tale of Love, Grief, and Spiritual Renewal on the Camino de Santiago*. New York: Doubleday.

Frey, N. 1998. *Pilgrim Stories: On and Off the Road to Santiago*. Berkeley: University of California Press.

Geertz, C. 1973. "Religion as a Cultural System." In *The Interpretation of Cultures: Selected Essays*, 87–125. New York: Basic Books.

Gitlitz, D., and M. Davidson. 2000. *The Pilgrimage Road to Santiago: The Complete Cultural Handbook*. New York: St. Martin's Griffin.

Gordon, A. 1997. *Ghostly Matters*. Minneapolis: University of Minnesota Press.

Herrero, N. 2008. "Reaching Land's End." *New Social Practices in the Pilgrimage to Santiago de Camino* 21 (2): 131–49.

Jackson, M. 2005. *Existential Anthropology*. New York: Berghahn Books.

Jackson, M. 2007. *Excursions*. Durham, NC: Duke University Press. https://doi.org/10.1215/9780822390640.

Jackson, M. 2009. *The Palm at the End of the Mind*. Durham, NC: Duke University Press. https://doi.org/10.1215/9780822392439.

Jackson, M. 2013. *The Wherewithal of Life*. Berkeley: University of California Press. https://doi.org/10.1525/california/9780520276703.001.0001.

Lodge, D. 2011 [1995]. *Therapy*. New York: Vintage Books.

MacLaine, S. 2001. *The Camino: A Journey of the Spirit*. New York: Atria.

Margry, P. 2007. *Shrines and Pilgrimage in the Modern World*. Amsterdam: Amsterdam University Press.

Nooteboom, C. 1997. *Roads to Santiago: Detours and Riddles in the Lands and History of Spain*. Amsterdam: Harvill.

Orsi, R. 2008. "Abundant Histories: Marian Apparitions as Alternative Modernity." *Historically Speaking* 9 (7): 12–16.

Reader, I. 2007. "Pilgrimage Growth in the Modern World: Meanings and Implications." *Religion* 20: 1–20.

Reader, I. 2013. *Pilgrimage in the Marketplace*. New York: Routledge.

Roseman, S. 2004. "Santiago de Compostela in the Year 2000: From Religious Center to European City of Culture." In *Intersecting Journeys: The Anthropology of Pilgrimage and Tourism*, ed. S. Roseman and E. Badone, 68–88. Urbana: University of Illinois Press.

Roseman, S., and W. Fife. 2008. "Souvenirs and Cultural Politics in Santiago de Compostela." *International Journal of Iberian Studies* 21 (2): 109–30. https://doi.org/10.1386/ijis.21.2.109_1.

Sheen, M., perf. 2011. *The Way*. Directed by E. Estevez. London: Icon Home Entertainment.

Solnit, R. 2002. *Wanderlust: A History of Walking*. London: Verso.

Starkie, W. 1957. *The Road to Santiago: Pilgrims of St. James*. London: John Murray.

Sumption, J. 1975. *Pilgrimage*. London: Faber and Faber.

Taussig, M. 2011. *I Swear I Saw This*. Chicago: University of Chicago Press. https://doi.org/10.7208/chicago/9780226789842.001.0001.

Turner, V. 1978. *Image and Pilgrimage in Christian Culture*. New York: Columbia University Press.

Webb, D. 2002. *Medieval European Pilgrimage*. New York: Palgrave.

3

Johan Huizinga Goes Tombstoning with the Devil

PATRICK LAVIOLETTE

> Living at risk is jumping off the cliff and building
> your wings on the way down
> (RAY BRADBURY 1988)

What name for a voluntary high-risk activity so evocatively captures the relationship among leisure, danger, and death as well as the term *tombstoning*? This practice, rather simply, consists of the action of throwing oneself off an overhanging ridge or cliff face into a body of water. Usually, this is done feet-first, without any protective apparatus save perhaps a wetsuit. The name derives from both the dangerous character of the act itself, which can result in serious injury or death, and a bodily posture that often requires the person's arms to be tucked in closely alongside the torso's flanks or crossed over the chest. Since such a still pose morbidly resembles a corpse in a sarcophagus, we get the apt enough idiom "tombstoning," at least in the southwest of Britain.

The origins and etymological roots of the term *risk* connect the word to cliffs and the hazards of navigation. A metaphorical expression dating back to classical Greek times, *rhizikon* was a nautical idiom identifying "difficulties to avoid in the sea." It became *resicum* in Latin, the derivatives of which, *risicum/riscus*, similarly referred to cliffs or reefs. The background for much of the research I present here originates from ethnographic work I've been carrying out in Cornwall, United Kingdom, for over a decade, as well as more recent fieldwork in New Zealand and Estonia. The idea behind some of this research is to explore the dynamics of certain hazardous games involving sea cliffs, coastal caves, flooded mining quarries, and other abandoned postindustrial landscape features. Based on participant observation research dealing with dangerous places and risky behavior, this work follows the anthropological tradition of reflecting upon playful techniques of the body. By considering spontaneous as well as calculated risk rituals that occur along the Cornish coastline, it considers how certain existential experiences get caught within the leveled verticality of recreational "adventure-scapes" (Laviolette 2007).

Beginning with tentative ethno-historical and auto-ethnographic findings, this chapter documents the phenomenon of tombstoning and similar risky cliff-related leisure activities. It does so from the perspective of individual as well as social anxieties, especially those radical reactions to taboo activities. Such questioning aligns itself with recent thematic developments regarding embodied leisure, dark tourism, playscapes, and the risks of adventure in landscapes of fright or death. In considering the growing concerns over "danger zones" (Stone 2006; Laviolette 2014), this study scrutinizes intimate, emotional perceptions. It chronicles the movements, sensorial reactions, and material interactions that take place as one skirts around steep edges or through sea caves. In other words, through the residue of embodied action, it strives to reconcile some of the structural dichotomies between place and non-places, worthlessness and heritage value, accessibility and local protectionism.

A central paradox exists between hyper-tourism and the appropriation of specific sites by marginal, subversive thrill seekers (Augé 1995). Such groups often propagate a "spatial infection," whereby fear and foreboding can spread. Yet through the prism of modernity's fascination with immediacy, such playfully serious activities also add value to restricted playgrounds or ludic, off-limit spaces (Stebbins 2007). For attention to the hyper-modern state of sensorial acceleration (Larsen 2008), one must look to a certain sociological impressionism that considers those effects and affects that stem from our faster pace of life. Here, leisure is not just conspicuous, it is landscaped in manifestly excessive and occasionally risky ways—ways consistent with Johan Huizinga's (1956 [1938]) theory of play and yet quite distant from his reflections on warfare and structural violence.

MAUSS-TRAP

Claude Lévi-Strauss starts his classic travel memoir *Tristes Tropiques* with what is, in my opinion, a fairly outlandish polemical comment about what anthropology is not. Or, at least, what it should not involve:

> Anthropology is a profession in which adventure plays no part; merely one of its bondages, it represents no more than a dead weight of weeks or months wasted en

route; hours spent in idleness when one's informant has given one the slip; hunger, exhaustion, illness as like as not; and those thousand and one routine duties which eat up most of our days to no purpose and reduce our perilous existence in the virgin forest to a simulacrum of military service ... That the object of our studies should be attainable only by continual struggle and vain expenditures does not mean that we should set any store by what we should rather consider as the negative aspect of our profession. (Lévi-Strauss 1961, 17)

Despite its rhetorical elegance, there is nonetheless much to disagree with here. My objective is not to deconstruct this quotation, however. Rather, it is to take the reader on an impressionistic, auto-ethnographic adventure. As this section heading suggests, we begin that journey with reference to the famous French social anthropologist Marcel Mauss (1872–1950). Mauss is especially pertinent to the study of the human body even though his exceptional work on the gift and reciprocity overshadows it. He introduced the concept of the "total social fact" in the 1920s and *l'habitus* in the 1930s; in his famous essay on "techniques of the body" (1992 [1934]) he proposed that our biological bodies are not only subject to evolutionary principles. Instead, they have complex tripartite relationships with social and psychological elements whereby these dimensions cannot be isolated or separated from each other.

In short, bodily techniques are corporeal ways of becoming en-skilled. They are also contingent and malleable, and they allow for an adaptable creative physicality. The processes of describing such techniques of the body may be understood as disciplining or punishing, as in Michel Foucault's (1977) now classic accounts, whereby the modern body is unintentionally subjected to risk. Indeed, it is one recent scholarship often portrays as mechanized, surveyed, patrolled, and thus never more regulated.

Nevertheless, such techniques of the body can also be seen as therapeutic and emancipatory—vehicles for transporting the imaginary (Robbins 2010). Hence, we need to ask whether corporeal regimentation is the only result of modernity, the only framework in which to consider risk taking. Or is there something else that is possible here, an alternative scenario that ethnography, perhaps inspired by multi-sited, postmodern, or phenomenological approaches, can tackle (Ravn and Ploug Hansen 2013)? My research on adventurous pursuits provides such a scenario in which the hazardous use of landscape, when linked to positive encounters with danger, allows extreme acts to exist beyond the levels that deal only with restraint and power to a more creative position in which some of them can be understood as existential acts of the social imagination (Laviolette 2011).

A significant conceptual parallel thus exists with Georg Simmel's likening of the adventurer to the artist: "A fragmentary incident, it [the adventure] is yet, like a work of art, enclosed by a beginning and an end. Like a dream, it gathers all passions into itself and yet, like a dream it is destined to be forgotten; like gaming, it contrasts with seriousness, yet like the *va banque* of the gambler, it involves the alternative between the highest gain and destruction" (Simmel 1997 [1911], 5). In this sense, the body itself can be a recording device for sensual data. Affects, feelings, and emotions embody the surrounding environment and embed themselves in our flesh, muscles, and bones to be recalled later. Indeed, as mnemonic devices in their own right, our bodies remember, demonstrating that memory is not only a mental or cerebral process. The cognitive psychologist and developer of "affect theory" Silvan Tomkins (2008) identifies six to nine primary bodily based affects: interest-excitement, enjoyment-pleasure, surprise-startle, distress-anguish, fear-terror, shame-humiliation, contempt-disgust, and anger-rage. Affective knowledge is central to the understanding of what are often split-second events and experiences. There is, however, an immediacy to affect, which means it must often be translated into words quickly after that fact. Otherwise it risks getting lost, distorted, and embellished into heavily refined or self-censured narratives.

These are some of the quagmires of researching accelerated, compressed, and condensed events—the phenomenology of now, as it were. Hence, instead of Lévi-Strauss's limited view of adventure, I find Marcel Griaule's early analogy between our discipline and that of the sporting world more cogent: "This study of traditions, customs, techniques and rites, which is the object of ethnographic sciences, doesn't separate as much as one could think its dedicated researchers from the sportsmen. Isn't sport itself made of traditions, rites and techniques" (Griaule 1931, cited in de Heusch 1984). These are much more suitable words from which to postulate a framework for sensual anthropologies and the comprehensive developments of embodiment theory (Stoller 1997; Howes 2003; see also Casserly's and Horner Brackett's chapters, this volume). Given the significant autobiographical nature of my own research material, I gladly endorse Clifton Evers's definition of affect as well as his general methodological approach: "Affects are how bodies feel and what motivate us ... I evidence the possibility of a shift from research about bodies to a way of researching through bodies. By positing my body as part of what it researches, it will become clear that feelings are the fundamental basis by which men who surf are made ... Affects leap from body to body" (Evers 2006, 230, 235). I would also be inclined to echo the warning of social theorist Anne Witz (2000)—we must be weary, mindful, cautious even of establishing an anthropology of the body at the expense of embodying the socio-cultural or the anthropological, as it were.

YE FAITHFUL DEVIL'S FRYING PAN

How did I get to this point of thinking that a study of euphoric places and adrenaline practices might make an interesting anthropological topic to explore? One part of the answer dates back to a set of identifiable incidents and observations midway through my fieldwork. Although I did not realize it at the time, I was witness to an unofficial risk ritual that would add an unanticipated dimension to my future research.

The Devil's Frying Pan is an infamous cove in Cornwall where young people participate in a rather extreme activity known locally as tombstoning. This site is owned by the National Trust and is located near the village of Cadgwith on the east side of the southernmost tip of the Lizard Peninsula (figure 3.1). For my informants in the village of Mullion, roughly 6 miles away, it is perhaps the quintessential cliff jump in the area, to which most new practitioners are eventually introduced once they have gained a bit of experience and developed a certain bravado from easier jumps. "Trust me, ya need to build up to this one. It's not called the Devil's Frying Pan for nothing," states Ally (age twenty-seven), who boasts having made the jump twice in her "youth" but would not dream of doing it again. She continues: "I think it gets its name from the actual shape of the cove and the way the water actually swells up and bubbles like oil in a frying pan . . . That's the worst part of this jump 'cause even if it's a safe-ish jump, it's still a really eerie and sinister kinda place, no *fooling*." The emphasis on fooling suggests that she might not have thought I was taking her seriously.

My first face-to-face encounter with the Devil's Frying Pan was also a mysterious leap of faith, for many reasons. First, it was a complete ordeal just to rally the enthusiasm to be taken by my friends. It was like pulling teeth. In May 2003 I had tried to convince the "Mullion Crew" to take me to the Frying Pan, but they were not interested. They kept saying I was too old to be engaging in these types of crazy teenager activities: "The advantage of reaching your thirties is that you don't have to do stupid things like that anymore . . . you clearly don't want to get any older, do you? Midlife crisis already, old boy?" These were the types of comments Ally's partner, Mike, kept making.

So I never made it that time, but I was determined to go during a later visit at the end of July 2003. After leaving the pub one night, I thought I had convinced Mike to go on Thursday afternoon. I rang him after lunch that day and got more banter about my being insane. He then said he had scheduled a band rehearsal. I was beginning to think this Devil's Frying Pan idea was cursed, but I eventually convinced him to go the following day. Five of us, plus a baby and a dog, set off from Mullion on Friday at midday: myself, Ally and Mike and their dog, and their friends Ron and Julie and their daughter, Pearl.

FIGURE 3.1. Devil's Frying Pan, Cadgwith, 2003. Author photo.

The Frying Pan would not give up its secrets that easily, however. This notorious jump also became a "leap of faith" because once we arrived we had considerable problems physically accessing the site. There was overgrowth of gorse, nettles, and thorns all around. It took sheer determination and even obsessiveness for me to reach it because of my conviction that I "had" to do this jump and because I had a wetsuit on that allowed me to fight my way through the otherwise impenetrable thicket of bushes. The Frying Pan seems to be such an important and symbolic jump in part because of its many barriers. Conquering the physical obstacles made the experience significant in my limited biography of jumping. But the barriers were also social (see Egan's chapter, this volume). Indeed, not being easily put off by my informants' reticence was important. All of them stipulated that the site had changed considerably over the past decade since they were last there, perhaps, one of them suggested, as a National Trust deterrent to the practice of cliff jumping.

This jump was a leap of faith for me not only because the others were unprepared to participate but also because, given the difficulty of access, they were unable to spectate either. In fact, no one saw me jump, so one has to take it on good faith that I actually did so. If you ask any of my four companions, I am sure there is no doubt in their minds that I jumped. They would testify, as they did to me, that they clearly heard the incredibly loud splashes when I hit the water. Given that I was upwind from them, they also explained that they distinctly heard my screams of terror, particularly on my second jump, which I felt I should mark by yelling something. Since I could not think of anything clever I simply shouted, leaving the others slightly worried, especially when I did not hear, and thus did not reply to, their inquiries as to my well-being. My point here is that even though my companions never saw my jumps, other sensorial indicators provided validity.

Given that no one was present to witness these jumps or to capture them on film, I was clearly doing them as a challenge to myself—for the pure experience factor—as well as to tell the tale, obviously. This was highlighted by Ron once we arrived at the site. He jested that it was surely enough that I had now seen the place and taken photos: "So you don't actually have to go through with it. We won't tell anyone; no one will know the difference, right? Let's go, then." He was, of course, being facetious. But he was also touching on the importance of overcoming the access barriers imposed by banter if I really wanted to understand what this was all about. The gauntlet was thrown down.

Similarly, the jump was again a leap of faith because my friends were not immediately present to reassure me or to be reassured that everything was going well. Further, they were unable to encourage me or share any strategic information about the site. Not having anyone there to "spot me"—jumping blind, as it were—was rather stressful and made the experience even more of a leap of faith. Hence, because it was so conscious-laden, it was much more part of an existential rather than an un-reflexive experience (Jackson 2005). There is a definite feeling that more can go wrong when one is jumping alone but also that it is a more individualistic, even liminal, moment. In a sense, then, even if it was not my first initiation to jumping, I nonetheless felt this was a type of ritual process.

In the end, my jumps lasted a few seconds in total, a quarter of an hour with the climbing. Nevertheless, the event itself lasted several hours and allowed me to tap into several years of stored-up lived experience that had been formative for the identity construction of my informants (Young 1990). This type of solo jumping means nobody is there to share the actual experience with you on the day it occurs. Consequently, I could not find out from anyone other than myself what the experience was like in situ. Ethnographically, this is a strange turn of events. I was participating in something my informants had not done for some time, thus engaging in a form of "subjective observation." What mattered was that I now had their "respect" and had potentially achieved a level of embodied empathy. I had done something that was once a significant part of their lives. And perhaps more important, the afternoon's jumping provided a good means of accessing certain social memories as well as soliciting several valuable jumping stories afterward.

This vignette demonstrates certain methodological aspects of studying cliff jumping from a phenomenological perspective. The experience of undergoing a moment of flow is often exceptionally difficult for participants to describe afterward. In fact, they often resist trying, sensing that doing so might contaminate the "magic" of the physical memory. So, one can always contrive a situation in which to talk with and interview people about an activity, but it is not until it becomes a genuine topic of conversation based on the day's events that you get to a level of understanding how the imagination exists in and through this fleeting embodied experience (Hunter and Csikszentmihalyi 2000). One of the points here is that certain visceral sensations are hard to fake; therefore, inter-subjective empathy is detectable.

"WHAT'S IN A GAME?"

Another reason I have gravitated to this kind of research is more personal. One event pre-dates my time as an anthropologist. I'm certainly not unique in freely admitting to enjoying precarious moments of solitude along the jagged shore and in wild landscapes. Those of us who do are a specific type; we do not have a death wish, as some would have it, and we are not particularly brave, either. Interestingly, my own research isn't really concerned with asking why people do these things, at least not at an individual level. This is largely the terrain of the psychologist or cognitive anthropologist. I'm interested in certain social whys—the contexts, narrative scenarios, and networks of relations that are created as well as the issues to do with how, when, and where such activities take place.

Hence, this description by Simone de Beauvoir in her memoir *La force de l'âge* (1960) [*The Prime of Life* (1976)] is worth considering for the many ways it resonates with experiences many of us have had at some point in our lives, if not recurrently:

> I had made up my mind to explore some higher-lying area than I had ever dared to tackle on foot hitherto. Pagniez suggested the parts around the Col d'Allos. I set out from Lauzet at midday, and slept in the rest hut at the foot of the Trois-Evêchés, which I attempted to scale the following morning. The track referred to in the *Guide Bleu* was practically invisible, and very soon I became terrified by the sheer drop below me. In an effort to get away from it I climbed higher and higher, which merely increased the void yawning under my feet. Eventually I came to a halt. The way I was going I could not possibly reach the summit; and yet, I thought, I was bound to break my neck if I tried to retrace my steps. So there I stuck, pressed into the rock face, heart beating madly. I made an effort to shift one foot, but exhaustion and fear made me stumble, and to recover my balance I jettisoned my rucksack, which went plummeting down into the valley below. How was I to follow it without being dashed to

pieces? Once again I moved a foot forward and struggled on very slowly, yard by yard. I felt as though I would never reach level ground again. Suddenly I lost my footing, slipped, grabbed frantically at some loose stones, and brought them tumbling down with me. "Well," I thought, "it's happened, and it's happened to me: this is the end." But I found myself at the bottom of the ravine with nothing worse than some skin abrasures on my thigh—not a single bone broken. It astonished me that I had felt so little emotional reaction when I believed myself on the very brink of death. I picked up my rucksack, ran back all the way to Lauzet, and thumbed a lift from a car, which took me across the mountains as far as my chalet-hotel on the Col d'Allos. As I fell asleep I remember saying to myself somberly "I've lost a day!" (Beauvoir 1960, 240–41, author translation)

This passage describes the setting and conditions of the event, as well as the protagonist's rationale and emotions. The story culminates in a potentially fatal accident with a fortunate outcome, not to mention a brief remark of a subsequent activity, hitchhiking, which many would hold to be an additional type of risk pursuit (cf. Laviolette 2016). Now compare this with one of my own "near misses." Together they reveal similarities in the autobiographical account of encountering fear full on. Such anecdotes might seem to be "individual." Yet as we shall see in subsequent examples in the chapter and in this volume more generally, they reveal many inter-subjective modalities, as described by Judith Okely and Helen Callaway in their edited compilation dealing with auto-ethnographic anthropology (Okely and Callaway 1992).

During one of my undergraduate summer breaks in 1993, a friend and I rented a car in Amsterdam and traveled across Europe to his uncle's place in Prato, just outside Florence. After a couple of weeks of driving and then a few days off in Italy, we headed toward Monaco and the south of France, crossing the Maritime Alps. We arrived in Monte Carlo one afternoon just after the Grand Prix had ended, unintentionally missing the event by a couple of hours.

As students, our travel itinerary did not always consist of a hotel or a B&B: we sometimes stayed with friends or relations and often chose to sleep in the car, especially—as you can expect—on the night of Monaco's busiest attraction. The evening's entertainments consisted of a few drinks with some local youth at an open square. A few more drinks followed at a beach campfire we had been invited to by some new acquaintances. As the driver, my mate was rather exhausted from the bendy route through the hills and decided to pack it in early, around midnight. I carried on for another hour or so. He was sound asleep when I made my way back to our little Fiat Cinquecento, such that it was.

We were parked a little bit out of town on a road along the beach, only meters from the Mediterranean (near the area of the Boulevard du Larvotto, with the "le

Sporting" headland on our left and the city center to our right as we looked out to sea). Up against the pavement behind our view rose a massive cliff. It was hard to accurately make out its height in the darkness, but it was probably a little over 40 meters. After about 30 meters the not-quite-vertical rock face appeared to taper off, with some grass and vegetation growing on the top 10 meters.

Restless and not wanting to disturb my companion, I decided that the view from the top of this section of the cliff must be incredible, since it looked out toward the harbor lights as well as, in the distance, little houses cut into the hills that contoured the sea. So, I started ascending what seemed to be a fairly easy part of this roadside sea cliff. After about 20 meters, however, things got slightly more complicated. As the surface became less vertical, the rock face became less sturdy, with loose bits of gravel crumbling from my grip and foothold. A look down revealed just how high I had gone. Taking stock of the fact that I was starting to feel quite fatigued, I had to finally accept that I was far from sober. I decided to start back down, but a couple of failed attempts to land a foothold that felt secure enough for descent left me clinging to the rock face, frozen. The combination of these circumstances resulted in an instant and severe sense of panic. With a pounding heart and a throbbing head, all sorts of racing thoughts entered my mind, obstructing any possibility of thinking clearly. Then again, I wasn't sober. And at this point in my life, I had little experience with free climbing, other than climbing the kinds of trees typical for children.

My naive bravado and sense of control of the situation were gone. Instead, I was left vulnerable to several visions of disaster. Looking down at the tiny blue Fiat, I imagined myself landing on it, breaking both legs if not my neck, leaving my friend traumatized by a violent crash and the discovery of my spattered body on the bonnet. After a couple of minutes of senseless dread, something came over me and I regained a certain calm. I started weighing options. Climbing further to reach the plateau was one, but a fall from higher up would surely be fatal. Besides, it was difficult to tell what it was like up there. I might simply end up having to make my way back down from whence I had come. As a clouded reasoning began to dissipate, another reassuring thought came to mind—it would be possible to stay put and scream for help. I probably had enough stamina to remain there for the hour or two it would take to summon the fire brigade, although that was not an ideal option.

With some trepidation, I resolved to turn around and do what I had set out to do in the first place: stare out across the bay. It was somehow manageable to do so without difficulty. Even though this was surely another unnecessary risk, the view was absolutely spectacular and strangely sobering as well. The successful completion of this action as well as the time it provided me to calm down and assess the situation gave me the confidence to make my way down, which occurred fairly smoothly. In total, the whole episode (incident) took about 45 minutes.

This type of practice often finds inspiration from, or at least parallels in, societies other than our own. Most cultures engage in risk behavior, as rites of passage or part of hunting expeditions or other events that mark different life-cycle changes (Harris and Park 1983). For instance, Oxford's Dangerous Sports Club transformed the earth dive rituals of Pentecost Island, Vanuatu, into the activity we now know as bungee jumping. This activity captured the public imagination and catapulted the club into the international spotlight. In Britain this event was pivotal in launching an era of innovation and media hype in the realm of public stunts, performance art, and risky games.

These activities reveal that not only is modern Western society obsessed with controlling risk but that we often present and conceptualize risk as a barrier to the full realization of our human potential. Depending on the levels of mitigation that take place, risk flows between various states of taboo-ness. The framework here, however, goes against that grain. Hence, without wishing to glorify the relationship between leisure and death for the sake of it, the aim is nonetheless to consider the emancipatory potential of what Huizinga (1956 [1938]) calls the innate ludic character of the human species.

ZERO-SUM GAME

> An accident may easily and naturally befall me on a mountain cliff.
> (GORDON CHILDE 1980, 3)

The world-renowned Marxist pre-historian Professor Vere Gordon Childe retired from his position as director of the University of London's Institute of Archaeology in 1956. The following year he returned to his native Australia for the first time in over three decades. While hiking in the Blue Mountains near Sydney to collect material for a book on the geomorphology of New South Wales, he fell to his death at Luchetti Lookout near Govett's Leap on October 19, 1957.

Rumors quickly circulated that he might have deliberately taken his own life. Troubled by increasingly complicated health issues, fearful that his intellectual capabilities were deteriorating, and (perhaps indicative of his staunch socialist values) mindful of becoming a burden on the state, such a conclusion seems more than plausible despite the coroner's decree of accidental death (Thomas 2003). A letter sent to Professor W. F. Grimes, his successor at the institute, published as the editorial to the first issue of the journal *Antiquity* in 1980, all but confirmed speculations about deliberation on Childe's part. Grimes had further added that during a conversation with Childe just prior to his retirement, the unexpected reply to the question "what are you going to do when you retire" had been "I know a 2,000 foot cliff in Australia. I intend to jump off it." Over the years, Childe is alleged to have made similar, seemingly flippant comments to a number of friends, colleagues, and acquaintances. The other well-known anthropological death caused by someone going over the edge of a precipice was that of Michelle Rosaldo in 1981 while doing fieldwork in the Philippines (Rosaldo 2013).

Jumping off cliffs, high bridges, buildings, or similar structures in order to commit suicide as well as to "show off" is an activity that has a rich history (see Kaul, this volume). Recall the Wall Street stockbrokers' mass suicides during the crash of the 1920s, which the Dangerous Sports Club parodied with its choice of attire when it did the first bungee jumps in 1979. Moreover, Ron Brown (2001) mentions the famous case of a daredevil in the nineteenth century who jumped off the Tower Bridge in London as a public stunt and did not survive. Andy Warhol also captured some of what could be called the "aesthetic" facets of precipitating danger in his screen print *Suicide: Purple Falling Man* (Hartley 2007). This piece was part of the somewhat controversial series *Death and Disaster* in the early 1960s, controversial largely because of the apolitical nature of Warhol's work and maybe his morals.

More recently, the documentary *The Bridge* by Eric Steel (2006) also depicts the "popularity" of jumping as a means of attempting suicide. The filming at San Francisco's Golden Gate Bridge during the year 2004 reported that an average of one person every fortnight throws him- or herself off the 220-foot-high suspension span with the intention of killing themselves. The Golden Gate remains the most frequent site for suicides in America and thus ranks among the most prominent in the world, along with such places as Govett's Leap, the Aokigahara Forest at the base of Mount Fuji, Niagara Falls on the US/Canadian border, Eiffel's famous Parisian Tower, the Grafton Bridge in Auckland, the cliffs of Beachy Head in Sussex, and the Clifton Suspension Bridge near Bristol.

Another well-known tragedy that caught the public imagination, this time at the turn of the new millennium, was the frequently reprinted and for a time heavily censored depiction of "the falling man" in New York City. Hundreds of people jumped or were blown out of the twin towers of the World Trade Center on September 11, 2001. Of course, we are no longer dealing with suicide for those who jumped; rather, it is a clear example of being pushed by circumstance. Some might even say that when faced with the inevitability of death, these jumpers were making a type of leap of faith, either for the unlikely chance of survival or to catch one last breath, to live one last moment (DeLillo 2007).

This level of the absurd perhaps illustrates part of what Alfred Camus (1957) and Jean-Paul Sartre (1956) were addressing in their own existential ways. Given that at least one person is reported to have been killed by being hit by a falling victim during 9/11, we see a tragic irony in the actual result of these jumps, not that I am suggesting the possibility of foresight in this case. In addition, we have the rejection by some people that their loved ones could have given up hope and "deliberately" leapt. This is captivatingly captured in the *9/11: The Falling Man* documentary when attempts are made to identify the protagonist of this affair and locate his family (Singer 2006).

One of the things that was so captivatingly disturbing about the Falling Man was the symmetry of his descent, which made it look like the man was diving rather than in free fall. This is one of the reasons the American press self-censored itself from reprinting the image for a few years after the catastrophe. But the case of the Falling Man had not been an isolated instance in terms of the form of the drop that some take. There are other, less famous accounts of people plunging in this way. Take, for instance, this description of a suicide in New Zealand in the 1990s:

> *Witness's description*: "At about 12:03 hours I noticed a male climbing over the protective railling [sic] on the top floor of the City Council Building. He moved out to the edge and then jumped. There was no hesitation from the time he mounted the barrier to the time he jumped. The victim appears not to fight the fall. He held a perfect swan dive the whole way down keeping his legs straight and arms extended. At no time did he kick his legs about in the usual manner. The victim landed face first on a small concrete path. He bounced and shifted about 10 foot [sic] sideways from the initial impact. When the victim was climbing over the protective barrier he was on his own. At no time was there anybody on the top floor with the victim." (Munro 2010, personal communication, cited in Laviolette 2011, 157)

Jumping with the desire to end one's life—attempted suicidal jumps—shares certain things in common with free falling and similar leisure-oriented thrill-seeking jumps. On a simple structuralist level, then, there could be two strands of jumps. On the one hand you have the person who wants to feel life at its extreme, that is, jumping off a cliff for the pure rush and exhilaration; on the other is the person for whom life itself has become too extreme. The notions of performance and appearance play an important part, both involving a considerable amount of planning, preparation, and determination. In the cases of jumping to celebrate life and those of jumping to die, the jumper is taking a risk of failure—the extreme sports enthusiast runs the risk of failing to execute the jump properly, for its proper enjoyment. These are persons who are hoping for extreme life experiences. They want to prove to themselves that they are fully alive, that they are in control of contingencies, the elements, themselves—mind and body. Some of their main exhilaration comes as they survive and master the perils, during those moments after they realize that they have executed the task correctly and perhaps in their own novel way.

Suicidal individuals also run the risk of failing to kill themselves, thus facing unbearable humiliation as well as serious injury and other psychological harm.

These are people for whom life itself has become too extreme, so much so that they can no longer stand to be alive. That is, they no longer want anything to do with the "extremity of life" and are searching to opt out. At the heart of each individual action is another meeting point—the rush. Indeed, many of those who experienced failed suicide attempts report a kind of release and euphoria that enters the faller's mind with the knowledge that life is ending (Staples and Widger 2011). Extreme sports jumpers equally articulate their experiences in terms of searches for freedom and adrenaline rushes. The free fall of jumping experiences can therefore quite literally be an end in itself as well as without end—endless. Consequently, at the heart of each individual action is a meeting point—existential extremity.

These more individualistic opposing perspectives have more ambiguous counterparts, such as the pseudo-accident and the charity campaign jump. The latter represent a form of symbolic social statement about the worthiness of a life-giving principle through the desire to help others by engaging in dangerous practices that can potentially entail a risk of death for the "giver." Here, spontaneity and a blurring of the distinction among accidents, jumping to live, and jumping to die are frequently involved.

VERTIGO-ING

Much of the literature in the area of high-risk recreation focuses on the immediately embodied and phenomenological experience of the participants (Le Breton 2010). There is less material regarding how such experiences relate to the social or cultural realm. A notable exception, and one of the most direct treatments of risky recreation and culture, is Stephen Lyng's (1990) theory of risk taking, which is decidedly culturalistic and sociological in its approach. In broad strokes, Lyng concludes that risk taking is mostly a response to institutionalization—it is a dependent rather than an independent variable, a phenomenon that is caused versus one that causes.

While reflective of some statistical empiricism, this type of top-down explanation tends to present itself as vacuous to those who regularly seek out and participate in dangerous recreation, as the reasons for undertaking those activities are often expressed in terms of the immediate experience. Notions surrounding embodiment, flow, skewing of time and place, surrealism, and momentary detachment from the bounds of the mundane are typical descriptions of the experience and worth of risky recreation. I have been keen here to explore the explanatory power of an inverted paradigm in the case of voluntary risk taking, one that begins with direct phenomenological experience and constructs culture accordingly instead of vice versa.

Since the confrontation with death is an ultimate condition of existence (Bloch and Parry 1982), the relationship free falling has with the possibility of physical injury

and death marks it as an act of foreboding, a true existential moment. Interpreted as such, tombstoning offers a radical critique of the culture of fear and the hyper health- and safety-conscious scaremongering of the risk society (Beck 1992). John Tomlinson (2007) talks of the inherent connections among danger, machine innovation, and socio-cultural acceleration. He highlights some interesting features that bind the social construction of rapidity to the prevalence of the risk society, when violence as well as the creation of moments for reflexivity or even existential realization are made possible. Drawing on Paul Virilio, he connects immediacy with the politics of violence: "Virilio has developed a complex and wide-ranging analysis of the relationship between speed, technology, cultural representation (particularly cinema), and what he calls the 'pure-war' of twentieth-century modernity... Virilio argues... that the increasing speed of modern weapons delivery systems linked to high-speed communications technologies is producing a shift in the very ontology of warfare. Wars are now not so much about gaining, holding, and pressing the initiative in terms of *territory*, as in terms of *temporality*" (emphasis in original; Tomlinson 2007, 58).

Here we see that it is not the sublime that is accelerated but rather the conditions of modernity through efficiency and an aggressive abolishment of frills, as well as an alienation from labor-time and nature. The escape from these hegemonic structures—which in more extreme cases can also be forms of oppression—is one of the things liminal rites of passage are orchestrated to permit. These come in many shapes and sizes, but hurling oneself away quite literally from such constraints is clearly an immediate and visually powerful symbol that exists in a number of cultures across a vast expanse of history; examples include the El Colacho baby-jumping festival performed by Spanish Catholics, the bull jumping of the Hamar tribe in Ethiopia, and the Alaturbi Turkish jump into the Black Sea. In the case explored here, the sped-up bodily liminality of tombstoning harbors its emancipatory value. While some people engage in it for its own sake, most do so as a mundane form of anarchism. Hence, such a sub-cultural form of leisure unites a certain hedonism, resistance, and moral concern whereby the action of protest in itself is consistent with risk, the need for which arises in extreme social circumstances (figure 3.2).

From *Homo Ludens*, playing emerges as a profoundly serious activity. Huizinga's (1956 [1938]) main argument is that there is consubstantiation between play and culture. That is, they are of the same essence. It would thus be too narrow or restrictive to interpret his study as defending any thesis purporting that play is only a non-serious form of activity. Indeed, on several occasions he cites games that require participants to risk their own lives, asserting that it is usually difficult to outline with any accuracy the features that distinguish between playful and serious relations with the world. For Huizinga, even children relate to play as a type of everyday activity

FIGURE 3.2. Piskie Cove, Praa Sands, United Kingdom, 2003. Author photo.

that is all-absorbing, essential, and essentializing. It is this essentializing as well as the existential character of dangerous leisure that is of concern in the act of tombstoning.

REFERENCES

Augé, Marc. 1995. *Non-Places: Introduction to an Anthropology of Supermodernity*. Trans. John Howe. London: Verso.

Beauvoir, Simone de. 1960 [1976]. *La force de l'âge*. Paris: Folio Gallimard. English edition (*The Prime of Life*) published in 1976.

Beck, Ulrich. 1992. *Risk Society: Towards a New Modernity*. London: Sage.

Bloch, Maurice, and Jonathan Parry. 1982. *Death and the Regeneration of Life*. Cambridge: Cambridge University Press. https://doi.org/10.1017/CBO9780511607646.

Bradbury, Ray. 1988. *Quotation from a Speech at the Future Style Symposium*.

Brown, Ron. 2001. *The Art of Suicide*. London: Reaktion Books.

Camus, Albert. 1957. *The Fall*. Trans. Justin O'Brien. London: H. Hamilton.

Childe, Vere Gordon. 1980. "Childe's Suicide." *Antiquity* 54 (210): 1–3.
de Heusch, Luc. 1984. *Sur les Traces du Renard Pâle: Recherches en pays Dogon, 1931–1983 (Tracking the Pale Fox)*. Brussels: Centre Audiovisuel à Bruxelles, 48 minutes.
DeLillo, Don. 2007. *The Falling Man*. London: Picador.
Evers, Clifton. 2006. "How to Surf." *Journal of Sport and Social Issues* 30 (3): 229–43. https://doi.org/10.1177/0193723506290394.
Foucault, Michel. 1977. *Discipline and Punish: The Birth of the Prison*. Trans. Alan Sheridan. New York: Vintage Books.
Harris, Janet C., and Roberta J. Park, eds. 1983. *Play, Games, and Sports in Cultural Contexts*. Champaign, IL: Kinetic.
Hartley, Keith. 2007. *Andy Warhol: A Celebration of Life . . . and Death*. Edinburgh: National Galleries of Scotland.
Howes, David. 2003. *Sensual Relations: Engaging the Senses in Culture and Social Theory*. Ann Arbor: University of Michigan Press. https://doi.org/10.3998/mpub.11852.
Huizinga, Johan. 1956 [1938]. *Homo Ludens*. Hamburg: Rowohlt Taschenbuch Verlag.
Hunter, Jeremy, and Mihalyi Csikszentmihalyi. 2000. "The Phenomenology of Body-Mind: The Contrasting Cases of Flow in Sports and Contemplation." *Anthropology of Consciousness* 11 (3–4): 5–24. https://doi.org/10.1525/ac.2000.11.3-4.5.
Jackson, Michael. 2005. *Existential Anthropology: Events, Exigencies, and Effects*. Oxford: Berghahn.
Larsen, Jonas. 2008. "De-exoticizing Tourist Travel: Everyday Life and Sociality on the Move." *Leisure Studies* 27 (1): 21–34. https://doi.org/10.1080/02614360701198030.
Laviolette, Patrick. 2007. "Guest Editorial: Hazardous Sport?" *Anthropology Today* 23 (6): 1–2. https://doi.org/10.1111/j.1467-8322.2007.00545.x.
Laviolette, Patrick. 2011. *Extreme Landscapes of Leisure: Not a Hap-hazardous Sport*. Farnham, GB: Ashgate.
Laviolette, Patrick. 2014. "The Neo-Flâneur amongst Irresistible Decay." In *Playgrounds and Battlefields*, ed. Francisco Martínez and Klemen Slabina, 243–70. Tallinn, Estonia: Tallinn University Press.
Laviolette, Patrick. 2016. "Why Did the Anthropologist Cross the Road?" *Ethnos: Journal of Anthropology* 80 (4): 1–23.
Le Breton, David. 2010. *Expériences de la Douleur: Entre Destruction et Renaissance*. Paris: Métailié.
Lévi-Strauss, Claude. 1961. *Tristes Tropiques*. Paris: Plon.
Lyng, Stephen. 1990. "Edgework: A Socio Psychological Analysis of Voluntary Risk Taking." *American Journal of Sociology* 95 (4): 851–86. https://doi.org/10.1086/229379.

Mauss, Marcel. 1992 [1934]. "Techniques of the Body." In *Incorporations*, ed. Jonathan Crary and Sanford Kwinter, 455–77. New York: Zone Books.

Okely, Judith, and Helen Callaway, eds. 1992. *Anthropology and Autobiography*. London: Routledge. https://doi.org/10.4324/9780203450536.

Ravn, Susanne, and Helle Ploug Hansen. 2013. "How to Explore Dancers' Sense Experiences? A Study of How Multi-Sited Fieldwork and Phenomenology Can Be Combined." *Qualitative Research in Sport, Exercise, and Health* 5 (2): 196–213. https://doi.org/10.1080/2159676X.2012.712991.

Robbins, Joel. 2010. "On Imagination and Creation: An Afterword." *Anthropological Forum* 20 (3): 305–13. https://doi.org/10.1080/00664677.2010.515296.

Rosaldo, Renato. 2013. *The Day of Shelly's Death: The Poetry and Ethnography of Grief*. Durham, NC: Duke University Press. https://doi.org/10.1215/9780822376736.

Sartre, Jean-Paul. 1956. *Being and Nothingness: A Phenomenological Essay on Ontology*. Trans. Hazel E. Barnes. Paris: Gallimard.

Simmel, Georg. 1997 [1911]. "The Adventure." In *Simmel on Culture*, ed. David Frisby and Mike Featherstone. London: Sage.

Singer, Henry. 2006. *9/11: The Falling Man*. London, Channel 4 television.

Staples, James, and Tom Widger. 2011. "Situating Suicide as an Anthropological Problem: Ethnographic Approaches to Understanding Self-Harm and Self-Inflicted Death." *Culture, Medicine, and Psychiatry* 15 (1): 183–203.

Stebbins, Robert A. 2007. *Serious Leisure: A Perspective for Our Time*. New Brunswick, NJ: Aldine/Transaction.

Steel, Eric. 2006. *The Bridge*. New York, Koch-Lorber Films, 95 minutes.

Stoller, Paul. 1997. *Sensuous Scholarship*. Philadelphia: University of Pennsylvania Press. https://doi.org/10.9783/9780812203134.

Stone, Philip. 2006. "A Dark Tourism Spectrum: Towards a Typology of Death and Macabre Related Tourist Sites, Attractions, and Exhibitions." *Tourism: An Interdisciplinary International Journal* 54 (2): 145–60.

Thomas, Martin. 2003. "Vere *Gordon Childe* and the Abyss of Time." In *The Artificial Horizon: Imagining the Blue Mountains*. Melbourne: Melbourne: University Press.

Tomkins, Silvan. 2008. *Affect, Imagery, Consciousness: The Complete Edition*. 2 vols. New York: Springer.

Tomlinson, John. 2007. *The Culture of Speed: The Coming of Immediacy*. London: Sage.

Witz, Anne. 2000. "Whose Body Matters? Feminist Sociology and the Corporeal Turn in Sociology and Feminism." *Body and Society* 6 (2): 1–24. https://doi.org/10.1177/13570 34X00006002001.

Young, Robert. 1990. *White Mythologies: Writing History and the West*. London: Routledge.

PART 2

Tourist Encounters with the Dead

4

Leisure in the "Land of the Walking Dead"

Western Mortuary Tourism, the Internet, and Zombie Pop Culture in Toraja, Indonesia

KATHLEEN M. ADAMS

> Do any research into the Torajan culture and you are bound to hear the rumors about real-life Zombies, and as they say, seeing is believing, my search was on.
> —OPENING PARAGRAPH, "TRAVELLING AMANDA" BLOG, MARCH 24, 2013[1]

In fall 2012, as I packed up my bags after a class lecture on my research among the Sa'dan Toraja of Sulawesi, Indonesia, a sophomore bounded up enthusiastically and asked if he could volunteer as a research assistant on my next return to the Toraja highlands. "I'm *dying* to go there. I'd do whatever it takes—learn the language, work long hours, carry heavy bags—anything!" he begged. Assuming that his fervor was inspired by the same Toraja icons that have drawn both anthropologists and tourists for decades, I queried, "Tell me, was it the PowerPoints of Toraja carved houses, sculpted graves, or funeral rituals that grabbed your attention?" His answer took me by surprise: "No, I want to see the zombies."

American zombie mania was not unknown to me at the time: I'd caught a few episodes of TV's *The Walking Dead*, thumbed through a bookstore copy of *Pride and Prejudice and Zombies* (Austen and Grahame-Smith 2009), and observed students dashing around the campus parking lot playing *Humans versus Zombie*. But this was the first I'd heard of "Torajan zombies" in three decades of conducting research on the Sa'dan Toraja. Perplexed, I returned to my office, googled "Toraja zombie," and found a bonanza of Web articles and blogs offering photos and descriptions of "The Creepy Walking Dead of Tana Toraja"[2] as well as video clips of "real Toraja walking zombies" bearing warnings advising "viewer discretion."[3] Alongside the haunting mix of online images and sensational descriptions were travel blogs titled "Searching for Zombies in Tana Toraja, Finding Bliss in Sulawesi,"[4] "Tana Toraja: Land of the Divine Kings . . . and Zombies?!?,"[5] and "Take the Kids Zombie Hunting in Tana Toraja, Indonesia."[6]

This chapter offers a critical analysis of the burgeoning cottage industry of cyber and actual Toraja zombie tourism. Various studies have chronicled tourists' fascination with cadavers and with touring the purported haunts of the undead (cf. Light 2009; Linke 2005; Stone 2011a), yet the ways in which new death-oriented leisure zones not only arise but become fetishized remain understudied. This chapter responds to the recent call for new research on the relationship between the media and dark tourism sites (Stone 2011b, 327). In the following pages I draw on data culled from fieldwork in the Toraja highlands of Indonesia and Web-based sources to demonstrate the role of both the internet and the anthropological imagination in this process. As I aim to show, decontextualized photographs and video clips in tandem with anthropologized narratives are central to the emerging association of Torajans with zombies, an association born and bred on the internet. Moreover, as my introductory vignette suggests, it is through leisure-time Web surfing that some zombie enthusiasts such as my student become entranced by the possibility of having their own firsthand touristic encounter with the (un)dead. It is also through pre-trip Web surfing that more mainstream tourists planning Indonesian vacations stumble upon the zombie narrative that further embellishers their pre-departure visions of their holidays in the Toraja highlands. Thus, one of my aims is to unpack how media and pop culture imagery are interwoven into the varied narratives underpinning cyber and touristic voyagers' accounts of the Toraja mortuary world.

A second theme in this chapter entails examining the often contradictory emotional dynamics underlying the pursuit of fun and fright by vacationers in what is touted as one of the most death-obsessed cultures on the planet. Many scholars have theorized about how dark tourism enables meditations on dying through firsthand leisure-time encounters with the physicality of death (cf. Seaton 1996, 236; Lennon and Foley 2010). Still others have hypothesized that our own cultural segregation of death from everyday life has fostered yearnings for leisure activities that mediate life and death through playful and serious encounters with cadavers (Durkin 2003; Stone and Sharpley 2008).[7] Cultural studies scholars have also analyzed the Western fascination with zombies and reanimated corpses (such as Frankenstein). Some have argued that the nineteenth- and twentieth-century literary and filmic tales of reanimated dead derive from our fear of science unharnessed and express anxieties of life in the post-atomic era (cf. Boon 2011; Christie and Lauro 2011). Others theorize that the popular culture interest in zombies stems from our postcolonial imperialist histories, since Hollywood zombies "represent enslavement at its most basic levels" (Bishop 2010, 66).[8] However, ethnographically based studies of the complex emotional terrain entailed in these firsthand encounters remain limited. In this chapter I contribute to our understanding of the emotional dynamics embodied in touristic pilgrimages to observe the mortuary rituals of another culture. In particular, I aim to highlight the simultaneous dimensions of attraction and revulsion revealed in tourists' actions and narratives, a theme echoed in many of the online commentaries about Toraja mortuary practices made by virtual tourists at "real zombie"–oriented websites.

This brings me to a third point. This is a chapter about what some might call a Western voyeuristic fascination with dead (and potentially undead) corpses, or what Geoffrey Gorer (1955) has so famously termed the "pornography of death." However, I am not interested in fueling the sensationalized imagery of yet another dark group in a dark place where dark activities are seemingly a part of everyday life. Nancy Scheper-Hughes and Philippe Bourgois's cautions regarding "pornographies of violence"—as captivating yet repelling chronicles of violence that circumvent critical analysis—strike me as equally apt for discussions of this particular genre of dark tourism (Scheper-Hughes and Bourgois 2003, 1). What I term "pornographies of the macabre," like pornographies of violence, can reify stigmatized perceptions of subordinated peoples while neglecting to spotlight the "chains of causality . . . link[ing] structural, political, and symbolic violence . . . buttress[ing] unequal power relations" (Bourgois 2003, 433). Thus, not only does this chapter aim to examine *how* the Toraja homeland emerged as a magnetic site for Western travelers pursuing encounters with the dead and the undead but also *why*. That is, one of my aims is to explore the cultural "logic" and structural, political, and symbolic asymmetries that buttress outsiders' sensationalized zombie-themed references to Toraja mortuary traditions, references that have lent the Toraja a new kind of global notoriety.

In striving to avoid fueling a pornography of the macabre, I also hope to foster a more complex portrait of the local experience by examining how Torajans deal with their new zombie notoriety. This chapter closes with a preliminary discussion of how Torajans make their own meanings out of their emergent status as both the "capital of the walking dead" in the Western imagination and a source of symbolic capital for dark tourists. From these preliminary examples, we can harvest more positive images of Torajans as active agents drawing upon Western misunderstandings of their mortuary rites to carve out new sources of revenue.

My data derive from over three decades of anthropological field research in the Toraja highlands beginning in the mid-1980s, with most recent follow-up fieldwork in summer 2012. I employed a mixed-methods approach (Bernard 1998), which included qualitative open-ended interviews and participant observation in various locales, including funerals, tours, and tourism planning meetings (Pelto and Pelto 1981). I supplemented this qualitative research with archival research, photo-documentation of tourists partaking in mortuary rituals and grave tours, and critical discourse analysis of tourists' commentary and internet pages concerning Toraja zombies.[9]

This chapter begins by tracing the shifting tourism imagery of the Toraja from the early 1980s to today. I then examine Western mortuary tourists' range of responses to their vacation encounters with death, from contemplative to playful to a compelling mixture of attraction and revulsion. Next, I examine the role of social media in the rise of Toraja zombie tourism. Finally, I offer a glimpse into Torajan ways of navigating their newfound zombie notoriety.

BACKGROUND: MORTUARY TOURISM AND TOURISTIC IMAGERY OF THE SA'DAN TORAJA

The Sa'dan Toraja are a Christian minority group of over 750,000 whose homeland is in the highlands of South Sulawesi. While Torajans have migrated throughout Indonesia and beyond, those remaining in the homeland work as farmers, small business employees, in the tourism sector, or as civil servants. Within Indonesia, the Toraja are renowned for their pageantry-filled mortuary traditions, which draw thousands of guests and can last up to a week (depending on the rank and wealth of the deceased). They are equally celebrated for their exquisitely carved ancestral houses and effigies of the dead. Although adventure travelers have been making the bone-shaking nine-hour bus ride to the Toraja highlands since the late 1970s, it was not until the 1980s, after the Indonesian government began promoting the region as the "next destination after Bali," that larger-scale domestic and international tourism began to flourish (Adams 2006). Whereas in 1972 only 650 foreign tourists visited the Toraja highlands, by tourism's heyday in the mid-1990s the region was hosting 59,388 foreign tourists and 176,949 domestic tourists annually. Following a period of Indonesian political and economic instability in the late 1990s and early 2000s, tourist visits plummeted. However, tourism to the Toraja highlands is rebounding, and in 2013 the region received 19,324 foreign and 42,319 domestic tourist visits (Adams 2006; data collected in the Tana Toraja Provincial Office of Statistics).

Throughout the 1980s and 1990s, tourist brochures heralded Tana Toraja as the "land of the heavenly kings"—a realm where people "believe that life is only a celebration before a happy eternity in heaven, [and] death a joyous occasion" (Hemphill Harris 1981). Likewise, more recent magazines and tourist-oriented Web articles spotlight the possibility of witnessing a Toraja mortuary ceremony replete with displays of coffins, corpses, and effigies of the dead as the pièce de résistance of a trip to the highlands (Adams 1991). Returning tourists I've interviewed all declared their experiences at Toraja funeral rituals as the highlight of their vacation visits. Descriptions of firsthand encounters with corpses, bloody animal sacrifices, and burial bones featured prominently in their travel reminiscences, as did accounts of excitement, confusion, and discomfort at being in the midst of what visitors often erroneously assume are "pagan" funeral rites, assumptions cultivated by the travel literature they had read prior to their trips (Adams 1984, 1993; Volkman 1987). As one blogger writes, "Torajans are all about death—This is . . . the grim reaper's playground—but in a good way. The main reason I had to visit Sulawesi was to see the Torajan culture, which intrigued me."[10]

Today, many Western tourists' comments echo the travel brochure and guidebook imagery of Torajans as Rousseauian exemplars of a more pristine era in human history: tourists I interviewed often spoke admiringly of Torajans as "living in harmony with the environment" and as enjoying "more authentic" lifestyles. For many tourists, this unique harmony is epitomized by Toraja attitudes toward death. A thirty-one-year-old Dutch woman's comments are fairly typical: "The people are so close to nature . . . even the way they treat their dead." And a journalist planning a Toraja vacation explained, "I want to go to Toraja because they don't seem to have the hangups we have about death. Their lives are not separated from death, and it does not seem to cause them anxiety."[11] For these tourists, a visit to Toraja seems to beckon as a kind of time travel to an imagined earlier era when death was more integrated into peoples' everyday lives. As one blogger writes, "We visited . . . a small village of traditional . . . houses, hanging graves, cave graves, rice paddies, collections of bones in open coffins with skulls placed to watch the goings and comings. It's a great example of how the Toraja . . . treat the dead like the living and shows their traditions have been the same for thousands of years."[12] As these comments suggest, tourists' narratives frequently bundle Torajans' unique mortuary practices with assertions about their timelessness. Ironically, bloggers and interviewees rarely note that most contemporary Toraja funerals feature Christian hymnals, loudspeakers, family videography sessions, and other modern-era accoutrements.

CONTEMPLATIVE AND PLAYFUL TOYING WITH DEATH

For many travelers, a visit to Toraja represents a way to positively engage with death, sometimes playfully and sometimes more contemplatively (figure 4.1). A major theme in tourist interviews and travel blog narratives was that witnessing a Toraja funeral, observing children playing with ancestral bones, or viewing

FIGURE 4.1. Crowds gathered to watch a water buffalo fight at a 2012 funeral ritual in Ke'te' Kesu', Toraja Utara, Indonesia. Photo by Kathleen M. Adams.

cliff-side tombs and babies' tree graves offered life-and-death lessons.[13] As one visitor observes:

> On the surface, it seems . . . Torajans are obsessed with death. But really, it's just the opposite. They are celebrants of life in some of the most beautiful ways. When their people die, they keep them in the house for a long time, allowing time to grieve, time to let go, time for life and death to fade together gently. Death isn't the sharp cutting of a cord and immediate detachment that quick burial is. I kind of like that.[14]

Another blogger writes:

> As my stay among these hospitable people drew to an end, I pondered what I had learnt about their magical philosophy, their constant efforts to balance the opposing forces of life and death [and] . . . I was just glad that I, as a western visitor . . . had been . . . the privileged observer of the expression of such unique spiritual beliefs.[15]

As these typical quotes suggest, for some, Toraja mortuary tourism dangles the promise of a more comfortable way of living with mortality. Perhaps not surprisingly, accounts of Torajan death-related practices are now featured on New Age blogs about embracing life's end[16] and have even become the subject of a TED talk.[17]

Benedict Anderson's observation concerning how national monuments face simultaneously backward and forward in time may help us understand these tourists' perceptions of Toraja mortuary practices (Anderson 1990, 174). As Anderson notes, monuments mediate between particular types of pasts and futures. Likewise, mortuary tourism may be understood as a way of mediating between the past and the future. That is, the potency and appeal of Toraja mortuary tourism may lie in its ability to offer tourists an opportunity to both contemplate the past and foresee the future of lived existence. In touring a culture imagined to embody a more pristine human past and in seeking firsthand encounters with death, Western tourists are simultaneously confronting human pasts and futures. That is, on the one hand they are envisioning Torajans as representative of humanity's living past, evocative of an earlier, simpler era when we were all presumably more comfortable with the natural processes of life and death. Yet these touristic pilgrimages to a "death-celebrating" culture are also future-looking: in their close encounters with corpses, blood, funerals, and graves, tourists can be said to be looking ahead to that which makes them most anxious—death. The underlying logic animating these Western mortuary tourists' experiences, then, is that if Torajans (as exemplars of our human past) can be so at ease with death and corpses, then perhaps even tourists' own fears evoked by death and "zombies" can be reframed, then tamed.

It is noteworthy that not all the mortuary tourists I encountered engaged in serious contemplation: some toured death in a more frivolous fashion. I occasionally witnessed younger male tourists at cliff-side graves snatch up human bones and wave them ghoulishly in the direction of their friends. Likewise, groups of friends sometimes jovially posed for pictures alongside rows of skulls and weathered wooden coffins at the base of burial cliffs. On occasion, these groups of younger Western tourists invoked "Indiana Jones" or "Laura Croft, Tomb-Raider" as they posed at the mouths of bone- and coffin-littered caves, but more often the laughter and bravado seemed edged with awkwardness or nervousness. In this regard, these playful and very physical interactions with the material world of death seemed to be small acts of defiance of the ultimate reality of our existence. For these more spirited tourists, the Toraja homeland appeared to function as a space where it was permissible to mock and physically toy with death. Whereas at home, frolicsomely handling human bones would be unthinkable, for these vacationers the touristic framing of Toraja space as a land of "death cultists"[18] offered an exotic, taboo-free zone where skulls and coffins became ludic settings for photo ops. In short, Torajaland serves as a mortuary-themed play-scape (Junemo

2004) for enacting and commemorating prior cinematic texts, dark adventurer fantasies, and cultural inversions.

SEEKING DEATH, FINDING AMBIVALENCE

Although lured by their fascination with death, a pervasive theme in many tourist narratives is that of ambivalence and sometimes even revulsion. As one traveler writes of his Toraja funeral experience:

> [Standing] ankle-deep in mud, I watched one of the most confusing, engrossing, and disturbing spectacles I've ever seen. The houses were arranged around a muddy square with a buffalo carcass with a gash across the throat . . . in front of a house with a cylindrical coffin. In front of the dead buffalo . . . was a man standing with a live buffalo and about ten pigs lying on the floor tied up . . . The pigs' screaming for everything that their lives were worth was bone-chilling. In front of the [livestock] was a circle of men chanting and . . . making more noise than the screaming pigs . . . Peter encouraged us to join this group's procession into the pavilion and I reluctantly accepted . . . The male relatives of the deceased . . . offered us cigarettes, followed by the women who came . . . with plates of cakes, tea, and coffee . . . in almost complete silence. The uncomfortable feeling of being an intruder and a voyeur of something I didn't understand never left.[19]

Added to the ambivalence entailed in being a tourist intruder is revulsion at the sight, sounds, and smells of the animal slaughters. The visceral experiences with blood, excrement, and death that are part and parcel of the Toraja funeral scene are often a focal point of touristic accounts. As a Spanish tourist wrote:

> Finally the ritual of killing buffaloes . . . The Toraja people put in line several dozens of buffalos and started killing them with a machete in a brutal way. I had pity for them. The blood of the buffalos would sprinkle to the faces of the numerous tourists that came close to take pictures. I did not want to see more slaughter of buffaloes . . . I am happy that in spite of their commercialization and disgusting slaughtering of buffaloes, I saw the Toraja funeral ritual.[20]

This combination of fascination and revulsion is an underlying theme in Toraja mortuary tourism. During their interviews with me, some tourists were apologetic about their squeamishness, often noting that at home they were unnaturally shielded from the slaughter of the animals they consume. Online, however, the "revulsion" dimension of tourists' experiences seems to find fuller expression.[21] For example, the author of a Toraja trip blog titled "The Macabre and the Massacre" describes her long-awaited arrival at a funeral arena:

As we walked about the setting, there were some horrifying scenes. Pigs being carried into the central ring, suspended by their legs and screaming as they went, to be then dumped on the ground and left to wait for their ultimate slaughter. Over in the second ring, the massacre was already under way! As we walked we passed buffalo heads and disemboweled pigs, vast quantities of blood staining the earth red and stifling the surrounding air with the smell of death. And as horrifying and outdated as some of these actions and traditions may seem, it was very difficult to take your eyes away![22]

Another tourist blog, "Toraja: A Culture Whose Views on Death Will Blow Your Mind," describes the Toraja funeral he witnessed as a "fascinating yet gruesome event" and goes on to recount the rumor that "some outlying villages still maintain an ancient practice where a Shaman puts a spell on the body at the end of the funeral and the deceased 'walk themselves' to their graves!" As proof, this tourist blogger cites the gruesome zombies yielded by googling "Toraja Death."[23] In this blog we glimpse how a tourist's experience with the "world of corporeal, physically encountered reality" can imaginatively meld with a fantasy-geography to "produce a sense of reality that . . . visitors . . . appropriate," a process Jorgen Bærenholdt and Michael Haldrup term "fantastic realism" (Bærenholdt and Haldrup 2004, 86). That is, we see the blogger's up-close, physical encounter with Toraja mortuary sacrifice, death, and blood bridged to the realm of fantasy and zombies.

RISE OF THE TORAJA ZOMBIE (OR LOST IN TRANSLATION . . .)

Let us now turn to these so-called Torajan zombies, the characters that so fascinate tourists and which embody one of the most intense postmodern fears: disfigurement and unresolved semi-death. The imagery of Torajans as a land of "zombie love"[24] is a relatively recent accretion that builds on the much longer tradition of Toraja mortuary tourism. As John Urry observed, "Places [to play] are not fixed and unchanging . . . [they] are economically, politically and culturally produced through the multiple mobilities of people but also of capital, objects, signs and information moving at rapid yet uneven speed across many borders" (Urry 2004, 205). As in an earlier era when Indonesia's tourism promotion machinery helped transform the Toraja highlands' image from that of a relatively unknown (beyond anthropological and adventure travel circles) "hinterland" of Indonesia into a celebrated "land of heavenly kings," in the past few years various factors have added a new wrinkle to the touristic portrait of Torajans. These factors include the expansion of the internet's reach and a renewed Western obsession with zombies.

As best I can ascertain, the first online mentions of Toraja "walking dead" began in Indonesian-language blogs in 2006. Generally, most of these blogs recounted how Torajans use black magic to walk the dead back to their home villages for their funerals and how corpses laid to rest in Toraja caves did not decay. Although the ethnicity of the Indonesian bloggers cannot be ascertained, significantly, this earliest wave of writers did not use the term *zombie* (although subsequent Indonesian bloggers use this English-language expression). Rather, they employed the Indonesian expression "*mayat berjalan*" (walking corpse). Lacking photos, these Indonesian language blogs did not gain much traction. It was not until 2010 (in the midst of the most recent Western wave of zombie television shows and films) that the online circulation of Toraja "zombie" images arose in full force. By 2011, net traffic on "Toraja zombies" had erupted: postings appeared on a wide array of internet sites, from blogs on Oddity Central to a National Geographic forum discussion of Torajan "walking dead rituals" to Zombie Research Society Web pages featuring research on whether "real walking dead" were to be found in the Toraja highlands.[25]

Most of these blogs and Web discussions feature the same photograph of a wrinkled, moldy faced Toraja woman with unkempt hair flowing to her knees. Her shriveled arms are crossed at her waist, and she is clad in a teal sarong and top. Uncropped versions of the image show her being assisted by a male sporting a red T-shirt, with one younger spectator slightly behind the woman and another younger spectator standing on the hillside in the background. In the foreground one can discern the edge of a raised hand clasping a cell phone to capture an image of the purported "zombie" (figure 4.2). Contrary to what one would expect, the people in the snapshot do not seem frightened—rather, they appear solicitous. For the past few years, this image and others like it have circulated on the Web, sometimes accompanied by a video depicting another "Toraja zombie." This walking dead photograph has been cut and re-posted on countless personal blogs and Pinterest sites.[26] It has also materialized on internet sites devoted to the supernatural or to "incredible" or "amazing things" (e.g., see the account of "Real Zombies Walking in Indonesia" at https://www.vyperlook.com/odd-strange/real-zombies-walking-in-indonesia). Snopes, the website dedicated to assessing the veracity of Web-circulated urban legends, summarizes the typical narrative:

> Only in Indonesia (especially Toraja), a corpse is usually being [*sic*] carried up to the grave, but in Toraja, the corpse is woken up; letting it walk to its grave (is rarely performed anymore). The corpse is woken up using black magic. This is done because in Toraja the graves/cemetries [*sic*] is [*sic*] placed above limestones [*sic*] mountains. The corpse walks by itself, and its [*sic*] guided by an expert in black magic behind it. But there is one prohibition, the corpse shouldn't be pointed [at], once pointed, the corpse falls down and isn't able to walk again.[27]

As early as September 2010, Snopes offered its assessment of these "Toraja zombie" accounts, as did the Zombie Research Society website. Both sites outline that

FIGURE 4.2. One of the most widely reproduced images of the so-called Toraja "walking dead" circulating on social media. Photographer unknown.

these supposed "zombies" are actually corpses being re-clothed several years after entombment, in keeping with the Torajan *ma'nene'* ritual.[28] Citing anthropological sources, these sites explain that the *ma'nene'* ritual does not entail reanimating the dead. Rather, these are snapshots of people supporting bodies as they are moved for a re-clothing ritual that occurs months or years after death.

How, then, did these ritual images come to proliferate the internet as "zombies"? Preliminary research suggests that these images were most likely photos taken by younger Torajans and by migrant Torajans returning home for family visits and heritage-oriented tourism. Over the past decade, as Indonesian cell phone connectivity expanded, Indonesians enthusiastically embraced social media, to the point that observers have declared Indonesia the world's most social media–oriented nation (Reed 2013).[29] As growing numbers of younger Torajans share their lives on social media, photos of Toraja family rites, including the *ma'nene'* ritual, have come to populate Facebook, Twitter, and other feeds, where they are shared and re-shared, often without contextual information.

Here, additional background on the *ma'nene'* ritual is warranted. My experiences with *ma'nene'* ceremonies suggest that, unlike funerals, they are much smaller affairs: though they draw extended family members, they are generally not promoted for tourists. In the Northern Toraja valley region where I've based my fieldwork, *ma'nene'* rituals are Christianized and often simply entail gravesite sweeping and cleaning, followed by a collective meal, prayers, and hymnals. If there are effigies of the dead (only elite individuals whose funerals adhered to certain ritual requirements are entitled to effigies), they are removed from the familial burial areas for dusting and re-clothing in "new" apparel, then returned to their original gravesite locations upon completion of the ritual. Some Christian families also clothe the deceased in new garments, something that was once part of the pre-Christian version of the *ma'nene'* ritual. In the *ma'nene'* rituals I observed, however, if coffins were opened for corpse dusting, families simply tucked the new apparel into the coffin.[30]

However, Elizabeth Coville (an anthropologist who works in Sa'dan Toraja's western hills) reports that in the 1980s *ma'nene'* rituals she observed, Torajans removed corpses from graves for cleansing and re-clothing (Elizabeth Coville, personal communication, September 25, 2014). In this era, the bodies remained horizontal during cleansing. It wasn't until 2012 that Coville witnessed bodies raised to standing positions so Toraja family members and visiting migrant kin could snap cell-phone "selfies" of themselves alongside the corpses (a selfie is a snapshot of oneself taken for sharing on social media). It seems reasonable to deduce that migration, social media, and the rise of the selfie converged and produced a flow of internet images of the so-called Toraja walking dead. As the original posters' social media "friends" re-shared these images, it seems that eventually these decontextualized selfies and video clips found their way into net zones frequented by Western zombie aficionados, and the images went viral. The snapshots of *ma'nene'* rituals were rapidly embraced as "proof" that zombies can and do exist.

English-language blogs about Toraja mortuary practices and zombies are rife with anthropologized narratives depicting the Toraja as an "isolated tribe" and as practitioners of "black magic" and ancient "supernatural rituals and traditions."[31] Torajan Christianity rarely surfaces in these online zombie-oriented narratives, and allusions to modernity are generally absent: there is no mention of the daily rush hour traffic jams in Toraja's largest towns or of the multitude of churches, hotels, shops, banks, and karaoke bars. We hear nothing of Torajan middle-class civil service workers, teachers, and engineers or of the many Torajan migrants who reside throughout the world. If modernity surfaces, it is usually invoked as an explanation for the difficulty of finding rituals in which Torajans use magic and mystical powers to awaken corpses so they can walk to their own graves. For instance, one blogger writes, "Today, there are roads and cars in Toraja and raising the dead is no longer needed to transport the body. Sometimes the villagers like to prove that they still know how to raise the dead so they use their rituals on dead animals."[32] However, far more zombie-oriented blogs paint a portrait of the Toraja highlands as a realm of timeless rural villages where people still practice an "ancient belief system" and "shamans" have the ability to reanimate the dead. In short, many online accounts of Torajan zombies traffic in tropes that would delight a budding structuralist: these accounts foster musings about the place of the zombie in the Western mind, along the lines of North : South : Life : Death (or, "Is the North to the South as Life to Death as Culture to Nature?").

However, my pilot survey of twenty-three college students on "zombie imaginaries" muddies these quasi-structuralist waters. Many of these students who self-identified as "interested in" or "curious about" zombies volunteered that they associated zombies with "tribal," "organic," "remote," or "barbaric" places. As one student wrote: "Voodoo is strong, mainly in countries of older origin and countries that believe strongly in the "organic" (herbal medicines, spirits of the Earth). In my mind, these countries [where zombies might be found] would be some African countries and particular African tribes and some areas of Mexico and Spanish areas." Another wrote: "For some reason I associate Siberia with Zombies. I would love to travel there. I feel like because of its location, rough terrain and harsh climate [*sic*]. It is one of the places in the world not very well-known or explored." A third student wrote:

> I definitely would associate indigenous people and tribes with zombies. For example the indigenous people of South America or the remote areas of Asia. These people are still barbaric and even their facial structure isn't normal. They tend to have bigger features and look mean. There [*sic*] way of life isn't like that of the 21st century. Many wear minimal clothing and still conduct in [*sic*] rituals and traditions that seem to encompass the idea of spirits within the body and transcending into another being. This seems the closest to what a "zombie" in our world today would be like.

Yet other students' answers disrupt these crude North-to-South/Life-to-Death equations. Some point simultaneously to "tribal areas" and to "cities like New York" or states like California or even post-nuclear disaster locales like Chernobyl as imagined zombie zones. As one student wrote of her conversation with a "zombie-fanatic" friend,

> I think those places . . . like Indonesia and other Indigenous places are associated with zombies . . . I can't really understand why, but their culture is really adaptive to

zombies. Also, America is huge with zombies! So many people here believe in them. Legends and myths point to places like Thailand, Indonesia and Southern Africa. It would be amazing to travel there.

Several of the students mentioned spending leisure time playing *Humans versus Zombies* with friends on campus, while others noted that they enjoyed online zombie-themed gaming. Given the popularity of these games (which feature humans battling hordes of ravenous zombies), it seems likely that zombie gaming websites (e.g., www.zombiegaming.org and www.zombiegames.net) have not only enlivened students' imaginations regarding geographic locales associated with zombies but have also prompted some to explore additional online zombie sites. Most zombie gaming websites feature discussion forums where members can exchange zombie book and film recommendations, as well as news items about "real-life zombies." The image of the teal-clad female Toraja zombie is a frequent celebrity on these discussion forums. Even the "off-topic" discussion board of a broadly focused site devoted to "hardcore online gamers" (www.neogaf.com) has a particularly lengthy discussion thread devoted to the Toraja "walking corpse" ritual.[33]

Whatever the sources of their "zombie geographical imaginaries," my more zombie-obsessed students' yearnings to graduate from their leisure-time zombie play and travel to actual places where "real" zombies may roam is telling: their desires offer a window onto the new type of mortuary tourist now surfacing in the Toraja highlands. The twin tropes of primitivity/tribalism and remoteness that dominate most of my zombie-oriented students' imagery suggest a broader cultural imaginary wherein the extreme cultural "other" lives in close proximity to the supernatural world of the undead.[34] I suggest that it is these sorts of images that spark the imagination of zombie tourists long before they purchase tickets to the Toraja highlands.

TORAJA REFRAMINGS OF THE WALKING DEAD: EMBRACING THE ZOMBIE

I now examine how Torajans make their own meanings out of their emergent status as the "center of the walking dead" in the Western imagination. There is a certain irony to this new twist to Torajans' international celebrity. Before the advent of large-scale tourism to the Sulawesi highlands, Torajans were frequently disparaged by other Indonesian groups as "primitives" only a couple of generations removed from head-hunting. Seen as "uncultured" and "backward," Torajans were a routine target for development projects designed to pull them into the "modern" world. However, by the late 1980s and 1990s, Torajans were successfully drawing on their international touristic fame to escape these stereotypes of yore (Adams 2006). Yet it is precisely because of the current flow of tourists, global migrants, and photographic images in and out the highlands that Torajans find themselves newly anointed as "zombie chic."[35]

As more tourists arrive in the Toraja highlands with zombies on their minds, some evidence suggests that their interests are sparking a certain degree of zombie entrepreneurship on the part of some business-savvy Torajans. While "zombie tours" are not yet a routine part of the Toraja tourism landscape, the Facebook page of one Toraja-owned mountaintop homestay features an image of the teal-clad female Toraja zombie. In addition, at least one guide claims that, for the right fee, he will locate someone who will demonstrate the zombification process on an animal. A 2013 series of Twitter "tweets" from one aspiring Toraja zombie tourist and adventure travel blogger who boasts of having "Danced with Corpses in Africa, Hitchhiked across Saudi Arabia, [and] Lived with Sea Gypsies, Tattoos Hammered in by Headhunters"[36] offers a glimpse of the genesis of zombie commodification by Torajans. As this potential Toraja zombie tourist tweets:

> Thanks for the tip on the creepy Toraja walking dead voodoo ritual! I found a guy who swears he can demonstrate this and show me ... the guy says he can kill a pig and reanimate it, zombie style ... and teach me how. I'm a little skeptical ... It's a bit complicated, the competing magicians must allow it and they must counteract the black magic to prevent a bad harvest.

A day later he reports:

> So, unfortunately they want 40 million to reanimate a dead pig. That's too much, so I will come back if they soften their position ... the guide will work with them to show the positives. This can legitimize what they do and create a new source of tourism for them ... We agreed on a price and Torajan magicians will zombify a dead pig using black magic and make it walk around the room and teach me![37]

Although his tweets end without a report on the zombification demonstration, his postings nevertheless offer further testimony that some Torajans are now embracing the zombie imagery for economic advancement.

When I began my research in the Toraja highlands in the 1980s, Torajans frequently warned me not to travel to the adjacent (yet more remote) region of Mamasa because it was "not safe." As they told me, when Christianity arrived in the early 1900s, it "drove all of the black magic off into the Mamasa Toraja hills" (also known as "Western Toraja" and locally considered a similar yet distinct group). The Sa'dan Toraja homeland was safe and civilized thanks to Christianity, they assured me, but the Mamasa region was the place where priests of the old religion could still make the dead walk and where magic still animated the world. Just as westerners envision the Sa'dan Toraja homeland as a space on the margins of the earth and therefore a logical zone for the undead, so, too, were the Sa'dan Toraja implicating the culturally and geographically more marginal Mamasa Toraja. As tourists arrived in the Toraja highlands seeking zombies, I observed Toraja guides and touts point toward the neighboring Mamasa mountains and declare that the walking dead might still be found in those rugged lands. Some invariably added that, for a fee, they could organize a private trekking expedition to this "remote" and supposedly more culturally pristine zone.

Comparatively difficult to access, the Mamasa area had long been dismissed by provincial-level government officials as relatively uninteresting for tourists. Thus, this region has never received the touristic stardom enjoyed by the Sa'dan Toraja area. However, certain Mamasa developers have recently seized upon zombie fanaticism as a possible path for economic development. Some are now embracing the negative imagery that once plagued them and exploring re-branding their region as a more authentic zombie homeland than that offered by their Sa'dan Toraja neighbors. In November 2009, Mamasa regency began promoting its "flagship walking corpses" (Stephanus 2009). While it is too early to determine whether this strategy will bring a significant influx of tourist dollars, it is clear that Mamasa tourism planners see this as their opportunity to best their neighbors at their own game: as one news article (titled "Mamasa's Walking Dead Tourism Potential") proclaimed, "Mamasa is regarded as the greatest center of mystical power for ethnic Torajans. Many Toraja admit they are reluctant to face the mystical powers of Mamasa, which are far stronger than that [*sic*] found in Tana Toraja" (Stephanus 2009). It should not surprise us that accompanying this article was the now ubiquitous photo of the so-called female Toraja zombie.

CLOSING OBSERVATIONS: FANTASTIC REALISM AND THE EMOTIONAL TERRAIN OF ZOMBIE TOURISM

The late twentieth- and early twenty-first-century fascination with death-related destinations has produced a flurry of scholarly work, including a small body of speculative work on the allure of the reanimated dead, largely by cultural studies and literary scholars. While explanations for the surge of interest in death-oriented leisure zones vary, the Toraja case reaffirms Lennon and Foley's observations that global communication technologies play a key role in propagating initial interest in dark tourism vacations (Lennon and Foley 2010, 11). Not only does the internet (and social media platforms) enable cyber-tourists to see photographs and videos of Toraja zombies, but the internet has also enlivened Torajans' association with zombie imagery in the global imaginary.

While the internet serves as an amplifier of potential leisure zones pertaining to death and zombies, the bigger question remains, why click on such links in the first place? And why make the considerable financial expenditure to travel halfway around the world to witness funerals for strangers or to pursue the undead? While some might aptly suggest that the pursuit of cultural capital lies at the heart of the matter, I believe the allure of death and zombie tourism involves far more than the simple pursuit of cultural capital. Despite the relatively small number of leisure-time zombie aficionados purchasing costly tickets to visit the Toraja homeland, their activities and fascinations reveal broader patterns in Western imaginings of distant lands. I suggest that zombie tourism represents an extreme case of the dynamics of ethnic tourism, where Othering is a key theme (Adams 1984; van den Berghe 1994). As Michael Hitchcock, Victor King, and Michael Parnwell summarized, "For the vast majority, otherness is what makes a destination worthy of consumption" (Hitchcock, King, and Parnwell 1993, 3). In zombie tourism, cyber and actual travelers pursue the ultimate Other: the undead.

My analysis suggests that the prospect of leisure-time encounters with alleged "zombies," human bodies, and sacrificial animal blood in so-called tribal societies enables the mediation of life-and-death narratives. Moreover, the "tribal" context promises heightened levels of "frisson" beyond the levels prompted by touristic encounters with death at home.[38] Just as Transylvania became a fitting homeland for a menacing supernatural creature because of its location on Europe's periphery, which resonated with established myths about peripheral zones as marginal, backward spaces (Seaton 2000; Light 2009, 243),[39] so, too, does Toraja's "remote" tropical location in a "developing" nation render it a space where the normative Western order of life and death may be plausibly or playfully imagined as inverted.

Moreover, as I have suggested in this chapter, mortuary tourism to rural zones on the periphery of the Western postindustrial world may also be productively envisioned as a way of mediating between the past and the future in a broader sense. In their touristic forays to Toraja, Western mortuary tourists pursue a locale where our shared human past is imagined as preserved and available for sampling, even as our shared human future of death takes center stage. In a sense, then, mortuary tourists to peripheral zones may be unconsciously engaging in a kind of fantasy time travel, simultaneously backward and forward on the human time line.

Bærenholdt and Haldrup's notion of fantastic realism also bears relevance for Toraja mortuary and zombie tourism. As noted, fantastic realism refers to instances where visitors' physical experiences reinforce an imaginative geography and enable tourists to "appropriate the experience and make it a part of their lives and identities" (Bærenholdt and Haldrup 2004, 86). In the Toraja case, dark tourists' firsthand sensory encounters with funerals, bones, graves, sacrificial animals, and (occasionally) corpses meld with their pre-departure diets of sensational online tales of native sorcerers reanimating the dead: in this manner, their tours serve to animate both the imaginative geography of zombies as well as tourists' primal emotions triggered by the realm of death.

It is worth underscoring the role of emotion in these macabre journeys, both cyber and actual. Despite a growing corpus of work addressing the ideological underpinnings, machinations, branding, and drawing powers of death-oriented leisure sites, the emotional dynamics entailed in touristic pilgrimages to these sites remain understudied. My ethnographic data suggest that emotional ambivalence is common among travelers engaged in Toraja mortuary tourism. Interviews and tourist observations in the field, as well as traveler narratives and even "armchair zombie tourist" Web commentaries on photos of Toraja "zombies," generally reveal equally potent doses of attraction and revulsion. Emotional attraction and revulsion may well be characteristic of much of postindustrial Western tourism to witness non-Western mortuary rites as well as other culturally unfamiliar practices entailing physical pain (or what might be perceived as "bodily mutilation"). Erik Cohen's description of tourists' reactions to observing Vegetarian Festival religious devotees parade through the streets of Phuket (Thailand) with knives, guns, and other sharp objects piercing their bodies suggests a similar set of tourist emotions and appears to reinforce this hypothesis (Cohen 2001, personal communication, 2012). As the Toraja case demonstrates, such dark travels elicit potent emotions, not all of them pleasurable. Even years after their travels, some tourists' vivid remembrances of the intense emotional discomfort they experienced as funeral "intruders" and of their difficulties averting their eyes from slaughtered animals and corpses suggest that the experience of these sorts of enlivening emotions is an important dimension of their dark travels. For anthropologists of tourism, the attraction and revulsion enacted and narrativized by mortuary-zombie tourists and bloggers offer a revealing metacommentary on our own metaphysical anxieties. Clearly, we need more studies of the emotional terrain of death-oriented leisure pursuits.

EPILOGUE

In 2014, some months after I presented a draft of this chapter at a conference, a journalist writing a piece for the *New York Times*'s high school supplement *Up Front Magazine* contacted me for an interview. She explained that she was drafting an article aimed at uncovering the "real story" of the ubiquitous Torajan "walking dead" meme. Eager to correct the sensationalized, Orientalist imagery surrounding the teal-clad Torajan "zombie," I agreed to an interview. In the lengthy interview, I explained how the so-called zombie photos were misunderstood images of a post-burial corpse- and grave-cleansing ritual. At the close of our conversation, the journalist asked, "If there were only one thing I could stress for the story, what would it be?" I responded that most important of all would be to emphasize that the Toraja people are almost entirely Christian today and that these rituals are not pagan reanimations of the dead but rather Christianized rituals where people show their respect and affection for deceased kin by cleaning graves and lovingly re-clothing the corpses.

Several months later, a colleague left a copy of the publication in my mailbox. I was stunned to see an enormous two-page photo depicting a male Toraja "zombie" surrounded by living kin, bearing the bold caption "The *Real* Walking Dead" ("The Big Picture" 2015). Several small text boxes had been added to the image, noting the identity and age of the corpse, mentioning that today Torajans take pictures of the corpses and post them on social media, and explaining how Torajans once used leaves to preserve the bodies. Yet another text box described the Toraja homeland and the rituals involving mummified corpses. A small box contained more extended explanatory text: my heart sank when I read the closing line, which offered an oddly mysterious quote from me ("the anthropologist") about how the line between life and death was "much thinner" for the Toraja.

With the exception of the allusion to social media, nowhere was there any mention of the fact that these were Christianized rituals performed by people who are very much a part of the global world. Moreover, the enormous zombie image trumped the small text, and I had visions of high school teens distractedly thumbing through the magazine during social studies classes and retaining only the image and the large caption. So much for my intentions to correct the record. Perhaps the moral of this story is that it is hard to kill the walking dead.

ACKNOWLEDGMENTS

I am very grateful to Andrew Causey, Elizabeth Coville, Erik Cohen, and this volume's editors for their wise suggestions. I also thank Peter Sanchez and Maribeth Erb for their support and Kristen Krueger for gifting me with her copy of the *Up Front Magazine* article.

NOTES

1. https://travellingamandablog.wordpress.com/2013/03/24/searching-for-zombies-in-tana-toraja-finding-bliss-in-sulawesi/, accessed October 12, 2013.

2. http://forums.steroid.com/anabolic-lounge-off-topic-discussion/456752-real-walking-dead-indonesia.html, accessed January 12, 2014.

3. For instance, see https://www.vyperlook.com/odd-strange/real-zombies-walking-in-indonesia, accessed November 8, 2014.

4. https://travellingamandablog.wordpress.com/2013/03/24/searching-for-zombies-in-tana-toraja-finding-bliss-in-sulawesi/, accessed October 12, 2013.

5. http://jdsteely.blogspot.com/2013/06/tana-toraja-land-of-divine-kings-and.html, accessed October 30, 2013.

6. http://www.itcheefeet.com/blog/travelling-with-kids-2/take-the-kids-zombie-hunting-in-tana-toraja-indonesia, accessed October 30, 2013.

7. Lennon and Foley (2010, 5) counterbalance this "segmentation" argument, noting that our postmodern media-saturated world enables us to consume graphic depictions of death on a daily basis. While certainly true, it is important to underscore that such media-based encounters with death are *secondhand* encounters. The mortuary tourists I interviewed sought *firsthand* encounters with funerals, corpses, and graves.

8. I am skeptical about the cross-cultural applicability of this "imperialist condition" hypothesis. Younger urban Indonesians appear equally fascinated by zombies, yet Indonesia was a Dutch colony and younger Indonesians tend to have scant awareness of Indonesia's own recent imperialist ventures in Timor L'Este and West Papua.

9. Critical discourse analysis was particularly salient, given its premise that "certain discourses are more powerful than others [and that these dynamics] can be revealed in the grammatical, semantic, and visual construction of texts and images" (Waterton 2009, 46).

10. http://www.travelblog.org/Asia/Indonesia/Sulawesi/Tana-Toraja/blog-778051.html, accessed November 12, 2013.

11. She was disappointed when I explained that death is a source of great anxiety for Torajans, largely because of the exorbitant costs of funerals, which can plunge families into crippling debt.

12. https://www.travelblog.org/Asia/Indonesia/Sulawesi/Tana-Toraja/blog "Rantepao by Scooter," accessed November 12, 2013.

13. The tourists I interviewed before, during, and after their visits generally conveyed an array of impressions of the Toraja highlands, including comments on tranquil landscapes and reflections on the disrupting forces of modernization, tourism, capitalism, and Christianity. However, most underscored mortuary tourism as a dominant travel motive. Likewise, in the Toraja travel blogs I surveyed, well over 50 percent of the photos included featured mortuary-related themes (funerals, graves, ritual animal slaughter).

14. http://edventureproject.com/death-in-tana-toraja, accessed November 19, 2010.

15. Chris Dunham, 2008 Online Travel Writing Contest runner-up, http://www.transitionsabroad.com/listings/travel/narrative_travel_writing/life_and_death_in_tana_toraja_indonesia.shtml, accessed October 4, 2013.

16. E.g., http://blog.sevenponds.com/cultural-perspectives/tana-toraja-indonesia-where-death-is-never-a-severe-goodbye, accessed October 22, 2014.

17. https://www.ted.com/talks/kelli_swazey_life_that_doesn_t_end_with_death.html, accessed September 26, 2014.

18. http://benedante.blogspot.com/2013/08/the-death-cultists-of-toraja-and.html, accessed October 23, 2014.

19. https://robpacker.wordpress.com/2009/10/17/death-in-toraja/, accessed October 1, 2014.

20. http://mosttraveledpeople.com/Locations.php?Locid=549&Location=Sulawesi&q=Sulawesi, accessed October 13, 2013.

21. Perhaps this is not surprising, since the Western tourists I interviewed were cognizant of my identity as an anthropologist and may have presumed I was desensitized to the blood-spattering that is part and parcel of these funerals. Thus, these tourists may have minimized their revulsion in their interviews with me. Nevertheless, the theme of revulsion in the context of funeral visits (and sometimes in the context of burial cave visits, upon seeing scattered bones of the dead) is palpable in the fieldwork interviews, albeit slightly attenuated in comparison to some travel blogs.

22. https://www.travelblog.org/Asia/Indonesia/Sulawesi/Tana-Toraja/blog, "The Macabre and the Massacre," accessed November 13, 2013.

23. http://www.aaronswwadventures.com/2013/10/tana-toraja-death-culture/, accessed November 25, 2013.

24. http://strangesounds.org/2014/09/zombie-love-torajas-dig-relatives-freshen-ancient-ceremony-cleaning-corpses-mainene.html, accessed November 1, 2014.

25. For the Oddity Central account of Toraja zombies, see http://www.odditycentral.com/pics/the-creepy-walking-dead-of-tana-toraja.html, accessed May 21, 2015. The Zombie Research Society website has updated its page on Toraja "real walking dead": the site now declares the "mystery solved." See http://zombieresearchsociety.com/archives/24871, accessed May 21, 2015. Similarly, the National Geographic discussion forum is now removed, though National Geographic's site hosts a four-minute film clip on the Toraja titled "Corpse Lives with Family." See http://video.nationalgeographic.com/video/indonesia_corpseliveswithfamily, accessed May 21, 2014.

26. Pinterest is a visually oriented site where members save images that interest them. Typically, Pinterest sites displaying these images bear headings such as "Unexplained Mysteries" and include a Web link to the image source. Occasionally, the Pinterest compiler will also include commentary. For example, one Pinterest compiler accompanied the cut-and-pasted image of the blue-clad female zombie with this commentary: "Indonesian Real Zombie Photo: Walking Corpse in Toraja—Toraja people do practice something akin to the rising of the dead. It seems that the people believe that death is a long process, sometimes taking years as the deceased gradually works their [sic] way toward Puya (the afterlife). Very elaborate measures must be taken during the funeral to ensure that the loved one makes it safely to that destination." See https://www.pinterest.com/pin/527695281308773788/, accessed May 21, 2015.

27. See http://message.snopes.com/showthread.php?t=65203, accessed October 10, 2014.

28. See http://message.snopes.com/showthread.php?t=65203 and http://zombieresearchsociety.com/archives/24871, accessed November 10, 2014.

29. Indonesia has over 74.6 million internet users, most of whom access the Web through cell phones (Markplus Insight 2013). Indonesia also outscores other nations in Twitter usage and is ranked as the world's fourth-biggest Facebook nation, with 64 million active Facebook users in 2013 (Grazella 2013; Lim 2013, 146).

30. In her 1986 book based on 1970s Torajan research, Nooy-Palm also reports observing people tucking new garments into coffins but does not mention bodies being removed from coffins (Nooy-Palm 1986).

31. http://freshinfos.com/2011/11/17/have-you-ever-seen-a-real-zombie/, accessed November 11, 2013.

32. http://zazenlife.com/2012/03/15/real-life-zombies-walking-dead-toraja/, accessed November 4, 2013.

33. http://www.neogaf.com/forum/showthread.php?t=422988, accessed May 22, 2015.

34. Likewise, Chernobyl and other post-nuclear disaster zones can be similarly imagined as remote spaces, beyond the familiar and taming reach of Western society.

35. https://thedancingrest.com/2014/09/06/zombie-chic-indonesian-villages-bizarre-annual-ritual-of-digging-up-its-dead/, accessed September 12, 2014.

36. See http://mywanderlist.com/, accessed May 21, 2015.

37. See https://twitter.com/mywanderlist/status/381024991564689408, accessed May 21, 2015.

38. See Desmond's discussion of frisson, this volume.

39. Albeit based on the actual iron-deficient impaler Vlad Tepes.

REFERENCES

Adams, Kathleen. 1984. "'Come to Tana Toraja, Land of the Heavenly Kings': Travel Agents as Brokers in Ethnicity." *Annals of Tourism Research* 11 (3): 469–85. https://doi.org/10.1016/0160-7383(84)90032-X.

Adams, Kathleen M. 1991. "Distant Encounters: Travel Literature and the Shifting Image of the Toraja of Sulawesi, Indonesia." *Terrae Incognitae* 23 (1): 81–92. https://doi.org/10.1179/tin.1991.23.1.81.

Adams, Kathleen M. 1993. "Club Dead, Not Club Med: Staging Death in Contemporary Tana Toraja (Indonesia)." *Southeast Asian Journal of Social Science* 21 (2): 59–69.

Adams, Kathleen M. 2006. *Art as Politics: Re-crafting Identities, Tourism, and Power in Tana Toraja, Indonesia*. Honolulu: University of Hawai'i Press.

Anderson, Benedict. 1990. "Cartoons and Monuments: The Evolution of Political Communication under the New Order." In *Language and Power: Exploring Political Cultures in Indonesia*, ed. Benedict Anderson, 152–93. Ithaca, NY: Cornell University Press.

Austen, Jane, and Seth Grahame-Smith. 2009. *Pride and Prejudice and Zombies*. Philadelphia: Quirk Books.

Bærenholdt, Jorgen O., and Michael Haldrup. 2004. "On the Tracks of the Vikings." In *Tourism Mobilities: Places to Play, Places in Play*, ed. Mimi Sheller and John Urry, 78–89. London: Routledge.

Bernard, H. Russell, ed. 1998. *Handbook of Methods in Cultural Anthropology*. Walnut Creek, CA: Altamira.

"The Big Picture: The *Real* Walking Dead." 2015. *Up Front Magazine* (supplement of the *New York Times*), January 12, 2–3.

Bishop, Kyle William. 2010. *American Zombie Gothic: The Rise and Fall (and Rise) of the Walking Dead in Popular Culture*. London: McFarland.

Boon, Kevin. 2011. "The Zombie as Other: Mortality and the Monstrous in the Post-Nuclear Era." In *Better Off Dead: The Evolution of the Zombie as Post-Human*, ed. Deborah Christie and Sarah Juliet Lauro, 50–60. New York: Fordham University Press. https://doi.org/10.5422/fordham/9780823234462.003.0005.

Bourgois, Philippe I. 2003. "The Continuum of Violence in War and Peace: Post–Cold War Lessons from El Salvador." In *Violence in War and Peace: An Anthology*, ed. Nancy Scheper-Hughes and Philippe I. Bourgois, 425–34. Oxford: Blackwell.

Christie, Deborah, and Sarah Juliet Lauro, eds. 2011. *Better Off Dead: The Evolution of the Zombie as Post-Human*. New York: Fordham University Press. https://doi.org/10.5422/fordham/9780823234462.001.0001.

Cohen, Erik. 2001. *The Chinese Vegetarian Festival in Phuket: Religion, Ethnicity, and Tourism on a Southern Thai Island*. Bangkok: White Lotus.

Durkin, Keith F. 2003. "Death, Dying, and the Dead in Popular Culture." In *Handbook of Death and Dying*, ed. Clifton D. Bryant, 43–49. London: Sage. https://doi.org/10.4135/9781412914291.n5.

Gorer, Geoffrey. 1955. "The Pornography of Death." *Encounter* 4 (October): 49–52.

Grazella, Mariel. 2013. "Facebook Has 64m Active Indonesian Users." *Jakarta Post*, June 18. Accessed March 18, 2014. http://www.thejakartapost.com/news/2013/06/18/facebook-has-64m-active-indonesian-users.html.

Hemphill Harris Travel Corp. 1981. "Orient: Including People's Republic of China and Circle Pacific." Los Angeles.

Hitchcock, Michael, Victor King, and Michael Parnwell. 1993. *Tourism in South-East Asia*. London: Routledge.

Junemo, Mattias. 2004. "Let's Build a Palm Island! Playfulness in Complex Times." In *Tourism Mobilities: Places to Play, Places in Play*, ed. Mimi Sheller and John Urry, 181–91. London: Routledge.

Lennon, John, and Malcolm Foley. 2010. *Dark Tourism: The Attraction of Death and Disaster*. Andover, UK: Cengage Learning.

Light, Duncan. 2009. "Performing Transylvania: Tourism, Fantasy, and Play in a Liminal Place." *Tourist Studies* 9 (3): 240–58. https://doi.org/10.1177/1468797610382707.

Lim, Merlyna. 2013. "The Internet and Everyday Life in Indonesia." *Bijdragen tot de Taal-, Land- en Volkenkunde* 169 (1): 133–47. https://doi.org/10.1163/22134379-12340008.

Linke, Uli. 2005. "Touching the Corpse: The Unmaking of Memory in the Body Museum." *Anthropology Today* 21 (5): 13–19. https://doi.org/10.1111/j.0268-540X.2005.00381.x.

Markplus Insight. 2013. "Report: Indonesia Now Has 74.6 Million Internet Users." http://www.markplusinc.com/markplusinsight/research-report/.

Nooy-Palm, Hetty. 1986. *The Sa'dan-Toraja: A Study of Their Social Life and Religion*, vol. 2: *Rituals of the East and West*. The Hague: Brill.

Pelto, Pertti J., and Gretel H. Pelto. 1981. *Anthropological Research: The Structure of Inquiry*. Cambridge: Cambridge University Press.

Reed, Chris J. 2013. *The World's Most Social Mobile Centric Country*. Indonesia: Campaign Asia-Pacific. Accessed March 18, 2014. http://www.campaignasia.com/article/indonesia-the-worlds-most-social-mobile-centric-country/426174.

Scheper-Hughes, Nancy, and Philippe I. Bourgois. 2003. *Violence in War and Peace: An Anthology*. 1st ed. Malden, MA: Blackwell.

Seaton, Anthony V. 1996. "Guided by the Dark: From Thanatopsis to Thanatourism." *International Journal of Heritage Studies* 2 (4): 234–44. https://doi.org/10.1080/13527259608722178.

Seaton, Anthony V. 2000. "The Worst of Journeys, the Best of Journeys: Travel and the Concept of the Periphery in European Culture." In *Expressions of Culture, Identity, and Meaning in Tourism*, ed. Mike Robinson, 321–46. Sunderland, UK: Centre for Travel and Tourism/Business Educational Publishers.

Stephanus, W. B. 2009. "Potensi Wisata Mayat Berjalan Mamasa" (Potential of Mamasa Walking Corpse Tourism). *Mamasa Online*, November 5. Accessed November 12, 2013. http://www.mamasaonline.com/2009/11/potensi-wisata-mamasa.html.

Stone, Philip. 2011a. "Dark Tourism and the Cadaveric Carnival: Mediating Life and Death Narratives at Gunter von Hagens' Body Worlds." *Current Issues in Tourism* 14 (7): 685–701. https://doi.org/10.1080/13683500.2011.563839.

Stone, Philip R. 2011b. "Dark Tourism: Towards a New Post-Disciplinary Research Agenda." *International Journal of Tourism Anthropology* 1 (3–4): 318–32. https://doi.org/10.1504/IJTA.2011.043713.

Stone, Philip R., and Richard Sharpley. 2008. "Consuming Dark Tourism: A Thanatological Perspective." *Annals of Tourism Research* 35 (2): 574–95. https://doi.org/10.1016/j.annals.2008.02.003.

Urry, John. 2004. "Death in Venice." In *Tourist Mobilities: Places to Play, Places in Play*, ed. Mimi Sheller and John Urry, 205–15. London: Routledge.

Van den Berghe, Pierre. 1994. *The Quest for the Other: Ethnic Tourism in San Cristóbal, Mexico*. Seattle: University of Washington Press.

Volkman, Toby. 1987. "Mortuary Tourism in Tana Toraja." In *Indonesian Religions in Transition*, ed. Rita Smith Kipp and Susan Rodgers Siregar, 161–68. Tucson: University of Arizona Press.

Waterton, Emma. 2009. "Sights of Sites: Picturing Heritage, Power, and Exclusion." *Journal of Heritage Tourism* 4 (1): 37–56. https://doi.org/10.1080/17438730802221117.

5

That "Awful Margin"

Tourism, Risk, and Death at the Cliffs of Moher

Adam Kaul

And when you look long into an abyss, the abyss also looks into you.
—Friedrich Nietzsche, *Beyond Good and Evil*

In 2007, a new interpretive center was opened at the Cliffs of Moher on the west coast of Ireland, a few kilometers from the small village of Doolin in County Clare where I began conducting ethnographic research in 2002.[1] The Cliffs are a dramatic and iconic Irish landscape, a 214-meter mountain of black shale that has been sheared in half by the relentless waves of the Atlantic Ocean. The Cliffs rise and fall in an undulating arc that stretches a total of 8 kilometers from Doolin on the north side to Liscannor on the south. The colossal size of the Cliffs themselves, the precipitous verticality of the cliff face, and the overwhelming expanse of the Atlantic make this a place have a powerful pull on the psyche. Irrationally, it draws us to the edge. Fintan O'Toole (2007, 16) probably put it best when he wrote that the Cliffs are "one of the world's most awful margins. The abrupt, harsh, and vertiginous confrontation between land and ocean has an elemental force. Yet it is also a strangely comforting location. Here, you can look at the end of the world and turn away from it." In many ways, the Cliffs of Moher have also become a metaphor for Irishness in a romantic conflation of culture and landscape (Kaul 2014, 37). Given the symbolic power of this site, its primordial beauty, and the risky but thrilling confrontation with such an awe-inspiring height, it is no wonder that this is one of the most popular tourist attractions in all of Ireland and that it boasts over a million

DOI: 10.5876/9781607327295.c005

visitors annually (Dunphy 2014). To put that number in perspective, that is close to a quarter of the population of the population of the Republic of Ireland.

Prior to 2007, there was little at the Cliffs besides a tower built in 1835 by local landlord Cornelius O'Brien as a "folly," a parking lot that charged a small fee for each car, bathroom facilities, a small number of booths where vendors sold souvenirs, and some busking musicians. By contrast, the new €32 million interpretive center, called the Cliffs of Moher Experience, is an impressive building set completely into the hillside, enticing tourists to quite literally enter the landscape. The center houses multiple exhibits, a large gift shop, a restaurant, and a virtual reality tour of the Cliffs, among other things. Prime Minister Bertie Ahern officially opened the center on February 8, 2007. It was cause for a great deal of excitement and media attention, but a shadowy pall darkened the celebrations. Only a few days before the opening, a twenty-six-year-old woman named Eileen Murphy and her four-year-old son were found dead at the base of the Cliffs in what was presumed at the time to be a murder-suicide. The tragedy was national news, but while the Murphy story was shocking, it was by no means extraordinary. Death at the Cliffs is an all-too-common occurrence. Some of these deaths are accidental, although the Cliffs of Moher has become not only one of the most popular *tourist* destinations in Ireland but also a well-known *suicide* destination. In an interview, the director of the new interpretive center acknowledged that "basically, the Cliffs are a known suicide hotspot." Some suicide victims are from the region, while others from outside the country make long journeys to the site with the explicit intent of committing suicide there (Bracken and Flynn 2012). Official numbers are not widely publicized. There are periods of time, for example, between 2005 and 2007, when no one dies at the Cliffs; but other years are worse, such as 2011, when eight people died purposefully or accidentally (Deegan 2012a, 2). "Every year it varies," one staff member at the interpretive center told me. "You know, it goes from one to much more than that, but, you know, I don't recall the year where it's ever been more than ten."

So for some, like O'Toole, the Cliffs provide a unique affirmation of life because we reject death by walking away from the cliff's edge. We approach that "awful margin" to get as close as possible to our own mortality, but we leave feeling revived in the knowledge that we must go on living. In this way, tourists' "edgework" at the Cliffs, to invoke Stephen Lyng's (1990) terminology, can be transformative and restorative. For others, though, the Cliffs provide a means of using their bodies not to affirm life but to reject it as they leap to their deaths. Suicide at the Cliffs evokes Foucault's analyses of the violent use of the body as the last vestige of agency for those who are tragically overwhelmed by a sense of powerlessness (Foucault 1984, 263).

Whether by accident or design, death at this beautiful natural site is perceived to be anything but natural. Local people speak of the tragedy of death at the Cliffs

FIGURE 5.1. A tourist taking a photo of the local Coast Guard unit as they look at the body of a suicide victim, Cliffs of Moher, 2002. Author photo.

in hushed tones, if they speak of it at all. By contrast, in her contribution to this volume, Pipyrou writes that locals in Greece "indulge in spreading rumors about the deceased" through gossip. Speech bubbles audibly around the dead. This chapter acts as a counterpoint to her case study in that sense because in Ireland, it is the silence about suicide that speaks volumes. This silence takes several forms. Suicide is notoriously underreported as the cause of death in many nations; however, underreporting is far more extensive in Ireland than elsewhere (Corcoran and Arensman 2010, 175). It is often misclassified as "accidental death" or "death by misadventure." In his book *Suicide: The Irish Experience*, Sean Spellissy writes that traditionally, "victims of suicide were simply buried, quietly . . . and few people referred to what happened" (Spellissy 1996, 9). These forms of silencing are often attributed to the fact that historically, Ireland has been a deeply Catholic nation. Not only is self-inflicted death deemed a mortal sin by the Catholic Church, but in Ireland it was also against the law until an act of decriminalization was passed in 1993, thus stigmatizing the act of suicide for the victim and his or her family in this world and the next. Because "both church and state were reluctant to discuss it until recently" (Spellissy 1996, 33), suicide in Ireland became a literally unspeakable tragedy. Pipyrou argues that in the Greek context the social construction of what she calls "death narratives" acts to domesticate and civilize "socially problematic deaths" (Pipyrou 2014, 189). In

Ireland, it seems that the "problem" in a socially problematic death is instead exorcised from the death narrative altogether. Echoing Émile Durkheim's (2002 [1897]) classic assessment that the act of suicide is driven at least in part by social and cultural factors, this silent stigmatization and denial of suicide are even more dramatic in a cultural context in which "death seems to enjoy an almost casual pre-eminence... as both possible and actual event, and the rural wake is still the quintessential expression of communal values and relations" (Taylor 1989, 175).

Even factoring in underreporting, rates of suicide in Ireland were relatively low up to the mid-1970s (Lucey et al. 2005, 90; Gallagher and Sheehy 1994, 147), but they increased steadily throughout the next three decades, especially among young men (Lucey et al. 2005, 93). Tragically, suicide rapidly became the leading cause of death for young men ages fifteen through thirty-four (Corcoran et al. 2004, 19), and "the Republic of Ireland experienced one of the fastest rising suicide rates in the world during the 1980s and 1990s" (Richardson, Clarke, and Fowler 2013, 25). The recent crash in the Irish economy seems to have sparked another surge of suicides (Richardson, Clarke, and Fowler 2013, 29), and it is now widely considered a key public health concern or even a "so-called suicide 'epidemic'" (Saris 2012, 6). In 2011 the coroner's office reported that in County Clare alone, nineteen suicides had occurred that year compared with only two fatal automobile accidents (Deegan 2012a).

It is not in my interest, nor is it central to my argument, to dwell further on the exact number of fatalities that occur at the Cliffs of Moher on an annual basis, whether by suicide or accident, or to speculate about suicide victims' motives.[2] Instead, this chapter explores the multitude of meanings people have ascribed to the Cliffs of Moher and how they create very different embodied behaviors there. The various ways people have interacted with and shaped the site are highly charged and highly symbolic; taken together, they imbue the Cliffs of Moher with inherent contradictions. As Talcott Parsons argued, unlike other types of death, suicide is inherently meaningful even before the act (Parsons 1994 [1978], 61–62), and its attempt or its completion creates dark and affective echoes in the minds of locals, staff, visitors, and friends and families of the victim. Accidental deaths resonate in the collective memory as well, although the nature of the tragedy is obviously quite different. An accidental death may seem meaningless, but its aftermath is tragically meaningful for those left behind.

In stark contrast to this dark reality of death and dying, the tourism industry has created its own, more luminous narratives about the Cliffs of Moher in the form of a major new interpretive center that attempts to mediate the leisurely tourist gaze. This chapter argues that death and dying—their actual occurrence but also macabre stories and even joking behavior about them—resist and punctuate the dominant tourism narrative. In one sense, this chapter sketches a cultural geography of death, analyzing how it imparts a macabre significance onto a particular landscape and how the idea and the actuality of death contradict and sully attempts to inscribe the place with other (postmodern, leisurely) meanings. Secondarily, I also engage with the literature on "dark tourism" and suggest a slight expansion of the analytical framework.

NARRATIVE-MAKING IN THE TOURIST ENCLAVE

To unravel the juxtaposition between tourism and death at the Cliffs of Moher, I am interested first in the story the elaborate new interpretive center at the site "tells" about the place. Among others, Barbara Bender (1998, 2001) has argued that *land* is elevated to land*scape* when humans circumscribe it and infuse it with meaning. Likewise, Keith Basso argues extensively that "place-making" (Basso 1996, 5) occurs when people saturate specific sites with cultural memories and stories. The process of interpreting the Cliffs by building an *interpretive center* is in and of itself an attempt to sequester and solidify the story of this landscape. In part, the official tourism narrative actively evokes tropes of modernity, purity, and a romantic fusion of Irish culture and Irish soil. Two aspects of the new interpretive center are worthy of detailed examination: first, the way the building evokes the feeling that we are literally entering into the landscape and, related to this, the postmodern elements of the tourist experience such as the virtual reality tour of the Cliffs, an exhibit titled *The Ledge*. In both instances the tourist experience is a manufactured interaction with the site, a simulacrum of sorts, with the real version of the Cliffs just outside the door. Multiple layers of interpretive representation have been created.

A darker story crowds in at the periphery of these understandings about the place. First and most tragically, actual deaths at the Cliffs cast a pall on the leisurely, carefree, and cheerful tourist experience. Also, a touristic discourse about death and dying often bubbles to the surface, especially as visitors approach the cliff face. There are warning signs everywhere asking visitors to stay away from the edge, but they are actively ignored (figure 5.3). There are also signs advertising a suicide hotline and a small memorial plaque at the south end of the visitors' center honoring the dead. Despite all this, visitors consistently walk past the signage to the very edge and naïvely look over the side, apparently unaware that the strong winds can sometimes send a person right off the edge or that on occasion entire sections of stone have crumbled off the side and into the sea below. Even if one does not approach the edge, it is typical—even perhaps something of a compulsion—for tourists to joke about jumping or falling off the Cliffs (figure 5.4). This dark humor may simply be a way to cope with facing the possibility of death, and one might suggest that it is also a psychological means of combatting it. Through action, accident, discourse, and memory, death turns the Cliffs of Moher into what Hannah Rumble in this volume calls a "deathscape."

As visitors drive into the site in rental cars or by bus, they are by no means compelled to enter the interpretive center before walking to the cliff edge, but most do. A recent study showed that around 85 percent of visitors enter the center (Healy, van Riper, and Boyd 2016, 579). The building is impressive to look at, in no small part because there is very little to see. The structure is set almost entirely into the hillside. Its grass-covered exterior blends in perfectly with the surrounding fields where cattle graze. Only the main entrance and two large windows, shaped something like winking eyes, are exposed (figure 5.2). The new building projects a powerful sense of environmental sustainability, purity, and raw, elemental nature. The structure itself is a kind of rhetorical move, making the case that Ireland has fully arrived in the twenty-first century. These narratives of elemental purity are told more literally in pamphlets on the center's website and in placards in the center's exhibits.

Tim Edensor would describe the Cliffs of Moher Experience as a "tourist enclave" in which there is a "continual maintenance of a clear boundary which demarcates which activities may occur" (Edensor 2000, 328). The tourist enclave is physical in the sense that the built environment attempts to restrict regions of interaction with the landscape. It seems clear that the architects, who have won multiple design awards for the building ("Awards" 2007), were consciously attempting to draw visitors into the center. The spatial flow of the sidewalks and the courtyard outside the main entrance pulls the crowd forward through the doors and into the subterranean building. Once inside, visitors are presented with a large gift shop, a restaurant, and an information kiosk staffed with employees ready to answer questions and direct traffic. The walls and floors are covered in stone, completing the manufactured feeling of having stepped inside the landscape. Off to the left, the tourist traffic flows toward the entrance of the main exhibit hall. The walls and floor curve up and around in smooth arcs, giving the subtle illusion that the center was not built so much as formed by natural processes over millennia.

After passing through a short hallway where a looped digital image of rippling water is projected onto the floor (placing into question whether one is at the top of the cliffs, inside them, or at the base of them), the visitor enters the cavernous expanse of the main hall. The walls curve up overhead and blend into a ceiling punctuated by skylights, creating the impression that this space is not manmade. The interior of the center is described several times on the center's website as "cave-like," suggesting that the structure is in harmony with the natural environment that envelops it. Inside the exhibit hall, tourist performances are well scripted. Educational kiosks and displays discuss the geology, biology, and geography of the Cliffs. There are four main exhibit themes in the main hall titled Ocean, Rock, Nature, and Man. The meta-narrative is that this is a place to experience the elemental forces of nature. The single-word labels capture the powerful simplicity of the Cliffs, as if words could never adequately describe the raw confrontation with the environment in its most primeval state. Instead, the suggestion seems to be that this landscape presents a gestalt vision of ocean, rock, and nature. The exhibit on people at the site called Man is interesting not only because one wonders where the women of Ireland have gone but also because it focuses on rather narrow aspects of local culture: traditional musicians, local folklore, and a single significant historical event—the destruction of the Spanish Armada along the County Clare coastline in 1588. It is common to conflate traditional music with landscape in Ireland (Kaul 2006–7, 53–54, 2014); while there is no direct claim to do so in the exhibit at the Cliffs of Moher interpretive center, the implication is forceful. Furthermore, it is interesting that the only aspect of the exhibit on people that does not include folklore or traditional music is a dramatic historical account about how a foreign culture in the form of the Spanish Armada was obliterated in the powerful clash between ocean and stone.

I have suggested elsewhere (Kaul 2012, 2014) that the Cliffs of Moher have become a condensed symbol of Irishness. More generally, tourists and the tourism industry foster an evocative conflation of people and nature in the wild west of Ireland. Locals are not immune to the powerful romance, either; on the contrary, many embrace it (Kaul 2011, 242–43). The land is romantically reified but also something to conquer. The trope contains a contradictory push-pull / repulsion-attraction / fission-fusion between nature and culture. Perhaps the most iconic representation of this confrontation is Robert Flaherty's 1934 film *Man of Aran*, in which the landscape is really the main character. The environment is depicted at once as compellingly beautiful, dangerously repulsive, and ultimately something people must overcome and domesticate. *Man of Aran* is not anomalous. In the plays of John Millington Synge, the paintings of Augustus John, and the photography of Dorothea Lange, local people in County Clare and the Aran Islands just off the coast have been depicted as strong and romantic, close to the earth and yet at war with it in an unending struggle for survival.

These motifs about tradition and landscape are central to the story the new interpretive center tells, but the center sends another message as well about global hyper-modernity. The lavish expense that went in to its construction (€32 million) and the state-of-the-art and environmentally sustainable facilities seem to project the notion that a twenty-first-century Ireland has arrived. This is far from the quaint postcard version of Ireland with its images of peasant cottages, ruined castles, and donkey carts full of peat turf. Intentional or not, several aspects of the Cliffs of Moher Experience are not simply hyper-modern but also hyper-real. A virtual reality film exhibit called *The Ledge* forcefully frames the tourist narrative, often before

FIGURE 5.2. The new visitor center, "The Cliffs of Moher Experience." Unaltered image by Ingo Mehling (own work) (CC BY-SA 3.0 [http://creativecommons.org/licenses/by-sa/3.0]), via Wikimedia Commons.

tourists go to see the real thing. The film literally takes a bird's-eye view of the Cliffs, seen through the point of view of a seagull. Like the physical structure of the exhibit hall, the film is fluid and in constant motion. The bird's perspective allows the camera to approach the Cliffs from the sea and zoom back out for broader views. It is not a minor point that late in the film the viewer is "flown" across the top of the Cliffs toward the edge and sent plummeting over the side, shooting at full speed headlong into the sea below. This is one of the most dramatic moments of *The Ledge*, one that provides tourists with a virtual reality experience it is hoped they will not have in reality once they approach the edge, which is to jump. It purposefully forces a sense of vertigo and frisson on the viewer, one that could be perceived as either terrifying or exciting. While the video is part of an effort to establish a modern design aesthetic, it does not always have that effect on visitors. A man who had recently moved from England to a town near the new interpretive center was confused by this exhibit when he first visited the site. "It reminded me of *Toy Story*, for one," he told me. "[It's] old technology. You know, there's supposed to be a bird flying around. It made me feel . . . it made me feel seasick. And then it's all over." In their recent study of the visitor experience at the Cliffs, Noel Healy and his colleagues also found that many tourists felt that exhibits like *The Ledge* exemplified the heavy-handed interpretation of the site (Healy, van Riper, and Boyd 2016, 579).

The film *The Ledge* is not the only example of hyper-reality. In the foyer, several displays create multiple layers of representation including *The Infinity Cascade*, which consists of a wall of photographs of tourists with the Cliffs in the background. In this exhibit, the viewer experiences a secondhand version of the landscape and also a secondhand version of the tourist interaction with it. The photographs *of* the Cliffs and of previous tourists *at* the Cliffs provide a script for how visitors might experience the site once they proceed outdoors. In the foyer there is also a large back-lit floor-to-ceiling photo of the cliffs at sunset that is meant for tourists to use as a backdrop for photos. Tourists take photos of themselves standing in front of a photo of something that is in reality just outside the door. What visitors walk away with is a representation of a representation.

It could be argued that the design of the Cliffs of Moher Experience does not simply tap into this set of tropes about a "traditional landscape" on the one hand and (hyper-)modernity on the other but in fact embodies and embeds them in its very structure. This is perhaps most obvious on the narrative fusion of "Ocean, Rock, Nature, Man" in the main exhibit hall. But the way the new building is set into the hillside and the emphasis on sustainability, conservation, and purity also forefront the very idea that the site is something to be preserved as pure in the first place.

In all these ways, the Cliffs of Moher Experience is intrinsically postmodern. As Fintan O'Toole adroitly points out in the same article from which I borrowed the title of this chapter, "The Cliffs of Moher are no more—they have been replaced by the 'Cliffs of Moher Experience'" (O'Toole 2007, 16). The center might be seen as a snapshot writ large, an entire built environment that acts to turn the *land* into a land*scape* by infusing it with meaning, by including romantic tropes and excluding unwanted narratives. Some stories, such as the ones about death and suicide, are purposefully left out of the frame. Still, in the same way we might try to exclude unwanted objects in our tourist photos—for example, other tourists—that are perceived to sully the supposed purity of the landscape, in spite of our efforts, sometimes they find their way in.

IMPROVISATION, RISK, AND DEATH

Outside the subterranean structure, tourist behaviors are far more improvisational. It is here, faced with the reality of the cliff edge, that visitors take risks and confront the possibility of death. Stone fencing has been in place for generations in an attempt to control visitors' approach to the cliff edge, but with very limited success.[3] As part of the new developments in 2007, more substantial stone walls were erected in front of the walking paths within the official boundaries of the center

FIGURE 5.3. Warning sign at the Cliffs of Moher defaced by tourists, 2011 (signs since removed). Author photo.

where traffic is heaviest. But there is a constant low-level tension between the staff of the Cliffs of Moher Experience who patrol the cliff edge in a failed attempt to contain visitors within the walls and the tourists who successfully defy their efforts. Until relatively recently, particularly at the two points farthest from the interpretive center, tourists actively and aggressively ignored the boundary walls meant to restrain them. There is technically nothing anyone can do to prevent visitors from jumping these fences to walk along the edge because the shoreline in Ireland is legally a public right-of-way (Kaul 2014, 35). In the years just after the center was opened, warning signs were posted to scare visitors away from the cliff edge in these spots; instead, they became the subject of ironic tourist performances that mocked the site's danger. The signs were defaced with stickers—a kind of reverse souvenir—so thoroughly and at such a constant rate that the staff could not keep them clean (see figure 5.3).

Likewise, the results of more improvisational performances by tourists as they ignored warning signs and walked around them became inscribed in the landscape itself. Tens of thousands of feet carved out compacted dirt paths that flowed around the signs and boundary walls like flooding water coursing around a boulder. Visitors were able to physically see that countless tourists before them had blatantly ignored the danger inherent in crossing these boundaries. It gave them the notion that their border-crossing "edgework" was either not as dangerous as the officials suggested or that the risks were worth taking. One employee told me "there's a huge amount of copycat behavior [that] goes on. So you see one person climbs over the wall . . . and if they're not caught, the ranger doesn't see them because he's dealing with the visitor at the other end of the pathway or something, you could suddenly find twenty people down there." On one fieldtrip to the Cliffs of Moher during the summer of 2011, I noticed a comment written in the guest book in the foyer of the center that summed up this popular tourist sentiment. It simply read, "Cross the 'no trespassing' sign—WELL WORTH IT!!!"

In 2013, the ineffective barriers at the north and south boundaries of the Cliffs of Moher Experience site were removed altogether, along with the defaced signage. The director of the interpretive center told me they had been planning to do this for some time, just as soon as they received formal permission from the remaining farm families to construct a more stable path along the entire 8-kilometer length of the cliffs' edge. Now, guided walking tours are available, but the vast majority of tourists walk these paths unaccompanied by experienced guides who know the risks. In effect, this new path has instantiated the tourist flow across boundaries and borders into an officially recognized route. The floodgates have opened, but far from reducing risky tourist performances, it may arguably only increase them. Parts of the path run very close to the edge, and in some places it empties out onto stony ledges that seem to invite tourists to walk right up to the precipice and lean over to look at the waves crashing hundreds of feet below them. The staff members at the site are trained to help reduce the risks to tourists and to spot danger, but the public right-of-way, combined with the sheer number of annual visitors, makes it impossible to prevent visitors from engaging in dangerous behavior.

While most people wisely approach the edge with caution, others naïvely take great risks, joking around at the edge, pretending to fall or push others over. A common, macabre form of visual "joke" about dying at the Cliffs consists of having a

FIGURE 5.4. Pretending to fall off the cliffs is common photographic joking behavior among tourists. Photo used by permission of Matt Heckel.

photo taken of oneself jumping into the air with the precipice and the Atlantic Ocean in the background to make it appear as though the person is leaping off the edge. Often, the subject is smiling or laughing. To provide another example among many, the last time I visited the site I watched a young American woman climb over the wall to hang off of it by her fingertips, pretending to be in peril while her friends took photos. Terrifyingly, there was nothing between her and the edge except a short, steep grassy slope slick with salt from the sea air. As their cackling laughter resounded and other groups of passing tourists looked on, I had to turn away from my horror at her actual peril.

This macabre joking extends into cyberspace as well. There are dozens of photos of tourists engaging in the behaviors described above. In addition, a series of disturbing examples can be found on sites like YouTube.com,[4] where tourists have posted mock-suicide videos. It is not only tourists who engage in playful dark humor about death and dying at the Cliffs. The center itself has started to do so by selling T-shirts emblazoned with one of the most commonly displayed warning signs that shows a stick figure falling off the edge of the crumbling cliff face with the universal red circle with a diagonal line through it. The director of the site told me that tourists started stealing the signs and that "one of the signs is so popular that we've turned it into a T-shirt. It's the picture of someone falling backward over the cliffs by accident, and so, you know, it's this 'stay away from the cliff edge' sign. Those were being pried off the walls and taken home as souvenirs." She also told me that one of the most common questions tourists have—especially Americans—is how many people die at the Cliffs each year. Presumably, much of this is simply morbid curiosity or brinksmanship. Understandably, the official policy is to acknowledge that suicide does happen but not to give out numbers.

"All of our rangers and front line staff have done an HSE [Health Services Executive] course on suicide prevention," the director told me, and a suicide hotline number is posted at regular intervals all along the official barriers. She linked these efforts to several dozen times staff members were able to prevent a suicide. Local authorities are regularly tipped off as well if, for instance, someone travels to the Cliffs using a one-way bus ticket or if arrangements are not made with a taxi driver for a return trip. Some of the staff and musicians who busk at the site have heart-wrenching stories about attempted or completed suicides, but again, these are not widely told to the general public. "There have been a couple that have been witnessed by visitors and staff," one worker told me, "but that's the exception." For the most part, those who attempt or complete suicide go somewhere "out of sight of others—they will try to find a location where there are not many people around." On the one hand, keeping the somber stories associated with actual deaths quiet reflects the taboo nature of suicide in Ireland, and one might more cynically suggest that there is anxiety about tarnishing the reputation of such a prominent tourist site. But there is also a very legitimate concern about preventing this locale from attracting copycat suicides, something known as "the Werther Effect" (Phillips 1985).

One might wonder why the Cliffs of Moher have become such a well-known suicide black spot. Suicide can take place almost anywhere, after all, and the west coast is riddled with cliff edges tall enough to end a person's life. As elsewhere in Europe, jumping is a somewhat unusual method of committing suicide; hanging is the most common means (Richardson, Clarke, and Fowler 2013, 33–34). Hanging is typically a very private act that takes place in enclosed locations in or around the home, unlike jumping in such an open, natural, and public location. And while each death is located somewhere, the decision to use a dramatic locale like the Cliffs of Moher as the method itself irrevocable tethers the act of dying to this place in a qualitatively different way than do private suicides. Dying at the Cliffs of Moher, by design or by accident, creates an association between victim and the locale that lives on in the collective memory of the person's extended social world, something Trudi Buck and Stavroula Pipyrou have labeled a narrative "prosthesis" of death, a "trace of an absence, an image of a person that has disappeared" (Buck and Pipyrou 2014, 263). In the case of suicides at the Cliffs, the site is given another layer of meaning because it was *chosen* as the place to die.

DARK TOURISM OR NARRATIVE RESISTANCE?

In this chapter I have suggested that the most dramatic rupture in the high gloss of the new ideological aesthetic of the tourist center with its tropes of nature, traditionalism, purity, and hyper-modernity is death. This occurs when the occasional visitor punctuates societal norms altogether and commits suicide by leaping over the edge of the Cliffs or when a visitor accidentally falls or is blown off the edge by strong winds. The rupture also occurs more regularly in the form of tourists' grisly, leisurely joking behavior. In addition, the signage posted throughout the site raises the issue of intentional or unintentional death for those who had not thought of it themselves.

This case study also begs an engagement with the burgeoning literature on "dark tourism." Peter Phipps has argued that "death itself becomes a macabre and fascinating tourist site" (Phipps 1999, 83). He continues: "The themes of death, the destructive forces of modern warfare and the dangers of the road are an inescapable part of tourist thought ... this threat of death and danger is something that tourism relishes so as to retain its imaginative power as a space for reconnection with that 'real' which remains so elusive, and thoroughly denied, in the order of highly stratified, regulated and abstracted capitalist postmodern society" (Phipps 1999, 83). These themes are brought into sharp relief and made real at tourist sites like the Cliffs of Moher, where the possibility of death and personal harm becomes obvious. But is this odd and horrible juxtaposition between leisure and suicide, joking and death, irony and tragedy an example of what has recently come to be known as "dark tourism"?

The fast-growing literature on dark tourism, which, broadly speaking, explores the intersection between tourism and trauma, began in earnest with John Lennon and Malcolm Foley's 2000 book *Dark Tourism*. Since then, a flurry of analysis has been done on the topic (cf. Dann and Seaton 2001; Edkins 2004; Sturken 2007; Seaton 2009; Sharpley and Stone 2009; Skinner 2010; Stone 2011). However, the idea had been brought up years earlier in a special issue of the *International Journal of Heritage Studies* (1996 2 [4]). In that issue Anthony Seaton provided a second influential label, "thanatourism," combining the notion of thanatopsis, a "contemplation of death," with tourism (Seaton 1996, 235). Seaton (1996, 240) defines thanatourism as "travel to a location wholly, or partially, motivated by the desire for actual or symbolic encounters with death, particularly, but not exclusively, violent death, which may, to a varying degree, be activated by the person-specific features of those whose deaths are its focal objects." To reuse Phipps's (1999, 83) phrasing, some "macabre and fascinating" analysis has been done on, among other things, tourism to Auschwitz, Ground Zero, war memorials, and the sites of battles and battle reenactments, assassinations, mass murder, slavery, dungeons, and ghost walks. It is a diverse list of horrors, though one key aspect of Seaton's definition remains constant: the idea that tourists are "wholly, or partially, motivated by a desire for actual or symbolic encounters with death" (Seaton 1996, 240). Given this parameter, this chapter does *not* fit neatly within the increasingly standardized definitions of dark tourism in which tourists actively seek out these encounters. Many visitors go to the Cliffs to enjoy the sublime beauty of the landscape, and only once they are there do they contemplate death and dying. I hope this analysis adds to the literature by proposing that we might broaden the scope of the discussion. Extending the definition to include leisurely, accidental encounters with death and dying seems productive. Sometimes we seek beauty but are instead faced with mortality.

The tragedy of death and dying at the Cliffs of Moher and the prominent discourse about it are examples of the failure of tourism to create a singular, sanitized interpretive frame about what this landscape is "all about," despite the forceful attempt to do so. Death and the recognition of the possibility of death resist the disciplining of the tourist enclave. The Cliffs of Moher Experience may represent a new Irish ideology, one that is decidedly embedded in the (now-defunct) Celtic Tiger era—consumerist, postmodern, hyper-real, glossy, and wealthy—but the enforcement of this new cultural regime at the site has not been hegemonic. The "monologic certitude" (Bruner and Gorfain 1984) of the new interpretive center has been resisted by local entrepreneurs, businesspeople, musicians, and the culture at large (Kaul 2012, 2014). The recent redevelopment of the site by tourism authorities attempts to control and discipline visitors' bodies in their interaction *with* the landscape and provides meaning to visitors *about* the landscape. In one sense, this chapter is about how that control fails.

NOTES

1. This research was generously supported by a Moore Institute Visiting Fellowship at the National University of Ireland in Galway and a grant from the Augustana College Friestat Center for Peace Studies. This chapter is based on dozens of visits to the Cliffs of Moher as well as many conversations with local residents, visitors, and employees at the site over the course of twelve years. Because of the sensitive nature of the topics, no names are used.

2. Experts in the mental health professions and "suicidology" are far more equipped than I am to draw conclusions about these issues (cf. a comprehensive report for the Men's Health Forum by Richardson, Clarke, and Fowler 2013). Honkasalo and Tuominen divide the scholarly approaches to understanding suicide into three categories: as a medical problem

to be "cured," as a "social phenomenon" (à la Durkheim), and as "a human act embedded in a cultural context" that seeks to understand the grassroots meaning given to the act at the local level (Honkasalo and Touminen 2014, 8–9). I follow Honkasalo and Tuominen in taking this third approach. I am not the first to develop an "anthropology of suicide" in Ireland. A 2012 special edition of the *Irish Journal of Anthropology* focused solely on suicide in relation to the LGBT community (Bryan and Maycock 2012), gender differences (Sheehan 2012), masculinity (Garcia 2012), and the Traveller community (Walker 2012).

3. Cornelius O'Brien, the local landlord, had the original fencing built in the 1830s out of flat Liscannor flagstones upended like grave markers all along the cliff edge. He also built a "folly" watchtower at the highest point of the Cliffs for friends who came to visit his estate.

REFERENCES

"Awards: The Atlantic Edge Exhibition." 2007. Association for Heritage Interpretation. http://www.ahi.org.uk/www/awards/view_details/3/award/view_details/20/.

Basso, Keith H. 1996. *Wisdom Sits in Places: Landscape and Language among the Western Apache*. Albuquerque: University of New Mexico Press.

Bender, Barbara. 1998. *Stonehenge: Making Space*. Oxford: Berg.

Bender, Barbara. 2001. "Introduction." In *Contested Landscapes: Movement, Exile, and Place*, ed. Barbara Bender and Margot Winer. Oxford: Berg. https://doi.org/10.1007/978-3-662-04419-3_1.

Bracken, Ali, and Pat Flynn. 2012. "Did She Come Here to Die: Cliffs of Moher Rescue Services on High Alert after 22-Year-Old Tourist Discusses Suicide Online." *Irish Daily Mail*, April 7, p. 12.

Bruner, Edward M., and Phyllis Gorfain. 1984. "Dialogic Narration and the Paradoxes of Masada." In *Text, Play, and Story: The Construction of Self and Society*, ed. Edward M. Bruner, 56–79. Washington, DC: American Ethnological Society.

Bryan, Audrey, and Paula Maycock. 2012. "Speaking Back to Dominant Constructions of LGBT Lives: Complexifying 'At Riskness' for Self-Harm and Suicidality among Lesbian, Gay, Bisexual, and Transgender Youth." *Irish Journal of Anthropology* 15 (2): 8–15.

Buck, Trudi, and Stavroula Pipyrou. 2014. "You Can Die but Once? Creativity, Narrative, and Epistemology in Western Death." *Mortality* 19 (3): 261–83. https://doi.org/10.1080/13576275.2014.929567.

Corcoran, Paul, and Ella Arensman. 2010. "A Study of the Irish System of Recording Suicide Deaths." *Crisis* 31 (4): 174–82. https://doi.org/10.1027/0027-5910/a000026.

Corcoran, Paul, Helen S. Keeley, Mary O'Sullivan, and Ivan J. Perry. 2004. "The Incidence and Repetition of Attempted Suicide in Ireland." *European Journal of Public Health* 14 (1): 19–23. https://doi.org/10.1093/eurpub/14.1.19.

Dann, Graham M.S., and Anthony V. Seaton, eds. 2001. *Slavery, Contested Heritage, and Thanatourism*. New York: Haworth Hospitality Press.

Deegan, Gordon. 2012a. "Clare Suicides Outweigh Road Deaths Tenfold." *Irish Examiner*, February 6. Accessed September 19, 2015. http://www.irishexaminer.com/ireland/clare-suicides-ouweigh-road-deaths-tenfold-182701.html.

Dunphy, Mark. 2014. "The Cliffs of Moher Visitor Experience Welcomes One Millionth Visitor." *Dunphy Public Relations*, October 14. Accessed September 18, 2015. https://www.cliffsofmoher.ie/the-cliffs-of-moher-visitor-experience-welcomes-one-millionth-visitor/.

Durkheim, Émile. 2002 [1897]. *Suicide: A Study in Sociology*. London: Routledge and Kegan Paul. https://doi.org/10.1522/cla.due.sui2.

Edensor, Tim. 2000. "Staging Tourism: Tourists as Performers." *Annals of Tourism Research* 27 (2): 322–44. https://doi.org/10.1016/S0160-7383(99)00082-1.

Edkins, Jenny. 2004. "Ground Zero: Reflections on Trauma, In/Distinction, and Response." *Journal for Cultural Research* 8 (3): 247–70. https://doi.org/10.1080/1479758042000264939.

Foucault, Michel. 1984. *The Foucault Reader*. Ed. and trans. Paul Rabinow. New York: Pantheon.

Gallagher, Anthony G., and Noel P. Sheehy. 1994. "Suicide in Rural Communities." *Journal of Community and Applied Social Psychology* 4 (3): 145–55. https://doi.org/10.1002/casp.2450040302.

Garcia, Felicia. 2012. "Coping and Suicide amongst 'the Lads': Expectations of Masculinity in Post-Traditional Ireland." *Irish Journal of Anthropology* 15 (2): 22–27.

Healy, Noel, Carena J. van Riper, and Stephen W. Boyd. 2016. "Low versus High Intensity Approaches to Interpretive Tourism Planning: The Case of the Cliffs of Moher, Ireland." *Tourism Management* 52: 574–83. https://doi.org/10.1016/j.tourman.2015.08.009.

Honkasalo, Marja-Liisa, and Miira Touminen. 2014. "Introduction." In *Culture, Suicide, and the Human Condition*, ed. Marja-Liisa Honkasalo and Miira Touminen. New York: Berghahn.

Kaul, Adam. 2006–7. "On 'Tradition': Between the Local and the Global in a Traditional Irish Music Scene." *Folk Life: The Journal of Ethnological Studies* 45 (1): 49–59. https://doi.org/10.1179/flk.2006.45.1.49.

Kaul, Adam. 2011. "The Village That Wasn't There: Appropriation, Domination, and Resistance." In *Ownership and Appropriation*, ed. Veronica Strang and Mark Busse, 239–59. Oxford: Berg.

Kaul, Adam. 2012. "Tourism in the West of Ireland: Solution to Economic Collapse or Part of the Problem?" *Practical Anthropology* 34 (3): 10–13. https://doi.org/10.17730/praa.34.3.p35qt81417110t30.

Kaul, Adam. 2014. "Music on the Edge: Busking at the Cliffs of Moher and the Commodification of a Musical Landscape." *Tourist Studies* 14 (1): 30–47. https://doi.org/10.1177/1468797613511684.

Lennon, John, and Malcolm Foley. 2000. *Dark Tourism*. London: Continuum.

Lucey, Siobhán, Paul Corcoran, Helen S. Keeley, Justin Brophy, Ella Arensman, and Ivan J. Perry. 2005. "Socio-Economic Change and Suicide: A Time-Series Study from the Republic of Ireland." *Crisis* 26 (2): 90–94. https://doi.org/10.1027/0227-5910.26.2.90.

Lyng, Stephen. 1990. "Edgework: A Social Psychological Analysis of Voluntary Risk Taking." *The American Journal of Sociology* 95 (4): 851–86.

Nietzsche, Friedrich. 1989 [1886]. *Beyond Good and Evil: A Prelude to a Philosophy of the Future*. Trans. Walter Kauffmann. New York: Vintage Books.

O'Toole, Fintan. 2007. "Taming the Cliffs of Moher." *Irish Times*, February 6, 16.

Parsons, Talcott. 1994 [1978]. "Death in the Western World." In *Death and Identity*, ed. Robert Fulton and Robert Bendiksen, 60–79. Philadelphia: Charles Press.

Phillips, David P. 1985. "The Werther Effect: Suicide, and Other Forms of Violence, Are Contagious." *Sciences* 25 (4): 32–39. https://doi.org/10.1002/j.2326-1951.1985.tb02929.x.

Phipps, Peter. 1999. "Tourists, Terrorists, Death, and Value." In *Travel Worlds: Journeys in Contemporary Cultural Politics*, ed. Ramninder Kaur and John Hutnyk, 74–93. London: Zed Books.

Pipyrou, Stavroula. 2014. "Narrating Death: Affective Reworking of Suicide in Rural Greece." *Social Anthropology* 22 (2): 189–99. https://doi.org/10.1111/1469-8676.12069.

Richardson, N., N. Clarke, and C. Fowler. 2013. *A Report on the All-Ireland Young Men and Suicide Project*. Men's Health Forum in Ireland.

Saris, A. Jamie. 2012. "Studying Suicide in Modern Ireland: New Directions and Old Conundrums." *Irish Journal of Anthropology* 15 (2): 6–7.

Seaton, Anthony V. 1996. "Guided by the Dark: From Thanatopsis to Thanatourism." *International Journal of Heritage Studies* 2 (4): 234–44. https://doi.org/10.1080/13527259608722178.

Seaton, Anthony V. 2009. "Thanatourism and Its Discontents: An Appraisal of a Decade's Work with Some Future Issues and Directions." In *The SAGE Handbook of Tourism Studies*, ed. Mike Robinson and Tazim Jamal, 521–42. London: Sage. https://doi.org/10.4135/9780857021076.n29.

Sharpley, Richard, and Phillip R. Stone, eds. 2009. *The Darker Side of Travel: The Theory and Practice of Dark Tourism*. Buffalo, NY: Channel View.

Sheehan, Cormac. 2012. "The Gender Paradox and Stories from the Edge of Living." *Irish Journal of Anthropology* 15 (2): 16–21.

Skinner, Jonathan. 2010. "Introduction: Writings on the Dark Side of Travel." *Journeys* 11 (1): 1–28. https://doi.org/10.3167/jys.2010.110101.

Spellissy, Sean. 1996. *Suicide: The Irish Experience*. Blarney, Ireland: On Stream.

Stone, Phillip R. 2011. "Dark Tourism: Towards a New Post-Disciplinary Research Agenda." *International Journal of Tourism Anthropology* 1 (3–4): 318–32. https://doi.org/10.1504/IJTA.2011.043713.

Sturken, Marita. 2007. *Tourists of History: Memory, Kitsch, and Consumerism from Oklahoma City to Ground Zero*. Durham, NC: Duke University Press. https://doi.org/10.1215/9780822390510.

Taylor, Lawrence. 1989. "Bas InEirrin: Cultural Constructions of Death in Ireland." *Anthropological Quarterly* 62 (4): 175–87. https://doi.org/10.2307/3317614.

Walker, Mary Rose. 2012. "An Explorative Study of Episodes of Suicides between 2000 and 2006 within Traveller Culture." *Irish Journal of Anthropology* 15 (2): 28–32.

6

Tourism of Darkness and Light

Japanese Commemorative Tourism to Paradise

SHINGO IITAKA

The Palau Pacific Resort is one of the most luxurious seaside resorts in the Palau Islands of Micronesia. It is situated on Ngerekebesang Island in Koror, which had been the capital of the Republic of Palau until 2006. The resort was built in 1984 by a Japanese real estate agent and has been frequented by numerous visitors from nearby Asian countries and the West. The guests enjoy a variety of facilities such as a private beach, pool and Jacuzzi, dive center, athletic gym, fishpond, nature trail, and duty-free shops. The resort's private beach lies toward the Rock Islands, the southern part of which was registered as a World Heritage Site in 2012 and is well-known as a mecca for divers from all over the world. Walking along this beach, a visitor reaches a small jetty where the entire beach comes into view. Here stands a small monument that could easily be overlooked. Although there is no information about the builder, this marker is titled "Southwest Seaplane Base Arakabesan Island." "Arakabesan" is a Romanized word for Ngerekebesang, derived from a Japanese Katakana word that was used during the Japanese administration.

Japan had administered Palau and other Micronesian islands north of the equator except Guam, which was called Nan'yō Guntō (South Seas Islands), from 1914 to 1945 (Peattie 1988). As the South Seas Bureau (Nan'yō-chō), which was established in Koror in 1922, and its related organizations promoted immigration to Micronesia, the population of Japanese immigrants grew rapidly and outnumbered the native population by the mid-1930s. The majority of Japanese immigrants were from Okinawa. They were particularly concentrated in the Mariana Islands and the

DOI: 10.5876/9781607327295.c006

Palau Islands and were engaged in agriculture, fisheries, mining, and other industries to exploit island resources (Purcell 1976). During the Pacific War (1941–45), Micronesia became a violent battlefield. The monument lies within the resort property because the entire island used to be in service of the military of the Empire of Japan during the Pacific War.

Referring to the colonial history, the inscription on the monument says: "This historic site was built in 1934 by South Seas Development Company when the first commercial air route was anticipated. Then during World War II the Japanese used this for military purposes . . . The small hill beside is where the control tower and associated small buildings were. A majority of the structures on this island were military in nature during the Japanese occupation of Palau."[1] In fact, there are remains of another seaplane base on Ngerekebesang. The site is now used as an open space for local and national festivals and events. Palauans call this place "Sukōjyō," a borrowed but accented Japanese word that is probably derived from *hikōjyō* (air base) in Japanese. There are other reminders of the Pacific War on this island as well. In the farms owned by Palauans are big craters made by bombs from numerous US air raids. Disposal of unexploded bombs and munitions continues to this day. The resort facility may have covered up some physical remains of the war, yet war memory could not be erased completely in Ngerekebesang.[2]

This illustration suggests that leisure and death coexist in contemporary tourism in Palau. Such an odd combination in tourism is common in Palau, which was once a violent battlefield of the Pacific War but is now famous for its beautiful ocean and attracts leisure tourists from around the world. With so much death and destruction in the past of its beautiful islands and waters, the image of darkness and light is complexly intertwined with tourism in Palau.

With reference to the recent studies on dark tourism (e.g., Lennon and Foley 2000; Urry 2004; Stone 2006; Sharpley 2006; Bowman and Pezzullo 2009; Skinner 2012; Azuma 2013), this chapter examines the ways the development of tourism and remembrance of/forgetting about the Pacific War in postwar Palau are deeply entangled. I chose three different kinds of Japanese tours to Palau: memorial tours, sightseeing tours, and heritage tours. Memorial tours to Palau began in the late 1960s among Japanese veterans and former immigrants who experienced and survived the war. Since the 1980s, the image of paradise that blossomed with the growth of tourism in Palau has attracted global tourists anxious to see one of the most beautiful marine and island habitats in the world. Heritage tours to war sites and war relics have developed recently in accordance with a growing consciousness about the cultural and historical value of the war sites in Palau. More often than not, Palau's tourism tends to be characterized as lighter or darker tourism, depending on whether the focus of tours is on leisurely activities and natural beauty in paradise or on the traces of deaths that occurred during the Pacific War. However, in practice, actual tours frequently incorporate both darkness and light to some degree.

As previous studies on postwar tourism in Micronesia have pointed out (e.g., Yamashita 2000; Yamaguchi 2007; Dvorak 2011), the general public in Japan in the postwar era, having partially inherited the pre-war image of Nan'yō (South Sea), (re)constructed Palau and other Micronesian islands as a paradise. Shinji Yamashita observed that "the popular image of the Pacific for many Japanese is that of a 'south seas paradise' with beautiful ocean and sunshine, where Japanese middle-class tourists can escape their busy and stressful urban lives in Japan" (Yamashita 2000, 441–42). Considering the general character of tourism as an escape from daily routines (Urry 1990), it is natural for Japanese visitors to overlook the colonial ties between Micronesia and the Japan of the past and forget the tragedy that occurred during the Pacific War.

However, narratives of paradise in Palau are always contradicted by alternative narratives of death caused by the Pacific War, just as "death and dying . . . resist and punctuate the dominant tourism narrative" on the Cliffs of Moher in Ireland, which is a magnificent tourist site but also a site of death (see Kaul, this volume). Japanese tourists, including those who stay at the Palau Pacific Resort, cannot escape from the dark side of the Palau Islands, which pops up in the midst of their tours, even though they come to enjoy the bright ocean and white sandy beach. At the same time, it is also common that tourists are fascinated with encountering the looming danger associated with death or dying. Kaul shows in chapter 5 that visitors to the Cliffs of Moher "consistently walk right past the signage to the very edge" or "joke about jumping or falling off the cliff." Adams also depicts in chapter 4 the way tourists, such as those who visit Tana Toraja, are fascinated with corpses in death rituals. It is clear that "various technological and commercial factors involved in reshaping tourists' encounters with death also shape tourist encounters with relaxation and pleasure" (Bowman and Pezzullo 2009, 190). A recent study on dark tourism in Fukushima, where serious accidents at nuclear power plants occurred after the mega-earthquake on March 11, 2011, also argues that various tourist facilities are necessary to attract visitors and preserve memories of the disaster (Azuma 2013). Dark tourism in Palau is closely related to the commercial tourism that has developed in the post–Pacific War era. With commercial tourism facilities, Japanese visitors who come to Palau to mourn the war dead also give themselves to the beautiful islands and oceans that highlight a poignant memory of the wartime.

DYING IN PALAU

As the war advanced closer to Micronesia, heavy militarization of its islands took place. Male Japanese immigrants were drafted locally while women, children, and elder immigrants who had no combat capacity were ordered to evacuate to Japan (Imaizumi 2005, 10). Yet the majority of immigrants remained on the islands and was involved in the battle, especially after the landings by US forces in the Marianas in June and July 1944 and in Peleliu and Angaur of the Palau Islands in September 1944 (BBS 1967, 1968).

According to the former Ministry of Health and Welfare, the number of deceased military personnel from Japan in "the central Pacific area," covering Guam, the Bonin Islands, and other Micronesian islands, was estimated to be 197,600 (BBS 1967, table 1). On Peleliu Island, known as one of the deadliest battlefields in the Pacific War, the death toll of Japanese military personnel was 10,022. Casualties among US military personnel on Peleliu were also heavy: 1,684 deaths out of 28,484 troops. On Angaur Island, 1,150 Japanese soldiers and servicemen fought to the death. Meanwhile, many of the Japanese military personnel stationed on Babeldaob Island starved to death, since the supply lines from the main island of Japan were cut off. In the Palau Islands a total of 10,732 army and 5,278 navy personnel from Japan died (BBS 1967, table 1).

Although there are no official records on the number of civilian deaths, the loss was still overwhelming. According to Stephen Murray's (2013, 52–54)estimation, about 5,000 Japanese, Asian, and Micronesian civilians died on Babeldaob Island, Palau. They were forced to live in remote jungles to escape from air raids, making non-indigenous people more vulnerable to death from sickness or malnutrition. When the Palau Battle ended, 6,571 Japanese civilians and 3,179 military laborers surrendered, many in a state of extreme hunger (BBS 1968, 235). When the war ended, all the people from Japan and its overseas territories, both civilians and military personnel, were evacuated from Micronesia by the US military administration (Richard 1957, 34–41).

MOURNING THE WAR DEAD IN PARADISE

Until the mid-1960s, US government policy closed Micronesia to travel or development from outside. Japanese citizens' travel to foreign countries was also restricted immediately after the war. Thus, it was not until the late 1960s that Japanese veterans and former immigrants were allowed to visit Micronesia to conduct memorial services for the war dead. These memorial tour groups are generally called *ireidan* in Japanese.[3] One of the most influential figures among the organizers of the tours to Palau in the initial stage was Hiroshi Funasaka, a survivor of the Angaur Battle. He is known as a writer of war histories in Palau, such as *Falling Blossoms* (Funasaka 1986).[4] The first memorial tour to Palau was organized in 1968, with around fifty total participants. They conducted memorial services and built war memorials on

Koror, Peleliu, and Angaur. The visitors had very little information about Palau, since its tourism industry was not well developed. Despite that fact, the tour was successful because of the assistance offered by local Palauans with Japanese ancestry. Minoru Ueki, a Palauan with a career as a medical doctor, a businessman, and a politician, who ultimately became Palau's ambassador to Japan in 2009, helped Japanese travelers with obtaining tourist visas and offered accommodation at his hotel facilities (Nihon Saura Kai 1968, 14).

Almost all Palauans with Japanese ancestry had Japanese fathers and Palauan mothers. Having lost their paternal ties when Japanese immigrants were evacuated to Japan, these Palauans formed an association called the Palau Cherry Blossom Association (Palau Sakura Kai) for mutual aid, such as exchanging information to locate Japanese relatives and helping each other find employment in the local public sector.[5] The association welcomed Japanese visitors for practical reasons: to restore relationships with their paternal relatives in Japan (Iitaka 2009). However, in the report of Funasaka's memorial tour to Palau, the association is represented as a group of pro-Japanese people "who have never lost the Japanese spirit and kept Japanese tradition" (Nihon Sakura Kai 1968, 8). Despite the veteran's overstatement, it is noteworthy that the Palauans' voluntary association functioned as a conduit for Japanese memorial tour groups at the earlier stage of the postwar memorial tours.

The 1968 memorial tour came to mourn the souls of dead Japanese soldiers. Tour participants visited major war sites on Peleliu, Angaur, and Babeldaob. They also visited remnants of the Japanese administration in Koror, such as the ruins of administrative buildings, the old Japanese graveyard, and the remains of Shinto shrines. Concurrently, the tour provided elements of leisure. When they landed on Palau, one of the participants, who had lived in Palau and been drafted locally during the war, expressed nostalgia in a warm remembrance of a place he found very much changed: "Once, a place called Nan'yō Ginza was very busy, but now it is declining in prosperity . . . No more Nan'yō Hotel here" (Nihon Sakura Kai 1968, 18). On the boat to Peleliu, they enjoyed the beautiful scenery and passed by the ship in which the famous Japanese actor Toshirō Mifune stayed to film the movie *Hell in the Pacific*.[6] Before the return to Japan, the Palau Cherry Blossom Association arranged a farewell party with a large amount of Japanese and Palauan food (Nihon Sakura Kai 1968, 29).

Former Japanese immigrants have also visited Micronesia since the late 1960s to conduct memorial services for the war dead. Unlike war veterans' memorial tours, which tend to be discontinued when core members grow older and die, some former immigrants, most noticeably Okinawan returnees, have maintained memorial tours and passed down war memory to the next generation. Although the number of attendees is declining, they still conduct memorial tours every year (Iitaka 2015).[7]

In September 2013, I joined a memorial tour to Palau organized by Okinawan returnees. There were nineteen participants. Fourteen were Okinawan returnees from Micronesia and their descendants: the oldest participant was in his nineties, and the younger ones were in their thirties. The rest of the participants included a Buddhist priest, a tour conductor, and researchers. Okinawan returnees and their descendants have strong motivation to keep visiting Palau, not only because they lost family members or colleagues during the war but because they maintain vivid memories of their peaceful life from the pre-war era. They have both dark and light memories of Palau.

The six-day tour, from Okinawa via Taipei to Palau, was arranged by a travel agency in Okinawa and was advertised in a local newspaper to attract potential participants. During their time in Koror, participants stayed at the Palasia Hotel, a large hotel under Taiwanese management, with a duty-free shop, a gym, restaurants, and an onsite Japanese travel agency. The memorial services, assisted by the Palau Cherry Blossom Association, were conducted on the second day at the old Japanese graveyard in Koror and on the third day at the public cemetery on Peleliu (figure 6.1). In both places there is *Okinawa no Tou*, a memorial column for the war dead. The memorial services were solemn and involved a Buddhist-style ceremony. The service held in Koror included a prayer by a local Catholic priest. The tour is dark in these aspects of the practice. At the same time, in the speeches delivered by former immigrants at the ceremony, the light of the Palau Islands was often mentioned together with the tragedy that happened during the Pacific War. At the ceremony on Koror, the oldest participant, in his nineties, said he felt sorry for the spirits of the deceased since this could be the last spirit-consoling tour to Palau. He added, however, that beautiful Palau was eternal and their second homeland. The youngest participant, in her thirties, also said in her speech that she could not believe great tragedy had happened during the Pacific War on these beautiful islands.

As if to confirm the lighter aspect of tourism in Palau, the participants also behaved as tourists during their stay. Since the schedule was open except for the two memorial services, they had enough time to enjoy what Palau offers leisure visitors. Some of the participants strolled around the places they had once lived or explored sites where their parents or grandparents had lived. They joined a bus tour arranged by a local travel agency in Koror and visited the Coral Reef Center, a local museum, gift shops, and a shopping center. Some participants took a sightseeing flight to enjoy the panoramic view of the Rock Islands from the sky. On the way back to Okinawa, the group stayed in Taipei for a one-day sightseeing tour on a chartered bus. The lighthearted elements of leisure were mixed in with the memorial practices, where the darker atmosphere permeated the participants. The beautiful landscape of Palau seemed to make the nostalgic memories of the peaceful prewar life and the

FIGURE 6.1. Okinawans' memorial service on Peleliu. Author photo.

grim memories of the dreadful wartime all the more poignant, as represented in the speech presented at the memorial service.

TOURISTS' ENCOUNTERS WITH DEATH IN PARADISE

The development of memorial tours in the 1960s was followed by the rise of mass tourism in Palau. Diving and other marine activities started to develop on a full scale in the 1970s. Francis Toribiong was the first Palauan who brought dive compressors and scuba tanks to Palau, and he opened a dive shop called Fish 'n Fins.[8] The tourism industry flourished in the 1980s when Palau became a self-governing political entity, even though domestic politics were unstable because of arguments over the future political relationship with the United States (Rechebei and McPhetres 1997, 323). Numerous businesses catering to the tourist trade opened in central Koror, including the Palau Pacific Resort in 1984. The number of visitors entering Palau was 5,640 in 1980, but it rose to 13,371 in 1985 and to 23,398 in 1990 (Yamashita 2000, 438).

Since tourism along with fishing was regarded as an important local industry for Palau's future development, the new republic strongly enforced tourism policies after its 1994 independence. Palau's attractiveness as a scuba-diving destination became known worldwide. As a result, the number of tourists grew rapidly in the late 1990s and 2000s. It reached 89,161 in 2004, when Palau hosted the Ninth

Festival of Pacific Arts.[9] In 2012 the Rock Islands Southern Lagoon was registered as a World Heritage Site for the "exceptional variety of habitats within a relatively limited area" and other criteria.[10] The number of tourists that year reached 115,629 (ROP 2013, table 10.3d, 10.3e, 10.3f), while the local population was around 20,000, including about 5,000 foreign workers such as Filipinos and Bangladeshi.

Memorial tours mentioned above tend to be regarded as an exceptional type of tour arranged by non-typical visitors, but in fact the development of tourism in Palau involved dealing with the deaths from the Pacific War from the start. In the 1980s, Fish 'n Fins' founder, Francis Toribiong, together with the German wreck diver Klaus Lindemann, investigated Japanese war shipwreck sites around the Rock Islands. They rediscovered over thirty Japanese warships sunk during the US Navy's air raid in late March 1944, called Operation Desecrate I. Along with regular diving tours, the wreck dive is also a popular activity within contemporary tourism in Palau. On the sixtieth anniversary of the Palau Battle, an eighty-seven-year-old Japanese veteran dove to see the Japanese naval oil tanker *Irou*, which was sunk on March 30, 1944, and discovered in 1995. He conducted a memorial service for his fellow soldiers who had died there. The activity was also part of the "2nd Wrexpedition," an event organized by Fish 'n Fins to enhance understanding of shipwrecks in Palau as a tourist attraction (Genova 2004, 7). In a local newspaper, the vice president of Palau at that time commented that it is "paying a respect to the dead so we can enjoy the peace and pleasure of diving" (Genova 2004, 7).

Even if tourists are not involved in wreck diving, they invariably encounter remnants of war and the image of death in tours to the Rock Islands. Local travel agencies, especially those that actively seek Japanese visitors, include visits to war sites in their tour plans. Thus, tourists are introduced to the darker side of Palau while placed within its lighter side, staying at hotels and enjoying the beautiful ocean. In August 2012 I joined a snorkeling tour to the Rock Islands with thirteen other tourists, mostly Japanese. On the way from the harbor in Koror to the Rock Islands, the boat stopped at a shallow point where a Japanese Zero fighter plane had sunk. Here, tourists could see the ruined body of the aircraft under water, which has been left behind since the war era. This encounter with a former Japanese warplane surprised the tourists in swimsuits who were eager to enjoy marine activities at the World Heritage Site, but they enthusiastically took photos of the ruin (figure 6.2).

The tourists did not have a deep feeling of grief or revulsion, even though they stopped at a war site where a Japanese warplane had fallen. Rather, it was important for them to take photos to show friends back home. It is true that the image of a "South Seas paradise" in postwar Japan was constructed and was possible as a result of collective amnesia about the Pacific War, which contributed to the flourishing of mass tourism in postwar Micronesia (e.g., Yamaguchi 2007). At the same time,

FIGURE 6.2. Sunken Zero fighter plane and tourists. Author photo.

many recent tourists know the broad outlines of what happened in Micronesia during the Pacific War from guidebooks and websites. The Japanese visitors taking photos of the Zero fighter was typical tourist behavior that represented an attempt to confirm the knowledge they had gained in advance. In addition, this odd encounter with death seemed to spice up their leisure activities and offer variety to the possibly fatiguing image of paradise. This is an example of commercialization of death, which covers the lighter spectrum of dark tourism (Stone and Sharpley 2008, 578), even though this type of tour potentially has an educational impact on the participants.

After the encounter with the submerged Zero fighter plane, the tour participants refreshed themselves and prepared to go to the Milky Way Lagoon, where they packed their bodies with white sand for cosmetic purpose; swam with millions of harmless jellyfish in Jellyfish Lake, famous for its unique ecosystem; marveled at schools of tropical fauna and corals at a couple of easy snorkeling points; then took lunch and a rest on an uninhabited island. On the way back, the participants were guided to other war sites. The boat passed by a small rocky island full of ruins that looked like gasoline drums. The tour guide, after explaining how the battles developed in the Rock Island area during the war, said that a small cave on the island had been used by Japanese military as a base for war supplies. The participants were surprised to know that these relics had never been removed, but their interest was slight since the ruins were too far away to allow them to take photos and looked unattractive. Besides, the tourists were tired after a long day on the water. Their attitude toward war sites was capricious; they were mainly concerned about the lagoon area registered as a World Heritage Site. Occasional encounters with the image of death were just another item on their list of activities in Palau.

HERITAGE TOURISM AT SITES OF WAR

Along with tours to underwater sites of death, tours to battlefields are developing today. The trend reflects a growing consciousness toward war sites among Palauans. The Historic Preservation Office in Palau has registered some sites related to the Pacific War as historic sites, along with indigenous historic sites that trace their origins to prehistoric times. In addition, local governments and travel agencies have started to make use of war artifacts as tourism resources.[11]

Peleliu Island, the bloodiest battlefield, offers rich resources for battlefield tours. Along with the ruins of battle tanks, a gun battery, storehouses, and Japanese headquarters, visitors are guided to the place where the Japanese commander committed suicide at the end of the battle. They also visit a local graveyard where various war memorials built by war veterans, voluntary associations, and bereaved families stand, as well as the southern end of the islands where in 1985 the Japanese government built an impressive stone structure and in 2015 the Japanese imperial couple visited for a memorial service. Peleliu attracts visitors from the United States, too. There are US memorials near "Orange Beach" where the US Marine Corps landed. Another memorial stands on "Bloody Nose Ridge" where fierce battles were fought. The US National Park Service intended to turn a vast area of the island into a memorial park, but the plan was not realized since the area overlapped private lands that belonged to Palauans (Murray 2016, 182–87). Although the actual battle ended more than seventy years ago, the symbolic struggle between Japan and the United States over war memory seems to continue.

Palauans are also playing an important role. There is Peleliu War Museum, a local museum managed by Peleliu State, whose building structure used to be an old Japanese storage bunker. Visitors find a space where war remnants such as guns, bullets, glass bottles, dishes, fabric, and other artifacts—most of which were collected by local Palauans—are arranged casually but carefully. Photography within the museum was prohibited but has recently been allowed. Here, war remnants do not belong to those from the countries that were engaged in the war but are tightly appropriated or even possessed by Palauans (cf. Busse and Strang 2011; Ishimura 2010).

Likewise, a different type of heritage tour was planned on Angaur Island, which was also a battlefield on which the US military landed. The island had been mined for phosphate during the German administration era (1899–1914), throughout the Japanese administration era until right before the war, and for a few years in the postwar era (Hanlon 1998, 63–73; Iitaka 2013, 16–17). The Oceanic Wildlife Society (OWS, a nonprofit organization based in Japan) and the local government of Angaur Island created a tour plan that combined natural environment tours with battlefield tours, joining in a single scheme the two very different types of tourism in Palau.

Since its establishment in 1998, the OWS has been focusing on the development of environmental awareness and ecotourism in Asia and the Pacific region. Another unique feature of the OWS is the scope of its activities, which cover former war sites such as Midway Atoll and Angaur.[12] The Angaur State Nature Park Project was launched in 2001 to make use of the entire island for tourism. This project was designed by Yōji Kurata, a Japanese oceanologist who was one of the founders and the vice president of OWS. He was also a survivor of the Angaur Battle and has led memorial activities for the war dead. The local counterpart was Angaur State; an Angaurese with Japanese ancestry, whose father had assisted Japanese memorial tour groups, supported the project. In 2004 the Angaur State Nature Park visitor center opened in a renovated former elementary school building provided by Angaur State. The center held exhibitions of the island's fauna and flora as well as historical photos from the Japanese administration era and the Pacific War. It was managed by Kurata and volunteer workers who were in charge of recording nature on the island, although they were not permanently stationed on Angaur.

The tour plan introduced visitors to historic sites from the Japanese administration era (1914–44) and the Pacific War period when the United States and the Empire of Japan fought against each other (1944) while also giving visitors the chance to appreciate rare fauna and flora on the island. Since Angaur is a flat, small island of raised coral, it is easy for visitors to go around by bike or on foot. Highlights of the tour included the remains of wrecked US airplanes, an artificial pond from the mining era, old mining company factories, traces of railroads that used to transport minerals, the ruin of a Japanese shrine, a lighthouse destroyed by the US naval bombardment, and memorials erected by Japanese,[13] Americans, and Angaurese. Numbered boards were installed at some of these spots as guideposts for visitors. Among these visiting spots, some places are registered as historic sites by Palau's Historic Preservation Office. These sites include the Angaurese monument built near the cave where about 200 Angaurese lived during the war and remains of the phosphate-drying factory built during the German administration.

Some relics are not situated at their original positions but have been relocated and preserved as tourism resources: for example, wrecked US airplanes were collected in one place, which was named the Airplanes' Graveyard (figure 6.3). Such relocations of war relics had already occurred on Peleliu and other places.[14] In

FIGURE 6.3. Airplanes' Graveyard on Angaur. Author photo.

general, arguments could develop over the authenticity of relocated artifacts if they are not in their original places (Stone 2006, 151). Yet no one in the local community seems to regard the relocation of the war relics as problematic, even though Micronesians highly value "physical remains associated with people and events of the past" (Falgout, Poyer, and Carucci 2008, 32). This shows that war relics do not strongly attract Paluans and still belong to foreigners while, at the same time, the need to use war relics as resources in the tourism industry is greater.

It is noteworthy that the project uniquely combined nature and battlefield tours: a mixture of hiking, nature watching, tours of historical site, and tours of war remains. Such disparate activities did not seem to confuse tourists. Just as the participants in memorial tours were deeply touched by the beautiful landscape while mourning the war dead, participants in heritage tours also vacillated between the darker and lighter sides of Palau, which has a complex history. However, the Angaur State Nature Park Project did not last long. One of the primary reasons for its failure was the difficult access to the area. The Cessna plane service that used to operate between central Palau and Angaur Island has not been available for more than fifteen years. Now, visitors can reach the island through only one ocean route, which is not easy to navigate since Angaur Island lies outside the protection of Palau's barrier reef. The failure of the Angaur State Nature Park Project tells us that battlefield tours need to be combined with commercial offerings, such as convenient transportation and comfortable accommodations (Bowman and Pezzullo 2009, 190).[15]

CONCLUSION

The term *dark tourism*, generally defined as tours to destinations where death and tragedy occurred in history, is too obscure to identify a particular type of tourism, as Michael Bowman and Phaedra Pezzullo (2009) pointed out in an article titled "What Is So 'Dark' about Dark Tourism." Philip Stone developed the idea of a dark tourism spectrum in which "particular sites may be conceivably 'darker' than others, dependent upon various defining characteristics, perceptions, and product" (Stone 2006, 146). There is a danger of essentialization in labeling particular type of tours associated with death sites as dark tourism. The binary oppositions such as "serious or frivolous, educational or entertaining, authentic or inauthentic, and historically accurate and edifying or devoted to nostalgia and tourist kitsch" dismiss deep connections between play and death in tourists' behavior and experiences (Bowman and Pezzullo 2009, 195).

As I investigated in this chapter, the three forms of tourism in Palau—whether memorial tours, standard sightseeing tours, or heritage tours—encounter death to some degree, regardless of whether the tourists are prepared for it. At the same time, all three types of tourism incorporate leisure in different ways. Rather than remain at odds with each other, Palau's dark tourism and light tourism are complementary. Traveling for leisure and touring sites of death are not separate activities but rather are integrated in tourists' itineraries. The image of death seems to be a tangent of leisure (Urry 2004, 206; Skinner 2012, 16).

Japanese veterans and former immigrants came back to Palau for memorial services while also frequently enjoying various elements of commercial tourism during their visits instead of devoting all of their energies to serious mourning of the war dead. Some former Japanese immigrants simultaneously returned for the lighter side of Palau, such as their happy memories from the prewar era. The speeches delivered by former immigrants at the memorial services often referred to the lighter side of Palau. The more strongly they felt about the tragic destruction and loss from the war, the more deeply they were touched by the ocean and nature.

Contemporary tourists from the postwar generation seek out lighter tours to the tropics, with bright sun over the ocean and white beaches, yet while doing so, they also stray into the darker side of the paradise. The encounter with the underwater Zero fighter plane during the Rock Island tour offered a striking counterpoint to those engrossed in enjoyment of marine leisure activities. Yet, since the image of death was commercialized in the context and did not pose an immediate danger, these tourists eagerly took photos from the boat to capture their visit. Recent heritage tours deliberately combine the image of death with the image of paradise. War remains have come to be considered heritage, which attracts tourists with no direct war experience and provides tourism resources to a local society that has little industry—although in the case of Angaur, local residents are not much involved in the tour project.

Death became a commodity for consumption in the late modern world (Lennon and Foley 2000, 3). Various technological and commercial factors contributed to the commercialization of death, which resulted in the entanglement of leisure and death in tourism (Bowman and Pezzullo 2009, 190). The flourish of dark tourism is also fueled by guests' motivation to consume the image of death as well as hosts' motivation to (re-)present the death sites (Sharpley 2006, 14). Palau's tourism of darkness and light demonstrates that these motivations intersect on the sites. If there is a strong demand to visit death sites, either by Japanese veterans and former immigrants who come back to console the war dead or postwar generations who are fascinated by the Pacific War legacy, Palau tourism agents offer visits to shipwrecks, battlefields, and war memorials and provide comfortable facilities. Even if Japanese tourists are not motivated to visit death sites, there will be an accidental supply of such sites, as in the case of the Rock Island tour.

In addition to the factors pertaining to late modernity or postmodernity, historical factors are also important in investigating the development of tourism in Palau. The islands experienced a turbulent colonial history. Palau has been a colony of Japanese settlers, a battlefield during the Pacific War, an important strategic point for the United States during the Cold War era, and a paradise for world tourists in the postwar era. Since various strangers such as settlers, soldiers, and tourists have crossed the beach in Palua's modern history, the landscape is enlivened by complexity, with many layers of meanings (cf. Mio 2010; Camacho 2011). Thus, Japanese visitors to Palau inevitably embark on a voyage through time and cultures and thus cross the boundary between leisure and death (cf. Denning 2004).

Finally, we must recognize that the Pacific War memory is tightly appropriated by local Palauans. The exhibition at the Peleliu War Museum, disordered but straightforward and heartfelt, provides an alternative image of death to visitors from Japan and the United States, who are accustomed to exhibitions with war stories told neatly and often in sanitized versions. Palauans' memories of war, which tend to be excluded from the contents of tourism, may have such potential. Japanese tourists might encounter alternative images of death when they leave the comfortable context of tourism. They are sometimes startled when addressed in fluent Japanese by older Palauans, who might tell stories about wartime experiences, such as their life in a refuge in the forest (*hinanba*, a borrowed word from Japanese meaning a shelter). The visitors may be astonished to listen to Palauan elders singing a mixture of Palauan and Japanese lyrics that describe their war experiences with specificity (Falgout, Poyer, and Carucci 2008). Further insight into the entanglement of Palauan memory and foreigners' memories of war is necessary before we can fully understand the entire range of experiences encountered by those who engage in journeys of darkness and light.

ACKNOWLEDGMENTS

I thank the editors of this book, Jonathan Skinner and Adam Kaul, for their comments on an earlier draft. I also thank Stephen Murray, who edited my English and provided comments on the Pacific War in Palau. Geoffrey White kindly introduced me to this collaborative project. This work was supported by JSPS KAKENHI grant no. 24720393 15K03049.

NOTES

1. The inscription is written in all capital letters without periods. I have rewritten it in lower case and added punctuation.

2. When the Japanese company started to build the resort, mud was leaking from inland into the sea as a result of the heavy use by the Japanese military and the damage caused by US air raids. The company website said that the development of the resort contributed to the recovery of the environment. https://www.tokyu-fudosan-hd.co.jp/csr/topics/discussion/index04.html, accessed April 1, 2015.

3. *Ireidan*'s main purpose is to conduct *ireisai* (spirit-consoling service), which is closely connected with the Japanese Buddhist tradition. The living family members are left with a religious duty to perform to make the departed souls (*rei*) of ancestors sacred enough to protect their descendants.

4. The original Japanese version, titled *Eirei no Zekkyo* (Screams of a Fallen Hero), was published in 1966 (Funasaka 1966). The royalties from this book were used to build war memorials in Palau.

5. Although the matrilineal social system and frequent adoption in Palau functioned as a safety net for Palauans with Japanese ancestry, they needed to help each other since they lacked support networks through paternal ties. See Iitaka (2009, 17).

6. This is a movie about two soldiers, one Japanese and one American, marooned on a deserted island, where they struggle with each other for survival. The movie was directed by John Boorman and released in 1968. Just two actors, Mifune and Lee Marvin, are featured in the film.

7. Okinawans have strong motivation since they had such horrific wartime experiences in Micronesia as well as in Okinawa. In addition, they have different viewpoints, as they were discriminated against by other Japanese immigrants. See Iitaka (2015).

8. See the Fish 'n Fins website, accessed April 1, 2015, http://www.fishnfins.com/v2/en/history.html.

9. The Festival of Pacific Arts has been held every four years since 1972. It was originally conceived by the governing conference of the Secretariat of the Pacific Community as "an attempt to combat the erosion of traditional customary practices." http://www.spc.int/hdp/index.php?option=com_content&task=view&id=24&Itemid=42, accessed April 1, 2015.

10. See UNESCO's website, accessed April 1, 2015, http://whc.unesco.org/en/list/1386.

11. War sites on Babeldaob Island became more accessible in the 2000s when the highway funded by the Compact of Free Association with the United States was built. In Ngerechelong State there are ruins of an old Japanese lighthouse that Palauans call "Todai," a borrowed word from Japanese meaning a lighthouse. In Ngeremlengui State there are remains of gun batteries built to defend against the US bombardment. In Ngatpan State, where the headquarters of the 14th Division of the Japanese Imperial Army was situated, are the ruins of a huge radio tower.

12. In 1999 the OWS launched "the Midway Project," which planned to guide Japanese on eco-tours to the Midway Atoll, known as one of the largest albatross habitats in the world and now registered as a US National Wildlife Refuge. The atoll is also famous in Japan, since the Japanese Navy was soundly defeated in June 1942 off the islands. This project was terminated in 2002 when flight services to the islands ended. See the OWS website, accessed April 1, 2015, http://www.ows-npo.org/activity/midway/index.html.

13. In the postwar era, Japanese veterans and bereaved families built numerous memorials on the west coast of Angaur, where Japanese soldiers fought to the death. In 2010 these memorials were relocated to the east coast, since the local landowner, who was born in the postwar era, refused to renew the lease for the land.

14. For example, in Airai State a ruin of a communication station bombed during the war is surrounded by anti-aircraft guns collected from other parts of Palau during the filming of *Hell in the Pacific* in 1968.

15. A similar failure happened to tourism on Tinian, an island of the Marianas from where the B-29 bombers with atomic bombs left for Hiroshima and Nagasaki in August 1945. In contrast, Saipan of the Marianas, which has a more advanced tourism infrastructure than Tinian, has many tourists who visit Banzai cliff, where many Japanese committed suicide at the end of the battle (Ide 2013, 152–54).

REFERENCES

Azuma, Hiroki, ed. 2013. *Fukushima Daiichi Genpatsu Kankōchika Keikaku* (Tourizing Fukushima: The Fukuichi Kanko Project). Tokyo: Genron.

BBS (Bōeichō Bōeikenshūjyo Senshishitu). 1967. *Senshi Shōsho: Chūbu Taiheiyo Rikugun Sakusen dai 1: Mariana Gyokusai made* (War History Series: Japanese Army Operations in the Central Pacific Area, vol. 1: Fight to the Death in the Marianas). Tokyo: Asagumo Shinbun Sha.

BBS (Bōeichō Bōeikenshūjyo Senshishitu). 1968. *Senshi Shōsho: Chūbu Taiheiyo Rikugun Sakusen dai 2: Peleliu, Angaur, Iwojima* (War History Series: Japanese Army Operations in the Central Pacific Area, vol. 2: Peleliu, Angaur, and Iwo Jima). Tokyo: Asagumo Shinbun Sha.

Bowman, Michael, and Phaedra Pezzullo. 2009. "What's So 'Dark' about 'Dark Tourism'? Death, Tours, and Performance." *Tourist Studies* 9 (3): 187–202. https://doi.org/10.1177/1468797610382699.

Busse, Mark, and Veronica Strang. 2011. "Introduction: Ownership and Appropriation." In *Ownership and Appropriation*, ed. Veronica Strang and Mark Busse, 1–20. New York: Berg.

Camacho, Keith. 2011. *Cultures of Commemoration: The Politics of War, Memory, and History in the Mariana Islands*. Honolulu: University of Hawai'i Press. https://doi.org/10.21313/hawaii/9780824835460.001.0001.

Denning, Greg. 2004. *Beach Crossings: Voyaging across Times, Cultures, and Self*. Philadelphia: University of Pennsylvania Press.

Dvorak, Greg. 2011. "Atolls of Amnesia: Touring Japan's Pacific Past in the Marshall Islands." *Pacific Asia Inquiry* 2 (1): 69–84.

Falgout, Suzanne, Lin Poyer, and Laurence Carucci. 2008. *Memories of War: Micronesians in the Pacific War*. Honolulu: University of Hawai'i Press.

Funasaka, Hiroshi. 1966. *Eirei no Zekkyo* (Screams of a Fallen Hero). Tokyo: Bungeishunjū.

Funasaka, Hiroshi. 1986. *Falling Blossoms*. Translation of *Eirei no Zekkyo* (1966). Trans. Jeffery Rubin. Singapore: Times Books International.

Genova, Windsor John. 2004. "War Survivor Dives to Shipwreck." *Koror: Tia Belau*, April 2–9, 1, 7.

Hanlon, David. 1998. *Remaking Micronesia: Discourses over Development in a Pacific Territory, 1944–1982*. Honolulu: University of Hawai'i Press.

Ide, Akira. 2013. "Dark Tourism kara Kangaeru (Reflection from Dark Tourism)." In *Fukushima Daiichi Genpatsu Kankōchika Keikaku* (Tourizing Fukushima: The Fukuichi Kanko Project), ed. Hiroki Azuma, 144–57. Tokyo: Genron.

Iitaka, Shingo. 2009. "Kyū Nan'yō Guntō ni okeru Konketsuji no Association: Palau Sakura Kai (An Association of Half-Japanese and Half-Palauans in Micronesia: The Palau Cherry Blossom Association)." *Imin Kenkyū* (Immigration Studies) 5: 1–26.

Iitaka, Shingo. 2013. "Saipan Town on Angaur Island, Palau: Contact among Micronesian Mine Workers under the Japanese Administration." *Bulletin of the University of Kochi, Faculty of Cultural Studies* 62: 13–24.

Iitaka, Shingo. 2015. "Remembering *Nan'yō* from Okinawa: Deconstructing the Former Empire of Japan through Memorial Practices." *History and Memory* 27 (2): 126–51. https://doi.org/10.2979/histmemo.27.2.126.

Imaizumi, Yumiko. 2005. "Nan'yō Guntō Hikiagesha no Dantai Keisei to Sono Katsudo: Nihon no Haisen Chokugo wo Chūshin toshite (Problems among the Postwar Repatriates from Japanese Mandate Micronesia: Their Mainland and Okinawan Associations)." *Bulletin of the Historiographical Institute* 30: 1–44.

Ishimura, Tomo. 2010. "Palau ni okeru Sensō no 'Kioku' to 'Ikotsu': Senbotsusha Ikotsu Shūshū to Kōkogaku (War Memory and Ruins in Palau: Collecting Human Remains of War Dead and the Role of Archaeology)." *Kindai Kōko* (Archaeological Journal of Kanazawa University) 66: 1–3.

Lennon, John, and Malcolm Foley. 2000. *Dark Tourism: The Attraction of Death and Disaster*. London: Continuum.

Mio, Yuko. 2010. "Historical Recognition Constructed under Control of Multi-Layered Foreign Powers, Including Japan: An Anthropological Perspective." Paper presented at the CAPAS-MARC Workshop: Migration, Network, and Colonial Legacies in Pacific Islands, Taipei, Academia Sinica, November 11–12.

Murray, Stephen. 2013. "The Palauan Kirikomi-tai Suicide Bombers of World War II and the Siege of Babeldaob: A Reconsideration." *Pacific Asia Inquiry* 4 (1): 30–57.

Murray, Stephen. 2016. *The Battle over Peleliu: Islander, Japanese, and American Memories of War*. Tuscaloosa: University of Alabama Press.

Nihon Saura Kai. 1968. *Sakura ni Musubarete: Palau Shotō Ireidan no Kiroku* (Connected by Cherry Blossom: A Record of a Memorial Tour to the Palau Islands). Tokyo: Nihon Saura Kai.

Peattie, Mark. 1988. *Nan'yō: The Rise and Fall of the Japanese in Micronesia, 1885–1945*. Honolulu: University of Hawai'i Press.

Purcell, David, Jr. 1976. "The Economics of Exploitation: The Japanese in the Mariana, Caroline, and Marshall Islands 1915–1940." *Journal of Pacific History* 11 (3): 189–211. https://doi.org/10.1080/00223347608572301.

Rechebei, Elizabeth, and Samuel McPhetres, eds. 1997. *History of Palau: Heritage of an Emerging Nation*. Koror: Ministry of Education, Republic of Palau.

Richard, Dorothy. 1957. *United States Naval Administration of the Trust Territory of the Pacific Islands*, vol. 2: *The Postwar Military Government Era 1945–1947*. Washington, DC: Office of the Chief of Naval Operations.

ROP (Republic of Palau). 2013. *2013 Statistical Yearbook*. Koror: Bureau of Budget and Planning, Ministry of Finance, Republic of Palau.

Sharpley, Richard. 2006. "Shedding Light on Dark Tourism: An Introduction." In *The Darker Side of Travel: The Theory and Practice of Dark Tourism*, ed. Richard Sharpley and Philip Stone, 3–22. Bristol, UK: Channel View.

Skinner, Jonathan, ed. 2012. *Writing the Dark Side of Travel*. New York: Berghahn Books.

Stone, Philip. 2006. "A Dark Tourism Spectrum: Towards a Typology of Death and Macabre Related Tourist Sites, Attractions, and Exhibitions." *Tourism: An Interdisciplinary International Journal* 54 (2): 145–60. Accessed April 1, 2015. https://works.bepress.com/philip_stone/4/.

Stone, Philip, and Richard Sharpley. 2008. "Consuming Dark Tourism: A Thanatological Perspective." *Annals of Tourism Research* 35 (2): 574–95. http://doi:10.1016/j.annals.2008.02.003.

Urry, John. 1990. *The Tourist Gaze: Leisure and Travel in Contemporary Societies*. London: Sage.

Urry, John. 2004. "Death in Venice." In *Tourism Mobilities: Places to Play, Places in Play*, ed. Mimi Sheller and John Urry, 205–15. London: Routledge.

Yamaguchi, Makoto. 2007. *Guam to Nihonjin: Sensō wo Umetateta Rakuen* (Guam and Japanese: A Paradise Made by the Reclamation of the War). Tokyo: Iwanamishoten.

Yamashita, Shinji. 2000. "The Japanese Encounter with the South: Japanese Tourists in Palau." *Contemporary Pacific* 12 (2): 437–63. https://doi.org/10.1353/cp.2000.0071.

PART 3

Life, Decay, and the Sensual Experience of Death

7

Memento Mori and Tourist Encounters with Authentic Death in European Ossuaries

CYRIL SCHÄFER WITH RUTH MCMANUS

In a world that offers tourists simulated experiences of cremation (Chow 2015), it appears that an increasing number of individuals are pursuing a remarkably diverse array of encounters with mortality.[1] Indeed, much of the contemporary dark tourism literature echoes current trends in popular death discourse that accentuates an emerging openness and honesty surrounding death. Drawing on the work of authors such as Gorer (1965), Becker (1973), and Aries (1974), who noted that twentieth-century death was denied, sequestered, or taboo, this discourse acclaims an emerging societal shift that confronts rather than conceals human mortality (Staudt 2008). While the accuracy and analytical value of the death-denial thesis have been problematized (Kellehear 1984; Lee 2008; Zimmermann and Rodin 2004), this putative shift has been represented as an enlightened approach to death, inextricably linked to notions of "healthy," "natural," and "authentic" engagement with mortality (Schäfer 2014).

The trope of confrontation has become a recurring theme in the dark tourism discourse. Discussions of demand and visitor motivation, for example, have repeatedly emphasized that death and dying are sequestered in modern life and that dark tourism provides individuals with one significant way of engaging with fundamental questions of mortality. The rise of dark tourism has been explicitly linked to Western society's privatization, medicalization, and professionalization of death, with some authors declaring that this form of tourism has contributed to a contemporary revival of death in the public sphere (Stone 2009). Dark tourism sites not only provide spaces that mediate contemplations of mortality (Sharpley and Stone 2012; Stone and Sharpley 2008; Stone 2009, 2011) but also allow visitors to construct ontological frameworks in secular society (Stone 2012; Stone and Sharpley 2014). Authors such as Seaton (2009) have augmented these assessments, arguing that interpretations of dark tourism that privilege a sequestration thesis neglect the prevalence of death and dying in contemporary society. Rather than constituting a distinctly modern phenomenon that emerged in response to a societal denial of death, dark tourism (or what Seaton [2009] describes as thanatourism) can also be located in a historical tradition of thanatopsis (contemplation of death) that has evolved since the Middle Ages and the Christian cult of the dead (Seaton 1996, 240). Other authors, such as Walter (2009), have extended this debate by arguing that dark tourism sites are rarely spaces that promote prosaic encounters with mortality, tending to instead accentuate certain forms of human suffering and death.

This chapter specifically examines one form of dark tourism that centers on the display of skeletal remains in ossuaries or charnel houses. Stone and Sharpley (2014, 56) argue that sites that display the dead have long been associated with societal taboos but that these proscribed spaces are increasingly translucent in late modern society. A number of authors have similarly asserted that displays of the dead provide one of the few available means for people to explore their own death and broader meaning frameworks. Sayer (2010), for example, has argued that funerary archaeology is one of the ways people can encounter a corpse and ponder their own demise. Another form of display that has received significant academic scrutiny has been Günther von Hagen's *Body Worlds* exhibition featuring plastinated bodies. Some authors have argued that these de-personalized bodies privilege a scientific gaze (Walter 2004; Moore and Brown 2007), presenting a purified form of death that eliminated physical signs of putrefaction and posed no risk of contamination or decay (Desmond 2008). Others have argued that such exhibits also raise existential questions about life and death (Jagger, Dubek, and Pedretti 2012) and the transience of human life (Leiberich et al. 2006). At a popular level, charnel houses themselves have been the subject of recent non-fiction writing that reiterates the significance of confronting death through encounters with skeletal remains (Inge 2014).

By drawing on participant observation at ossuaries in Germany and the Czech Republic over a three-month period (January–March 2015), this chapter explicates some of these themes to examine a disconnect between organizers' and visitors' ways of seeking engagements with death that inform these encounters. On close inspection, this disconnect suggests a more complex and multilayered engagement than a simple shift from sequestering to confronting death.

A BRIEF HISTORY OF CHARNEL HOUSES

In Europe, charnel houses or ossuaries have been repositories for the remains of the dead since at least the twelfth century (Kenzler 2014, 12–13). Limited cemetery space and the Catholic belief in resurrection[2] (Walker Bynum, 1995) were two significant factors that contributed to the proliferation of double burial (Hertz 1960), where skeletons were exhumed after the decomposition of the flesh and placed in consecrated and dedicated buildings close to churchyards. The linked practices of double burial and constructing charnel houses meant that these constructions were not only "associated with an intense reverence for the dead" (Goody and Poppi 1994, 147) but also provided waiting places for souls and "a space where the living could engage in a dialogue with the dead" (Höpfl 1989, 27–28). This combined materiality and symbolism and early descriptions indicate that the sites became important Christian *memento mori* (remember you are mortal).

While *memento mori* provide visible reminders of human mortality and are not specific to Christianity (Inge 2014, 84), they are seen as core Christian eschatological emblems because *memento mori* "remind the beholder of death and urge him [*sic*] to behave morally" (Cohen 1973, 3). More often than not, these charnel houses contained gathered skulls and femurs arranged in no particular order. As the most durable bones in the human body, skulls and femurs (or crossbones) were the least likely to decay in the first burial. This physical phenomenon is also linked to their symbolic status as highly potent death symbols, in particular their association with Christian resurrection; "common tradition has it that a femur and a skull were prerequisite for a resurrection, and to this day you will see many more femurs and skulls than anything else preserved in charnel houses and ossuaries" (Inge 2014, 87).

Although charnel houses may initially have been little more than storage spaces for bones exhumed to make more room in consecrated burial ground, especially in times of increased mortality such as the plague, they became a contextually specific form of *memento mori*, providing "tangibly present instances of disappearance" (Hallam 2010, 471). This form, in line with contemporary understandings of the Resurrection, "erased unique individuality and imposed anonymity on human remains waiting for Judgement Day" (Koudounaris 2011, 101).

In line with the increasingly prominent place of the church in late medieval life and its focus on organizing people's lives, charnel houses became prominent symbolic structures that accentuated the visibility of human transience; their role was increasingly associated with "a range of sacred functions" (Koudounaris 2011, 22–23). During these times the hierarchy of senses associated with spiritual significance shifted from touch (as in being able to touch religious relics that may confer spiritual connection) to sight; being able to see a religious object became the dominant organizing principle for people's engagement with religious artifacts (Hallam and Hockey 2001, 47–48). By the end of the fourteenth century, they became exhibits or literal reminders of the need for piety, with skeletal remains "arranged around the courtyard of the church so as to form a backdrop for the daily life of those sensual times" (Aries 1981, 61).

Ossuaries have undergone significant change over the past centuries. A number of historical factors, including changing relationships between the living and the dead, "contributed to the eventual disappearance of these ossuaries" (Guerrini, 2015, 100–101). For instance, many "charnels were probably cleared at the Reformation, when the notion of bones as sacred relics and an encouragement to intercessory prayer was suppressed, and the practice of respectfully storing them was discontinued" (Harding 2002, 64). Although the Counter-Reformation initiated an escalation in the elaborate display of the dead, many but not all of the ossuaries were abandoned in the increasingly modern eighteenth and nineteenth centuries. Some charnels were lost, only to be discovered in more recent times; others, such as at Sedlec, were maintained through recent centuries. Those that remained, like the one at Sedlec, entered a new phase of display in the nineteenth century. These ossuaries were rearranged in ways that not only characterized a "Romantic sensibility" that increasingly recognized individuality but also marked a more general shift from sacred meaning to secular attitudes and popular culture as Europe moved toward the Enlightenment (Koudounaris 2011, 93). Rearrangements toward individualization included, for instance, the boxed skulls at the ossuary of St. Hilaire Cemetery in Marville, France, that "record the name and date of death and sometimes also list names of spouses, as well as inscribing the names and date of death on the deceased's skull," as in the Chapel of S. Michael Hallstatt, Austria" (Koudounaris 2011, 125, 126). These ossuaries are now significant tourist sites (Seaton 2002; Tanaś 2008).

OSSUARIES AS AUTHENTIC TOURIST EXPERIENCES OF THANATOPSIS: THE RESEARCH SITES

Fieldwork was conducted in five ossuaries across Czechoslovakia and Germany during the northern winter of 2013–14. The primary site included in the study was the cemetery of the Church of All Saints in Sedlec, Czechoslovakia. Following the foundation of a Cistercian monastery in Sedlec in 1142 and a cemetery in the thirteenth century, the site became a particularly desirable burial space after an abbot returned from his pilgrimage to the Holy Land and scattered soil from Golgotha in the graveyard. The popularity of this site throughout central Europe—augmented by fables, plagues, and, later, wars—contributed to a profusion of burials and the construction of a charnel house in 1400.

A folktale tells of a belief held around Europe that the ground at Sedlec could "rot the body swiftly, thus releasing the soul to Paradise. This theory spawned a myth that burial at Sedlec would guarantee a place in heaven within three days of death" (Inge 2014, 71). Accorded great popularity, the cemetery filled many times over, and bones were piled up in local churches. The bones of the dead were removed after primary burial, deposited in the chapel, and later transferred to the charnel house on the lower level of the cemetery chapel (Kratzke 2009, 201; Hornya 2001, 36).

While a fable recalls that it was a half-blind monk who first piled the bones into pyramids in 1512 to make order from the chaos, the chapel was redesigned a number of times in the ensuing centuries, including Baroque modifications completed in the eighteenth century by Jan Santini Aichl. The monastery was dissolved by Josef II in 1784 and sold to the Schwarzenberg family, which hired artist Frantisek Rint to remodel the chapel in the 1860s. In addition to four of the earlier pyramids, Rint added bone chandeliers, chalices, monstrances (an open or transparent receptacle in which the consecrated Host is displayed for veneration), a series of garlands, and four spires lined with skulls in the center of the ossuary. His bone creations also included the Schwarzenberg coat of arms and so reflected the ossuary's shift from religious to secular times, from medieval to modern hands. More recently, the ossuary's proximity to Prague "contributed to the increasing popularity of this site as a tourist attraction after the fall of communism, becoming the focus of numerous films and documentaries" (Koudounaris 2011, 100).

The other sites included in this study are perhaps less well-known than Sedlec but are nevertheless important tourist attractions in Germany. St. Martin's Basilica in Greding in Bavaria, Germany, features a chapel and charnel constructed in the fourteenth century to accommodate the growing population in the region. The ossuary underwent a number of reconstructions, including Romantic and Baroque additions, before renovations in 1905 re-created the style and character of the medieval charnel. Constituting the skulls and femurs of approximately 2,500 bodies, "the bones at St. Martin's Basilica were reorganised at this time into their present arrangement" (Braun 1999–2000, 219–20). A similar charnel and cemetery chapel can be found in the church of St. Michael in the Franconian town of Iphofen. The ossuary (*beinhaus* in German) was used to store the skeletal remains of people who had been buried in the constrained cemetery spaces from the fourteenth century until 1690, when the graveyard was abandoned for nearly 300 years. In 1960 the bones in the ossuary were removed to a local burial site, and it was not until 1998 that the buried remains were transferred back to the ossuary and the charnel was reconstructed using historical photographs (fig. 7.1).

FIGURE 7.1. Ossuary, Iphofen, Germany. Image by Cyril Schäfer.

Two further ossuaries in this ethnographic study include the charnel houses in Chammünster and Oppenheim, both in Germany. The small ossuary in Chammünster is located in the cemetery at St. Mary's church. Established in the thirteenth century, the charnel was abandoned after the Reformation and only rediscovered in 1820. In response to community concerns about groundwater contamination and damage to the bones from groundwater seepage, a new floor was made when the ossuary was repaired and reorganized in 1902 by a local teacher, who separated the skulls and bones into their present arrangement.

FIGURE 7.2. Michaelskapelle ossuary, Oppenheim, Germany, contains the skeletal remains of over 20,000 people. Image by Cyril Schäfer.

Finally, the largest remaining ossuary in Germany, containing the bones of an estimated 20,000 people, can be found in the Rhineland-Palatinate town of Oppenheim (fig. 7.2). Located next to the church of St. Catherine, the chapel of St. Michael (Michaelskapelle) was first used in the early fifteenth century and was continually used for secondary burials until 1750 (Wieser 2006). The "current arrangement of bones appears to date from the latter 19th century" (Koudounaris 2011, 36), although local villagers renovated the ossuary in the 1950s and at that time erected the gate that now separates visitors from the skeletal remains.

These ossuaries are predominantly filled with skulls and femurs. This is partly due because of the likely disintegration of small bones during first burial but also because they embody the Christian symbolism that underpinned their existence; keeping these particular bones was linked to pervading Resurrection beliefs that they would suffice on Judgment Day. Linked to the desire of the living for the salvation of the souls of the dead on Resurrection Day, "the living engaged with these sites as places to encounter the bones as powerful relics to whom they pray for intercessionary help both for the dead and for the living" (Cohen 1973, 70).

AUTHENTICATING ENCOUNTER: CHARNEL HOUSE RULES

Using an ethnographic approach, this project includes observation, informal interviews, and discourse analysis in an attempt to elucidate contemporary tourist experiences of these four ossuaries and their displays of skeletal remains. Drawing on the interdisciplinary work of dark tourism scholars and anthropological studies of authenticity, tourist encounters with displays of the dead are assessed by contextualizing these responses with the discourses of site administrators and affiliated tourist services.

The analytical approach was to draw on Bruner's tactic of examining authenticity "only when the tourists, the locals, or the producers themselves use the term" (Bruner 2005, 5) and Kaul's strategy of employing the notion of credibility as a means to conceptually examine the use of authenticity so as to "leave room for the existentially authentic experiences of any actor with any level of knowledge about a performance," or in this case bone exhibit, while also recognizing that some actors "have a deeper epistemological ability to assess a particular performance [exhibit] in relation to its quality and its historical continuity" (Kaul 2009,161).

Authenticity emerged as a fundamental term employed by both site administrators and tourists in their attempts to emphasize the significance of encounters with skeletal remains. The manner in which each group framed authenticity is revealing. Both groups juxtaposed themselves against a jointly perceived modernist superficiality and a concomitant disengagement with death, from which both groups sought to distance themselves. This distancing is akin to what Bruner calls the deprecation of tourists by other tourists. This deprecation of others' superficiality sets "them apart from those other travellers, who, they said, were mere tourists" (Bruner 2005, 7). Anthropologically, this distancing from perceived superficiality reveals pervading Western narratives about not only social hierarchy but also the complexity of equivocation over perceived anxieties of modern society as death denying. Both groups underscored the importance of identifying and extracting meanings that transcended the materiality of the bones. They did this through recourse to diverse discourses of authenticity. Both managers and visitors sought "authentic encounters"; however, each group approached its understandings of authenticity through distinctive and at times competing logics. Managers discussed authenticity in terms of transparency, while visitors talked about it in terms of veracity, trying to suspend their disbelief that the bones were real. Yet despite these aspirations of authentic encounters and in line with Rapport (2009) in the challenge of attaining the desired connection, both expressed doubts about their ability to achieve the authentic encounters they sought. The manner of their doubts is revealed through problematic engagements with the materiality of the bones. Managers struggled with the limits of transparency, while visitors wrestled with limits to their capacity to believe in the veracity of the bones. Such aspirations and doubts suggest a partial and complex acceptance of death in which death as an event is no longer denied but the material putrefaction associated with death remains taboo.

Fieldwork involved meeting with various ossuary officials—people involved with the ossuary in some capacity or another as tour guide, administrator, working archaeologist, retired sexton, or manager. Meeting at the sites and walking around the exhibits with them elicited impromptu commentaries that were supplemented by more formalized interviews where they were asked about their opinions on and, if relevant, how they were involved in managing tourist experiences of the ossuaries. Tourists were approached after their visit to the ossuary; approximately a dozen who were willing were interviewed onsite about their experiences.

READING BONES: TRANSPARENCY AND REVERENCE

The discourse generated by the dark site managers prioritized transparency about death as well as educational objectives to demonstrate requisite levels of respect and dignity for the dead as a means to generate the context for authentic encounters, or a full emotional engagement with death for visitors. In addition to providing access to socially sequestered spaces, managers and administrators emphasized the need for visitors to be guided to move beyond perfunctory perusals of the bones and engage with substantive existential or ontological themes, and they planned the spaces and tours to achieve that goal.

One of the salient themes in the responses of ossuary administrators and tour guides was the significance of *memento mori* in late modern society. *Memento mori*, or reminders of mortality, found expression in a variety of artistic forms in the late medieval and early modern periods. These historic versions included the *danse macabre*, a medieval allegorical concept of the all-conquering and equalizing power of death expressed in the drama, poetry, and visual arts of Western Europe. It is a "literal or pictoral representation of a procession or dance of both living and dead figures, the living arranged in order of their rank, from pope and emperor to child, clerk, and hermit, and the dead leading them to the grave" (Encyclopedia Britannica, accessed February 9, 2016, https://www.britannica.com/art/dance-of-death-art-motif). The *danse macabre* represented the frailty and vanity of earthly things, as well as the universality and unpredictability of human death (Huizinga 1999 [1924]). Other well-known *memento mori* included the legend of the Three Living and Three Dead, which illustrated the human embodiment of decay, and the *transi* (cadaver tombs), which featured the effigy of a decomposing corpse (Binski 1997, 134–52). These *memento mori* "contained observations on the mortality of man, and . . . used [the following] device for appealing directly to the spectator: the words 'I was like you and you will be like me.' In the *memento mori* inscriptions these words were followed by admonitory phrases such as 'Do good to all while you can' or 'Only good works will count' . . . stressing the need for good behavior" (Cohen 1973, 44).

Memento mori differ from mementos, as mementos are keepsakes associated with specific individuals or events; they hold private memories rather than social messages. The skulls, bones, and decaying flesh that featured in these representations accentuated the brevity of earthly life and the salvation of the soul, encouraging viewers to contemplate their own mortality. Such reflection emphasized the significance of piety and reminded the living of the sin inextricably linked with salvation (Oosterwijk 2004, 64), demonstrating that the relations of the living and the dead were intrinsically embedded in religious cultures (Gordon and Marshall 2000, 3). Although the style and emphasis of *memento mori* evolved in the ensuing centuries, certain images such as skulls remained popular on jewelry and memorial headstones. During the seventeenth and eighteenth centuries the macabre images were superseded by a new variant of *memento mori* that expressed increasing interest in anatomical knowledge and eventually incorporated increasingly secularized representations that combined playful and romantic images with skeletal crania in the nineteenth century (Kearl 2014, 4; Guerrini 2015, 94).

These historical expressions varied significantly from contemporary understandings proffered by participants. The site administrators and tour guides included in this study linked *memento mori* with changing attitudes toward death in late modern society. Instead of understanding these displays as reminders of one's earthly moral responsibilities, as in their original medieval intent, site administrators and tour guides across all sites saw these ossuaries as indicative of increasing death acceptance. Their point of reference for this claim was a disavowal of what they saw as the superficiality of modern life. Frequently alluding to the taboo nature of death in modern life, informants argued that life and death were inextricably linked but that the processes of individualization, medicalization, and secularization in the twentieth century had created a superficial and detrimental separation. Participants emphasized the importance of transparency and honesty in discussions of death, noting that modern life was pervaded by impediments to "openness," understanding "their" ossuaries as part of that edification. They asserted that displays of the dead were one significant way of proliferating transparency surrounding death, echoing Birchall's (2011, 8) contention that transparency has become a virtue: "the secular version of a born-again cleanliness that few can fail to praise."

Showing Cyril around the exhibits, administrators specifically noted that ossuaries had a clear educational role in transforming attitudes of denial and promoting a greater openness around death and dying by providing tourists with access to skeletal remains. Transparency in this context was associated with the visual display of the bones, with site managers and administrators emphasizing that modern secrecy surrounding death had been replaced with late modern pellucidity (allowing maximum passage of undistorted light). This emphasis "reflects the cultural importance of sight within western epistemology" and its intrinsic link to transparency and knowledge (Classen 1997, 402). Concerned that tourists may leave the exhibits without fully engaging with theirs' and others' mortality, site managers, administrators, and guides were ambivalent about what strategies contributed most effectively to this educational objective. This ambivalence can be linked to critiques of "the tourist gaze," in that the sense of sight is similarly associated with a "superficial form of engagement that neglected other sensory experiences and the time required for adequate immersion and cognizance" (Urry and Larsen 2011, 18).

This ambivalence can be found in the differing ways those involved in the organization and management of the ossuaries approached the displays of bones. On the one hand, administrators felt the dramatic bone displays enforced the universality of death and accentuated the superficiality of socially constructed categories such as ethnicity, religion, and gender. Two German guides, for example, stressed that the ossuaries in Oppenheim and Greding contained the remains of former political and religious enemies from past centuries that now lay undifferentiated in the charnel houses, providing a potent reminder of the physical homogeneity of human remains. An archaeologist involved in a reconstruction of the Sedlec ossuary, on the other hand, explained that historically, the large number of bones would have had an impact on visitors but that few contemporary visitors would engage with these remains at a "deeper level." Together with the manager of the site, he articulated the need to provide more contextual information for tourists and to make the anonymous bones more familiar. Skulls and bones created a very "flat history of the dead" (Mark, archaeologist) and did little to engage the sustained interest of the visitor. One way to instill more respect and comprehension, according to this informant, was to re-personalize the remains. Archaeological attempts to re-create some of the physical features of the face and body, in addition to the provision of more detailed information about the dead, would contribute to the construction of a biography and counter the culture of "selfies" that eroded any respect for the dead.

Selfies (photographs taken of oneself with a smartphone and shared through social media) (see Kohn et al., this volume) were frequently described by the resident archaeologist at Sedlec as an exemplar of triviality that epitomized narcissism, conceit, and a lack of respect for, in this case, death and the dead. Authors such as Hornya (2001, 46–48), when describing a similar ambivalence about tourist behavior, have further argued that the tourist gaze is itself indicative of an unhealthy relationship with death and that contemporary visitor motivations associated with unrestricted access to human remains are a conspicuous component of the banalization of death and dying. Recent research has critically assessed the significance of these images, arguing that debates over the meaning and import of taking such selfies is an aspect of the "heightened public discourse" that brings disparagement of the perceived modern eschewal of death together with moral panic narratives "associated with young people and their use of digital media" (Meese et al. 2015, 1818–19). Nevertheless, managers of charnel houses stipulated that this form of representation rarely progressed beyond what they called "a surface reading," or superficial engagement with the bones.

Although selfies were described disparagingly as shallow and perfunctory, there was considerable disagreement about the control and restriction of photography. While some sites, such as the Polish Kaplica Czazek, strictly precluded all forms of photography, others felt such restrictions simply contributed to the aforementioned sequestration of death. Currently Sedlec, for example, allows unrestricted amateur photography, as do the ossuaries visited in southern Germany. Although the parish at Sedlec had previously considered restricting the use of cameras, when interviewed, the director emphasized that it was extremely difficult to monitor all forms of photography and that photographs were a very productive way of promoting the site—as the thousands of micro-blogging, social networking, and photo-sharing websites appear to confirm.[3]

Related to concerns about photography at the sites were discussions about the requisite respect and reverence "paid" to the dead by managers and tourists. Brochures produced by a number of sites, including Sedlec, emphasized that ossuaries were linked to notions of piety. Piety was described by managers as incompatible with "tourist attraction," which they felt was itself the nomenclature of banality. In the ephemeral literature produced, such as tour pamphlets and tourist website pages, ossuaries were frequently defined as places that retained some connection to Christian-meaning frameworks and that an element of veneration for the dead was ideally a component of visitor motivations. Some managers maintained, however, that such expectations were increasingly unrealistic in a secular age and that these frameworks had been superseded by a profusion of spiritual forms. This spirituality provided an opportunity for "implanting in people the meaning of the place" (Michael, site manager) and for visitors to derive meaning that transcended a cursory perusal of the physical remains.

The former sexton at St. Catherine's church in Oppenheim felt that one of his crucial tasks was to guide people to the appropriate interpretation of the bones in the ossuary. His concern was that contemporary visitors rarely had the relevant knowledge or background to comprehend the intended significance of these skeletal remains. He explained that people from former communist countries, for example, were unfamiliar with religious frameworks that would allow them to extract the meanings the sexton was familiar with from their encounter with the bones. According to this former sexton, these people's ignorance of Christian doctrine was conspicuous and contributed to a presumed superficial engagement that involved very limited contemplation of mortality. One of his roles was therefore to mediate between the living and the dead; he saw himself balancing decorum and respect with the appropriate interest and information so that tourists would extract some personal meaning from the remains in ways that could in some way resonate with the "domestic" and thus, according to this sexton, create an authentic engagement with the ossuary. This mirrors Bruner's point that while they may be articulated through essentializing discourses, as is the case with this sexton, "sites themselves are not passive for they are given meaning and are constituted by the narratives that envelope them" (Bruner 2005, 12).

Site managers and administrators discussed the significance of the physical ossuary space and how the condition of the ossuary contributed to visitor experiences. Although all of the ossuaries were hundreds of years old—and some in serious disrepair after decades and often centuries of neglect—managers noted that this was not the form of authenticity desired by tourists. The Sedlec manager, for example, explained that restoration of the deteriorating ossuary might itself create a less "distracting" space that would avoid any possible Disneyified displays. For Sedlec's manager, "Disneyified" meant displays that were too peculiar and acted as curios that would distract visitors from the desired experience of reverence and respect rather than referring to the process of vulgarization of the presented cultural content (Bryman 1999). Supporting Taussig's (2006, 198) assessment that the ossuary at Sedlec goes beyond art and converts the bone displays into "pure kitsch, draining the bones of whatever reverential and religious potential they might have," the manager reiterated the need to create a deeper engagement with the skeletal remains through the elimination of extraneous factors. These factors included tourists getting in the way of each other's engagement with the exhibits, for example, jostling for position to take photographs, which was believed to be incongruous with the managers' expectation that visitors would engage with the ossuary with dignity and understanding.

One further concern for some site managers was the condition of the skeletal remains. Discussions of the bones typically shifted to their presentation, color, and arrangement, with participants emphasizing the need for ordered displays that reflected the requisite reverence and dignity:

> "As an anthropologist you will want to see the bones more closely," the administrator [at the diocese office] remarked as she led me to the Totenkappelle [chapel for the dead]. Behind the imposing church tower, she shuffled to the iron gate that protected the dead from the living and carefully descended the small stairs into the ossuary with

ancient vaulted ceilings. She closed the gate, declaring that some of her colleagues were extremely uncomfortable in the presence of death as she did so. She glanced at the carefully arranged strata of skulls and femurs that lined the ossuary wall before motioning to a chaotic accumulation of bones in the far corner of the ossuary. Unlike the gray edentate skulls so deliberately arranged to peer benignly at any visitors, these bones lay in disarray on the floor, perfectly hidden from the tourists standing at the gate. The bones had not been cleaned and displayed the unmistakable signs of burial and decomposition, while the tufts of orange and brown hair provided potent signs of personhood. "Those unsavory remains," she remarked, "do not need to be seen." (Field notes, February 11, 2015)

The bones she was describing referred to the remains that had been uncovered in more recent excavation and building projects and not been incorporated into the historical ossuary display. As with a number of smaller ossuaries in surrounding areas that were not publicly accessible, it was clear that certain forms of disposal and burial were not appropriate forms of *memento mori* or suitable for public display. This sense of appropriate or inappropriate displays is a theme explored in Kathleen Adams's chapter in this volume on "zombie" mortuary tourism. It also underpins Desmond's (2008) study of taxidermied animals and plastinated corpses. As several site managers and tour guides noted, clean bones made people feel safe while any reference to the process of decay generated distress and potential fear. As one tour guide in Greding articulated, the absence of any recognizable forms of personhood contributed to the creation of a space that paradoxically allowed visitors to contemplate death without being overwhelmed by the physical signs of corporeal deterioration. Unlike the historical *memento mori* outlined above, managerial participants in the project felt that decomposition and decay constituted an element of death that needed to be extricated from displays, as they got in the way of the exhibits' transparency and authenticity because such processes disrupted the desired level of engagement with mortality. While these participant responses accentuated transparency, it became clear that this shift to openness had contours that privileged a reading of the bones that avoided some obvious features of death and encouraged tourists to move beyond a focus on the physical. In sum, professional participants were ambivalent about what precisely constituted engagement with the displays but articulated the significance of religious frameworks, spirituality, and reverence for the dead.

READING BONES: "MACABRE BUT DELICIOUSLY CREEPY"

Tourists, in contrast, proffered accounts that centered on a desire to identify elements of "real" death. Their logic for achieving an authentic encounter was embedded in close examination and recording (through photos) the physical displays of bone.

Although few tourists in this study were specifically motivated to visit ossuaries to engage with mortality as suggested by Walter (2009), many described their experiences as gruesome, macabre, or creepy and an opportunity to encounter real death in an undomesticated setting. Despite their professed fascination, however, tourists also expressed a certain ambivalence about the purpose, function, and effect of the displays. Many tourist responses recalled the historical details produced by ossuary administrators and tour guides, with an emphasis on the establishment of the ossuary and the cultural significance of secondary burials. Tourists cited the religious importance of resurrection, with a specific interest in the causes of death and the number of bones contained in the ossuaries. Nevertheless, beyond these cursory assessments informed by the touristic literature, visitors provided varying interpretations of these dark sites that revealed how the concept of authenticity was mobilized to derive meaning from the displays. Authenticity was mobilized through seeking a sense of "realness" or veracity.

For some, ossuaries were an educational display that provided a form of prefatory, or introduction, to a scientific gaze, as also occurs in *Body Worlds* (Walter 2004). Of particular interest were the displayed bones that exhibited structural deformities, war injuries, or evidence of diseases (such as syphilis or arthritis), prompting a few tourists to consider the physical suffering associated with archaic ways of life. The trephination (drilling a hole in the skull while the individual was still alive) of a skull displayed at Sedlec was a particular source of fascination, with tourists emphasizing the crudeness and brutality of early medicine. Other tourists noted that the vast number of bones made profound statements about the universality of death and the fragility of human life. The assemblages of bones and the recurrent motifs created an apparent uniformity (Hallam 2010, 475–76) that encouraged some tourists to ponder the contemporary significance of a distinct individuality. A few visitors, in contrast, interpreted their exploration of dark tourist sites as abstruse encounters that contributed to their own biographical projects (commonly described as "bucket lists"), providing a tangible measure of biographical completeness in late modernity (see Jacobsen and Kearl 2013).

While some tourists felt that the impersonal and anonymized bones were a synecdoche of human mortality, others considered the de-personalized remains problematic, as they erased all features of an embodied presence and offered no biographical context to the objects before them. Objectifying the dead in this way eliminated all residues of individual biography and memory for a significant number of visitors. One of the frequent questions for tour guides focused on the appropriateness of publicly displaying the dead and, indeed, whether viewing the dead constituted a respectful practice. While some tourists acclaimed the artistic value of the bones—emphasizing the beauty and creativity of the displays—others felt such representations were undignified and degraded the dead. Numerous comparisons were made with more contemporary ossuaries (viz. those in Cambodia), which tourists claimed exuded a reverence that was absent at sites such as Sedlec. A few visitors also noted that the uniform bone arrangements attempted to divest the dead of potency but that after they entered the ossuary they became aware of the presence of the dead housed in the charnel. For instance, one notably timorous tourist spent a considerable period hovering outside the ossuary entrance receiving insistent encouragement from her husband and the local tour guide, both asseverating that the chapel was decorated with "harmless bones." Upon tentatively entering the ossuary, she declared that she could "feel the dead" before abruptly turning and running out of the cemetery gates, her flustered husband announcing to the tour guide that her attitude was entirely "irrational and embarrassing."

Some tourists asserted that it was not the displays of the dead themselves that generated unease but the commodification of sites associated with death. These visitors noted that the entrance fees at some sites and the mass touristic appeal destroyed the requisite sanctity and solemnity of the site. For a few tourists, the souvenirs available at the affiliated gift shops vulgarized and depreciated the value of the site by prioritizing capitalist concerns and exploiting the dead.

Prolonged observation over several days also revealed other prominent themes that were not immediately evident in tourist explanations. One of the themes that emerged during the project was a desire for a degree of intimacy with the bones. While managers explained that the bones needed to be protected from the living and that enclosures provided necessary distance between the living and the dead, visitors frequently lamented the inaccessibility of bones in German ossuaries. Visitors would carefully maneuver their cameras through the iron bars to take photographs that provided an illusory proximity to the bones. These tourists explained that the displays were reminiscent of museum exhibits that only allowed for a very remote engagement with the remains. In the ossuary at Sedlec, in contrast, visitors deliberated on their accessibility to the skeletal remains and their ability to take unrestricted photographs. The skulls in particular were described by one tourist as "extremely photogenic," while another stated that it was exceedingly difficult to take a "bad photograph" in the ossuary. During most days of my research, the ossuary resonated with the monotonous sounds of digital cameras tirelessly capturing carefully orchestrated bone arrangements. In addition to eliminating extraneous elements (such as other tourists), visitors positioned their cameras to identify the surface features of the bones and to peer "deeply" into the apertures of the skulls. For some visitors this constituted an attempt to capture the essence of "real" bones and what they described as authentic representations of death.

Proximity and photography also contributed to a feeling of affinity with the dead. Some visitors described the beauty of the macabre, noting that initial anxieties about viewing the bones were often transformed into feelings of admiration or reverence. Associated with this perceived connection and a quest for the real was an express desire for an encounter that transcended the physicality of the remains and included elements of the spiritual, supernatural, or sacred. While a few tourists with religious backgrounds were familiar with prescribed rituals for the dead, many non-religious visitors felt that they *wanted* to experience something that transcended the materiality of the bones and that they were receptive to spiritual possibilities. One tourist clearly stated that she felt a perpetual impulse to pray but had no idea what to pray for, while another noted that he was waiting for a sensory experience linked to the presence of so many dead: "I'm not the kind of person who goes to séances, but I thought there might have been something. I don't know. Like maybe a gust of wind or some type of energy or emotion. There are so many bones and so many dead people, but I didn't get any feeling."

Both of these participants specifically noted that the bones created a presumed level of intimacy with death but that there was something contrived about this relationship. In contrast to the majority of participants who referred to a disassociation between the bones and their own experiences of death, one participant explicitly noted that there were simply no frameworks to help her make sense of the display. Death is typically associated with prescribed mourning practices and emotional responses, which provide some context for these encounters. As this participant emphasized, however, the ossuaries were simply "piles of bones of people that died a long time ago." Along with other visitors who assessed the effect of the bones on any contemplation of mortality, this participant found herself asking particularly contemporary questions about the disposal of the bones in the hope of creating some connection to the dead: Was a charnel house their preferred method of disposal? What kinds of lives and personalities had been associated with the remains? Would the people mind that their bones were so intimately connected to other (potentially unrelated) bones? The temporal and spatial separation identified by administrators and tour guides as significant for contemplation of mortality were precisely the factors that contributed to a feeling of disassociation with the dead in this instance.

These responses resonate with Linke's (2005, 13) assessment of displays of plastinated bodies that "presented anonymised, aestheticized corpses devoid of any emotional engagement." Participants in the present project felt that this paucity of affect applied to spirituality. As one visitor recounted her experience of visiting the ossuary, she emphasized that she had felt "sad and somber" but that there was nothing more substantive—even though "there *should* have been a moment that was vaguely spiritual." The sense that this visitor's personal symbolic landscape was out of harmony with the ossuary manager's intended effect of the displays recalls Rapport's (2009, 37) discussion of the impossibility of reconciling gruesome historical happenings "with any notion of everyday life." While site managers accentuated the need to derive meaning that transcended superficial scrutiny, non-religious participants frequently stated that the sites did not "feel truly spiritual." Some participants explained that they had imagined that a site replete with so many physical remains of death would exude a "natural spirituality" but that the elaborate displays detracted from spiritual reflection and the disarticulated bones exhibited a disorder of identity that appeared incongruous with spirituality. Participants frequently described spirituality as a universal human essence located inside each individual (see Hornborg 2011; Knoblauch 2010 for a discussion of culturally specific articulations of universal spirituality), and this spirituality contributed to the authenticity and gravitas of death. These descriptions emphasize "the significance of contemporary containment and boundedness after death" (Krmpotich, Fontein, and Harries 2010, 377) and the fact that the loss of skeletal integrity was "associated with erasure of individual identity" (Hallam 2010, 475).

Other tourists indicated that their quest for authentic death was closely connected to a semblance of silence and solitude but that the large numbers of tourists dissipated any such emanation. Although many tourists arrived in tour groups, these individuals also explained that the site required solitude to create a feeling of something transcendental but that the tourists at sites such as Sedlec diluted the experience they were searching for. While this distaste for the presence of other tourists displays the irony of tourism, these visitors also noted that death was traditionally associated with silence and that the inevitable auditory elements accompanying mass tourism subverted any attempts to create a feeling of the supernatural that might transcend the materiality of the remains.

These assessments also indicated that a focus on the visual was perceived by some individuals to be inextricably connected to the sanitizing tendencies of Western death practices. Such evaluations were characterized by an ambivalence surrounding sensory experiences. Visitors expressed relief that the ossuaries themselves were not marked by visual or olfactory signs that accompanied the process of putrefaction, yet this itself detracted from the authenticity of the experience. While anthropological explorations have elucidated the boundary-transgressing nature of smell and its proclivity to evade linear classificatory schema (Lawton 1998), Edensor (2006) has also suggested that contemporary concerns for sensory security coexist with desires for certain transcendent experiences. He goes on to note that certain modes of tourism engage with these sensualities, suggesting that "delight is found in the contingent and opening up of the body to sensation" (Edensor 2006, 42). Such experiences are intrinsically linked to the pursuance of the authentic other, as well as the desire for cultural capital and projects of the self. Smell in particular was identified as something that many expected to confront in their encounters, but the bones themselves were significantly "cleaner" than many had anticipated. Some visitors noted that this created a display that reduced the potency or intensity of the remains and made the experience less "real" than they had anticipated.

Tourists explained that there was a current trend to use bones—particularly crania—in popular culture but that this "did not mean anything" in contemporary contexts (Scott, tourist in Greding). As Kearl (2014) has argued, depictions of skulls have been transformed from potent symbols of danger or reminders of human mortality to meaningless skulls that diminish the presence of the dead. He goes on to suggest that such insignificant symbols preclude any reflection on mortality (Kearl 2014, 15). Other authors have proffered a similar assessment, noting that "skull style" is an indication of a paradoxical preoccupation with death in a culture where ordinary death is sequestered from view (Foltyn 2010). While these authors stress that contemporary representations of bones disregard rather than confront mortality, the tourists emphasized that they tried to extract meaning from their encounters but felt, on reflection, that the meanings were impenetrable or, to use Rapport's phrase, "unencompassable" (Rapport 2009, 37), equivocal, or ambivalent. Unable to elicit the desired meaning or uncover the imagined authenticity, tourists felt that photographs were at least one way to capture—although only partially—a remnant of their experience.

Some visitors also discovered that the displays were simply "not real" enough or that the reality they envisioned did not coincide with their preconceived visions of the ossuary. Visitor assessments repeatedly noted that the charnel houses were small physical spaces that did not exude the authenticity they had anticipated. As one tourist explicitly elaborated, the ossuary *should* have resembled an extensive subterranean cavern lit only by flickering candles and shafts of light filtering in through cracks in the dilapidated exterior. Others similarly noted that the images of the ossuaries on the internet, television, and cinema had created an expectation of charnels that was not evident at the physical site. Descriptions reiterated that the ossuaries felt like "elaborate Halloween displays, "haunted houses," or "film sets" that felt spurious and contrived. Perhaps in resonance with the insights of Baudrillard (1994, 2), who suggested that there is a blurring between reality and its representation in a world of layered reproductions ("a question of substituting the signs of the real for the real"), tourists emphasized that they had to remind themselves that the bones in the ossuaries were in fact not fake representations but *"real"* human remains.

A general point about their shared aim of experiencing an authentic encounter with death was that while both managers and visitors were willing participants in a "touristic border zone" (Bruner 2005, 17), both groups were uncertain about the genuineness and appropriateness of these displays and struggled to achieve their desired aim of an authentic experience. Both groups failed to achieve a seamless sense of authenticity as they struggled with the materiality of the bones. On the one hand, managers felt impelled to exclude from public view those bones that carried remnants of decomposition (such as hair and skin) that were also markers of individuality. On the other hand, visitors struggled with their inability to appreciate the bones as real because of the perceived lack of individuation in the displays. They resolved this through an invented individuality, attempting to fabricate a sense of connection with the dead through imagining what it would feel like emotionally to be jumbled up with strangers and put on show, given that they were prevented from viewing "less tidy" exhibits that would allow them to imagine the smells of putrefaction or the dried, wrinkled, and scarred skin and the remnants of brown, blond, black, or gray hair that testify to the singular struggles of that particular life and "our understanding of each human body as a unique subject" (Desmond 2008, 349).

THE SEARCH FOR AUTHENTIC DEATH

This discussion highlights the importance of authenticity for site administrators and tourists, where this concept emerged as an overarching theme in discussions of ossuary displays. Authenticity has been problematized in the field of tourism studies since the formative work of MacCannell (1973), who explored the staged and commodified dimensions of this concept. Debates in the literature have shifted from objectivist, essentialist ideologies to subjective forms of authenticity, such as existential authenticity (Wang 1999; Chhabra 2005; Olsen 2002). These studies have also elucidated the limitations and validity of this term, with authors such as Cohen (2012, 261) asserting that simulacra in the postmodern age may supersede the "longing for the wholeness of the pre-modern other." The current findings in this chapter, however, can be contextualized by drawing on some of the classic and recent anthropological explorations of authenticity (see, for example, the seminal work of Trilling [1972] and the more recent analyses of Ferrara [2013], Bendix [1997], Fillitz and Saris [2013], and Vannini and Williams [2009]). Authors such as Bruner (2005), Theodossopoulos (2013), Carse (2014), and Schäfer (2014) have argued for studies of authenticity that explore the coexistence of varying forms of authenticity and the cultural contexts of its production. As Theodossopoulos (2013, 340–41) goes on to argue, this shift in anthropological inquiry is not simply an indication of academic verbalism but an attempt to understand the multiple vernacular uses of the term and the multiplicity of meanings under negotiation.

The current project has revealed that authenticity was used in a number of ways to assess meaning related to displays of the dead. Ossuary administrators and managers emphasized that these sites had a significant role to play in making death more accessible and transparent in a society that had experienced professionalized and medicalized encounters with death and dying. The focus of transparency was therefore partially reliant on visual displays of the bones that provided visitors with authentic, "unmediated" representations of death. At the same time, however, professionals asserted that this focus was unsatisfactory and needed to be supplemented with meaning that included some supernatural or spiritual understanding and reverence.

Tourists also mobilized the concept of authenticity in their consideration of these sites, and it became evident that their gaze was structured by a desire to assess what constituted the "realness" of death. While some admired the artistic creativity of the displays or the profound quantities of bone, many emphasized that these skeletal remains were little more than curiosities, with limited applicability to contemporary contemplations of mortality. Although some visitors proposed that photography was a way of capturing the realness of death, others explained that the profusion of images already available on the internet failed to contribute anything more substantive to their interpretations. Despite a distinct *memento mori* theme in the touristic discourse, visitors asserted that the bones lacked agency because the disarticulated remains and the display setting provided no familiar means with which to access meaning; displayed bones lacked certain indicators of death, created limited affective response, or felt contrived and fixated on tourist consumption. Of particular significance for many tourists (and administrators) was the role of spirituality, which some argued constituted a fundamental form of authenticity. Visitors specifically asserted that sites such as ossuaries saturated with the remains of the dead should exude a form of spirituality and meaning that transcended the physical bones. For some of these visitors, authenticity became a "trope for transcendence" and a way for these individuals to articulate their quest for meaning (Lindholm 2013, 361).

While the death sequestration thesis outlined at the beginning of this chapter emphasized the importance of transparency and confronting death, this chapter went on to elucidate some of the contours of this engagement. Rather than demonstrating a developmental sequence indicating a fundamental shift in societal attitudes toward death (Goody and Poppi 1994), this project emphasized that dark sites such as ossuaries provided visitors with the opportunity to consider what constituted meaningful mortuary practices and their relationship with the dead. Rather than the existence of a universal *memento mori* that transcended spatial and temporal boundaries, the research highlighted the fact that contemporary encounters with bones—and the meaning derived from these encounters—were intrinsically related to contemporary concerns such as bodily integrity and personalized identity. Discussions with visitors regarding these experiences, in turn, revealed that authenticity not only provided an "extra-historical, endlessly renewable resource"

(Muir 2014, 491) for meaning making but that an examination of the "polysemy of authenticity" itself provides some understanding of this concept within the cultural context of its production (Theodossopoulos 2013, 341).

Ossuaries are sites where both visitors and managers seek authentic experiences of death. Yet ironically, in their quests to accept death for what it is, they shy away from deterioration and decay. Perhaps we have come around to rejecting the idea of "death denial," but we are certainly not ready for decay. Are we therefore in an age of "denial of decay," a denial of the process of death rather than the fact of it?

NOTES

1. Cyril Schäfer died suddenly of an aneurism while he was working on the final edits for this chapter in June 2015. His good friend and long-term research colleague Ruth McManus, with the help of editors Adam Kaul and Jonathan Skinner, completed the final edits in a way that, it is hoped, reflects Cyril's style of writing and ideas. *Poroporoaki hoa*.

2. As Gordon and Marshall (2000, 3) elaborate, the significance of the dead in late medieval Christianity was inextricably linked to a belief in Purgatory and the conviction that the living had a duty to ease the suffering of the dead.

3. See Cemetery Travel: Adventures in Graveyards around the World—Travelblog, accessed February 16, 2016, https://cemeterytravel.com/2011/10/27/the-ossuary-as-memento-mori/; also http://www.thebohemianblog.com/2014/09/bone-churches-of-bohemia-the-sedlec-ossuary-at-kutna-hora.html, accessed February 16, 2016.

REFERENCES

Aries, P. 1974. "The Reversal of Death: Changes in Attitudes toward Death in Western Societies." *American Quarterly* 26 (5): 536–60. https://doi.org/10.2307/2711889.

Aries, P. 1981. *The Hour of Our Death*. Trans. H. Weaver. New York: Alfred A. Knopf.

Baudrillard, J. 1994. *Simulacra and Simulation*. Trans. S. F. Glaser. Ann Arbor: University of Michigan Press.

Becker, E. 1973. *The Denial of Death*. New York: Collier-Macmillan.

Bendix, R. 1997. *In Search of Authenticity: The Formation of Folklore Studies*. Madison: University of Wisconsin Press.

Binski, P. 1997. *Medieval Death: Ritual and Representation*. Ithaca, NY: Cornell University Press.

Birchall, C. 2011. "Introduction to 'Secrecy and Transparency': The Politics of Opacity and Openness." *Theory, Culture, and Society* 28 (7–8): 7–25. https://doi.org/10.1177/0263276411427744.

Braun, E. 1999–2000. "Der mittelalterliche Karner von Greding: Neue Erkenntnisse zur seiner Baugeschichte und seine Rolle im Lichte der Karner in der Oberpfalz." *Sammelblatt des Historischen Vereins Eichstätt Bd.* 92–93: 211–32.

Bruner, E. M. 2005. *Culture on Tour: Ethnographies of Travel*. Chicago: University of Chicago Press.

Bryman, A. 1999. "The Disneyization of Society." *Sociological Review* 47 (1): 25–47. https://doi.org/10.1111/1467-954X.00161.

Carse, A. 2014. "The Year 2013 in Sociocultural Anthropology: Cultures of Circulation and Anthropological Facts." *American Anthropologist* 116 (2): 390–403. https://doi.org/10.1111/aman.12108.

Chhabra, D. 2005. "Defining Authenticity and Its Determinants: Toward an Authenticity Flow Model." *Journal of Travel Research* 44 (1): 64–73. https://doi.org/10.1177/0047287505276592.

Chow, E. 2015. "The Sickest Theme Park Ever? Tourists Flock to Experience Real-Life Cremation in 'Death Simulator' at Chinese Amusement Park." *Daily Mail*. Accessed May 10, 2015. http://www.dailymail.co.uk/news/peoplesdaily/article-3073742/Tourists-experience-real-life-CREMATION-death-simulator-Chinese-amusement-park.html.

Classen, C. 1997. "Foundations for an Anthropology of the Senses." *International Social Science Journal* 49 (153): 401–12. https://doi.org/10.1111/j.1468-2451.1997.tb00032.x.

Cohen, E. 2012. "Authenticity in Tourism Studies: Aprés la Lutte." In *Critical Debates in Tourism*, ed. T. Singh, 250–61. Bristol, UK: Channel View.

Cohen, K. 1973. *Metamorphosis of a Death Symbol: The Transi Tomb in the Late Middle Ages and the Renaissance*. Los Angeles: University of California Press.

Desmond, J. 2008. "Postmortem Exhibitions: Taxidermied Animals and Plastinated Corpses in the Theatres of the Dead." *Configurations* 16 (3): 347–78. https://doi.org/10.1353/con.0.0062.

Edensor, T. 2006. "Sensing Tourist Spaces." In *Travels in Paradox: Remapping Tourism*, ed. C. Minca and T. Oakes, 23–45. Lanham, MD: Rowman and Littlefield.

Fillitz, T., and A. J. Saris, eds. 2013. *Debating Authenticity: Concepts of Modernity in Anthropological Perspective*. Oxford: Berghahn Books.

Ferrara, A. 2013. *Reflective Authenticity: Rethinking the Project of Modernity*. London: Routledge.

Foltyn, J. 2010. "To Die For: Skull Style and Corpse Chic in Fashion Design, Imagery, and Branding." *Scan Journal* 7 (2). Accessed May 10, 2015. http://scan.net.au/scan/journal/print.php?journal_id=151&j_id=20.

Gordon, B., and P. Marshall. 2000. "Introduction: Placing the Dead in Late Medieval and Early Modern Europe." In *The Place of the Dead: Death and Remembrance in Late*

Medieval and Early Modern Europe, ed. B. Gordon and P. Marshall, 1–16. Cambridge: Cambridge University Press.

Gorer, G. 1965. *Death, Grief, and Mourning in Contemporary Britain*. London: Cresset.

Goody, J., and C. Poppi. 1994. "Flowers and Bones: Approaches to the Dead in Anglo-American and Italian Cemeteries." *Comparative Studies in Society and History* 36 (1): 146–75. https://doi.org/10.1017/S0010417500018922.

Guerrini, A. 2015. "Inside the Charnel House: The Display of Skeletons in Europe, 1500–1800." In *Fate of Anatomical Collections*, ed. R. Knoeff, R. Zwijnenberg, and O. P. Grell, 93–109. Farnham, GB: Ashgate.

Hallam, E. 2010. "Articulating Bones: An Epilogue." *Journal of Material Culture* 15 (4): 465–92. https://doi.org/10.1177/1359183510382963.

Hallam, E., and J. Hockey. 2001. *Death, Memory, and Material Culture*. Oxford: Berg.

Harding, V. 2002. *The Dead and the Living in Paris and London, 1500–1670*. Cambridge: Cambridge University Press.

Hertz, R. 1960. *Death and the Right Hand*. London: Cohen and West.

Höpfl, J. 1989. "Der Karner von Chammünster." In *1250 Jahre Chammünster: Festschrift der Pfarrei*, 15–20. City of Chammünster: Parish of Chammünster.

Hornborg, A.-C. 2011. "Are We All Spiritual? A Comparative Perspective on the Appropriation of a New Concept of Spirituality." *Journal for the Study of Spirituality* 1 (2): 249–68. https://doi.org/10.1558/jss.v1i2.249.

Hornya, M. 2001. "The Church of All Saints and the Ossuary at Sedlec, Kutna Hora." In *Memento mori*, ed. B. Chlibec, M. Hornya, V. Jirasek, R. Novak, and I. Pinkava, 34–50. Prague: Torst.

Huizinga, J. 1999 [1924]. *The Waning of the Middle Ages*. Toronto: General Publishing.

Inge, D. 2014. *A Tour of Bones: Facing Fear and Looking for Life*. London: Bloomsbury.

Jacobsen, M. H., and M. C. Kearl. 2013. "Time, Late Modernity, and the Demise of Forever: From Eternal Salvation to Completed Bucket Lists." In *Taming Time, Timing Death: Social Technologies and Ritual*, ed. D. R. Christensen and R. Willerslev, 59–78. Farnham, GB: Ashgate.

Jagger, S. L., M. M. Dubek, and E. Pedretti. 2012. " 'It's a Personal Thing': Visitors' Responses to Body Worlds." *Museum Management and Curatorship* 27 (4): 357–74. https://doi.org/10.1080/09647775.2012.720185.

Kaul, A. 2009. *Turning the Tune: Traditional Music, Tourism, and Social Change in an Irish Village*. Oxford: Berghahn Books.

Kearl, M. C. 2014. "The Proliferation of Skulls in Popular Culture: A Case Study of How the Traditional Symbol of Mortality Was Rendered Meaningless." *Mortality* 20 (1): 1–18.

Kellehear, Allan. 1984. "Are We a 'Death-Denying' Society? A Sociological Review." *Social Science and Medicine* 18 (9): 713–21. https://doi.org/10.1016/0277-9536(84)90094-7.

Kenzler, H. 2014. "Totenbrauch und Reformation: Wandel und Kontinuität." *Mitteilungen der Deutschen Gesellschaft für Archäologie des Mittelalters und der Neuzeit* 23 (1): 9–34.

Knoblauch, H. 2010. "Popular Spirituality." *Anthropological Journal on European Cultures* 19 (1): 24–39.

Koudounaris, P. 2011. *The Empire of Death: A Cultural History of Ossuaries and Charnel Houses*. London: Thames and Hudson.

Kratzke, C. 2009. "Die Abtei Sedletz im Kontext der Spulkralkultur des Zisterzienserordens." In *Sedletz: Geschichte, Architektur und Kunstschaffen im Sedletzer Kloster im mitteleuropäischen Kontext um die Jahre 1300 und 1700: Internationales Sympozium, Kuttenberg, 18–20 September 2008*, 185–213. Prague: Togga.

Krmpotich, C., J. Fontein, and J. Harries. 2010. "The Substance of Bones: The Emotive Materiality and Affective Presence of Human Remains." *Journal of Material Culture* 15 (4): 371–84. https://doi.org/10.1177/1359183510382965.

Lawton, J. 1998. "Contemporary Hospice Care: The Sequestration of the Unbounded Body and 'Dirty Dying.'" *Sociology of Health and Illness* 20 (2): 121–43. https://doi.org/10.1111/1467-9566.00094.

Lee, R.L.M. 2008. "Modernity, Mortality, and Re-Enchantment: The Death Taboo Revisited." *Sociology* 42 (4): 745–59. https://doi.org/10.1177/0038038508091626.

Leiberich, P., T. Loew, K. Tritt, C. Lahmann, and M. Nickel. 2006. "Body Worlds Exhibition—Visitor Attitudes and Emotions." *Annals of Anatomy—Anatomischer Anzeiger* 188 (6): 567–73. https://doi.org/10.1016/j.aanat.2006.03.005.

Lindholm, C. 2013. "The Rise of Expressive Authenticity." *Anthropological Quarterly* 86 (2): 361–95. https://doi.org/10.1353/anq.2013.0020.

Linke, U. 2005. "Touching the Corpse: The Unmaking of Memory in the Body Museum." *Anthropology Today* 21 (5): 13–19. https://doi.org/10.1111/j.0268-540X.2005.00381.x.

MacCannell, D. 1973. "Staged Authenticity: Arrangements of Social Space in Tourist Settings." *American Journal of Sociology* 79 (3): 589–603. https://doi.org/10.1086/225585.

Meese, J., M. Gibbs, M. Carter, M. Arnold, B. Nansen, and T. Kohn. 2015. "Selfies at Funerals: Mourning and Presencing on Social Media Platforms." *International Journal of Communication* 9: 1818–31.

Moore, C. M., and C. M. Brown. 2007. "Experiencing Body Worlds: Voyeurism, Education, or Enlightenment?" *Journal of Medical Humanities* 28 (4): 231–54. https://doi.org/10.1007/s10912-007-9042-0.

Muir, S. 2014. "Real People: Authenticity and Aboriginality in the Australian Holistic Milieu." *Ethnos* 79 (4): 473–95. https://doi.org/10.1080/00141844.2013.770411.

Olsen, K. 2002. "Authenticity as a Concept in Tourism Research: The Social Organization of the Experience of Authenticity." *Tourist Studies* 2 (2): 159–82. https://doi.org/10.1177/146879702761936644.

Oosterwijk, S. 2004. "Of Corpses, Constables, and Kings: The Danse Macabre in Late Medieval and Renaissance Culture." *Journal of the British Archaeological Association* 157 (1): 61–90. https://doi.org/10.1179/006812804799451385.

Rapport, N. 2009. "Walking Auschwitz, Walking without Arriving." *Journeys* 9 (2): 32–54.

Sayer, D. 2010. "Who's Afraid of the Dead? Archaeology, Modernity, and the Death Taboo." *World Archaeology* 42 (3): 481–91. https://doi.org/10.1080/00438243.2010.498665.

Schäfer, C. 2014. "Biography, Authenticity, and Personalised Postmortem Practices in Aotearoa/New Zealand." *Ethnos* 81 (5): 759–91.

Seaton, A. V. 1996. "Guided by the Dark: From Thanatopsis to Thanatourism." *International Journal of Heritage Studies* 2 (4): 234–44. https://doi.org/10.1080/13527259608722178.

Seaton, A. V. 2002. "Thanatourism's Final Frontiers? Visits to Cemeteries, Churchyards, and Funerary Sites as Sacred and Secular Pilgrimage." *Tourism Recreation Research* 27 (2): 73–82. https://doi.org/10.1080/02508281.2002.11081223.

Seaton, A. 2009. "Purposeful Otherness: Approaches to the Management of Thanatourism." In *The Darker Side of Travel: The Theory and Practice of Dark Tourism*, ed. R. Sharpley and P. R. Stone, 75–108. Bristol, GB: Channel View.

Sharpley, R., and P. R. Stone. 2012. "Introduction." In *Contemporary Tourist Experiences: Concepts and Consequences*, ed. R. Sharpley and P. R. Stone, 1–8. London: Routledge.

Staudt, C. 2008. "From Concealment to Recognition: The Discourse on Death, Dying, and Grief." In *Speaking of Death: America's New Sense of Mortality*, ed. M. K. Bartalos, 3–41. Westport, CT: Greenwood.

Stone, P. R. 2009. "Making Absent Death Present: Consuming Dark Tourism in Contemporary Society." In *The Darker Side of Travel: The Theory and Practice of Dark Tourism*, ed. R. Sharpley and P. R. Stone, 23–38. Bristol, GB: Channel View.

Stone, P. R. 2011. "Dark Tourism and the Cadaveric Carnival: Mediating Life and Death Narratives at Gunther von Hagens' Body Worlds." *Current Issues in Tourism* 14 (7): 685–701. https://doi.org/10.1080/13683500.2011.563839.

Stone, P. R. 2012. "Dark Tourism as Mortality Capital." In *Contemporary Tourist Experiences: Concepts and Consequences*, ed. R. Sharpley and P. R. Stone, 71–94. London: Routledge.

Stone, P. R., and R. Sharpley. 2008. "Consuming Dark Tourism: A Thanatological Perspective." *Annals of Tourism Research* 35 (2): 574–95. https://doi.org/10.1016/j.annals.2008.02.003.

Stone, P. R., and R. Sharpley. 2014. "Deviance, Dark Tourism, and Dark Leisure." In *Contemporary Perspectives in Leisure: Meanings, Motives, and Lifelong Learning*, ed. S. Elkington and S. J. Gammon, 54–64. London: Routledge.

Tanaś, S. 2008. "The Perception of Death in Cultural Tourism." *Turyzm* (Lódz) 18 (1): 51–63.

Taussig, M. 2006. *Walter Benjamin's Grave*. Chicago: University of Chicago Press. https://doi.org/10.7208/chicago/9780226790008.001.0001.

Theodossopoulos, D. 2013. "Laying Claim to Authenticity: Five Anthropological Dilemmas." *Anthropological Quarterly* 86 (2): 337–60. https://doi.org/10.1353/anq.2013.0032.

Trilling, L. 1972. *Sincerity and Authenticity*. London: Oxford University Press.

Urry, J., and J. Larsen. 2011. *The Tourist Gaze 3.0*. London: Sage. https://doi.org/10.4135/9781446251904.

Vannini, P., and J. P. Williams, eds. 2009. *Authenticity in Culture, Self, and Society*. Farnham, GB: Ashgate.

Walker Bynum, C. 1995. *The Resurrection of the Body in Western Christianity, 200–1336*. New York: Columbia University Press.

Walter, T. 2004. "Body Worlds: Clinical Detachment and Anatomical Awe." *Sociology of Health and Illness* 26 (4): 464–88. https://doi.org/10.1111/j.0141-9889.2004.00401.x.

Walter, T. 2009. "Dark Tourism: Mediating between the Dead and the Living." In *The Darker Side of Travel: The Theory and Practice of Dark Tourism*, ed. R. Sharpley and P. R. Stone, 39–55. Bristol, GB: Channel View.

Wang, N. 1999. "Rethinking Authenticity in Tourism Experience." *Annals of Tourism Research* 26 (2): 349–70. https://doi.org/10.1016/S0160-7383(98)00103-0.

Wieser, M. 2006. *St. Michael in Iphofen: Beiträge zu Baugeschichte und Instandsetzung einer gotischen Friedhofskapelle mit erhaltenem Beinhaus (no. 46)*. Gesellschaft für Fränkische Geschichte. Stegaurach: Wissenschaftlicher Kommissionsverlag.

Zimmermann, C., and G. Rodin. 2004. "The Denial of Death Thesis: Sociological Critique and Implications for Palliative Care." *Palliative Medicine* 18 (2): 121–28. https://doi.org/10.1191/0269216304pm858oa.

8

Parading through the Storm

Risk, Death, and Parades in Northern Ireland

RAY CASSERLY

Music in Northern Ireland is an often contested and complex art form, interwoven into a legacy of conflict rising from divisions tracing back several centuries. Here, public performances are often an artistic and creative series of declarations, statements of identity, history, and claims of legitimacy (Bryan 2000). These divides through performance are further reinforced when different musical forms are appropriated by political ideologies. Music becomes associated with events, peoples, and places where the "boundaries constructed in musical contexts defining 'Irish' and 'British' are as much part of the violence of the political situation as shootings and bombs" (Stokes 1994, 10). With such profound sensitivities apparent in the performance of music, an activity of leisure for many is regularly considered the new form of attack and defense in what politicians frequently refer to as part of the "Culture War."[1] An uncomfortable connection forms between leisure and death as these public performances, often recalling tragic fatal events in history, become awkwardly associated with serious public disorder and violence—risking severe injury or loss of life to the musicians, their supporters, their detractors, and members of the Police Service of Northern Ireland (PSNI).

This molding of a leisurely and entertaining pastime, the performance and enjoyment of music, into a socio-political collection of proclamations from one community to another is not an extreme or exceptional event in Northern Ireland. This small province within the United Kingdom is not unlike many other Western European societies when we consider the range and type of leisurely pursuits enjoyed by local communities. Many sports, traditional arts, and cultural displays of heritage coexist alongside live music as exceptionally popular leisurely activities across society. However, among the lower socioeconomic sectors of Northern Ireland, many of these forms of leisure and entertainment are contested, imbued with political rhetoric in the context of a post-conflict society that divides the Roman Catholic community from its Protestant neighbors. The further down the socioeconomic spectrum of society one travels, the more pronounced these divisions become, particularly in urban areas where the residential districts for each community exist in close proximity to one another. Few, if any, leisurely activities or entertaining pastimes are shared across the divide in urban working-class areas. In sports, soccer is segregated by communities based on what international, local, or Scottish soccer team one supports. Similarly, in Northern Ireland, Gaelic football is considered a virtually exclusive Roman Catholic sport (Wilson and Donnan 2006, 98–103). In west Belfast, the city council owns and operates two large health and fitness centers half a mile apart, one for each side of the dividing concrete and steel peace wall.

Music, especially traditional music, is also divided between the communities, with traditional Irish music typically considered part of the cultural domain of Roman Catholics and military marching music that of Protestants. When we envisage the performance of traditional music in Ireland, we stereotypically recall the session, a public house–based recital of music (Hast and Scott 2004). As an inclusive, relaxed, social, and leisurely experience that invites musicians and audiences to enjoy performances, contemporary Irish music sessions prioritize the enjoyment and entertainment of music, even when popular traditional songs reflecting somber aspects of Irish heritage often recollect morbid tragedies of famine and war. In an ironic contrast to these inclusive and audience-entertaining performances of morbid historical tragedies, in Northern Ireland the performance of traditional music in public is regarded as exclusive and is often found in the context of tense, politically charged, and sometimes violent displays of culture and protest during the marching season.[2] Popular examples of traditional songs that evoke violence and death in Irish history include "The Minstrel Boy," a song recalling the failed 1798 United Irishman rebellion, and "The Fields of Athenry," a song recalling the mid-nineteenth-century struggles of famine, rebellion, forced immigration, and indentured servitude. The music's strong association with Irish Roman Catholic identity presented a challenge to radical views within Protestant loyalism during the recent conflict in Northern Ireland when the paramilitary group the Red Hand Commando bombed the Jolly Judge Bar in Newtownards, County Down, in August 1993, claiming that any venue hosting traditional Irish music was a legitimate target (Vallely 2008, 5).

Existing predominantly at the opposite end of the community spectrum, parading is a comparatively large Protestant tradition. The parades and associated protests can lead to significant political and inter-community tension, as they often pass points of contestation, peace walls, or interface areas where community boundaries meet. It is at these points that leisurely activities such as music performance and symbolic display are most sensitive. Engagement in these leisurely pursuits at junctions or interfaces of two opposing communities and their respective ideologies collides with the often large-scale security operations by the PSNI. The reality of these three groups involved in aggressive confrontation with each other raises the risk of death or significant injury for participants, supporters, protesters, observers, and police, as violence is common at these performances. At these junctions where violence occurs, the meaning embedded within the leisurely activity—the performance of music and display of cultural heritage—changes dramatically for participants and observers as the emotional impact of performance in the midst of aggressive and antagonistic displays, offensive symbols, and noise from police announcements, protester chants, water cannons, and plastic bullets alters the meaning of the music. In the face of perceived threats, both the musical sounds and their associated meanings can change as the threats of death from the paramilitaries, parade participants, police, or protestors—real or perceived—impact the music and symbols and their respective interpretations for performers, supporters, protesters, and observers.

For example, the Union flag of the United Kingdom of Great Britain and Northern Ireland is carried in parades throughout the province at the front of most Protestant marching bands and loyal Protestant fraternities as a means of legitimizing the state of Northern Ireland as British (Bryan 2000; Jarman 1997). This interpretation is not contested, but the appropriateness of that symbolic statement is challenged by sections of the Roman Catholic community. For some, the flag draws upon associations with British security and military forces, thus becoming increasingly problematic for Roman Catholic radical republicans who regard aspects of the British forces as akin to a cruel and violent occupation. For the Irish republican living in Belfast, the Union flag does not merely represent the Protestant claim of Northern Ireland as British; it also symbolizes the death and destruction from the British forces' atrocities against Irish people, most notably in recent decades the massacres of Ballymurphy in Belfast in 1971 and Bloody Sunday in Londonderry in 1972. Alongside the Union flag in this discourse between the communities regarding symbolic displays on parade is the Northern Ireland flag, used to represent the Belfast-based government prior to the introduction of direct rule by the Westminster government in 1972. One of the most precarious and unpredictable parades in Northern Ireland in which such symbolism and associated musical performance intertwines with leisure, risk, and the commemoration of death and conflict is the Protestant loyalist Twelfth of July parade in north Belfast.

THE CHALLENGE OF THE TWELFTH

The annual loyalist parade organized in Belfast by local counties, districts, and lodges from the Grand Orange Lodge of Ireland on July 12 is known throughout the wider Protestant community in Northern Ireland simply as "the Twelfth."[3] Although the day is contested as one of either a commemorative or a sectarian display, the Orange Order argues that this highlight of the parade calendar provides substantial economic benefits to Northern Ireland (Grand Orange Lodge of Ireland 2013). In Belfast, where the commemorative, solemn parade recalling the great Battle of the Boyne is re-branded by the Orange Order as the leisurely celebration Orangefest. In tandem with these efforts to highlight the positive aspects of the Twelfth, in 2013 the Orange Order released a report estimating that the economic activities of the overall Protestant parading tradition include "economic and social benefits" (Grand Orange Lodge of Ireland 2013, 9) of over 54 million pounds sterling, with the cost of policing loyalist parades at nearly 5.5 million pounds sterling per annum (Grand Orange Lodge of Ireland 2013, 76). However, despite attempts to represent the parade as a celebration for the city of Belfast and presumably all of its population to enjoy, the Twelfth celebrations remain a predominantly exclusive social experience and cultural display for Protestant unionists and loyalists in Belfast, as Roman Catholic nationalists and republicans contend that the commemoration of the Battle of the Boyne in this celebratory manner is a triumphalist display of supremacy.

Although there are other Twelfth parades throughout Northern Ireland on this day, in Belfast this parade travels through several parts of the city. The predominantly male flute bands dress in quasi-military attire, and many parade supporters drape British flags over their shoulders (Bell 1990; Radford 2001; Witherow 2011). The parades start as a collective of separate feeder parades in outlying residential areas and later come together near the city center as one large demonstration, with tens of thousands of participants and supporters making their way southward along the main arterial road in south Belfast, Lisburn Road. At the end of the parade route is "the Field," where a temporary stage hosts a number of speakers and sermons purporting the Protestant Christian faith and unionist politics to a small but constant audience. The majority of parade participants and supporters take advantage of the rest, mingling between the food and beverage stalls or watching the lambeg drum competitions.

In the late afternoon, after the events in the Field have concluded, the Orange Order lodges and bands come together for the return leg of the daylong parade. Some bands change into humorous costumes, sometimes wearing clown costumes or other "fancy dress" outfits. Crowds stand along the footpaths for most of the route, which is several miles long. However, as with the morning parade, the crowds congregate at "hotspots," the particular points and junctions along the route, such as Shaftesbury Square to the south of Belfast city center, known locally as more enjoyable than others because of the increased density of the crowd and the lively atmosphere. Although the majority of the supporting crowd remains sitting on deck chairs or standing in observation of the parade, a smaller segment of the audience—the young friends and girlfriends of the band members, known as the blue bag brigade (Radford 2001)—weaves its way through the dense crowds on the footpaths to keep favorite bands within earshot. The route is peppered with hot-food stands, flag and souvenir vendors, and snack and beverage vans, which, alongside the local alcohol stores, are typically bustling with business. Friends from across Belfast meet serendipitously, and warm, enthusiastic greetings are exchanged. Be it the bands on the street, an empty beer can resting on a wall, a thrown-away plastic carton of potato fries, or the laughter, conversations, singing, and chanting enveloping the waiting parade audience, the streets of Belfast look, sound, and feel like any urban community-based festival celebration throughout much of the Western world. Here, the tone of the days' events is in a state of flux, moving between moments of commemorative, somber display of a ghastly history to boisterous encounters between friends and families from the Protestant community.

In contrast to this relaxing atmosphere, a police presence remains at the typical flashpoints of the northern routes of the Twelfth feeder parade and main parade in Belfast. In the morning of the Twelfth, these parades pass through predominantly Protestant loyalist areas yet skirt along the edges of two Catholic republican enclaves, Ardoyne and Carrickhill, presenting a challenge to these communities. It is at these interfaces where tensions typically increase, and violence in recent years has become a common feature among parade participants, supporters, and associated protestors. Although the morning parades can be relatively peaceful, some tension and displays of aggression are present as protestors hold signs and placards along the roadside and within eyesight of parade supporters, who chant and sing in support of the bands as they march. Although the morning parade has an uncomfortable atmosphere, it is the return parade in the late afternoon and early evening—after the resting time at "the Field"—that typical leads to serious conflict between the communities and the police.

In recent years the Parades Commission has restricted the outward morning Ardoyne feeder parade to just one band and one lodge, with no music or drum tap of any kind as the parade passes the shops. The Parades Commission ruled in 2013 and again in 2014 that in the evening the parade must divert away from the shops to return home. In 2013 this led to widespread violence from supporters of the Orange Order and the loyalist bands as they attempted to force their way through the police lines along their preferred route. For four nights in the summer warmth, large groups of loyalists congregated at the police lines to chant, taunt, throw missiles, and perform band tunes among the din of police loudspeakers, sirens, dogs, helicopters, and water cannons. During these four nights of rioting, more than seventy police officers were injured.

Throughout the violence an almost jovial attitude toward the conflict existed despite the significant levels of serious injury among both police and rioters. People dressed in shorts and T-shirts, some men topless, stood around drinking as the sound of a flute band was heard approaching.[4] As the band reached the police lines where the loyalist protesters were waiting, the level of violence increased as men and women jumped on the bonnets of the armored police vehicles—dancing, kicking, and striking at the riot police standing their ground in a form of recreational rioting (Jarman and O'Halloran 2001). These riots involved significant disruption for the people of Belfast through the blocking of roads, hijacking of vehicles, and communities coming under siege while stones, petrol bombs, and paint bombs were hurled at the PSNI or the opposing community by young—often male—rioters (Leonard 2010, 38). Rioting in this circumstance is not only a means of expressing one's frustration at socio-political developments in Northern Ireland or the marking of territorial boundaries but is also a means of providing a dangerous and challenging pastime in Belfast's most divided areas. From the respondents in Leonard's (2010) research, it was clear that these threefold perspectives on the cause of engaging, and the invitation to engage, in rioting were not exclusive, that is, all three areas informed the decision to engage in rioting.

The 2013 Twelfth parade in Belfast was also subject to restrictions by the Parades Commission as it passed by the Carrickhill area and the local Roman Catholic Church. On July 5, 2013, the commission determined that "on the outward morning and return evening parade only respectful hymn tunes shall be played" (Parades Commission for Northern Ireland 2013, 6) as the parade passed St. Patrick's Roman Catholic Church. The commission also determined that those on parade "must behave with due regard for the rights, traditions and feelings of others in the vicinity; refrain from using words or behaviour which could reasonably be perceived as intentionally sectarian, provocative, threatening, abusive, insulting or lewd" (Parades Commission for Northern Ireland 2013, 6). In reaction to the previous Twelfth parade, during which the Protestant YCV flute band (known as the Young Conway Volunteers and Young Citizen Volunteers) performed the offensive "Famine Song" while supporters sang along outside the church, the commission determined that "there shall be no singing, chanting, or loud drumming and that marching should be dignified" (Parades Commission for Northern Ireland 2013, 7). The performance of the "Famine Song" in 2012, referring in a taunting manner to the mass emigration of Irish people to avoid the death, disease, and destruction of the mid-nineteenth-century Potato Famine, became popular among Protestant loyalists as a football supporter's chant during Glasgow Rangers' games. In this case the performance was recorded on a mobile phone by a nearby Roman Catholic resident,[5] who was threatened, physically attacked, and chased away by members of the YCV band. When the song was sung before the steps of St. Patrick's Church, the performance on that day was deemed as "outrageous and inflammatory behaviour which could have precipitated serious public disorder" by District Judge Paul Copeland, as thirteen members of the band were convicted at Belfast Magistrates Court on April 29, 2015, for provocatively playing a sectarian tune (British Broadcasting Corporation 2015).

Having perceived the Parades Commission's determination as a challenge to their right to perform as they wished, during the 2013 parade some bands performed immediately in front of the church as they would at any other parade, opting to play, in unambiguous defiance of the Parades Commission's determination, the popular traditional Protestant song "The Sash My Father Wore." In addition to the lyrics referring to the Battle of the Boyne, in 2013 the singing of this song outside St. Patrick's Church was an antagonistic display of aggression equal to the previous year's performance of the "Famine Song." With the precedent of violence stemming from the performance of music in the area having been established in 2012 (British Broadcasting Corporation 2012), performing a song that recalled and celebrated a battle that led to significant loss of life for both Protestants and Roman Catholics was not only an act of defiance of the Parades Commission but a musical and lyrical assault on nearby Roman Catholic residents. Such displays reinforce the republican view that these parades are not sincere commemorations of significant historical events, as advocated by the Orange Order, but instead triumphalist displays of authority, or challenges to authority, by the bands.

What is it that leads the two communities to consider a commemorative parade as either of vital importance to their cultural heritage or in gross violation of the same? How can one group of people view the concerns of another as a direct challenge to its cultural rights to commemorate the past? There is no single, all-inclusive answer to these questions, but an understanding of the communal memory (Connerton 1989), the historical narratives of conflict that interconnect in this parade, provides critical insights into how violent actions can arise without being considered contradictory to the meaning of the parade. Albeit an often predictable outcome, what is regarded by some as a cultural performance is perceived as a visual and acoustic assault by others. Conversely, the protest or surveillance of these performances is regarded by the former as a preemptive display of aggression. Regardless, these leisurely musical displays present a challenge to some or are conversely met with challenge, which can successfully conjoin the marking of territory with a cathartic outburst and be combined with relief from boredom to encourage young persons to engage in the hostile, dangerous, and potentially lethal activity of rioting.

CONFLICT REENACTMENT AND RECREATIONAL CONFLICT

Although to outside observers the parade for most of its route is overtly festive and celebratory, there is also an overt commemorative element to the Twelfth. However, the historical narrative surrounding the latter is a conflation of three distinct historical events for Ulster Protestants. First, the Twelfth of July parade, or demonstration as referred to by the Orange Order, is conceived and explained by organizers as a solemn commemoration of the great battle between the English Catholic king James and the victorious Dutch Protestant king William of Orange in 1690 along the banks of the River Boyne, just outside the walled port town of Drogheda (Bryan 2000). The significance of this event is not entirely lost in the midst of the festivities, as a member of the Hounds of Ulster, a predominantly Protestant flute band from north Belfast, once said, "We [Protestants] were always told it was where we beat the Taigs" (anonymous source, November 19, 2008).[6] However, the context, symbolism, and displays of the Ulster Volunteer Force in the Twelfth parade in north Belfast conflate this commemoration with another significant event in Protestant unionist communal memory: the 1916 Battle of the Somme.

As Europe eagerly engaged in the arms race prior to World War I, Ireland was in the midst of significant political changes through the nationalist-led Home Rule movement (Elliot 2001), leading to the development of the opposing Ulster Volunteer Force (UVF). Members of the UVF later enlisted en masse in Kitchener's Third Army as the 36th Ulster Division, where they fought in the Battle of the Somme. This epic battle is regarded among Protestant unionists as the blood sacrifice by the men of Ulster for the preservation of their rights as British Protestants in Ireland: the fulfillment of commitments made in the Ulster Covenant to protect and maintain Ulster from the perceived perils of Home Rule and Catholic domination (Loughlin 2002; Novick 2002). The Battle of the Somme and the commemoration thereof, despite having a festive and celebratory overtone in Belfast, is more than a leisurely or passive communal recollection of a key historical event for Great Britain. It is also the performance statement, or performance reminder, to the British State and its obligation to the British Protestant community in Northern Ireland. The suffering and loss experienced by the Ulster units in the battle has been described to me by David Scott, education officer for the Grand Orange Lodge of Ireland, as a great "betrayal of the Protestant people" (July 3, 2013).

What further complicates the context of this commemorative parade is the fact that World War I was not the last time the name UVF appeared as a viable paramilitary force. In the 1960s an organization that formed in Northern Ireland, led by Gusty Spence, named itself the Ulster Volunteer Force. This force argued that Northern Ireland was under threat from Roman Catholic nationalist and republican agitation and considered acts of violence the only suitable recourse. For the

1960s UVF, the conflict between Catholics and Protestants over civil rights and liberties in Northern Ireland was, in the unionist mythic tradition, the continuation or next phase in ensuring British Protestant ascendancy in Northern Ireland. It is contested both within and outside the Protestant community whether the 1960s organization is a re-formation of the original UVF or an entirely new organization. Unionists who argue that the two are not the same contend that the original UVF recalled during the Twelfth has no connection to the newer organization that has usurped the title of the original paramilitary force. Loyalists who support the claim that the newer organization is the same reformed version of the original contend that the parade reflects the link between the two. This argument by loyalists who support the idea that the newer UVF is a reformed version of the original is strengthened in the parade, as bands supported by the contemporary UVF display banners and flags, wear period militaristic uniforms, and perform tunes and songs that refer unambiguously to the UVF and its role in the Battle of the Somme. Connections between paramilitary organizations and marching bands is not a recent trend, as throughout the Troubles, groups like the UVF supported the formation and maintenance of numerous marching bands throughout the province as a means of displaying their presence within the Protestant community, providing a social or political activity for young people in the area, and developing a potential recruitment arena. However, the UVF has in recent times become openly and overtly involved in the communal commemorations of the Battle of the Somme and other centenary events relating to the Home Rule crisis.

These three histories are conflated through the display of symbols and performance of tunes and songs relating to the Battle of the Boyne, the Battle of the Somme, and the Troubles during one parade performance. Tunes that recall the Battle of the Somme are played by bands supported by the contemporary UVF while dressed in regalia and uniforms that recall the 1916 UVF. Equally, tunes that recall the role of the UVF in 1916 are performed in front of Orange Lodges with banners that reflect the significance of the Battle of the Boyne. Juxtaposed to these are the flags and banners that recall the UVF, none of which are presented passively at the front of a band parade for all in the crowd to merely observe. The flags, in tandem with the tunes, become important symbolic artifacts actively engaged by the bands in the rituals commemorating conflict and death along the parade route.

Throughout the day the parade passes by commemorative sites and war memorials, including the memorials at Belfast City Hall, where selected bands and lodges stop to tilt the flags forward as a salute to the dead of World War I and the Troubles while the band performs a religious hymn. As David Scott describes the Orange Order perspective, "We would play our normal march tunes on parade [for entertainment], but as soon as we arrive in close proximity of the war memorial it would be hymn tunes. The tone would change. So, for me it's all about remembrance" (July 3, 2013). However, despite this ritual in the parade echoing the commemorative purpose of the event, Scott believes younger audience members still see the overall experience as primarily a social, leisurely opportunity and entertainment. According to Scott, "The first thing they see, and having spoken to a number of young people from youth projects I work with, the first thing that they do see is the band parade. So, it is a traditional band parade... People under the age of twenty-five would not see the significance of the day. They just see it as an Orange thing where 'ach, they're just laying another wreath'" (July 3, 2013). Although Scott questions the level of young people's critical engagement with the legacy of the conflicts, there is little doubt that the historical narrative of Ulster Protestants fighting for their survival resonates with young male working-class loyalist Protestants during a contemporary contested parade. A member of the Shankill Protestant Boys Flute Band once argued to me that without the successful outcome of the Battle of the Boyne, "we [Protestants] wouldn't exist here" (January 25, 2008).

Through webs of association (Reily 2002), the historical narrative evolves from a commemoration of a historical event to a message that Protestant Ulster was and is in need of defensive, aggressive, and proactive paramilitary organizations like the UVF. Essentially, these performances by large numbers of young working-class Protestants are a means of legitimizing the contemporary UVF by articulating through performance an imagined correlation in the circumstances the organizations faced. In World War I the original UVF joined British military forces to protect its interests at home in the face of rising Irish nationalism. In facing a compulsive and profound fear that Home Rule in Ireland would equate to rule by the Roman Catholic Church, members of the UVF enlisted in support of the British war effort as a means of securing British government support for their agenda. In other centenary celebrations Billy Hutchinson, a contemporary public figure and convicted member of the UVF, dressed as anti–Home Rule politician Lord Carson as part of the commemorations of the Ulster Covenant. This attempt to draw a correlation between the events in 1916 and those in the 1960s, with the UVF the continuing presence in both, appears to have achieved its aims. A member of the south Belfast faction of the Ulster Defense Association (UDA), an organization formed at the outset of the Troubles, shared an anecdotal story in June 2014 of a young teenager in his area approaching him to ask why the UDA didn't fight alongside the UVF in the Battle of the Somme.

The blurring of these historical lines is not accidental, and the timing of this shift toward overt commemorations of 1916—even during 1690 commemorations—is not coincidental. In recent years Belfast has witnessed an increase in sectarian violence along the Ardoyne and Carrickhill interfaces as groups within loyalism express frustration at the peace process, arguing that historical and retrospective investigations into their actions by the police, city council decisions regarding the flying of flags over civic buildings, and perceived concessions to nationalists and republicans—particularly the decisions of the Parades Commission—are all products of the peace process and evidence of victories for the republican agenda. It is here where the display by the UVF through flags, emblems, uniforms, and tunes among the bands legitimizes its contemporary role as a perceived defender of loyalist Ulster. By raising the profile of the UVF and creating an air of legitimacy around its existence and contemporary purpose, the political wing of the UVF, the Progressive Unionist Party, can hope to mimic the electoral success of radical Irish republicanism. This also increases the UVF's influence over competing loyalist paramilitary organizations such as the UDA.

As the peace process progresses, increasing numbers of young loyalists are becoming disaffected with feelings of social exclusion, isolation from politics, educational underachievement, and economic depravity. All of this is juxtaposed against constant media images of Sinn Féin representatives in government, which for many loyalist commentators reflects the rewards of violence. When Catholic communities object to these commemorative parades, young loyalists view this as a republican strategy to challenge and repress the cultural identity of Ulster Protestants. This, in tandem with the increasing visual presence of the UVF in Belfast loyalist areas during parades and riots and on murals, presents the angry young loyalists with a paramilitary force and a conviction of historical legitimacy. Just as the conflicts during the Troubles recalled and reenacted the Battle of the Somme and the Somme recalled and reenacted the Battle of the Boyne, today's parading loyalists recall all of the conflicts as defending their rights as British Protestants in Northern Ireland.

In situations where flags and music relating to the UVF are displayed and performed during a Protestant parade, a contest of meaning takes place in the public discourse regarding the flag and the historical role of the UVF. However, the presence of UVF symbols and music on certain parade routes creates a totally different interpretation among nationalist and republican residents. For them, the context of the display appears as an attempt to demarcate territory and intimidate residents through a show of strength for the contemporary UVF, the organization that appeared in the 1960s. For republicans, the large numbers of bands and crowds in the area constitute a triumphalist display and restrict the movements of the community while the parade and security operation is in effect; this is the first stage of a siege.

The PSNI tactic in recent years has been to create a physical gulf by placing temporary barriers, steel walls, and rows of armored police vehicles where possible to keep the communities apart. However, it is not always possible for the PSNI to ensure that the two communities do not come into contact and conflict when dealing with large parades and protests. Inevitably, for many young loyalists the march toward police lines or through Catholic areas during these parades resonates with a legacy of violence. When a band like the Shankill Protestant Boys, which has strong associations with the proscribed paramilitary organization, the UVF, marches toward the police line, the images evoke communal recollections of the Troubles and the struggle against republicanism but equally the significance of World War I and the Battle of the Somme. Just as the men of Ulster went over the top to march toward the enemy with the sound of military music echoing in their ears, incensed parading loyalists not only reenact but also relive the conflicts, albeit in circumstances that are less immediately fatal but still dangerous. Here, in the heat of a contested parade, the young loyalist can "do their bit" for Ulster in preserving their cultural heritage and rights. The recreational riot is a reference to violence as exclusive entertainment but also a means through which one can engage in violent conduct to express and demonstrate a reading of history and contemporary political contexts. In the midst of fervent opposition from republicans, these parades move from commemorative and festive to a source of open conflict, a performative reenactment of a violent division that traces back three centuries. With the tense presence of the protestors and parade participants, divided along this particular interface only by a line of police officers and armored vehicles, bottles and other missiles are sometimes thrown from one side to the other.

CONCLUSION

Martin Stokes (1994, 12) argues that music in itself is an experience in which "social identity is literally 'embodied,'" one through which our ethnic boundaries are constructed, reinforced, and maintained. It becomes one of the less innocent ways in which dominant categories, or boundaries, are enforced and resisted. In this respect, music in the north Belfast Twelfth parades emulates a tangible, socio-political, and historical divide by constructing or reinforcing cultural boundaries between the different communities. The fact that so many visual and acoustic displays in the parading tradition reflect the past, or at least perceptions of the past, correlates the past with the present whether the parade is organized by a republican or a loyalist organization.

Every year a number of parades fall on or near the anniversary of significant battles and other morbid events in the histories of the Protestant and Roman Catholic communities. Just as a republican historical narrative can conflate substantially different periods in history by performing songs that tell British soldiers to "go on home," soon followed by a song recalling the foggy dew in Dublin during the 1916 Easter Rising, the Twelfth parade displays by loyalists conflate the contemporary conflict with the Battles of the Somme and the Boyne. Unlike an indoor republican rebel band performance, loyalist parades travel to and through interface areas where their songs, symbols, and associated meanings are aggressively challenged by Catholic republicans. As the police intervene to keep the sides apart, the "battle lines" are redrawn, but instead of the conflict taking place along the grassy slopes of a river near Drogheda or near a river in the French countryside, this particular no-man's land exists on streets between the footpaths and sidewalks of north Belfast.

The ability for the communities to reach an accommodation or mutual compromise through discussion is unlikely in the near future, as senior members of the Orange Order are publically critical of engaging with the republican Sinn Féin political party. Even in the city of Londonderry, where discussions between the Apprentice Boys of Derry (ABOD) and republicans have led to an understanding on parades, Billy Moore, secretary of the ABOD, who was involved in the initial talks, spoke to me of how the decision to meet with the republicans was considered drastic by some who considered that they were "meeting with the enemy" (June 24, 2014). Similarly, power struggles in north Belfast between republicans in support of the peace process and those against it lead both groups to compete for the most obdurate position on parading. Prior to the failed 2013 Haass and O'Sullivan peace talks in Belfast—an initiative supported by the US, UK, and Irish governments to finalize arrangements on how both communities can agree to deal with the legacy of the past, the display of symbols, and parading—an agreement was previously reached by the two main parties, the Democratic Unionist Party (DUP) and Sinn Féin, on parading. This proposal was rejected by the Orange Order and failed to proceed further, with the perspective of the women's Orange Order never featuring in public discourse.

The contested parade and protest is an adrenaline-fueled opportunity to vent frustration against decisions by the Parades Commission, the government, the Police Service of Northern Ireland, and those considered the opposite community. Described to me as "recreational rioting" by a police officer at the Closing of the Gates parade in Londonderry in December 2008, the age profile of rioters in recent years appears, according to police reports in the media, to be thirteen–eighteen.[7] This is not to suggest that rioting around a parade or associated protest is merely done for fun. There is little doubt that those who commit themselves to street violence are angry at the circumstances surrounding their lives and are encouraged to take action against their "opposition" by local paramilitaries. This does raise concern about the trajectory of Northern Ireland and the ability for cultural performances to become shared experiences across the divide. Violence will likely remain a romanticized feature of the historical narratives in Northern Ireland: even in 2012 a government minister of the Stormont Executive in Belfast, Nelson McCausland, refused to condemn those who engage in illegal violence in reaction to Parades

Commission determinations.[8] Here, street violence surrounding parades, when compared to the history of violence in Northern Ireland, is a means of "dipping your toe." Parading and violence is a means of being present to the risk of death—the metaphorical walking to the edge of the cliff—without the final, ultimate, and irreversible leap into eternity.

NOTES

1. "Culture War" is popular term among Democratic Unionist Party figures and other representatives from the Protestant community who contend that support for Irish language, culture, and arts is part of a campaign to isolate the Protestant British identity (the Newsletter 2015).

2. The marching season in Northern Ireland is an annual period of extensive parading from Easter to the end of August, with some exceptions occurring outside this parameter.

3. The Grand Orange Lodge of Ireland is also known as the Orange Order and is the largest Protestant fraternity in Northern Ireland. The overwhelming majority of cultural and religious organizations that parade as part of Protestant culture in Northern Ireland are exclusively male fraternities. These include the Grand Orange Lodge of Ireland, the Apprentice Boys of Derry, and the Royal Black Preceptory. A women's Orange Order exists, but this organization is smaller in number and is considered less significant in the local political context.

4. http://youtu.be/miSccViaoK4, accessed August 30, 2014. This YouTube video provides an ideal vantage point of the start of the 2013 riot at Ardoyne.

5. https://youtu.be/My5cf2zlkp0, accessed April 30, 2015.

6. Taig is a derogatory term for Roman Catholics in Northern Ireland.

7. https://www.theguardian.com/uk/2012/dec/18/northern-ireland-police-arrest-children-riots, accessed September 24, 2014.

8. http://www.bbc.co.uk/news/uk-northern-ireland-politics-19636275, accessed September 24, 2014.

REFERENCES

Bell, Desmond. 1990. *Acts of Union: Youth Culture and Sectarianism in Northern Ireland.* London: Macmillan. https://doi.org/10.1007/978-1-349-21014-5.

British Broadcasting Corporation. 2012. *Timeline of North Belfast Trouble.* http://www.bbc.co.uk/news/uk-northern-ireland-19489545.

British Broadcasting Corporation. 2015. *Young Conway Volunteers: Band Members Convicted in "Sectarian Song" Case.* Accessed April 30, 2015. http://www.bbc.co.uk/news/uk-northern-ireland-32523364.

Bryan, Dominic. 2000. *Orange Parades: The Politics of Ritual, Tradition, and Control.* London: Pluto.

Connerton, Paul. 1989. *How Societies Remember.* Cambridge: Cambridge University Press. https://doi.org/10.1017/CBO9780511628061.

Elliot, Marianne. 2001. *The Catholics of Ulster: A History.* London: Penguin.

Grand Orange Lodge of Ireland. 2013. "The Socio-Economic Impact of the Traditional Protestant Parading Sector in Northern Ireland." Belfast: RSM McClure Watters. Accessed July 9, 2014. http://www.grandorangelodge.co.uk/docs/may13-report.pdf.

Hast, Dorothea, and Stanley Scott. 2004. *Music in Ireland: Experiencing Music, Expressing Culture.* Oxford: Oxford University Press.

Jarman, Neil. 1997. *Material Conflicts: Parades and Visual Displays in Northern Ireland.* Oxford: Berg.

Jarman, Neil, and Chris O'Halloran. 2001. "Recreational Rioting: Young People, Interface Areas, and Violence." *Child Care in Practice* 7 (1): 2–16. https://doi.org/10.1080/13575270108413230.

Leonard, Madeleine. 2010. "What's Recreational about Recreational Rioting? Children on the Streets in Belfast." *Children and Society* 24 (1): 38–49. https://doi.org/10.1111/j.1099-0860.2008.00190.x.

Loughlin, James. 2002. "Mobilising the Sacred Dead: Ulster Unionism, the Great War, and the Politics of Remembrance." In *Ireland and the Great War: A War to Unite Us All?* ed. Adrian Gregory and Senia Paseta, 133–54. Manchester, GB: Manchester University Press.

The Newsletter. 2015. *Irish Schools Initiative "Stepping up SF Cultural War."* Accessed April 30, 2015. http://www.newsletter.co.uk/news/education/irish-schools-initiative-stepping-up-sf-cultural-war-1-6567119.

Novick, Ben. 2002. "The Arming of Ireland: Gun-Running and the Great War." In *Ireland and the Great War: A War to Unite Us All?* ed. Adrian Gregory and Senia Paseta, 94–112. Manchester, GB: Manchester University Press.

Parades Commission for Northern Ireland. 2013. *Determination Made in Relation to County Grand Orange Lodge of Belfast Parade Notified to Take Place in Belfast on Friday 12th July 2013.* Accessed September 1, 2014. http://www.paradescommission.org/viewparade.aspx?id=42592.

Radford, Katy. 2001. "Drum Rolls and Gender Roles in Protestant Marching Bands in Belfast." *British Journal of Ethnomusicology* 10 (2): 37–59. https://doi.org/10.1080/09681220108567319.

Reily, Suzel. 2002. *Voices of the Magi: Enchanted Journeys in Southeast Brazil.* London: University of Chicago Press.

Stokes, Martin. 1994. *Ethnicity, Identity, and Music: The Musical Construction of Place*. Oxford: Berg.

Vallely, Fintan. 2008. *Tuned Out: Traditional Music and Identity in Northern Ireland*. Cork: Cork University Press.

Wilson, Thomas, and Hastings Donnan. 2006. *Anthropology of Ireland*. Oxford: Berg.

Witherow, Jackie. 2011. "Marching Bands in Northern Ireland." A study carried out on behalf of the Department of Culture, Arts, and Leisure, in partnership with the Confederation of Ulster Bands. Accessed June 26, 2011. https://www.dcalni.gov.uk/marching_bands_study.pdf.

9

How to Eat an Endangered Species

Gastronomic Tourism and Cinta Senese Pigs

RACHEL A. HORNER BRACKETT

The undulating hills of Chianti vineyards and olive groves dotted with cypress trees nestle deep within the tourist's imagination of Tuscany. Medieval towers rise up unfettered by craggy landscapes or the whine of Piaggio *Ape* three-wheeled tractors and Vespa scooters. At the table, a two-inch-thick *Bistecca Fiorentina* T-bone steak epitomizes the carnivorous rusticity of an Italian hearth. Between the wine tastings, glimpses of Renaissance frescoes, and a late afternoon sunlight that renders the world into soft focus, it is easy to understand why so many seek the bucolic pleasures of Tuscany. In a region so frequently and ardently visited, savored, and acclaimed, what novel forms of tourism remain?

Eating well remains central to an experience of the Italian countryside for many, but gastronomic tourists in particular strive to access "authentic" foods and may seek out direct connections with the region's food producers themselves. In this chapter I present ethnographic research on an agritourism estate in Tuscany, the Tenuta di Spannocchia, where the endangered Cinta Senese pig is raised, butchered, and consumed. Here, eating Cinta Senese ("Siena Belted") pork operates as a distinctive form of gastronomic tourism. Visitors arrive at Spannocchia keen to observe the pastoral life of the pigs in their natural environment and then, paradoxically, to savor the essence of that life and death at the dining table. They seek out the unique culinary experience of dining on artisanal meat products within feet of where the animals are born, raised, and butchered. Cinta Senese pork production brings the normally unexamined death and subsequent butchery of animals to the forefront of the tourist experience.

DOI: 10.5876/9781607327295.c009

The visceral transformation of Cinta Senese pigs into celebrated pork products attracts new visitors to a region long distinguished—and, some may argue, oversaturated—by tourism. Whereas most definitions of dark tourism encompass the acts, sites, or attractions surrounding *human* death (cf. Lennon and Foley 2000; Seaton 1996; Stone 2006), here I focus on the life and postmortem transformation of a rare livestock breed. Normally, when we think of endangered animal species, the idea of *eating* them is far from our minds. Lingering on the margins between life and permanent annihilation, the survival of many endangered species relies on wildlife conservation strategies. However, in the case of domesticated heritage livestock breeds, cultivating consumer demand for animal food products is central to conservation efforts. Ironically, to conserve a rare species of domesticated livestock, we must sometimes quite literally "eat it to save it." As such, sustainable and artisanal food production methods carry a new form of social distinction. Consumers hold positive attitudes toward "traditional" methods of breeding, rearing, and butchering; and they value foods produced in this way for their taste and prestige. Likewise, producers explicitly link their products to local geography, history, and cultural identity when marketing to tourists and locals alike. The Cinta Senese pig symbolically represents the cultural traditions of agriculture in southern Tuscany. To explore the intersection of gastronomic tourism, butchering, and rare breed livestock, I conducted participant observation research at Spannocchia in 2008–9. My unique position there as an anthropologist-turned–volunteer farmworker and butchering assistant provided insight not only on the everyday activities of food producers and pigs but also on how these activities are reframed and presented for a tourist audience hungry for new experiences.

FOOD AND PLEASURE IN ITALY

Culinary tourism has existed in Italy at least since the British encountered the Neapolitan *maccheroni* eaters in the late eighteenth century (Dickie 2008). With heads tilted back, lips curling luxuriously around long strands of pasta descending from hands above, the pasta eaters shocked and delighted those on the Grand Tour. Both then and today, "Culinary tourism is about food; exploring and discovering culture and history through food and food-related activities in the creation of memorable experiences" (Long 2005). Tuscany is saturated with Sangiovese-stained tour groups, olive oil tastings, and culinary expeditions promising four-course lunches with a view of the countryside. In light of this inundation, an increasing number of tourists seeking an "authentic" experience of Tuscany look beyond the Chianti and bruschetta (delicious and ubiquitous though they may be) to rediscover the *prodotti tipici*, or typical dishes/products, of the region. For these gastronomic tourists, dishes like *lampredotto* (tripe) sandwiches, *ribolitta* vegetable and bread soup, chestnut flour cakes, and *buristo* (blood sausage) signify the "real" Tuscany.

Rosario Scarpato argues that *gastronomic* tourism, when compared with *culinary* tourism, includes both a wider range of foods and a deeper consideration of the cultural practices surrounding the production and consumption of those foods (Scarpato 2002). In this definition, gastronomy *is* culture, and food serves as one medium of meaningful cultural exploration. As such, the connection between "taste" and "place" is understood not only as a sensory experience of a particular food but also as a social index of the individuals who produce it and those who travel to consume it (Paxson 2008; Trubek 2008; Weiss 2011). The useful Italian phrase *saperi e sapori* (knowledge and taste) phonetically connects gustatory pleasure with cultural and material conceptions of food.

Because of its intrinsic role in the preservation of certain agricultural products such as the Cinta Senese discussed here, gastronomic tourism in Tuscany is also closely tied to the presentation of rural culture (Corigliano 2002). The success of Frances Mayes's 1997 book (and subsequent film) *Under the Tuscan Sun*, an autobiographical account of restoring a crumbling villa and the sensual pleasures of life therein, opened the gates for a flood of memoirs and novels—always peppered with recipes from the region—related to discovering authentic life in rural *Toscana* (cf. de Blasi 2004; Elon 2009; Máté 1998; Tucker 2007). Unfortunately, these authors often present local Italian inhabitants as cultural Others living, working, and eating in a mythologized or essentialized peasant past (Ross 2010). Such stereotyping results in an imprudent version of the realities of rural Tuscan life. Anthropologist Anne Meneley worked with olive producers in Tuscany, who reported that they found *Under the Tuscan Sun* "often saccharine, inaccurate and boring, [but] they argued that it had had a positive impact on the tourist trade" (Meneley 2004, 167). Meneley argues that "the commodification of Tuscany itself depends on foreign imaginings of it as a desirable place" (Meneley 2004, 167). She describes this positive discursive production as "reverse orientalism," or the inverse of Edward Said's (1979) formulation regarding the negative discursive productions and social stereotypes of the Middle East. As such, Tuscany offers a rich context for the expression and pursuit of cultural capital by outsiders, although local residents and producers may exist far outside the idealized mythology of the region. Moreover, this leisurely pursuit of gastronomic knowledge and pleasure largely overlooks the region's underlying histories of poverty and death.

Throughout Tuscany, reification of an agricultural past plays a central role in the ideology of food, and the typical dishes sought by gastronomic tourists are celebrated for their rustic simplicity. However, for centuries this agricultural past was based on the *mezzadria* sharecropping system, in which a handful of wealthy urban landowners contracted peasant families to live on and work the land in exchange for half (*mezza*) of the products made there. This system has been viewed variously as either a relatively balanced system of economic sharing or as one marked by extremes in poverty that grossly exploited peasant labor (Black 2002). Carole Counihan's (2004) ethnographic work on food and memory in Tuscany reveals that the sharecroppers' diet was largely one of bread and thin minestrone soups, with very little meat, cheese, or variety. Items like tripe sandwiches and blood sausages currently celebrated for their typicality and authenticity are in fact the foods once consumed by the poor out of necessity rather than culinary adventure. Dishes formerly associated with poverty, monotony, and poor nutrition are now heralded as typical regional specialties. For example, polenta (cornmeal) saw a surge in popularity among urbanite American foodies in the late 1980s, but as Scarpato points out: "The rise of Italian polenta in the media and on tables around the world happened in the name of these myths . . . no nostalgic editors of glossy food magazines ever told their readers the other story of polenta, which in the past killed hundreds of peasants forced to eat only that 'authentic, simple' food" (Scarpato 2002, 63).

The story of *lardo*, a charcuterie pork product made from salted and cured back fat, offers a similar tale. Once used as a proletarian hunger-killer consumed by impoverished marble miners, *lardo* is currently marketed to gourmands as an exotic delicacy. In the past, the miners who consumed *lardo* were both united through its consumption and distinguished from those who did not; as Deborah Gewertz and Frederick Errington point out, eaters of undesirable cuts of meat "know that they are eating what others reject because they have decidedly less efficacy in the world" (Gewertz and Errington 2010, 26). Yet today, a producer of *lardo* is viewed as the "quintessential modern subject, a holder par excellence of national heritage" (Leitch 2003, 447). The *New York Times* travel column outlined overnight excursions for tourists to sample *lardo* onsite (Williams 2010), and demand for traditional *Lardo di Colonnata* currently outstrips supply.

Even when gustatory mythologies turn a blind eye to certain historical realities, gastronomic tourism in Italy continues to offer a rich context for the expression and pursuit of cultural capital and leisure by outsiders. Pierre Bourdieu posited that it is the dominant socioeconomic class that marks certain foods and ways of eating as both gastronomically and metaphorically "in good taste" (Bourdieu 1984). For Bourdieu, highbrow tastes marked by an intellectualized appreciation of food are pitted against the seemingly un-reflexive consumption of the lower classes. Carefully refined aesthetic preferences operated to bolster and reproduce social inequality, and taste served as a marker of distinction between social groups. However, the reappropriation of traditional peasant foods as a new form of cultural capital for today's gastronomic tourists complicates this notion of "good taste."

Richard Peterson and Roger Kern (1996) restructure the significance of distinction by introducing the concept of a "cultural omnivore," an individual who claims to have an appreciation for all forms of culture, including those created by socially marginal groups such as isolated rural people and racial minorities. Rather than embrace an exclusionary ideology of taste, the cultural omnivore transgresses the boundaries between high and low culture to consume the exotic and "authentic" as a means to achieve distinction (Warde, Wright, and Gayo-Cal 2007). Here, distinction is found in foods like fresh hand-rolled tortillas (Bordi 2006), organic mesclun salads (Guthman 2003), or sausages made from sustainably raised, antibiotic-free pigs. No longer the *habitus* of a bourgeois gourmand, the consumption of foods marked as heritage, Slow, fair, sustainable, and so on advances a viewpoint in which "taste can be developed as a form of human capital and common consumption practices allow one to acquire a form of cultural capital" (Pietrykowski 2004, 315). The omnivore creates a new breed of culinary cultural relativism. In contrast, Josée Johnston and Shyon Baumann (2007) argue that omnivorous consumption strategies simply denote a qualitative shift in the ways elite status is marked. Suddenly, cultural and gastronomic eclecticism functions as an alternative strategy for generating status rather than an end to social distinction per se. The gastronomic tourist is both reflective and reflexive at the table. How does this new breed of enlightened pleasure seekers respond when the topic of death is brought, sometimes quite literally, to the table?

FROM FIELD TO TABLE WITH THE CULTURAL OMNIVORE

The sustainable and artisanal food production methods used at the Tenuta di Spannocchia embody this new form of social distinction. According to the foundation's executive director, there has been a shift in awareness among the people visiting Spannocchia. "Ten years ago, visitors came to Tuscany to see art," she says. "Now they want to understand what's going on with agriculture and the environment." Spannocchia is a roughly 1,100-acre estate located approximately 30 kilometers southwest of Siena. Even for those with a car, the estate is moderately difficult to access, as it is located several kilometers up a steep hillside off a winding rural road. Atop this forested hill, Spannocchia's 800-year-old stone tower overlooks organic wine and olive oil production, an active rare breed animal husbandry program, and a range of tourist activities including cooking classes, wild herb collection, and hikes to the ruins of a medieval fortress nestled in the woods. With only a single internet-accessible computer, a handful of telephones, and no television to speak of, the site feels remote. Hundreds of people visit Spannocchia each year anticipating an experience of rural Tuscany rooted in food and pastoral life. The tourist high season at Spannocchia extends from late May to mid-September. With seven guesthouses that can hold anywhere from four to nine people and sixteen guest rooms in the central villa, it is possible for dozens of visitors to be on the estate at any given time.

When planning their trip online, visitors are warned that Spannocchia is "truly rural and not a vacation resort; rather it is an historic working farm, a wildlife preserve, and an educational center" (http://www.spannocchia.com/rentals/, accessed November 11, 2017). Guests must join the Spannocchia Foundation prior to arrival, at a minimum cost of forty-five dollars for individuals. Richard, the American-born husband of the estate's owner, explained to me that this process weeds out many of those who want to "drink red wine by the pool under the Tuscan sun." Yet Spannocchia creates a unique opportunity for tourists to engage in unscripted interactions with the cooks, farmers, viticulturists, and butchers working onsite and carrying out daily activities. The estate is well-suited for the cultural omnivore; during nightly communal meals visitors excitedly regaled me with experiences from their day, which might include watching Cinta Senese pigs rooting beneath fig trees, discussions in broken Italian with the head gardener, or simply a relaxed stroll with one of the resident farm dogs. As Janet Chrzan writes, "What would normally be considered the back stage area from a tourist perspective dissolves into the foreground, creating authentic experiences for Spannocchia's guests" (Chrzan 2007, 26). However, this means that food producers at Spannocchia must attend not only to locally situated economic and ecologic concerns but also to the expectations and demands of an increasingly international audience.

Both local and international visitors noted that the Cinta Senese tours held on the farm were highlights of their time on the estate. These tours, which take place weekly and last approximately two hours, introduce tourists to the rare breeds program at Spannocchia. According to a flyer available in the estate's villa, the tour includes a walk to the fields and forests where the hogs live, a visit to the curing room where butchering and preserving take place, a climb up the twelfth-century tower, a visit to the small cantina where organic red and white wine and *vin santo* are made, and a grand finale wine and cured meat tasting on the villa terrace. The tour emphasizes Spannocchia's work to protect the rare breed Cinta Senese and links these efforts directly to the enjoyment of eating delicious pork products in the dining room. Tour participants first visit the pigs wallowing in the red Tuscan mud of Spannocchia's forested pastures, rooting for acorns, and generally enjoying a porcine high life. Within the hour this living "Noah's Ark" is juxtaposed against the curing rooms and small butchery kitchen, where the same hogs undergo preparation for human consumption. Tourists sip wine and savor Cinta Senese prosciutto while simultaneously learning about the near extinction of the breed and their own role in preserving the species. In this way, the ethos of "eat it to save it" is consumed by the gastronomic tourist.

Although the tour includes a visit to the aptly named "transformation kitchen" where butchering takes place, many tourists I spoke with during my months at Spannocchia showed less interest in understanding the ins and outs of the full butchering process. In a handful of cases, individuals chose to skip over this portion of the tour entirely, and some told me they simply did not want to see "that part" of the Cinta Senese life cycle. The tour actively links the life, death, and transformation of Cinta hogs into food products, but even for those who consumed pork, this was not a universally desirable experience.[1] To be clear, Spannocchia cannot legally slaughter hogs used for meat processing and sales onsite. Rather, the moment of death occurs off the estate at a small state-regulated butchering facility several kilometers away. Cinta Senese tours were not held on days when full sides of pork were broken down and blood puddled on the marble butchering tables in the transformation kitchen. Yet while some tourists did not want to witness any part of the butchering process, others showed a strong interest in the "full cycle" of meat production on the farm. The valorization of traditional forms of meat processing and their associated cultural nostalgia were central to some tourists' gastronomic agendas on the estate. For these visitors, death and leisure were not only linked but considered central to the Spannocchia experience. On more than one occasion during my time working as a butchering assistant, tourists wandered in to the transformation kitchen with cameras in hand, eager to capture this "raw" moment in the food cycle.

The Cinta Senese tours bring the normally invisible death and subsequent butchery of animals to the forefront of the tourist experience. A. V. Seaton posits that the tourism of death involves "travel to a location wholly, or partially, motivated by the desire for actual or symbolic encounters with death, particularly, but not exclusively, violent death" (Seaton 1996, 240). Working within the margins of this definition, might we consider animal butchery a motivation for some forms of gastronomic tourism? Eating Cinta Senese pork at Spannocchia invokes the largely unexamined relationship between contemporary socio-cultural perspectives on death and mortality with everyday acts of eating. Furthermore, this perspective dovetails with larger gastronomic pursuits and food-related social movements that emerged during the last twenty years in Europe and the United States. With the rise of "foodie" culture, the carnivore is encouraged to engage with information about how the animal on her plate was raised and how it met its eventual demise. Although the pleasures of eating meat remain central for a gastronomic tourist, an emphasis on a "good" life and a humane death for livestock is considered equally important. Widespread public disapproval of factory farms and slaughterhouse conditions for both livestock and employees continues to grow (see Fink 1998).[2] The specter of unclean, unethical, or uncontrolled livestock production stands in stark contrast to, and perhaps ultimately drives, the tourist's desire to witness free-range hogs and small-scale artisanal pork processing. Concerned consumers have a positive response to "traditional" methods of breeding, rearing, and butchering; and they value foods produced in this way for their taste and prestige. As such, sustainable and artisanal food production methods carry a new form of social distinction, and new tourist pursuits follow livestock destined for the plate.

BEHIND THE SCENES OF BUTCHERING

During the winter months, Spannocchia hibernates. The pool is covered, the guesthouses are sealed up, and some employees are released until the following spring. Living and working with this pared-down staff, I discovered new opportunities to participate in the everyday operations of the farm alongside its Italian residents. It was during this period that I was able to gather the bulk of my information regarding hog production and meat processing at Spannocchia. Late fall and early winter are historically the times when most butchering takes place in Tuscany. For practical reasons—including lower temperatures, a relative lack of insects, and a decreased availability of wild foods for the pigs to forage—farmers traditionally slaughter animals around this time of year.

The transformation kitchen occupies a small corner adjacent to a wing of guest rooms. On my first day at the estate, while hauling luggage to my room, I happened to glance out of a second-story window. Expecting a view of the villa courtyard surrounded by Tuscan flora, I was instead greeted by three men unloading a hog carcass from a refrigerated truck (see figure 9.1). I rushed to take a photo, unaware of how familiar this scene would become during the many hours I would spend processing Cinta Senese meat in the coming months. Although I grew up on a small midwestern hog farm, my presence in the transformation kitchen during this time had nothing to do with any preexisting knowledge of meat processing. Rather, I was drafted out of necessity: the fulltime farmhand was too busy with the rapidly expanding herds to help on a regular basis. Despite my lack of experience, I was equipped to complete unskilled but necessary labor in the transformation kitchen. Although most participant-observation research does not include mopping up hog blood on a daily basis,[3] my work in the transformation kitchen allowed me to access the everyday conversations, challenges, and rhythms associated with *salumi* production.

In 2005 the farm butchered between twenty-eight and thirty pigs, a figure that increased to forty–fifty per year in 2008–9. Every two to three weeks the farm manager, Giacomo, would select three or four animals to send to slaughter. The process at the slaughterhouse is relatively straightforward. One at a time, the pigs are stunned unconscious with an electric jolt and then immediately killed with a metal bolt to the

FIGURE 9.1. A Cinta Senese pig returns from the slaughterhouse for further processing.

forehead. The entire process takes only seconds. Giacomo believes that excessive fear and confusion at the moment of death affect the taste of meat negatively and that all possible care should be taken to make the slaughter process as stress-free as possible. It could be argued that in this case a "leisurely" death leads to a tastier final product.

The pigs arrive from the slaughterhouse sawn in half lengthwise. In addition to our regular white coats, we donned long plastic aprons and hung the carcasses from large metal hooks in front of the window. In the winter, steam would rise from the bodies, which were still warm from slaughter a few hours before. The majority of the wiry hair on the body of each hog is removed through a scalding process at the slaughterhouse, but the first step at Spannocchia is to use a small butane torch to burn off any remainder. Breaking down the carcass into its relative pork components—prosciutto, fresh loin chops, liver, and so forth—takes the better part of two days. Significant care is given to a less expensive preparation of meat such as *salsiccia* (fresh sweet sausage links) or *salame*. As Giacomo explained, if a customer buys the cheapest meat we have and finds it to be outstanding, it would indicate that our most expensive cuts would be even more phenomenal.

Two of the cheapest meats Spannocchia sells are *sopressata* and *buristo*, a headcheese and blood sausage, respectively. These products are made on the final day

FIGURE 9.2. Dry-cured prosciutto is first cured in salt and then air-dried for over twelve months.

of a butchering cycle, after all the sausages, prosciutto, *lardo*, and other items have been processed. At this point, all that remains of the pig—the skin, the head, and leftover bones and flesh—is tossed into a large cauldron filled with boiling saltwater. There it cooks for several hours, eventually emerging as a gelatinous slurry that must be strained for bones and inedible cartilage. Spices are added, and the entire mix is diced by hand using a large knife and a wooden board, a difficult process because of the hot steam that continues to rise up from the mix. The finished *sopressata* is then hung over a plastic bin, where it continues to ooze gelatin stalactites for several hours. For *buristo*, the hog's blood is added back to the mix and funneled into the hog's emptied and cleaned stomach, then re-boiled. Unlike the other Cinta Senese products, *sopressata* and *buristo* are not aged. These products go directly to the refrigerator, where they remain until market day.

While most tourists at Spannocchia were anxious to sample Cinta Senese prosciutto and salami and even *lardo* (as a result of the publicity noted above), I repeatedly watched individuals turn down *sopressata* and *buristo* or take a minimal nibble for the sake of "trying it." Although these products were equally artisanal and arguably even more distinctive, as they are difficult to access and hold deep ties to the peasants who consumed them in the past, they were not considered equally pleasurable. It is possible that headcheese and blood sausage simply lack the positive marketing associated with other Cinta products. Furthermore, disinterest in these products was not limited to tourists. When I worked at local markets with Giacomo, we sold very little of either product, and it was often difficult to get many middle-aged and younger Italian residents even to take a sample. Here, there is an almost Sausserian dichotomy between pleasure and disgust, between cured and cooked. This dimension of gustatory pleasure—namely, the lack thereof—speaks a great deal about the power of gastronomic distinction and how it interplays with deeply held notions about food purity and constructions of individual taste.

THE INCREDIBLE, EDIBLE ENDANGERED PIG

In the years following World War II, the advent of industrial farming and the subsequent introduction of larger, more prolific breeds like the Yorkshire hog (often known as the "Great White") nearly wiped out the Cinta Senese population in Italy. The Cinta Senese is the only breed of native Tuscan swine to survive extinction, and only a few dozen of these pigs survived in the late twentieth century. Several factors led to the decreased popularity of the breed among area farmers. First, the Cinta is a "grazing" pig and requires extensive wooded areas for foraging in addition to a typical grain diet. The Cinta Senese originated in the hills around Siena where their distinctive white belt, or *cinta*, was carefully selected for by medieval breeders who needed to separate their stock from feral breeds living in forests nearby (Pacini and Scatena 2005). However, in a country where 75 percent of agricultural holdings is dedicated to crop production and nearly a third of hog farmers operate on less than 20 hectares, space for adventurous foraging pigs comes at a premium today (Martins 2009). The biggest drawback for the Cinta Senese breed, however, is that it takes up to two years to reach market weight (300 kg for males, 250 kg for females). In a competitive market dominated by industrial production methods that can bring a Yorkshire to market weight in less than six months, small-scale Cinta breeders are not in a position to compete directly. Although the Cinta Senese is not an "economical" or particularly profitable animal in the age of industrial agriculture, ironically, this may be exactly what enhances its popularity in niche markets. Increasingly, the Cinta is raised for commercial production of *lardo*, salami, prosciutto, and other specialty meat products explicitly sought out by gastronomic tourists and others interested in artisanal, "traditional" food production in Tuscany. In addition, the hogs' status as endangered lends a degree of distinction, in a very Bourdieuian sense, to the final pork products.

The Cinta Senese is considered a heritage breed, one of the traditional livestock breeds raised by farmers prior to the drastic reduction of breed variety and genetic diversity caused by the rise of modern industrial agriculture. Heritage breeds retain key attributes that ensure survival and self-sufficiency in their native environments, such as foraging ability, longevity, maternal instincts, ability to mate naturally, and resistance to diseases and parasites. Although such features helped to ensure farmers' success in the past, they do not typically equate to economic profits today. Currently, industrial food production favors the use of a few highly specialized breeds selected for maximum output in a carefully controlled environment. Developed to produce a lot of milk or eggs, to put on weight quickly, or to yield particular types of meat within confined facilities, a narrow sliver of genetic diversity underpins the bulk of meat products available to consumers. Today, 21 percent of the world's 8,000 livestock breeds are in danger of extinction (Livestock Conservancy 2014). Worldwide, from 1999 to 2005, roughly one livestock breed per month fell into extinction (FAO 2007, 9). In Europe, half of the breeds living on farms in 1900 are now extinct, a staggering loss of agrarian and genetic diversity. Although modern industrial production and market pressures have literally caused the extinction of many livestock breeds, it is paradoxically this brush with extinction and endangered status that creates interest in breeds like the Cinta Senese today. The irony, of course, is that it is only through the death and increasingly distinctive consumption of these endangered breeds that they are surviving in specialized contexts like agritourism. The connection with the near-extinction of these animals appears to drive consumers' desire for, and pleasure in, their end products.

Consuming the Cinta Senese creates a visceral connection not only with Tuscan producers but also with a rarified slice of the Tuscan landscape itself. The Cinta Senese pig is not only a survivor of postindustrial agriculture; it is a re-branded and carefully designed cultural icon. For example, the Slow Food Movement, a worldwide organization founded on the principle of enjoying food that is not only delicious but also sustainable and ethical, supports Cinta Senese production through its Ark of Taste. The Cinta Senese was an early arrival on the Ark of Taste in 1996, and Slow Food's international scope introduced consumers far from Tuscany to this breed. The Ark of Taste aims to rediscover, catalog, and promote foods that are at risk of extinction but have productive and commercial potential and are closely linked to specific communities and cultures (Petrini 2003). As of March 2015, the Slow Food Foundation for Biodiversity website listed over 2,500 unique foods from dozens of countries around the world on the Ark of Taste, all of which are threatened by industrial standardization. In addition to profiling rare foods, it is a tool that helps farmers, ranchers, fishers, chefs, retail grocers, educators, and consumers celebrate the diverse biological, cultural, and culinary heritage of a particular place. To reiterate, in the case of heritage livestock breeds like the Cinta Senese, cultivating a consumer demand for animal food products is central to conservation efforts.

When a food product boards Slow Food's Ark of Taste, it is indexed as a culturally and gastronomically important item, making it highly desirable to our omnivorous, socially and ecologically conscious consumer. The examination of the milieu of local knowledge and memory of "endangered" foods connects the consumer to the "exterior landscapes" of local history and ecology (Nazarea 2006; see also Belasco 2006). Gastronomic tourists, such as those who visit Spannocchia, seek out the pleasure of this experience during their travels.

The Slow Food Movement claims to be democratic and based on the voluntary membership of those with shared cultural and gastronomic interests. The notion of "virtuous consumerism" is central to the movement, which increasingly focuses on cultural and symbolic strategies as means of achieving increased autonomy or democratization of social and cultural arenas. Elaine Tyler May first coined the phrase *virtuous consumerism* in her depiction of Cold War–era American mothers, who were encouraged to make purchases that emphasized pragmatism, morality, and an idealized domesticity over opulence and luxury (May 1988). As such, commodities gained distinction not through their monetary value but rather by way of an underlying greater good or moral standard. In the case of Slow Food, food commodities gain a similar political or moral distinction because they are believed to be connected to environmentally and economically sustainable practices. Individuals who take a Cinta Senese tour at Spannocchia can experience a field-to-table, snout-to-tail tour that links them to the Tuscan landscape, the individuals working on the farm, and the animals themselves.

However, some argue that this type of consumer democracy remains available only to those with the social and economic capital to join. Ironically, the people whose ancestors survived on Cinta Senese *salumi* may not be able to afford the product today. Alison Leitch (2003) argues that the Slow Food Movement is about the (re)invention not of tradition but of commoditization—herein, the cultural politics of "marketing nostalgia" to an audience eager for foods considered to be traditional, rural, and fresh becomes apparent. In other words, by eating Cinta Senese meat, one is symbolically connected to a long history of Tuscan food traditions. In a sense, visitors and locals alike are able to literally "consume" Tuscany. Renewed ideals of locality, typicality, and artisanal production bolster the market for Cinta Senese products in Tuscany. By attaching positive values to these products, tourist consumers value foods not only for their flavors but also for the cultural distinction they connote.

CONCLUSION

Cinta Senese pork is typically only available in the local markets and restaurants surrounding Siena. What could be deemed more "distinctive"—from a Bourdieuian perspective—than eating a food product that is difficult to obtain, must be raised in highly unique contexts, and can only be enjoyed by a few dedicated gastronomic pioneers? In their exploration of "foodie" discourse, sociologists Johnston and Baumann (2010) begin to untangle the rhetoric surrounding such distinctions. They identify the tension between two ideological poles useful for framing the activities of gastronomic tourists: (1) a democratic pole that eschews cultural elite standards by valorizing the cultural products of "everyday" non-elite people and (2) a pole that valorizes rare, difficult to access, and often economically inaccessible foods that represent possession of high cultural capital.

Cinta Senese hogs are culturally defined—they occupy symbolic space in addition to being a material, economic product. Visitors to places like Spannocchia value Cinta Senese products for their flavor as well as the prestige associated with consuming an endangered and artisanally produced meat. Marketing Cinta Senese meat products involves a conscious manipulation of cultural ideals, even as "traditional" foods are turned into commodities that must face the global market and meet criteria imposed by hygiene regulations, protocols, and possibly the standardization of flavor (Grassini 2011). Capturing a niche market, such as the international gastronomic tourist, is critical to the success and survival of the Cinta Senese breed, but a larger connection can be drawn between the pleasures of eating and the realities of animal death.

Food "quality" is a multidimensional concept—in addition to sensory valuations, it encompasses attributes of morality and aesthetics, as well as connotations with particular geographies, organizations, and institutions (Harvey, McMeekin, and Warde 2004). For some tourists, learning about the butchering process itself is central to gustatory pleasure and ideas of quality. At Spannocchia the experience of seeing living pigs in a celebrated cultural landscape is closely tied to the enjoyment of consuming Cinta Senese pork. For some tourists, the acquisition of cultural capital extends to participation in the butchery process itself. For example, a 2013 NBC news piece highlights the trend in the United States: "Nothing says vacation like getting elbow deep in a bloody pig carcass. At least not for the growing number of travelers looking to add butchery to the repertoire of culinary skills they've picked up around the country (or globe). While cooking classes and farm tours are long-time staples of foodie vacation activities, butchery workshops are picking up steam. The visceral, hands-on, seriously know-where-your-meat-comes-from aspect isn't for everyone. But the thought of donning chainmail and wielding a knife appeals to enough people that classes with master butchers are popping up from coast to coast" (McMahan 2013).

As butchery gains popularity among audiences eager to take a hands-on approach to food, new discourses surrounding death and leisure continue to emerge. For instance, an all-women's "Meat Camp" is now offered in Northern California, where for $2,000 women can learn basic meat-processing skills over a three-day period. The camp is geared toward the higher-end foodie and includes not only an overview of grilling techniques and butchery skills but also lodging in luxury safari platform tents. Some may view a vacation spent learning to process meat or consuming a rare breed as a logical extension of the pleasures of food, yet such activities continue to be driven by the ongoing search for cultural capital. The life and death of animals and their subsequent transformation into food products are central to the leisurely pursuit of new gastronomic experiences in this context.

NOTES

1 See Adams, this volume, for another perspective on the "ambivalence and revulsion" that surrounds animal death during the tourist experience.

2. Although the ethics and politics of eating animals are not my focus here, they also continue to shape the food choices and consumption behaviors of locals and tourists alike. Publications from other academics (cf. Fiddes 1991; Sapontzis 2004) and popular authors (cf. Foer 2009; Schlosser 2001) discuss the subject from a US/European perspective in greater detail.

3. Notable exceptions include Fink's (1998) and Rémy's (2004) ethnographies of industrial slaughterhouse work and Weiss's (2012) discussion of snout-to-tail pork production.

REFERENCES

Belasco, Warren. 2006. *Meals to Come: A History of the Future of Food*. Berkeley: University of California Press.

Black, Christopher. 2002. *Early Modern Italy: A Social History*. London: Routledge.

Bordi, Ivonne Vizcarra. 2006. "The 'Authentic' Taco and Peasant Women: Nostalgic Consumption in the Era of Globalization." *Culture and Agriculture* 28 (2): 97–107. https://doi.org/10.1525/cag.2006.28.2.97.

Bourdieu, Pierre. 1984. *Distinction: A Social Critique of the Judgement of Taste*. Cambridge, MA: Harvard University Press.

Chrzan, Janet. 2007. "Dreaming of Tuscany: Pursuing the Anthropology of Culinary Tourism." *Expedition* 49 (2): 21–27.

Corigliano, Magda Antonioli. 2002. "The Route to Quality: Italian Gastronomy Networks in Operation." In *Tourism and Gastronomy*, ed. Anne-Mette Hjalager and Greg Richards, 166–85. London: Routledge.

Counihan, Carole. 2004. *Around the Tuscan Table*. New York: Routledge.

de Blasi, Marlena. 2004. *A Thousand Days in Tuscany*. Chapel Hill, NC: Algonquin Books.
Dickie, John. 2008. *Delizia! The Epic History of the Italians and Their Food*. New York: Free Press.
Elon, Beth. 2009. *A Culinary Traveller in Tuscany: Exploring and Eating off the Beaten Track*. New York: Little Bookroom.
FAO (Food and Agriculture Organization of the United Nations). 2007. *The State of the World's Animal Genetic Resources for Food and Agriculture*. Ed. Dafydd Pilling and Barbara Rischkowsky. Rome: Communication Division, FAO.
Fiddes, Nick. 1991. *Meat: A Natural Symbol*. New York: Routledge.
Fink, Deborah. 1998. *Cutting into the Meatpacking Line: Workers and Change in the Rural Midwest*. Chapel Hill: University of North Carolina Press.
Foer, Jonathan Safran. 2009. *Eating Animals*. New York: Little, Brown.
Gewertz, Deborah, and Frederick Errington. 2010. *Cheap Meat: Flap Food Nations in the Pacific Islands*. Berkeley: University of California Press.
Grassini, Cristina. 2011. "Anthropology of Food [Online]." Accessed November 20, 2017. http://aof.revues.org/6819.
Guthman, Julie. 2003. "Fast Food/Organic Food: Reflexive Tastes and the Making of 'Yuppie Chow.'" *Social and Cultural Geography* 4 (1): 45–58. https://doi.org/10.1080/1464936032000049306.
Harvey, Mark, Andrew McMeekin, and Alan Warde. 2004. "Introduction." In *Qualities of Food*, ed. Mark Harvey, Andrew McMeekin, and Alan Warde, 1–18. New York: Manchester University Press. https://doi.org/10.9760/MUPOA/9780719068546.
Johnston, Josée, and Shyon Baumann. 2007. "Democracy versus Distinction: A Study of Omnivorousness in Gourmet Food Writing." *American Journal of Sociology* 113 (1): 165–204. https://doi.org/10.1086/518923.
Johnston, Josée, and Shyon Baumann. 2010. *Foodies: Democracy and Distinction in the Gourmet Foodscape*. New York: Routledge.
Leitch, Alison. 2003. "Slow Food and the Politics of Pork Fat: Italian Food and European Identity." *Ethnos* 68 (4): 437–62. https://doi.org/10.1080/0014184032000160514.
Lennon, John, and Malcolm Foley. 2000. *Dark Tourism*. New York: Continuum.
Livestock Conservancy. 2014. "Resources: About Us." Accessed May 27, 2015. http://livestockconservancy.org/index.php/resources/internal/about-us.
Long, Lucy. 2005. Presentation at the First Culinary Tourism Symposium. Lecture. George Brown College, Toronto, Ontario. March 8.
Martins, Carla. 2009. "Farm Structure Survey in Italy—2007." *Eurostat Statistics in Focus* 28. Accessed May 27, 2015. http://ec.europa.eu/eurostat/en/web/products-statistics-in-focus/-/KS-SF-09-038.

Máté, Ferenc. 1998. *The Hills of Tuscany: A New Life in an Old Land*. New York: Albatross Books.

May, Elaine Tyler. 1988. *Homeward Bound: American Families in the Cold War Era*. New York: Basic Books.

Mayes, Frances. 1997. *Under the Tuscan Sun: At Home in Italy*. New York: Broadway Books.

McMahan, Dana. 2013. "Cutting-Edge Travel: Tourists Take Stab at Butchery." *NBC News*, March 1. Accessed March 15, 2015. http://nbcnews75.rssing.com/browser.php?indx =6644644&item=84.

Meneley, Anne. 2004. "Extra Virgin Olive Oil and Slow Food." *Anthropologica* 46 (2): 165–76. https://doi.org/10.2307/25606192.

Nazarea, Virginia. 2006. "Local Knowledge and Memory in Biodiversity Conservation." *Annual Review of Anthropology* 35 (1): 317–35. https://doi.org/10.1146/annurev.anthro.35 .081705.123252.

Pacini, Giovanni, and Arianna Scatena. 2005. *Cinta Senese*. Monteriggioni, Italy: Industria Grafica Pistolesi Editrice Il Leccio.

Paxson, Heather. 2008. "Post-Pasteurian Cultures: The Microbiopolitics of Raw-Milk Cheese in the United States." *Cultural Anthropology* 23 (1): 15–47. https://doi.org/10 .1111/j.1548-1360.2008.00002.x.

Peterson, Richard, and Roger Kern. 1996. "Changing Highbrow Taste: From Snob to Omnivore." *American Sociological Review* 61 (5): 900–907. https://doi.org/10.2307 /2096460.

Petrini, Carlo. 2003. *Slow Food: The Case for Taste*. New York: Columbia University Press. https://doi.org/10.7312/petr12844.

Pietrykowski, Bruce. 2004. "You Are What You Eat: The Social Economy of the Slow Food Movement." *Review of Social Economy* 62 (3): 307–21. https://doi.org/10.1080/00 34676042000253927.

Rémy, Catherine. 2004. "L'espace de la Mise à Mort de L'animal." *Espaces et Sociétés* 118 (3): 223–49. https://doi.org/10.3917/esp.118.0223.

Ross, Silvia. 2010. *Tuscan Spaces: Literary Constructions of Place*. Toronto: University of Toronto Press. https://doi.org/10.3138/9781442698918.

Said, Edward. 1979. *Orientalism*. New York: Pantheon Books.

Sapontzis, Steve, ed. 2004. *Food for Thought: The Debate over Eating Meat*. Amherst, NY: Prometheus Books.

Scarpato, Rosario. 2002. "Gastronomy as a Tourist Product: The Perspective of Gastronomy Studies." In *Tourism and Gastronomy*, ed. Anne-Mette Hjalager and Greg Richards, 51–70. New York: Routledge.

Schlosser, Eric. 2001. *Fast Food Nation: The Dark Side of the All-American Meal*. New York: Perennial.

Seaton, A. V. 1996. "Guided by the Dark: From Thanatopsis to Thanatourism." *International Journal of Heritage Studies* 2 (4): 234–44. https://doi.org/10.1080/13527259608722178.

Stone, Philip. 2006. "A Dark Tourism Spectrum: Towards a Typology of Death and Macabre Related Tourist Sites, Attractions, and Exhibitions." *Tourism: An Interdisciplinary International Journal* 54 (2): 145–60.

Trubek, Amy. 2008. *The Taste of Place: A Cultural Journey into Terroir*. Berkeley: University of California Press.

Tucker, Michael. 2007. *Living in a Foreign Language: A Memoir of Food, Wine, and Love in Italy*. New York: Grove.

Warde, Alan, David Wright, and Modesto Gayo-Cal. 2007. "Understanding Cultural Omnivorousness: Or, the Myth of the Cultural Omnivore." *Cultural Sociology* 1 (2): 143–64. https://doi.org/10.1177/1749975507078185.

Weiss, Brad. 2011. "Making Pigs Local: Discerning the Sensory Character of Place." *Cultural Anthropology* 26 (3): 438–61. https://doi.org/10.1111/j.1548-1360.2011.01106.x.

Weiss, Brad. 2012. "Configuring the Authentic Value of Real Food: Farm-to-Fork, Snout-to-Tail, and Local Food Movements." *American Ethnologist* 39 (3): 614–26. https://doi.org/10.1111/j.1548-1425.2012.01384.x.

Williams, Ingrid K. 2010. "In Tuscany, Carrara Tempts Eyes and Mouth." *New York Times*, September 29. Accessed March 15, 2015. http://www.nytimes.com/2010/10/03/travel/03overnighter.html?smid=pl-share.

PART 4
Afterlife and After-Leisure

10

The Social Life of the Dead and the Leisured Life of the Living Online

TAMARA KOHN, MICHAEL ARNOLD, MARTIN GIBBS,
JAMES MEESE, AND BJORN NANSEN

Tamara: It was 6 a.m. As usual, I reached for my iPhone to press the snooze button, and then my sleepy eyes squinted at the bright screen to check my two email accounts. Nothing much there, so I moved on to see what my many friends and acquaintances on Facebook had found important or interesting or funny enough to post on their "walls." On one side of the Facebook page, a memo popped up and reminded me that it was Jim's birthday. Jim[1] *was a boyfriend from my undergraduate days who I had reconnected with after twenty lost years through email and then occasional interactions on Facebook. I responded to the birthday prompt by immediately writing a chatty short message ("Hey! Happy Bday!—when are you coming down to Australia for a visit?"). I posted it on his wall, and then my eye caught the messages below mine.*

"Can't believe it's been seven months yesterday. Still miss you so much." (Where would he have gone, I thought—on a long trip?)

"You have a piece of my heart. Mother."

"Happy Birthday! My vocabulary will never be the same."

An itch of concern turned to a horrible catch of breath as the truth dawned on me. My friend must be dead.

Jim died suddenly at age forty-nine in 2009. In 2015 he still had forty-three friends on Facebook. Messages are posted to him by some individuals (and thus shared with all his "friends") on his birthday, Father's Day, the anniversary of his death, Valentine's Day, and quite a few unmarked days in between. His personal details (found in the

DOI: 10.5876/9781607327295.c010   227

"About" section of a Facebook profile) are still written in the present tense, as when he was alive. Jim is "doing consulting" work for a firm, "lives in New York," and is "in a relationship with Maria." His photos never age. Eight days before his death he posted "Jim . . . is totally alive." Then eight days after a message read "Jim . . . is being missed by all his loved ones and out there experiencing one amazing afterlife!" Perhaps Jim's "spirit" is still "out there" while his physical body has long since been disposed of, but his social person lingers on social media, occasionally animated in living memories by the individual voices addressing him with semi-public intimacy.

This chapter explores what this intimacy conducted through social media entails, contributing to our understanding of how the dead are brought into these leisure spaces of the living. Through an analysis of personhood and sociality (Hallam and Hockey 2001; Hallam, Hockey, and Howarth 1999) in an important contemporary leisure space, we consider how the gravitas of death rubs against both the structures and sentiments of leisure on social media and the desires of those who occupy them. To show some of that diversity, we describe Facebook memorialization in its various forms before going on to briefly consider two other socially mediated trends through which online death and leisure closely interact: "selfies" taken at funerals (see Gibbs et al. 2014; Meese et al. 2015) and "selfies" taken moments before the subjects' unexpected and tragic deaths. The chapter is informed by current scholarship in digital ethnography and our own ongoing research on digital commemoration (Arnold et al. 2018; Mori et al. 2012; Meese et al. 2015; Nansen et al. 2014; Kohn et al. 2012), which has examined online commemoration sites, public discourse around digital commemoration, and the technical properties and policies of online platforms regarding death.

An analysis of these different sites of leisure will contribute to a more detailed understanding of how digital leisure practices intersect with death and the subsequent process of commemoration. For example, what do current practices tell us about how a deceased Facebook user's identity and personhood are constituted and animated in absentia through memorial sites and social network sites? Does continually engaging with a dead person's online social world alter processes of the sequestration of the dead, of memorialization, grieving, and social interaction with the living and between the living and the dead? How do digital media practices interact with traditional, often deeply historic rituals and codes of conduct established in relation to the deceased? How does an understanding of "leisure" become refigured as it confronts sentiments and activities associated with death and grieving? The way we are framing "leisure" in this chapter refers both to the way everyday social networks are nurtured through online interactions as well as, in the final case, to the spaces and times that are often physically separated from the everyday and then shared through social media.

Contemporary identities are continually transformed and expressed through digitally mediated leisure practices (see Hjorth and Arnold 2013; Arnold et al. 2006; Coleman and Kohn 2007; Christensen 2003; Jones 1994), and the power of social media as a site of leisure stems from its capacity to collapse and confound. Indeed, "context collapse" (Marwick and boyd 2011) is central to our contemporary experience of the online world, with "social media technologies collapsing multiple contexts and bring[ing] together commonly distinct audiences" (Marwick and boyd 2011, 115). These jarring contexts and multiplicity of online audiences are particularly notable in the case of a death. Social media commonly used for the latest cute-cat video and other lighthearted leisure practices are, of course, also deployed for notifying others about a death, sharing grief, and ongoing memorial practices. One moment my screen is claiming my attention with a status update about a parking fine and the next with a notification from my dead partner.

Moreover, compounding the discomfort that may emerge from the screen's disinterest is the uneven distribution of our experience with technology and death. Those who are immersed in networked communicative media are only ever partially disconnected and largely lead life through the screen (Arnold 2002). In this world it is unthinkable not to use networked media to commune with an intimate public about the experience of death. However, in another social world, networked communications do not play a constant role in people's lives, and grief is an emotion not automatically revealed or concealed online. To draw a generalization that is no doubt subject to many caveats, those most experienced with technology (the affluent young) are least experienced with death, and those most experienced with death (the impecunious old) are least experienced with technology. This provides plenty of opportunity for cultural tension, as seen in the recent controversy around selfies at funerals (Meese et al. 2015).

THE LIVELY DEAD ON FACEBOOK

Facebook is a popular and global contemporary site for leisure practice, a place where a huge number of people participate in an ever-increasing range of "lively" social connections. Facebook began as a simple online website that would allow people to decide who was "hot" (and who was "not") on the university campus by sharing, discussing, and comparing mug shots (Kirkpatrick 2010). Clearly, this social media company was driven more by sex than by death. But as Facebook grew and increased its membership base, people of all ages started to die (including the young), and their profiles lived on. In 2012 Facebook had over 1.3 billion active users and an estimated 30 million dead users, with a further 19,000 people with a Facebook profile dying daily (Kaleem 2012; Lustig 2012). If Facebook lasts long

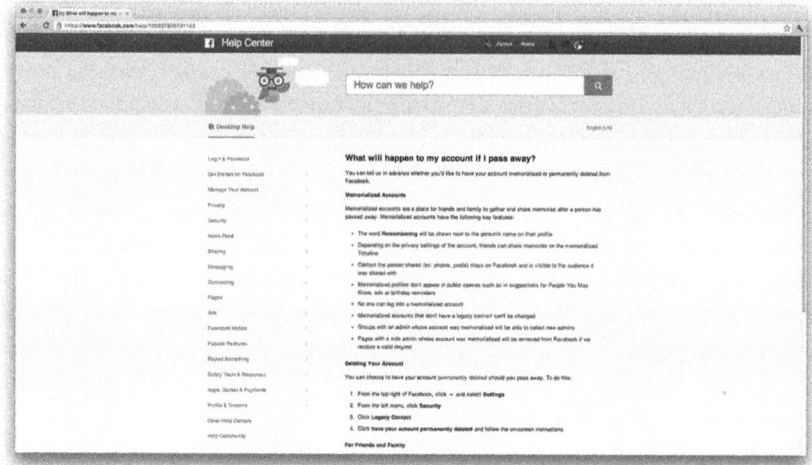

FIGURE 10.1. Facebook informs its users on profile management options after death. Screenshot from Facebook.

enough, it is inevitable that dead profiles will outnumber the living, and unquestionably, Facebook's design and management teams have a huge ongoing task to create, maintain, and adapt software controls to deal with this enormous and ever-growing "dead" population and its networks of living "friends." As social scientists, we have the challenging and fascinating task of understanding how notions of death and dying are replicated and refigured in and through social media and its affordances.

Facebook policy on how to manage the profiles of the dead has shifted over time as the result of a number of key events. There was no official policy on what to do with the accounts of the dead until a public relations disaster in 2009 forced Facebook's hand.[2] Among various other changes, Facebook activated a set of algorithms that monitored interaction among "friends" and prompted people to "reconnect" with those who had fallen out of touch. However, an unintended consequence was that people were prompted to reconnect with dead friends—no doubt causing distress for many users. Facebook was consequently forced to respond and tackle the issue of dead users head-on. Facebook policy ("Memorialized Accounts" 2015) now allows dead people's next of kin to "memorialize" the profile, in which case the word "Remembering" appears before the deceased's name on the profile. Automated prompts and public links to the profile are deactivated, and new friends are not permitted, although existing friends may continue to post in accordance with existing privacy settings. In late 2014 Facebook also enabled profile owners to nominate a "Legacy Contact" who would assume responsibility for the profile on the occasion of the owner's death, but at the time of writing this feature was only available in North America (see "Memorialized Accounts" 2015). There are also two alternative possibilities, neither officially supported by Facebook—to leave the profile exactly as it is by not reporting the death, in which case automatic features will continue to function and the profile will be open to posts, prompts, advertising, and so on; or to access the dead user's profile with the person's password, which contravenes Facebook's terms of use agreement but also enables the profile to live on (see Karppi 2013).

Facebook's preferred policy is to memorialize the profile, and so the process of memorialization is more straightforward than the process of account deletion: "It is our policy to memorialize all deceased users' accounts on the site. When an account is memorialized, only confirmed friends can see the profile (time line) or locate it in Search. The profile (time line) will also no longer appear in the Suggestions section of the Home page. Friends and family can leave posts in remembrance" (Lucas 2012). This is the case because Facebook can still extract value from data mining all profiles, dead or not, to resource the construction of consumption profiles for third parties and for its own advertising, a major source of revenue (see Karppi 2013). As Stanyek and Piekut remark: "In late capitalism, the dead are highly productive. Of course, all capital is dead labor, but the dead also generate capital in collaboration with the living" (Stanyek and Piekut 2010, 14). Memorialized Facebook accounts cannot make new connections, and the dead person's social circle is closed, but they remain an active node in the social network. The data-bodies of the memorialized dead are perfectly preserved on Facebook; they continue to be active as necro–click bait and thus continue to be mined and act as an important part of the company's business model.

People may also set up a Facebook memorial page—not a "profile" or "time line" but a "page" or "group"[3]—that is open to the public. The memorial page is rather different in its construction and tone: it is far less personal and often established for celebrities or to communicate around tragic deaths captured by the media (Kohn et al. 2012). Anyone can set up a memorial page or group for anyone, and in the case of high-profile deaths, it is not uncommon for more than one to be set up in competition or collaboration. Such pages have the potential to attract vast publics that gather physically or virtually after death and commonly extend far beyond family and friends to include strangers (also known as "grief tourists") and sometimes malevolent trolls (Phillips 2011). Such public memorials have often been subject to forms of defacement or "cyber-vandalism," prompting public debate about crime, privacy, security, and responsibility (Kohn et al. 2012).

While the memorialization of profiles may be Facebook's preferred option for its 30 million (plus) dead users, only around 3 million profiles have been memorialized at this point. The remaining 27 million have therefore either been deleted or remain online in a "live" state. Given that remaining "live" is the default position (if nothing

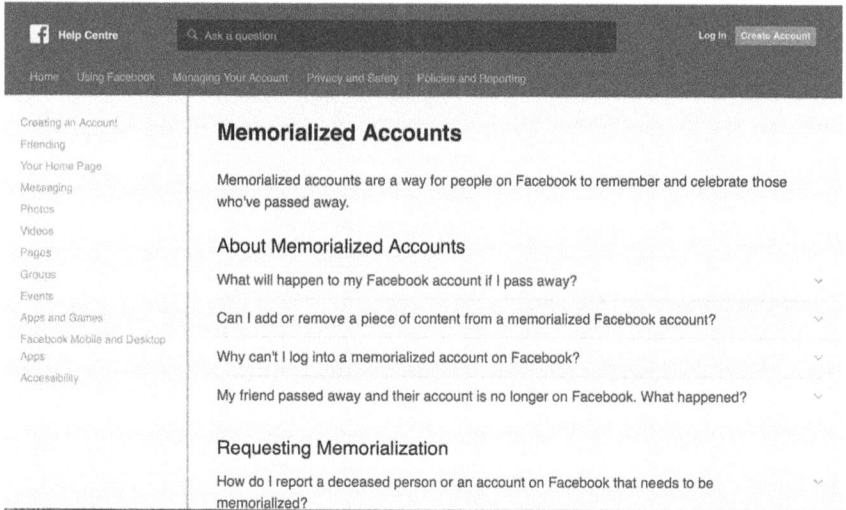

FIGURE 10.2. Facebook's information page on Memorialized Accounts. Screenshot from Facebook.

is done to the contrary) and given the barriers Facebook has created for deletion (a family member needs to provide Facebook with a death certificate, court document confirming power of attorney, birth certificate, or last will and testament), it follows that many of the 27 million remain present to the deceased's social networks as they were when the users were alive. The implication is that the deletion or memorializing of posthumous profiles is not serving the wishes of many users, including living persons preparing for their "afterlife" on Facebook. Instead, posthumous profiles are increasingly repurposed, often kept open through proxy users and intermittently buoyed and transformed by their continued engagement with the living (see Brubaker and Hayes 2011). This sees the community of the living representing or historicizing the dead by maintaining communications and relations with the dead in an *ongoing* and *diachronic* way rather than in a static fashion. Users of these online memorial sites continue to post and develop posthumous biographies to represent the dead, continue to maintain and develop their relationship with the dead by integrating them into their ongoing social networks, and continue to communicate directly with the dead. A living Facebook site is thus repurposed after death, not only as a marker of online life but also as a social meeting place for those who knew the deceased but didn't necessarily always know each other.

Jim's profile, for example, is a memorialized site and remains active through the efforts of friends posting new messages and photos that give it a sense of growth and change. Furthermore, it does not appear that any people listed as Jim's friends have "unfriended" him.[4] Ironically, as this quote (by a contributor to the "SocialTimes" online Facebook news site) makes clear, it feels wrong to "unfriend" a dead person even years later, regardless of whether one is an active Facebook user: "My friend has 303 people on her Facebook site. It has now been four months since her passing and not one person has unfriended her. I visit her page each day, several times a day in fact and still, friends have continued to post comments, share stories and pictures, plus even hold one-sided conversations with her. She still receives pokes and offers to play games" (http://adweek.com/digital/should-you-unfriend-a-dead-friend-on-facebook/). This example shows how Facebook is operating as a new medium through which to conduct an ongoing "wake"—a means for mourners to express and share their grief. On these sites bereaved friends and relatives not only provide biographical narratives relating to the dead but also provide representations of their unique relationships with the dead, with each other, and with their changing experience of grief, in a process that may extend for years (see Carroll and Landry 2010). In the following section, we consider how these methods of grieving and commemoration through social media reconfigure our understandings of social and biological death and instantiate a set of new relations between the living and the dead.

THE BORDERS OF LIFE AND DEATH: CLASSIFICATION AND RITUAL ON SOCIAL MEDIA

The borders of life and death have long reigned as a premier location from which to consider how different socio-cultural groups classify their worlds. Anthropological studies of death draw from debates on comparative "primitive" ritual practices (see Hertz 1960 [1907]; Rivers 1999 [1926]; Bloch and Parry 1983) and from highly politicized debates often focused closer to home, on euthanasia, abortion, organ transplantation, or reproductive technologies (e.g., Scheper-Hughes 2004; Strathern 1992; Lock 2001). A consideration of the position of the dead and the social spaces constructed on Facebook and other media that interact with death allows us to extend some of those ambiguities lurking at the hazy border of life and death.

Robert Hertz, a member of *L'Année Sociologique*,[5] published a series of essays on death in 1907 (translated into English in 1960 as *Death and the Right Hand*). He described the corpse (drawing data from around the world but particularly Indonesia) as a social entity as well as a physical or biological entity, suggesting that mortuary rites are variously constructed to mark the movement of the living to join previously departed members of society. Such rites entail the "painful psychological process" of separating the dead from the consciousness of the living. Ties with the dead, suggested Hertz (1960 [1907], 81), are not "severed in one day"; rather, memories continue through a number of "internal partings."

William H.R. Rivers (1999 [1926]) supported Hertz's observations in his ethnographically informed study about death rituals in the Solomon Islands in the 1920s. Rivers's description of the local term *mate* further outlines these links between social and biological death: "It is true that the word *mate* is used for a dead man, but it is also used for a person who is seriously ill and likely to die, and also often for a person who is healthy but so old that, from the native point of view, if he is not dead he ought to be" (Rivers 1999 [1926], 40). The community would bury a person whose physical body was still breathing but whose social body had died—who was no longer seen to have a productive role in the community. Žižek later called this social body a "symbolic body" (as opposed to the body's material death or death in "the real"), and the symbolic body would die as a result of a collapse in the symbolic order and the extermination of its subject position (Žižek 1992). For Žižek, the death of the symbolic body occurs when we no longer exist for the Other. For Hertz, Rivers, and Žižek, the social liveliness of the dead hinges on how they are understood and interacted with by the living. In this sense, biological death and social death are loosely coupled. One may be biologically alive but socially dead (the homeless, the lonely, the incarcerated) or biologically dead but socially alive (the dead who live in memory and continue to express social agency through the contemporary lives of the living). We therefore die twice: once when our bodies cease to function and again when we are forgotten—but this process does not necessarily occur in that order.

If we return to the challenges and innovations presented by Facebook use following the death of a user, an interesting extension of social life emerges. At first glance, we can see an inversion of the example above from the Solomons. The physical body is biologically dead (and disposed of with or without ritual), but the social and symbolic body is still maintained by the "liveliness" of techno-social networks established by the communications of the dead person's "friends," which draw the deceased into his or her friends' present and their plans for the immediate future. Where a deceased person's profile is adopted by a partner or a friend or a legacy contact has been appointed, old friends continue to visit and socialize, and indeed, the dead can make new friends. In this contemporary iteration, *if he is not alive, he ought to be*. What is interesting in our socially networked present is that the rules of social life and death still pertain: the memories that sustain individuals' connections with the dead are to some extent symbolically severed through the physical rituals of burial and the funeral. However, at the same time, relations with the deceased can be buoyed and nurtured on a social media platform. The social/symbolic body is kept alive and present by being addressed through messages and postings the dead person's profile receives from the living in the presence of other living social media users, each of whom possesses his or her own private memories of the deceased.

This online and ongoing "*talking to*" dead persons on active Facebook pages also interacts with the still important face-to-face religious or secular and embodied rituals of death (as studied by Hertz and many others up to the present—see Hallam, Hockey, and Howarth 1999) in a range of interesting ways. This talk is often quite ordinary and generally focused on the present and the future, sharing the new and the everyday rather than lingering on memory. It includes, for example, posted photos of grandchildren never met, jokes heard at work, plans for the next holiday, and lots of sentences starting with "you would have loved . . ." The messages on these sites, therefore, are often intimate and routinely employ the first-person pronoun (Brubaker and Hayes 2011). And yet they are also semi-public, with the semi-public witnessing of many personal responses creating multi-author social narrative built around grief and responses to death, a blending of interpersonal communication and mass communication via the Web. What was once very private communication—messages to the deceased—thus becomes very public (Carroll and Landry 2010; Hutchings 2012). In this multi-author, interpersonal, but public narrative, the personhood and character of the interlocutor are constructed (say, as a caring friend) and the personhood and character of the deceased are publicly reconstructed (say, as a life-loving person).

However, it is quite different to imagine or speak these things in private to the dead, perhaps kneeling alone at a graveside, than to do so in the guise of a conversation with the dead person and with the knowledge that the dead person's articulated and often unknown circle of friends, relations, and strangers is viewing posted pictures and associated texts. This example contrasts with offline social displays of individual grief that occur immediately after death, such as at a "wake," in at least three respects: the wake is circumscribed in time, in space, and in participants, none of which necessarily applies to Facebook. On Facebook, there is the potential for and expectation of a continued pseudo-social engagement into the future, involving an uncertain and ill-defined network of participants and observers. We describe this relationship as "pseudo-social" because it consists of a series of "conversations" that are better described as monologues—addressed to the dead person but never replied to and overheard and sometimes responded to by other lurking "friends" who may or may not be known to the declaimer.

Another interesting, though less common, mode of commemoration occurs when the dead person's user name and password are used by a close relative or friend not only for the purpose of access and maintenance but to appropriate the online *persona* of the dead and continue social interaction on the deceased person's behalf just as if that person were alive. Nicole Russell (2014) writes about an instance when "the husband of Auckland cancer patient Natalie Murphy, who lost her public battle with breast cancer in Dec, has kept his wife's profile going. Greg Murphy obtained Natalie's password after her death and updates her page regularly, so it seems to users that Natalie herself is still posting comments. He sees it as a way to continue Natalie's work in raising awareness for breast cancer prevention, and networking for fundraising events." A comparable example saw Roger Ebert—a Pulitzer Prize–winning *Chicago Sun-Times* film critic and Twitter pioneer—ask his wife, Chaz, to become the manager of his Twitter account when he fell ill. Although Ebert died in April 2013, Chaz continued this practice by posting links to old reviews and photos.

These practices present a layer of complexity around identity, as it is clear that the "identity work" (Watson 2008) is conducted by the living others who traverse the space and weave their own personal identifications through their interactions there. The dead person's identity on the site is thus imaginatively produced through others' semi-public musings that are continually consumed and reflected upon and reincorporated into living memories. As noted earlier, there is a clear self-consciousness in the way those others reveal in their postings their own understandings of the tastes, ideas, and desires of the dead. There are multiple ways of viewing this extension of the deceased's social life online. Daniel Miller (2010) offers one approach, suggesting that "the truth about yourself is revealed to you by what you post on Facebook." Indeed, one of Miller's informants in Trinidad felt that the most "real" person was not the one met face to face but the one revealed through representations crafted and carefully chosen for posting by that person on Facebook (Miller 2010).

In one sense, Miller's observation is appropriate. On social media we are what we do, and what we do is "post." It is clear that personally meaningful relationships are established and maintained through the exchange of posts. There is also ample evidence that bodily co-presence is not required for a full range of social and psychological responses, such as love, jealousy, anger, sympathy, sexual arousal, and so on (Stone 1995a; Stone 1995b). In this sense, the social network post is best understood through the "pragmatic" view of communications (Coyne 1999) that suggests that text on the profile page acts in the world. In this "pragmatic" view of text, the postings that appear on the profile are not a simulacra or a metaphor for embodied relations and do not look to embodiment for their rationale or context but may be understood as the locus of social agency. With its postings, the social network provides and constructs its own context, its own discourse of practice, and its own world of social meaning (Arnold 2002).

But whose truth counts on a dead loved one's site where the dead person can never protest your claims and can never "unfriend" *you*? To what extent is a dead person, animated in a social network, able to surprise, to veer off track and unhinge the audience with a new turn of phrase, to answer back with a meaningful glance that demonstrates his or her *inter*-subjectivity (see Lyotard 1991)? Such inter-subjectivity, we argue, goes a step beyond the subjectivity produced, in Žižek's (1992) terms, through our existence for the Other. Here, then, is where the "liveliness" of the dead finds itself at a dead end. In the following section we move from Facebook to consider two further online practices that shed further light on the various interactions that are occurring around leisure and death online.

NETWORKED IMAGES: SELFIES TAKEN AT FUNERALS AND SELFIES TAKEN BEFORE DYING

Perhaps unsurprisingly, considering the state of contemporary digital culture, both of our examples of networked images involve people taking selfies. A selfie is a self-portrait taken with a smartphone, sometimes accessorized with a "selfie stick," that can be instantly sent out to a network of friends—often with a caption—using an app such as Instagram, Snapchat, or Airdrop. This became such a popular media practice that the term *selfie* was announced as the Oxford Dictionary's international "word of the year" in November 2013. Perhaps not coincidently, this announcement emerged at the same time as a Tumblr blog called *Selfies at Funerals*—the second case study of this chapter.

The blog in question featured commentary around images of young people "turning their cellphone cameras on themselves during one of life's most solemn moments" (Clark-Flory 2013). The blog immediately "went viral" and, reflecting the blog's indignant tone, a public outcry followed (see Gibbs et al. 2014; Huffington Post 2013; Meese et al. 2015). Intrigued by the moral panic, we examined hundreds of instances of the actual *practice* of taking selfies as part of our wider project on Digital Commemoration (see Meese et al. 2015), and it offered another perspective on how the worlds of death and leisure are interacting through the use of digital technology.

A feature of this interaction that became apparent in our examination of the funeral selfie was that it affords the immediate mixing of seemingly incompatible publics. The funeral selfie inveigles a social network and invites it to a funeral to glimpse an embodied ritual traditionally constructed as private or by invitation only. However, the posted picture also situates the mourner's emotional circumstances and solemn ritual location into the social and leisured milieu of contemporary youth culture and online social networks. A frisson of subversion is achieved through mixing these publics and rituals, providing a clear example of "context collapse" (Marwick and boyd 2011). Through the funeral selfie, those physically gathering to share senses of loss and grief through "traditional" ritual processes become interconnected with those hanging out on Tumblr or Facebook for the fun and social engagements most often associated with leisure practice.

The selfie in this context may be seen in a number of different ways. It situates a practice that is for many an everyday, casual leisure pursuit in the midst of a ritual that is unique, formal, and somber. In this way, it is often deliberatively transgressive. Alongside transgression, the selfie posted at a funeral is playing on senses of irony. For many young users of social media, irony is an important cultural currency and one that would not necessarily be appreciated by older people (often the ones who feel the most outraged by the thought of it). On yet another level, the selfie is also readily understood as a form of communication, in particular a type of "presencing" that co-locates the subject at the funeral within the network and the network at the funeral (Meese et al. 2015) rather than a contributing form of memorialization.

Similar frissons of transgression, irony, and communication are felt around an even more recently exposed and discussed phenomenon: selfies taken by people just before their unexpected death. These photos are then found and posted by friends and relations online and collated by strangers to produce a visual catalog of immanent tragedies posted online. Most interesting, these pictures tend to be taken in a space of leisure associated with holidays and lively adventures. These pictures range from high-risk–taking solo shots (e.g., people perched on cliffs [see Kaul, this volume] or on high building ledges moments before a tragic fall) to happy social snaps (such as people in a car with friends before a fatal crash). A generous interpretation of the phenomena is that such images chill the viewer, who is reminded of the fragility of life that blossoms in a broad grin captured in one moment and snuffed out in the next. The selfie reminds the viewer that "it could have been me," as the image dramatically marks the points at which physical life and death are just moments apart. The idea of the abruptness of death interrupting the pictured joy of a healthy and happy life can be extremely touching. The tragedy becomes repackaged and alluring to a public through this uneasy and extraordinary juxtaposition.

A less generous interpretation is that the people who aggregate, curate, and publish these images as "click bait" do so to appeal to gratuitous and morbid voyeurism and that the many thousands who view these collated images comprise a new form of "grief tourist" (Phillips 2011) within the larger category of "dark tourism" (Lennon and Foley 2000; Stone 2011). The internet is not by any means unique in this regard. Our mass media is saturated with content that regularly employs sensational depictions of death and violence as entertainment (see Adams, this volume) and to derive profit. In this context, images of people prior to death are subdued and poignant by comparison.

Online sites that post these pictures include Viralnova, BoredBug—cure your boredom, and Runt of the Web. A collection posted on Sliptalk starts with: "There's something incredibly powerful when we look at the last picture a person took or a text they sent before a tragedy. It's almost like you're looking at a ghost. You can see the vibrant life in their eyes having a great time but knowing that that was one of the last times they smiled." These selfies ply their effect in a dramatically different

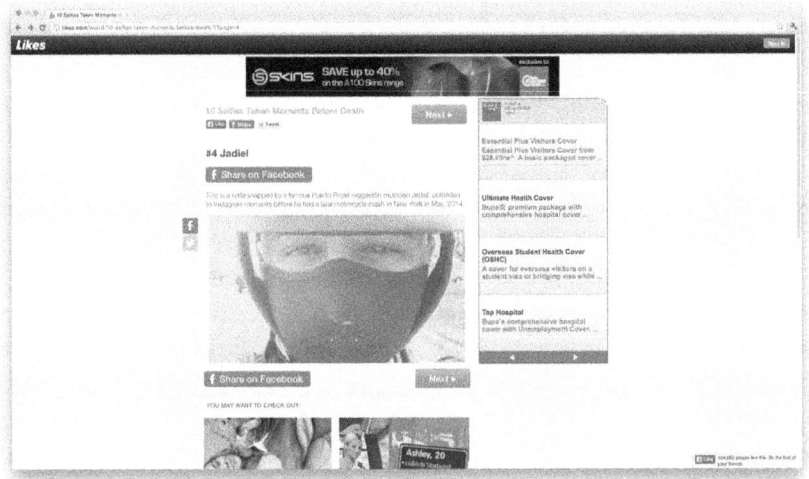

FIGURE 10.3. "Selfies Taken Moments Before Death." Screenshot from Likes.com (no longer active).

fashion from the Facebook profiles discussed earlier in this chapter. On Facebook, there is a relatively seamless transition from social media life to death, as captured in the very subtle but easily missed transitions in the tone of textual postings on Jim's site from before and after his physical demise. In contrast, these selfies are teleological: they are notable for flagging the powerlessness of the subject, who has "a destiny" made obvious to all, and the powerlessness of the viewer, who can't intervene but can only witness.

It is the tragic "it should not be so" of such deaths that attracts the curious and makes them vulnerable to collection and distribution on social media (cf. Erb, this volume). The French writer Georges Perec has eloquently addressed the problem of our attention in the news (or, in the present case, online) to the big events rather than the everyday in his essay "Approaches to What" (Perec 1999 [1973], 209): "Railway trains only begin to exist when they are derailed... Behind the event there has to be a scandal, a fissure, a danger, as if life reveals itself only by way of the spectacular." He bemoans the loss of the everyday in daily newspapers' reportage: the banal, the quotidian, the "infra-ordinary" (Perec 1999 [1973], 209). His views translate well into the digital age, where people are attracted to publicly posted stories and pictures that capture the tragic extraordinary and spectacular deaths of unknown Others. Leisure that rubs up against death in this way directly invites the emotional response of strangers. Because the image we gaze upon is a happy one, we are not—as in news footage and photos of war—directly "regarding the pain of others" à la Sontag (2003) but imagining its subjects' pain in the immediate future.

Perec identifies a dialectic that features in a long critical tradition of scholarship around the everyday, which approaches everyday life as both extraordinary and tedious (see Highmore 2002). In our case, the everyday of these digital spaces features both the act of leisure and, more jarring, the fact of death. This perhaps explains why these two examples of selfies taken during a funeral or immediately prior to death are so rife with tension. In the case of selfies at funerals, death rituals are re-presented in online spaces defined around leisurely acts and framed around largely positive discourses of "friends" and "sharing" (see Burgess 2015; Kennedy 2013). As we argue elsewhere (Gibbs et al. 2015), these selfies therefore respond to the normative discourses and vernacular that social media platforms present to their audiences. However, by sharing selfies in unexpected locations, like that of a funeral, these practices can also establish new vernaculars that challenge our normative expectations of what leisure entails both online and offline. Similarly, the spectatorship invited by the publication of people's pre-death selfies presents various interactions between leisure and death: the deceased subject engaging in leisure immediately prior to death and the powerless viewer who is only able to consume these poignant images as a form of leisured viewing and nothing more.

CONCLUSION

In this chapter we have introduced a range of different cases that address the various ways death is meeting leisure online. In the first example, we considered how new trends enabled through the policy framework of Facebook as well as driven by human desire have allowed people to continue relations with the dead online. Those online spaces of social intimacy with the dead are felt to be "real," and the postings there demonstrate a continuity in affect and inclusiveness with the everyday that the dead cannot see firsthand. The living—who interact on that site or simply observe it—may feel sadness about the loss of their friend, but they also continue to *include* their dead friend and his or her network alongside the numerous other friends they "hang out with" online. In a similar vein, we have pointed out that the leisure life of those now dead is not only preserved but lives on in the service of capital. The flesh is gone but the data remain, the processing continues, and it was only ever the data that were of value in any case.

In the second example, we examined the trend of "Selfies at Funerals" where youths escape to the leisure space of social media to post photos of themselves posing in mourning garb. Here, death meets leisure in a way that can be felt by audiences and critics to be tasteless, narcissistic, and "wrong" or, alternatively, as socially sensible, communicative, and in some sense inventively inclusive. This latter case particularly underlines the tensions that often emerge when leisure occurs in the shadow of death: leisure becomes a contested and political practice that challenges normative ideas around ritual practice and continues the wider social trend of commemoration increasingly becoming a vernacular and everyday practice (Walter 2015).

The third case assembled death and leisure together in a rather different way—in this case within a selfie, taken not at a place or location associated with death like a church or burial site or digital memorial site but in physical spaces associated with leisure and tourism. When images of leisure are posted into the everyday leisure space of social media yet are framed by death, they move from ordinary to extraordinary and become particularly consumable online because of the pictures' juxtaposition of content and context. All three forms allow us to consider how social networks facilitate a moving beyond the physicality of death through social network spaces of leisure. They challenge us to think carefully about our own futures into the hereafter online.

ACKNOWLEDGMENTS

This research was supported through funding from the Australian Research Council (DP140101871). We are grateful for helpful comments from the editors of this volume.

NOTES

1. "Jim" and other names in this vignette are pseudonyms, and location details have been changed.

2. This version of history is challenged by Facebook, which claims to have considered the memorialization of profiles years earlier (see Chan 2009).

3. https://www.facebook.com/help/103897939701143, accessed November 17, 2017.

4. "Unfriending" happens on Facebook pages when friends fall out of touch.

5. *L'Annee Sociologique* is a journal that was established by Durkheim in 1898 and also refers to a group of Durkheim's students and other scholars who shared their research in the early twentieth century.

REFERENCES

Arnold, Michael. 2002. "The Glass Screen." *Information Communication and Society* 5 (2): 225–36. https://doi.org/10.1080/13691180210130752.

Arnold, Michael, Martin Gibbs, Tamara Kohn, James Meese, and Bjorn Nansen. 2018. *Death and Digital Media*. London: Routledge.

Arnold, Michael, Chris Shepherd, Martin Gibbs, and Karen Mecoles. 2006. "Domestic Information and Communication Technologies and Subject-Object Relations: Gender, Identity, and Family Life." *Journal of Family Studies* 12 (1): 95–112. https://doi.org/10.5172/jfs.327.12.1.95.

Bloch, Maurice, and Jonathan Parry. 1983. *Death and the Regeneration of Life*. Cambridge: Cambridge University Press.

Brubaker, Jed R., and Gillian R. Hayes. 2011. "'We Will Never Forget You [online]': An Empirical Investigation of Postmortem Myspace Comments." In *Proceedings of the ACM 2011 Conference on Computer Supported Cooperative Work (CSCW '11)*, 123–32. New York: ACM. https://doi.org/10.1145/1958824.1958843.

Burgess, Jean. 2015. "From 'Broadcast Yourself' to 'Follow Your Interests': Making over Social Media." *International Journal of Cultural Studies* 18 (3): 281–85. 1367877913513684.

Carroll, Brian, and Katie Landry. 2010. "Logging On and Letting Out: Using Online Social Networks to Grieve and to Mourn." *Bulletin of Science, Technology, and Society* 30 (5): 341–49. https://doi.org/10.1177/0270467610380006.

Chan, Kathy H. 2009. "Memories of Friends Departed Endure on Facebook." Facebook, October 26. Accessed November 17, 2017. https://www.facebook.com/notes/facebook/memories-of-friends-departed-endure-on-facebook/163091042130.

Christensen, Neil Blair. 2003. *Inuit in Cyberspace: Embedding Offline Identities Online*. Gylling, Denmark: Museum Tusculanum Press.

Clark-Flory, T. 2013. "In Defense of Funeral Selfies." *Salon*, October 30. Accessed November 17, 2017. http://www.salon.com/2013/10/30/in_defense_of_funeral_selfies.

Coleman, Simon, and Tamara Kohn, eds. 2007. *The Discipline of Leisure: Embodying Cultures of "Recreation."*. Oxford: Berghahn.

Coyne, Richard. 1999. *Technoromanticism: Digital Narrative, Holism, and the Romance of the Real*. Cambridge, MA: MIT Press.

Gibbs, Martin, Marcus Carter, Bjorn Nansen, and Tamara Kohn. 2014. "Selfies at Funerals." In *Proceedings of the 15th Annual Conference of the Association of Internet Researchers (AoIR)*. https://spir.aoir.org/index.php/spir/article/view/944/613.

Gibbs, Martin, James Meese, Michael Arnold, Bjorn Nansen, and Marcus Carter. 2015. "#Funeral and Instagram: Death, Social Media, and Platform Vernacular." *Information Communication and Society* 18 (3): 255–68; Advanced online publication. https://doi.org/10.1080/1369118X.2014.987152.

Hallam, Elizabeth, and Jenny Hockey. 2001. *Death, Memory, and Material Culture*. London: Berg.

Hallam, Elizabeth, Jenny Hockey, and Glennys Howarth. 1999. *Beyond the Body: Death and Social Identity*. London: Routledge.

Hertz, Robert. 1960 [1907]. *Death and the Right Hand*. Trans. Rodney Needham and Claudia Needham. London: Cohen and West.

Highmore, Ben. 2002. *The Everyday Life Reader*. London: Routledge.

Hjorth, Larissa, and Michael Arnold. 2013. "Playing at Being Social: A Cross-Generational Case Study of Social Gaming in Shanghai, China." In *Gaming Globally: Production, Play, and Place*, ed. Nina Huntemann and Ben Aslinger, 101–17. New York: Palgrave Macmillan. https://doi.org/10.1057/9781137006332_9.

Huffington Post. 2013. "Funeral Selfies Are the Latest Evidence Apocalypse Can't Come Soon Enough." October 29. Accessed November 17, 2017. http://www.huffingtonpost.com/2013/10/29/funeral-selfies_n_4175153.html.

Hutchings, Tim. 2012. "Wiring Death: Dying, Grieving, and Remembering on the Internet." In *Emotion, Identity, and Death: Mortality across Disciplines*, ed. Douglas Davies and Chang-Won Park, 43–58. Farnham, UK: Ashgate.

Jones, Steven G. 1994. *Cybersociety: Computer-Mediated Communication and Community*. Thousand Oaks, CA: Sage.

Kaleem, Jaweed. 2012. "Death on Facebook Now Common as 'Dead Profiles' Create Vast Virtual Cemetery." *Huffington Post*, December 7. Accessed November 17, 2017. http://www.huffingtonpost.com/2012/12/07/death-facebook-dead-profiles_n_2245397.html.

Karppi, Tero. 2013. "Death Proof: On the Biopolitics and Noopolitics of Memorializing Dead Facebook Users." *Culture Machine* 14: 120.

Kennedy, Jenny. 2013. "Rhetorics of Sharing: Data, Imagination, and Desire." In *Unlike Us Reader: Social Media Monopolies and Their Alternatives*, ed. Geert Lovink and Miriam Rasch, 127–36. Amsterdam: Institute of Network Cultures.

Kirkpatrick, David. 2010. *The Facebook Effect: The Real Inside Story of Mark Zuckerman and the World's Fastest Growing Company*. London: Ebury.

Kohn, Tamara, Martin Gibbs, Michael Arnold, and Bjorn Nansen. 2012. "Facebook and the Other: Administering to and Caring for the Dead Online." In *Responsibility*, ed. Ghassan Hage, 128–41. Melbourne: Melbourne University Press.

Lennon, John, and Malcolm Foley. 2000. *Dark Tourism: The Attraction of Death and Disaster*. London: Thomson.

Lock, Margaret. 2001. *Twice Dead: Organ Transplants and the Reinvention of Death*. Berkeley: University of California Press.

Lucas, Forrest. 2012. "Is Your Social Media Account Now Part of Your Estate?" *Socially Skilled*, April 29. Accessed November 17, 2017. http://www.sociallyskilled.com.au/2012/04/is-your-social-media-account-now-part-of-your-estate/.

Lustig, Nathan. 2012. "Facebook Death Rate." Accessed November 17, 2017. www.nathanlustig.com/tag/facebook-death-rate/.

Lyotard, Jean-François. 1991. *The Inhuman: Reflections on Time*. Stanford, CA: Stanford University Press.

Marwick, Alice E., and danah boyd. 2011. "I Tweet Honestly, I Tweet Passionately: Twitter Users, Context Collapse, and the Imagined Audience." *New Media and Society* 13 (1): 114–33. https://doi.org/10.1177/1461444810365313.

Meese, James, Bjorn Nansen, Michael Arnold, Martin Gibbs, Tamara Kohn, and Marcus Carter. 2015. "Selfies at Funerals: Digital Commemoration, Presencing, and Platform Vernacular." *International Journal of Communication* 9: 1818–31.

"Memorialized Accounts." 2015. Facebook. Accessed November 17, 2017. https://www.facebook.com/help/1506822589577997/.

Miller, Daniel. 2010. "An Extreme Reading of Facebook." Accessed November 17, 2017. http://openanthcoop.net/press/2010/10/22/an-extreme-reading-of-facebook/.

Mori, Joji, Martin Gibbs, Michael Arnold, Bjorn Nansen, and Tamara Kohn. 2012. "Design Considerations for after Death: Comparing the Affordances of Three Online Platforms." In *Proceedings of the 24th Australian Computer-Human Interaction Conference (OzCHI '12)*, ed. Vivienne Farrell, Graham Farrell, Caslon Chua, Weidong Huang, Raj Vasa, and Clinton Woodward, 395–404. New York: ACM. https://doi.org/10.1145/2414536.2414599.

Nansen, Bjorn, Michael Arnold, Martin Gibbs, and Tamara Kohn. 2014. "From Repose to Restless in the Digital Cemetery." In *Digital Death: Mortality and Beyond in the Online Age*, ed. Christopher Moreman and David Lewis, 111–24. Santa Barbara, CA: Praeger.

Perec, Georges. 1999 [1973]. "Approaches to What." In *Species of Spaces and Other Pieces* by Georges Perec, 209–11. New York: Penguin Books.

Phillips, Whitney. 2011. "LOLing at Tragedy: Facebook Trolls, Memorial Pages, and Resistance to Grief Online." *First Monday* 16 (12). https://doi.org/10.5210/fm.v16i12.3168.

Rivers, William H.R. 1999 [1926]. *Psychology and Ethnology*. London: Routledge.

Russell, Nicola. 2014. "Death and Life in Cyberspace." *Sunday Star Times*, March 11. Accessed November 17, 2017. http://www.stuff.co.nz/sunday-star-times/latest-edition/6555760/Death-and-life-in-cyberspace. http://www.stuff.co.nz/sunday-star-times/latest-edition/6555760/Death-and-life-in-cyberspace.

Scheper-Hughes, Nancy. 2004. "The Last Commodity: Post-Human Ethics and the Global Traffic in 'Fresh' Organs." In *Global Assemblages*, ed. Aihwa Ong and Stephen Collier, 145–68. London: Basil Blackwell.

Sontag, Susan. 2003. *Regarding the Pain of Others*. New York: Picadour.

Stanyek, Jason, and Benjamin Piekut. 2010. "Deadness: Technologies of the Intermundane." *Drama Review* 54 (1): 14–38. https://doi.org/10.1162/dram.2010.54.1.14.

Stone, Allucquére Rosanne. 1995a. *The War of Desire and Technology at the Close of the Mechanical Age*. Cambridge: MIT Press.

Stone, Allucquére Rosanne. 1995b. "Sex and Death among the Disembodied: VR, Cyberspace, and the Nature of Academic Discourse." In *The Cultures of Computing*, ed. Susan Leigh Star, 243–55. Oxford: Blackwell.

Stone, Phillip R. 2011. "Dark Tourism: Towards a New Post-Disciplinary Research Agenda." *International Journal of Tourism Anthropology* 1 (3–4): 318–32. https://doi.org/10.1504/IJTA.2011.043713.

Strathern, Marilyn. 1992. *Reproducing the Future: Anthropology, Kinship, and the New Reproductive Technologies*. London: Routledge.

Walter, Tony. 2015. "New Mourners, Old Mourners: Online Memorial Culture as a Chapter in the History of Mourning." *New Review of Hypermedia and Multimedia* 21 (1–2): 10–24.

Watson, Tony J. 2008. "Managing Identity: Identity Work, Personal Predicaments, and Structural Circumstances." *Organization* 15 (1): 121–43. https://doi.org/10.1177/1350508407084488.

Žižek, Slavoj. 1992. *Looking Awry: An Introduction to Jacques Lacan through Popular Culture*. Cambridge, MA: MIT Press.

11

Rumor Has It

Leisure, Gossip, and Distortion at Funerals in Central Greece

STAVROULA PIPYROU

Ernest Becker (1973, ix–x) argued that death invites a discussion to make sense of "mountains of facts" and "truths." By incorporating rumors into an analysis of death, this chapter creatively engages with the contrasting pleasure-seeking activity of spreading rumors and gossip at funerals and leisurely distorting the "real proportions" of the facts. In his study of death in Greece, Loring Danforth (1982) argued that through the death of others, humans are able to contemplate their own death (see the example of Montaigne in Kaul and Skinner, this volume). In a reflexive fashion, Danforth, while conducting fieldwork in the village of Potamia, central Greece, visualized his own death while studying the "exotic" rites of passage of the "Other." Deeply affected by the study of "Others who die," Danforth concluded that approaching the death of the Other was the path to understanding how the "Self" dies, how "death comes to all, Self and Other alike" (Danforth 1982, 7).

This chapter examines an ethnographic case of death that occurred in my hometown Trikala, also in central Greece, and is a continuation of my own analytical attempts to anthropologically decipher death (Pipyrou 2014; Buck and Pipyrou 2014) within a wider framework of Greek death studies (for instance, Danforth 1982; Seremetakis 1991; Panourgia 1995). Directly engaging with the awkward nexus between leisure and death, the chapter is primarily a personal story—for I am one of the locals—in the reflexive first-person tone of many recent works, including Michael Herzfeld (2011) and parts of Neni Panourgia (2009). In the loaded emotional context of funeral mourning, I examine leisure practices such as gossip and the spreading of rumor in which funeral-goers appear to figuratively "play" with death. Since this is a favorite component of leisure time in Greece, I examine how and why rumors spread at funerals distort the narrative of death, playing a creative role in the politics of (mis)information. When funeral-goers indulge in spreading rumors about the deceased, the person's family, and the circumstances of death, the rumors beget mutual suspicion and conspiracy theories about the "facts" of death fed by the morbid indulgence of distorting information. Playing on well-established stereotypes, distortion, and hyperbole allows heightened visibility of crucial points of the rumor, including its origins, motivations, and responses. Despite the eruption of radical difference and controversy, distorted rumors and gossip further allow for evaluation of the dead person's life and interrogate the social differences of status, power, and control (Gluckman 1963) between gossipers and gossiped.

Funerals are occasions when feelings of bitterness, anger, admiration, and envy are openly expressed. In central Greece they are communal events that entail a gathering of the consanguineous and affinal relatives of the deceased as well as members of the local community (Just 2000, 189; Panourgia 1995, 139). The idea of the local community as "one family," where relationships are built on mutual interest and care, renders an individual's sorrow a collective concern (Du Boulay 1974, 46; Just 2000, 37). This close relationship, however, also invites excessive gossiping.

A longstanding form of leisure in Greece and the wider Mediterranean (cf. Gilmore 1978), gossiping provides amusement and entertainment, a source of immense enjoyment for a plethora of "enthusiastic perpetrators" who indulge in "imaginative scenarios" (Zinovieff 1991, 120–21). Sofka Zinovieff (1991, 125) notes that theories of gossip usually fail to recognize that it is indeed a significant form of entertainment, never more so than in the context of a funeral. To put it bluntly but accurately, in Diego Gambetta's (1994, 199, 202) words, gossiping is "fun," it is "pleasurable." Gossiping demonstrates that a person belongs to a community to some degree, and funerals in particular trigger "active speculation on the nature of the villagers' own lives and worlds" (Rapport 1998, 267). Locals revel in the wealth of "current information" (Rapport 1998, 267) available during funerals to create and circulate stories that rouse feelings of pleasure and self-satisfaction. Even though funerals may not at first appear to be the most appropriate place to gossip (cf. Du Boulay 1974, 206), the attendants grasp the opportunity to indulge in their favorite pastime, continually disassembling, evaluating, and reconstituting the everyday world through fervent gossip (Rapport 1998, 267). Similar to Peter Phipps's (1999, 83) comments on dark tourist sites, at a Greek funeral "death is a macabre and fascinating site" that invites leisurely, pleasurable gossip.

AN AWKWARD SCENE

In 2010, during summer vacation in Trikala, I received a distressed phone call from my childhood friend Antonis. Amid his tears and gasping breath, Antonis informed me that his father, Panos, had unexpectedly passed away that morning outside his parked car while in the middle of a phone conversation. This devastating news hit me hard, not only because it was completely unexpected but also because I had never had any indication that Panos was suffering from ill health. The postmortem showed that Panos died of cardiac arrest, a fact that shocked his immediate family and close friends.

The funeral was scheduled for two days after the death, which was exceptionally stressful and painful for Antonis because in addition to dealing with his own grief, he had to organize the funeral arrangements and navigate the bureaucratic system that surrounds a death in Greece. It was perhaps fortunate that Antonis has a large network of kin and friends prepared to alleviate emotional and practical distress. As a childhood friend of Antonis's I knew the family intimately, and some of my fondest memories of growing up in Trikala were deeply associated with Panos and his wife, Maria, driving us to the family's farm and allowing us to play freely with their animals. These memories, sensual hybrids of smells and colorful images of endless fields, now seemed tarnished by Panos's undeserved and untimely death.

Panos's family is of Vlach origin, from a small village in the nearby Pindos Mountains. They moved to Trikala during the civil war (1946–49), as a result of a government policy to effectively create "dead zones" in the mountains to minimize the communist danger. They arrived in Trikala when Panos was two years old, bringing only the clothes they had on their backs and a loaf of bread. They were forced to abandon their livestock in the village and thus leave behind their only source of income.

The history of the Vlach presence in Trikala has two distinct epochs, and the stereotypes surrounding Vlach identity are pertinent to this case of funeral rumors. In the fledgling Greek state (the region of Thessaly was annexed from the Ottoman Empire in 1881), Vlach and Sarakatsan shepherds were seasonal migrants to Trikala from mountainous regions near the Yugoslav border, renting land in the vicinity of the town to winter their livestock. This activity proved troublesome for the Greek government, as the main agricultural plain was not used to its optimum level. The second edition of the *Baedeker Guide to Greece*, published in 1894, noted that the population of Trikala rose from 14,800 in the summer to 18,000 in the winter because of the seasonal relocation of local shepherds (Baedeker cited in Knight 2015, 45).

The second phase of Vlach relocation to Trikala came in a more permanent form during the civil war. In an attempt to disrupt communist supply chains through the Pindos Mountains from Yugoslavia, the Greek government introduced policies encouraging people to relocate from mountainous areas to the urban centers of Trikala, Larisa, and Thessaloniki. Promising employment and security, the policies were aimed at controlling the influence of communist guerrillas and were a strategic scheme to discourage people from collaborating with the communist side. The national government sought to create "dead zones" to dilute communist influence, which appealed to anti-communists, guerrilla supporters, and neutrals alike. Therefore, during 1946 and 1947, many Vlachs from the mountainous areas of northern and central Greece relocated to urban centers on the Plain of Thessaly or to the city of Thessaloniki in Greek Macedonia (Knight 2014, 185–86). Today, despite overt historical consciousness of other eras of violence and social upheaval, people in Trikala rarely discuss the civil war; it has become a piece of history that is viewed as poisonous and divisive and as pitting brother against brother (Knight 2012a, 360, 370, 2015; cf. Hart 1992).

In the twenty-first century, Trikala is home to a variety of cultural groups, all of which are associated with a set of stereotypes accorded to cultural traits that, in turn, incite different topics of gossip (cf. Kirtsoglou and Sistani 2003; Sutton 2003; Theodossopoulos 2007). The descendants of the civil war migrants from Greek Macedonia are mainly, although not exclusively, of Vlach or Sarakatsan background. With their own language and cultural values, Vlachs continue to be stereotyped as the people of the highlands (cf. Cowan 2000). Trikalinoi may argue that Vlachs are not as "Hellenized" as other cultural groups and that they openly patronize their own people, showing open disregard for other Greeks. Often, the term *Vlach* is used in everyday discourse to denote the second-class citizen, the uneducated, and the vulgar. The claim that a local person from Trikala had ancestors of Vlach blood is met with suspicion, even disdain and mistrust, because of the association of Slavic (non-Greek) origins. Therefore, it could be said that gossip about Vlachs is usually intended to remind people of their inferior origins and impose a form of social control (cf. Gluckman 1963, 309). The category "Vlach," Jane Cowan argues, is notorious for the variety of meanings dependent on geographic context; a person living on the Greek side of the Macedonian border inhabits the category rather differently than another in the former Yugoslav Republic of Macedonia (Cowan 2000, 12).

In Trikala, one may hear the statement "the Vlachs are cunning and successful entrepreneurs." Such assertions are reinforced by proverbs and folk tales, songs, and short stories in which traits such as intelligence and cunning are exaggerated. Trikalinoi stereotype Vlachs as "taking care of their own," as Vlach men are often required to marry women of the same cultural origins. Vlach men have often gone against such family wishes, however, only for their partner, sadly, to be rejected by their families.[1]

The first years in which Panos's family lived in Trikala were exceptionally difficult, but amid their abject poverty they had happy memories of solidarity and sharing a sense of common fate with relatives and friends and a wider sector of people in the town who did not enjoy the privileges of secure financial and social status. Panos's parents were proud people and they did not indulge in recounting the suffering of those postwar years, as silence was their *techne* of dealing with the "critical event" (Das 1995) that irrevocably divided their extensive family between "communist" and "nationalist" loyalties. Yet while singing a Vlach song, a tear in the eye of Panos's father could reveal much more than any eloquent narrative. A brief sigh would conclude the only instances of the "unspoken" and "absent" and leave traces of a deeper pain about a decade of conflict in the 1940s and the village abandonment.

Accustomed to working with animals, Panos's parents found it only natural to continue with the same occupation in Trikala, although in a more systematic way. They started humbly by purchasing five sheep for their immediate needs; through doing odd jobs, from working in the fields to cleaning houses, they gradually raised the capital to buy more sheep. Panos remembered these years with mixed feelings. He missed his parents, as the only times he saw them were at lunch and before he went to sleep at night. He was lucky, however, because he lived on the outskirts of the town where more Vlachs came to settle, thus creating a strong network that cared for children whose parents had to work hard and compensated for the lack of immediate parental care. They were usually older people who, long past their working prime, provided a safe and emotional buffer from the ugliness of the surrounding poverty.

Panos's first home was a one-room dwelling where the room functioned as a kitchen, bedroom, and living room. How fond he was of that one-room house. During my childhood, he often took Antonis and me in his car with the specific purpose of passing outside his old house in his former neighborhood. Lacking his parents' reserve, Panos frequently recounted events of those first years in Trikala when the family gradually but steadily built the base for a brighter future. He often became emotional and revealed a deeper experiential suffering the years of this struggle had left in him. By working closely with other Vlachs and expanding their network, the family managed to build their first substantial sheep farm. By the end of the 1960s, they had 100 sheep and successfully supplied the local market with milk while gradually expanding their trade to the rest of central Greece.

Panos took over this successful business at the beginning of the 1970s after being awarded a degree in finance from Athens University of Economics and Business. Despite having tasted the rich social and political life of the capital city during his university years, for Panos it was an easy decision to return to Trikala and run the family business. It was not only a "sense of obligation toward the parents" instilled in him since he was a child but also a wider appreciation of the Greek periphery that reached its peak during his years in Athens, when he felt he did not belong anywhere other than his hometown. Under Panos's administration, the business achieved unprecedented expansion and development. In the 1980s Panos was one of the first people in Greece to successfully tap into the newly opened European markets, and through relevant European Union funding schemes the business prospered. His name appeared regularly in daily gossip in Trikala, as well as in local and national news, as a very successful entrepreneur. The family lived in a 400-square-meter house, a beacon of Panos's financial and social success. Everybody invited him to their celebrations during seasonal festivities and wanted to include him on their various civic boards. His word mattered.

Of course, not everything was that rosy. There were endless rumors in the city about his financial success and personal life (cf. Zinovieff 1991). Because it was so expansive during the years Daniel Knight (2015) characterizes as the "prosperity" of post-dictatorship Greece, Panos's success begot rumors of corruption and financial mismanagement. He was accused of abusing his European Union money to create more capital by investing in the stock market, which during the 1990s turned everybody in Greece into a "financial investor" (Knight 2012b, 2015). It was rumored that he engaged in money laundering through charity and other philanthropic activities. Locals gossiped endlessly about his personal life, hinting that he was no longer faithful to his wife, Maria, and that he indulged in extramarital relations with "imported" (migrant) women (see Zinovieff 1991 and Gambetta 1994 on gossip surrounding sex and adultery). The gossip was contextualized within wider narratives of kinship and stereotypes of his Vlach origin, questioning his position in the social hierarchy (cf. Gluckman 1963).

As local socialites, Antonis and I were often audience to such rumors. Our social circles commented on the family's success, speculating about Panos's financial and personal mistrust. "I do admire him for what he has managed in his life, *but* . . ." This *but* was the prelude to gossip and rumor that intended to convey specific information about Panos and his family and ultimately tell an alternative story about success. His Vlach origin was essentialized within an overarching understanding of otherness, itself the outcome of stereotyping Vlachs as possessing traits such as cunningness, untrustworthiness, and entrepreneurship.

Panos's death shocked Trikala and re-ignited already active rumors about his life. People speculated about the reason behind his unexpected end as they were trying to reconcile their own ideas about power, status, and untouchability. In the eyes of locals, Panos's power made him untouchable, even by death. But in the end, not even he escaped the reaper, people would say, thus regaining confidence in a "higher system of justice" in which the only certainty is that death comes to us all, rich or poor. Panos was kind and generous to his wife and son, but he was a hardnosed businessman. People who knew him only professionally would testify to his brilliant mind and ability to close the best deals. Panos's only vulnerability was in his home life—that was the only thing that could be targeted. "It could not have been a business matter that finished him. It had to do with his personal life," rumor had it.

During the two days leading up to his funeral, Panos's sister and cousins managed to organize everything, from making elaborate funeral arrangements and booking the church to informing relatives, friends, and business associates from across Greece. The night before the funeral, family and friends shared time with Maria and Antonis in their house, where Panos would spend his last night. Despite the short notice, the large house was flooded by relatives, friends, and business associates who came to pay their last respects to Panos and his family. And there he was, Panos, in the grand living room in his elaborate coffin, lying in a bed of flowers, with Maria and Antonis sitting by the coffin in a semi-drugged state. Immediately after the announcement of her husband's death, Maria collapsed and the family doctor had to administer a light sedative so she could cope with the event. More than drugged, Antonis was numb to the bone with a searing pain, and he could not stop crying. When a familiar face approached the coffin to offer condolences, the family would again burst into tears and fall into each other's arms.

We stayed all night at the wake, keeping Panos company for the last time before we escorted him to his "final home." My duties were to my childhood friend, trying to leave him space for mourning and holding him in my arms when his suffering reached uncontrollable levels. Antonis was in shock. I paced back and forth from the living room to the kitchen and dining room. As the living quarters had an open plan, I could keep an eye on Antonis while I was in the kitchen or dining room helping relatives serve coffee and water.

Even in the midst of all these people, I found the opportunity to lean against a wall and externalize my personal grief. Hiding behind two middle-aged women dressed in black, I could let my tears go and mourn silently. But suddenly...

"I find the whole thing strange. There is something weird about his death."

"Yes, I agree with you. I don't buy any of this. What does it mean that he died during a phone conversation?"

"I do believe that he was having an affair. That phone call was strange."

Suddenly, my silent mourning stopped and I was drawn to this conversation. Did I hear correctly? I looked at the dead body of Panos in the background and then at these two women in front of me, contemplating the incongruity. They continued.

"You know, since he became so rich, many women besiege him."

"Yes, all these trips away from Trikala, what do you expect?"

"Poor Maria, what is the meaning of all this wealth when your husband sleeps around?"

I felt my blood pressure rising and my face burning, and I had to resort to "the anthropological armor" to calm myself down. I tried to objectify a very personal and highly stressful situation. They continued . . .

"Ha, that is true. What is the point of all this wealth when you are betrayed and ridiculed by your husband?"

"I could not bear the deception for all the wealth of the world. I have my pride . . ."

"I believe that it was the girlfriend who must have threatened him during the phone call . . ."

"Yes, she must have threatened that she would reveal their relationship to Maria, and then he dropped dead."

A third woman entered the conversation with a smirk on her face. She seemed to enjoy the discourse and was ready to contribute further.

"Ssshhh, keep your voices down, I could hear what you were saying."

"We say nothing but the truth. The Vlach was cunning and manipulative, ha ha."

The women appeared to be having great fun, taking pleasure in putting together hypotheses about the cause of Panos's death. They speculated as to what his girlfriend may have been threatening to reveal, her identity, and her youthful age. One woman stated that she had heard that the girlfriend was "a young Russian girl who worked as a barmaid at the local club." The women snickered at the fact that Panos had been tempted by the exotic beauty of a young girl, smiling and breaking into open laughter while the dead Panos lay in rest just a few meters behind them. The women obviously felt good about themselves, as the image of the wealthy but unfaithful husband reified their own sense of morality and made them feel better about their relatively "poorer but purer" social situation. They compared their husbands' superior behavior to Panos's deception and belittled the Russian girl for destroying a Greek family, criticizing the morals of "her type." For the gossiping women, the wake was as good a source of fun as a theme park or a shopping trip to Athens.

But all this speculation had no basis. It was easy for Antonis to trace the last phone call from his father's mobile phone. The phone call that ended Panos's life was a business call from Panos's bank that revealed to him that—similar to hundreds of other businesses in Greece during the fiscal crisis—his company was experiencing financial difficulties. Two years earlier, Antonis had apologetically revealed to me that he had discretely followed his father for a long period of time, alarmed by the "imported girlfriend" rumors. He kept the operation covert, a secret from his mother, who would have felt betrayed by her son's absurd behavior. Panos was simply a workaholic who devoted endless hours to his business, so he was away from home for long periods of time, feeding the infidelity rumors.

RUMOR HAS IT

The gossiping women's macabre critique fed on commonly held stereotypes of Vlachs as cunning, manipulative, and deceptive. Employed as explanatory and classificatory devices, in this instance stereotypes were derogatory metaphorical characterizations that emphasized the status difference between the deceased Panos and the women. Unable to enjoy the wealth of Panos's family, the women situated themselves in positions of moral superiority by pigeonholing Panos's cultural identity into a well-known set of criteria (Kirtsoglou and Sistani 2003, 190). Yet the substantiation of the stereotypes is full of inconsistencies—they are "hollow categories" not because they are meaningless but rather because they are "incomplete, permeable, and imprecise" (Kirtsoglou and Sistani 2003, 200; Theodossopoulos 2007). The inherent dynamism in stereotypical markers of "the Other" directly relates to their classificatory and explanatory potential, which contains composite but simultaneously open-ended categorical ideas about collectivities (Kirtsoglou and Sistani 2003, 207–8; Theodossopoulos 2003; also Gluckman 1963).

Consistent with "the verbal and stylistic conventions of everyday gossip" (for details and examples, see Gambetta 1994), the women at Panos's funeral did not actually spell out their motives behind creating Panos as a "character"—the circulated rumors were characterized by an overt ambivalence toward their facticity. Instead, the women fed upon each other's narrative, thus revealing Panos "in story" (Hamilakis 2002, 121; Buck and Pipyrou 2014, 263). Michael Herzfeld argued that the Greek novelist Andreas Nenedakis "captures the formulaic character of gossip with a nicely sardonic eye for the external that legitimate[s] it, so that we are drawn into the cultural logic by which people infer each other's motives in a society that explicitly denies that possibility" (Herzfeld 1997, 245). Herzfeld further argues that "the gossip's delicately insistent whisper does its work twice over, in the event described and in the narration, and so it lends itself to the projection of these speculations about motive to a readership far larger than the small society of Rethemnos then and now: this is the canyon of echoes stretching into posterity" (Herzfeld 1997, 245).

In a small town like Trikala, gossip transcends the boundaries between private and public life. Gossip creates individual and collective histories and "continually disassembles, evaluates, and reconstitutes the everyday world" (Rapport 1998, 267; also Paine 1967; Zinovieff 1991). The early work of John Campbell (1964) in Greece sees rumor and gossip not as mere reflection but as constitutive of the social world, where gossip is competitive and largely distractive and annihilating. Juliet Du Boulay (1974, 204) points in another direction that is central to this chapter: rumor and gossip as a form of entertainment, something developed by Sofka Zinovieff (1991), who highlights that gossip is an intense source of pleasure. "A rumor," Jean-Noel Kapferer argues (1990, 14), "constitutes a relation to authority," and the women's attempt to handle constitutive categories such as kinship and status reveals their own interest in managing such categories to "expose the conditionality of the leading citizens' status" (Herzfeld 1997, 245).

Anthony Cohen and Nigel Rapport argue that individuals "own—and perhaps come to be owned by—unique narratives that unfold and mutate as these individuals situate themselves within moral, social, cultural, and historical habitats" (Cohen and Rapport 1995, 7; Rapport 1993). In cases of death, drawing on historically and cultural accepted repertoires of bereavement, narratives encourage particular public responses and often justify socially problematic deaths such as suicide (Pipyrou 2014, 189; Kaul, this volume). Through affective narratives, actors play with notions of presence and absence, truth and imagination (Navaro-Yashin 2007, 80). Especially in socially problematic cases, silencing and re-fabrication or distortion (Kaul, this volume), as well as affectively re-directing narratives, are put forward as coping mechanisms (Pipyrou 2014). In such attempts, dead subjects are reenacted, re-created, and reclaimed as they are pulled by narrative forces in different and often competing directions.

This pulling is prosthesis, multiplying the dead subject and changing the very nature of his or her death, summoning inventive answers to penetrating questions, and demonstrating the ingenuity of actors to negotiate social pressures. From the Greek verb *prosthéto*, prosthesis is to add something extra to or replace an aspect of the original story. The narrative of the dead person created through gossip conjures a different interpretation of the story, re-creating an alternative image of the individual in narrative form (see Buck and Pipyrou 2014, 263). The narrative embroilment of affective subjects and objects thus influences interactions between the individual and society (Stewart 2012, 2). Where the unspoken haunting presence of troubling events remains, affective narratives bridge the blurred spaces where personal suffering meets communal acceptability (Navaro-Yashin 2012, 17; see also chapters by Kohn and colleagues and Erb, this volume). The narrative becomes a trace of an absence, an image of a person that has disappeared or has never existed except in narrative form (cf. Bille, Hastrup, and Sørensen 2010; Vernant and Doueihi 1986, 58–59; Buck and Pipyrou 2014, 263).

But narratives unfold and mutate as individuals situate themselves within moral, social, cultural, and historical contexts (Cohen and Rapport 1995, 7; Rapport 1993, 78; Pipyrou 2014, 191). A sense of context is understood as a "domain or arena of significance" and is determined by the questions people ask of events, "signalling an important link between [sic] context, perception, and intention, between [sic] context, knowledge, and desire" (quotation in Rapport 1999, 190; also see Bateson with Reusch 1951, 238). These questions merge personal with collective perceptions, intentions, and desires and are accommodated "in story," in a narrative form that informs and is informed by the local toolkit to make sense of death (Pipyrou 2014, 197). As the circumstances of death continue to facilitate the "evaluation of the character and reputation of the deceased" and his or her family (Danforth 1982, 51), gossip and rumor about the deceased may have a long-lasting effect on wider groups of people (Pipyrou 2014).

Human beings as well as anthropologists are "invited" by death to make a comment, a discussion, and an "epistemological meta-commentary on what we say, think, and imagine in quotidian and academic environments" about other human beings who are themselves caught "in story"; their trajectories are a product of narratives that target both the dead and the living (Buck and Pipyrou 2014, 264). As Greek anthropologists have argued for other social phenomena, dichotomies such as real/unreal and orality/textuality may compartmentalize experience, thus foreclosing "our understanding of agency, creativity, and the power of the radical imagination" (Kirtsoglou 2010, 332). Nadia Seremetakis (1991) argued that death is not a bounded event but one that contains all aspects of culture.

In this sense, the "geography of death" (Kaul, this volume) should not be viewed as radically different from the geography of life, with all its associated pleasures and pains. In his reading of the fascination with suicide at the Cliffs of Moher, Ireland, Adam Kaul (this volume) shows that playful dark humor about death and dying can be extended to various aspects of everyday life, such as cyberspace (also Kohn et al., this volume). Drawing on larger overarching narratives such as kinship, status, and cultural origin, gossip and rumors operate like messengers that sustain informal communication (Paine 1967, 278; Du Boulay 1974, 204; Just 2000, 160). Funerals in Greece are events that entail the gathering of large collectivities associated through kinship, friendship, and business. Such gatherings unavoidably generate excessive gossip and rumor spreading because attendants have the opportunity to indulge in their favorite pastime (Just 2000, 40; Du Boulay 1974, 206; Panourgia 1995, 70). Some funeral-goers simply cannot wait for a large communal gathering, anticipating the opportunity to engage in exchanging information about mutual acquaintances and filling the plot with dark humor, as well as suspicious and salacious speculation (cf. Zinovieff 1991).

CONCLUSION

Rumors and gossip express concerns about power discrepancies in the community (Kroeger 2003) and are regularly linked to critical expressions of ethnic or cultural identity (Harney 2006), in this case the stereotype of "the Vlach" as cunning and manipulative. Constituting a range of conversational properties aimed at holding listeners' attention (Guerin and Miyazaki 2006), rumor and gossip should be regarded as recurrent forms of communication through which people in an ambiguous situation attempt to construct a meaningful interpretation of that situation by pooling their conversational resources. They might be regarded as a form of collective problem solving (Shibutani 1966, 17), as communicative devices offering "news" that travels across social fields. Nicholas Harney has argued that rumor acts as an improvised form of news in the absence of more formal and verifiable sources. Rumor offers an interpretative frame for those participating in "rumor publics, making use of the limited knowledge they possess, to solve problems, make sense of changing or uncertain conditions, and construct explanatory narratives in the face of fluid and ambiguous situations" (Harney 2006, 376). The news is substantiated to the extent that it is received by word of mouth from someone with whom the receiver has an interpersonal relationship and that it is subjectively evaluated against standards of experience, knowledge, and trust in those who deliver it (Harney 2006; Kapferer 1990).

Above all, in the context of a personal account of a Greek funeral presented in this chapter, gossip is a pleasurable activity, a form of entertainment that is constructed around one of the most prominent events in community life: death. Rumors are building blocks of wider overarching narratives such as kinship, status, and origin. They are snapshots of these narratives, and their plasticity allows a reworking into the creation of new accounts, the reinforcing of already existing ones, or the proposing of completely new interpretations. Precisely because they are concise and easy to grasp, such as the idea that Panos had a Russian girlfriend, rumors travel fast, and their combinatory capacity is endless and unpredictable (Allport and Postman 1947). Regardless of their own facticity, rumors are in "constant construction" (Shibutani 1966, 9), often acquiring a subversive capacity, especially when they contradict institutionalized channels that control information dissemination (Stewart and Strathern 2004, 43).

As a leading citizen of his town, Panos could not escape rumors about his life and the *value* of his life. In their facticity or lack thereof, rumors about his death, circulated at his funeral, were not devoid of a pleasure-creating capacity for their generators. Pleasure seeking in death-associated contexts reveals the fragility of the dichotomy between life and death. Like playing with Legos, the building blocks of our childhood, the women at Panos's funeral were pleasurably engaging with something bigger than Panos himself. They were having fun playing with the overarching categories of social life in Greece, such as kinship, status, and origin. By constantly remodeling, removing, or adding fundamental building blocks in the form of rumor, they challenged the rhetorical capacity of these categories, revealing their malleable character.

NOTE

1. In one case a Vlach, Theodoros, has been married to a woman of non-Vlach origin for thirty-five years, yet she remains "outside the family." If anything goes wrong in their lives or their relationship, Theodoros is reminded that "he should have married a Vlach." What did he expect? "A Vlach woman would not behave like that" (Knight, personal communication, 2009).

REFERENCES

Allport, G. W., and L. Postman. 1947. *The Psychology of Rumor*. New York: Holt, Rinehart and Winston.

Bateson, G., with J. Reusch. 1951. *Communication: The Social Matrix of Psychiatry*. New York: Norton.

Becker, E. 1973. *The Denial of Death*. New York: Free Press.

Bille, M., F. Hastrup, and T. F. Sørensen. 2010. "Introduction: An Anthropology of Absence." In *An Anthropology of Absence: Materializations of Transcendence and Loss*, ed. M. Bille, F. Hastrup, and T. F. Sørensen, 3–22. London: Springer. https://doi.org/10.1007/978-1-4419-5529-6_1.

Buck, T., and S. Pipyrou. 2014. "You Can Die But Once? Rhetoric, Narrative, and Epistemology in Western Death." *Mortality: Promoting the Interdisciplinary Study of Death and Dying* 19 (3): 261–83. https://doi.org/10.1080/13576275.2014.929567.

Campbell, J. K. 1964. *Honour Family and Patronage: A Study of Institutions and Moral Values in a Greek Mountain Community*. Oxford: Clarendon.

Cohen, A., and N. Rapport. 1995. *Questions of Consciousness*. London: Routledge.

Cowan, J. K., ed. 2000. *Macedonia: The Politics of Identity and Difference*. London: Pluto.

Danforth, L. 1982. *Death Rituals in Rural Greece*. Princeton, NJ: Princeton University Press.

Das, V. 1995. *Critical Events: An Anthropological Perspective on Contemporary India*. Delhi: Oxford University Press.

Du Boulay, J. 1974. *Portrait of a Greek Mountain Village*. Limni, Greece: Denise Harvey.

Gambetta, D. 1994. "Godfather's Gossip." *Archives Européennes de Sociologie* 35 (2): 199–223. https://doi.org/10.1017/S0003975600006846.

Gilmore, D. 1978. "Varieties of Gossip in a Spanish Rural Community." *Ethnology* 17 (1): 89–99. https://doi.org/10.2307/3773282.

Gluckman, M. 1963. "Gossip and Scandal." *Current Anthropology* 4 (3): 307–16. https://doi.org/10.1086/200378.

Guerin, B., and Y. Miyazaki. 2006. "Analyzing Rumors, Gossip, and Urban Legends through Their Conversational Properties." *Psychological Record* 56 (1): 23–33. https://doi.org/10.1007/BF03395535.

Hamilakis, Y. 2002. "The Past as Oral History: Towards an Archaeology of the Senses." In *Thinking through the Body: Archaeologies of Corporeality*, ed. Y. Hamilakis, M. Pluciennik, and S. Tarlow, 121–36. New York: Kluwer Academic/Plenum. https://doi.org/10.1007/978-1-4615-0693-5_7.

Harney, N. 2006. "Rumour, Migrants, and the Informal Economies of Naples, Italy." *International Journal of Sociology and Social Policy* 26 (9–10): 374–84. https://doi.org/10.1108/14433306106905 23.

Hart, L. 1992. *Time, Religion, and Social Experience in Rural Greece*. Lanham, MD: Rowman and Littlefield.

Herzfeld, M. 1997. *Portrait of a Greek Imagination: An Ethnographic Biography of Andreas Nenedakis*. Chicago: University of Chicago Press.

Herzfeld, M. 2011. "Crisis Attack: Impromptu Ethnography in the Greek Maelstrom." *Anthropology Today* 27 (5): 22–26. https://doi.org/10.1111/j.1467-8322.2011.00829.x.

Just, R. 2000. *A Greek Island Cosmos: Kinship and Community on Meganisi*. Oxford: James Currey Press.

Kapferer, J.-N. 1990. *Rumors: Uses, Interpretations, Images*. New Brunswick, NJ: Transaction.

Kirtsoglou, E. 2010. "Dreaming the Self: A Unified Approach towards Dreams, Subjectivity, and the Radical Imagination." *History and Anthropology* 21 (3): 321–35. https://doi.org/10.1080/02757206.2010.499908.

Kirtsoglou, E., and L. Sistani. 2003. "The Other *Then*, the Other *Now*, the Other *Within*: Stereotypical Images and Narrative Captions of the Turk in Northern and Central Greece." *Journal of Mediterranean Studies* 13 (2): 189–213.

Knight, D. M. 2012a. "Cultural Proximity: Crisis, Time, and Social Memory in Central Greece." *History and Anthropology* 23 (3): 349–74. https://doi.org/10.1080/02757206.2012.697064.

Knight, D. M. 2012b. "Turn of the Screw: Narratives of History and Economy in the Greek Crisis." *Journal of Mediterranean Studies* 21: 53–76.

Knight, D. M. 2014. "Mushrooms, Knowledge Exchange, and Polytemporality in Kalloni, Greek Macedonia." *Food, Culture, and Society* 17 (2): 183–201. https://doi.org/10.2752/175174414X13871910532105.

Knight, D. M. 2015. *History, Time, and Economic Crisis in Central Greece*. New York: Palgrave Macmillan.

Kroeger, K. 2003. "AIDS Rumors, Imaginary Enemies, and the Body Politic in Indonesia." *American Ethnologist* 30 (2): 243–57. https://doi.org/10.1525/ae.2003.30.2.243.

Navaro-Yashin, Y. 2007. "Make-Believe Papers, Legal Forms, and the Counterfeit: Affective Interactions between Documents and People in Britain and Cyprus." *Anthropological Theory* 7 (1): 79–98. https://doi.org/10.1177/1463499607074294.

Navaro-Yashin, Y. 2012. *The Make-Believe Space: Affective Geography in a Postwar Polity*. Durham, NC: Duke University Press.

Paine, R. 1967. "What Is Gossip About? An Alternative Hypothesis." *Man* 2 (2): 278–85. https://doi.org/10.2307/2799493.

Panourgia, N. 1995. *Fragments of Death, Fables of Identity*. Madison: University of Wisconsin Press.

Panourgia, N. 2009. *Dangerous Citizens: The Greek Left and the Terror of the State*. New York: Fordham University Press.

Phipps, P. 1999. "Tourists, Terrorists, Death, and Value." In *Travel Worlds: Journeys in Contemporary Cultural Politics*, ed. Raminder Kaur and John Hutnyk, 74–93. London: Zed Books.

Pipyrou, S. 2014. "Narrating Death: Affective Reworking of Suicide in Rural Greece." *Social Anthropology* 22 (2): 189–99. https://doi.org/10.1111/1469-8676.12069.

Rapport, N. 1993. *Diverse World-Views in an English Village*. Edinburgh: Edinburgh University Press.

Rapport, N. 1998. "Gossip." In *Encyclopaedia of Social and Cultural Anthropology*, ed. A. Barnard and J. Spencer, 266–67. London: Routledge.

Rapport, N. 1999. "Context as an Act of Personal Externalization: Gregory Bateson and the Harvey Family in the English Village of Wanet." In *The Problem of Context*, ed. R. Dilley, 187–211. Oxford: Berghahn.

Seremetakis, N. 1991. *The Last Word: Women, Death, and Divination in Inner Mani*. Chicago: University of Chicago Press.

Shibutani, T. 1966. *Improvised News: A Sociological Study of Rumor*. Indianapolis: Bobbs-Merrill.

Stewart, C. 2012. *Dreaming and Historical Consciousness in Island Greece*. Cambridge, MA: Harvard University Press.

Stewart, P. J., and A. Strathern. 2004. *Witchcraft, Rumors, Sorcery, and Gossip*. Cambridge: Cambridge University Press.

Sutton, D. 2003. "Poked by the 'Foreign Finger' in Greece: Conspiracy Theory or the Hermeneutics of Suspicion?" In *The Usable Past: Greek Metahistories*, ed. K. S. Brown and Y. Hamilakis, 191–210. Lanham, MD: Lexington Books.

Theodossopoulos, D. 2003. "Degrading Others and Honouring Ourselves: Ethnic Stereotypes as Categories and as Explanations." *Journal of Mediterranean Studies* 13 (2): 177–88.

Theodossopoulos, D., ed. 2007. *When Greeks Think about Turks: The View from Anthropology*. London: Routledge.

Vernant, J., and A. Doueihi. 1986. "Feminine Figures of Death in Greece." *Diacritics* 16 (2): 54–64. https://doi.org/10.2307/465071.

Zinovieff, S. 1991. "Inside Out and Outside In: Gossip, Hospitality, and the Greek Character." *Journal of Mediterranean Studies* 1: 120–34.

12

"If You Go Down in the Woods"

British Woodland Burial, Leisurely Funerals, and Recreational Burial Grounds

HANNAH RUMBLE

As every child who is familiar with the nursery rhyme "Teddy Bears' Picnic" knows, "If you go down in the woods today you're sure of a big surprise," but people who visit established or establishing woodland in Britain today may also be in for a surprise. What may appear to be a recreational woodland could in fact be a "natural burial ground," where visitors can be found picnicking, reading, or dog walking, as this middle-aged widow did:

> I used to go and lie where my grave is next to [my husband] and I'd take a sandwich quite often actually, but I don't do it now. There's a little shop in Barton and they do takeaway coffee, and I sometimes used to go early in the morning on my bicycle and buy a croissant or something, and . . . if you're very careful, you can balance it in your bicycle basket and I'd just go and sit and have my coffee and croissant next to [his] grave. Or I'd take a sandwich out and just go and lie there and read. If there's somebody else around I don't do it, but most of the time there isn't somebody around, so, you know, if it's a nice day I just take a sandwich out there . . . it is a place that I love. I used to lie down where I'm going to be buried and I'd be thinking, gosh, this is where I'll be! (Author interview with the widow)

You may wonder what the appeal is and why this widow feels inclined to visit a natural burial ground in Cambridgeshire and read a book beside the grave of her deceased husband. How is it that British natural burial grounds appeal to, among others, dog walkers and families with young children attending an Easter egg hunt, all the while knowing that the(ir) dead lie beneath them? In this chapter I argue that such varied, informal leisure activities and visiting behaviors are facilitated by the reduced topographic visibility of the dead in the burial ground while explicit attention is granted to trees and wildflowers by the burial grounds' management, mimicking practices more often seen in conservation areas. Such practices ultimately bring both the living and the dead together more informally in a myriad of leisure activities not popularly associated with British burial grounds from the mid-twentieth century onward.

As the editors and contributors of this volume remind us, while death has certainly become a macabre tourist site, it is also a borderland in which a multitude of leisure practices appear; these are numerous and diverse (see the chapters by Adams, Erb, and Iitaka, this volume, for example). In fact, there are endless entanglements of death and leisure in tourism, but writing from a death studies perspective, I highlight that the entanglements of leisure and death also have a long history in British cemetery use, not least with the latest "deathscape" (Maddrell and Sidaway 2010) to appear in Britain known as "natural," "eco," "green," or "woodland" burial. While historians and death studies scholars have long argued that in much of Western Europe by the thirteenth century churchyards had an extended social role, playing host to a variety of activities and leisure pursuits such as markets, fairs, gambling, theatrical performances, carriage driving, music, and dancing (Deering 2010, 75; Ariès 1994; Dunk and Rugg 1994; Worpole 2003), scholars of tourism have tended to focus on what is perceived as the tense or seemingly contradictory connections among leisure, risk, tourism, and death (Lennon and Foley 2000; Stone 2011, 2012).

Yet my fieldwork at a natural burial ground in Cambridgeshire, England, between 2008 and 2010 revealed that these connections are not necessarily tense or contradictory at all; indeed, such connections are often celebrated and emphasized by natural burial ground owners/managers. So, just as this volume seeks to situate and extend the current focus on "dark tourism" into a larger framework of leisure practices, I seek to highlight the various ways natural burial grounds are fostering leisurely funerals and supporting a range of recreational activities within burial grounds in Britain today. Further, just as labeling particular tourist destinations or experiences "dark tourism" (Lennon and Foley 2000) along a spectrum of "light" to "dark" is a construction largely open to debate, the same applies to the construction of defining a burial space as "natural" and categorizing burial grounds as places that sequester the "dead" from the "living" (see Rumble et al. 2014). With the recent emergence of an innovative "deathscape" popularly known as "natural burial"—a distinct mortuary practice and burial space I describe below—came a new place and mode of burial that accommodates dog walkers, birdwatchers, schoolchildren, and picnicking bereaved visitors (among others). In natural burial grounds there are attempts to reconcile, or at least undermine, the juxtaposition "life"-"death"; subsequently, the entanglements of leisure and death are not necessarily tense or peculiar for all people, all of the time, or necessarily encountered in a borderland.

NATURAL BURIAL?

One way natural burial is perceived to be "natural" is in the capacity for these burial places to bring the living and the dead together more informally in a myriad of leisure activities not commonly associated with contemporary burial grounds, thus reinforcing the view held by natural burial supporters that it is a place and practice that firmly establishes life-death in a continuous cycle. For example, a widow whose husband is buried at Barton Glebe Woodland Burial Ground takes comfort from the growth of trees through the seasons, which she articulates as metaphors for death and life (author interview with the widow): "It's a comfort. The *continuity* of seeing things go on. You know, it makes *dying* just like leaves falling off a tree. It's all circular, isn't it?"

Natural burial is popularly understood as a mode of burial that is environmentally advantageous, and many natural burial supporters would agree with the funeral director who said in an interview with me that natural burial is "about trees and sustainability and putting something back and having the thought that your loved one is part of the continuance you know, the *land* and sustaining that." By choosing to have a natural burial, the dead will "return to nature" and, by doing so, "give something back" by "sustaining" the land through what is perceived as fecund decomposition (Davies and Rumble 2012; Rumble et al. 2014). Rather than eliciting a "yuck" factor, this notion of "putting something back" is celebrated and understood as bringing life and death conceptually closer together in a continuum in which they are not necessarily mutually exclusive. Often, those who favor natural burial perceive cemeteries and crematoria as the very opposite of what natural burial represents and affords them. So, for example, a woman who has pre-registered for a grave plot at Barton Glebe Woodland Burial Ground says the natural burial ground provides

> a very natural, very *positive* sort of atmosphere. Whereas graveyards, you know, people don't *go* there. It's a separation. It emphasizes the separation between life and death, and it emphasizes to me even more that we want to sanitize [death]. Whereas for me, death is part of life ... life comes out of something and goes back into it. It seems to me ... that although there is a separation in that it's a designated site, it's *not done* in the same way. I mean, me walking along the road there, I just think that there's a field with trees—you know, it's a *part* of nature. Unless you knew it's there, you wouldn't

think "oh, there's a graveyard," whereas you do with a cemetery. So that distinction isn't quite as strong with woodland burial. (Author interview with the woman)

It is precisely because the life-death "distinction isn't quite as strong with woodland burial" that these latest places of burial have utility beyond that of a singular mortuary purpose; they are equally places that are used for environmental and social sustainability enterprises in which the possibilities for recreation in these places of human bodily interment are not assumed to be awkward, tense, or troublesome.

Just as Britain was the first European country to popularize crematoria in the late nineteenth and early twentieth centuries (Davies and Mates 2005; Jupp 2006), it is also where natural burial emerged in the early 1990s. This latest deathscape marks the most significant development in the disposal of the dead in Britain since the first official cremation was conducted in 1885 at Woking Crematorium (Clayden et al. 2010; Grainger 2005; Green 2008; Joyce 2009). Natural burial—also known as woodland, green, or eco burial—was pioneered in Britain by Ken West in 1993. West, then the bereavement services manager of Carlisle Cemetery, instigated woodland burial in an unused part of Carlisle's municipal Victorian cemetery in response to his conversation with two women who, voicing their disapproval of cemeteries as ecologically barren, wanted to be buried in their back garden: "The scheme was originally intended for people who had expressed a need for an alternative to conventional cemeteries and cremation e.g. back garden burials. A secondary appeal was that native woodland would be created thereby providing wildlife habitats, especially for the diminishing red squirrel" (West 2008, 104). Since West's first woodland burial ground opened in 1993, over 200 natural burial grounds have been developed across the United Kingdom. This burial innovation has been subsequently adopted by and fostered in other countries worldwide.[1]

The guiding principles behind natural burial stipulate that corpses cannot be embalmed because embalming chemicals are regarded as environmentally hazardous. A corpse must be buried in a shroud or a biodegradable coffin or urn[2] in a grave not marked by a headstone. Some natural burial sites do allow the bereaved to plant a *native* tree on or close to the grave in place of a stone memorial, but a commonly held principle is that graveside memorialization and gardening should not be permitted. Nevertheless, because this is difficult to "police" and many mourners find it difficult to completely accept this principle, many natural burial sites allow some grave memorialization; in keeping with the concept and landscape, however, memorials should be biodegradable: wood plaques, wildflower bouquets without cellophane wrapping, grave decorations made from biodegradable found objects (figure 12.1). Often, natural burial sites are managed to encourage native flora and fauna, though what is regarded as "native" is often open to heated, public

FIGURE 12.1. Bouquet made of naturally occurring materials laid on a grave in a woodland burial ground. Author photo.

contestation (see Davies and Rumble 2012; Rumble 2010). Yet while natural burial sites cohere around sharing a broad concept in burial provision, the management, landscape, and ownership of these sites vary enormously (see Clayden et al. 2010, 2015; Davies and Rumble 2012; Harris 2007; Rumble 2010).

While the first natural burial grounds that opened were intended for whole body burial only—therefore offered as an alternative to cremation—over the years natural burial grounds have increasingly accommodated the interment or scattering of cremated remains because of customer demand. Subsequently, natural burial and cremation are no longer necessarily mutually exclusive, though some natural burial ground operators do maintain an anti-cremation stance because they are guided by strong ecological principles in which they understand that cremation is a major

FIGURE 12.2. A farmer's "green burial ground" in northeast England located on his pastureland. The graves are identifiable by those areas in the foreground where the meadow grasses have not yet been reestablished on disturbed soil. Author photo.

source of airborne pollutants and involves a process that requires great amounts of nonrenewable energy resources (Cowling 2010; Speyer 2006). Research has shown, nevertheless, that there is "an inconsistency in the extent to which below-ground environmental aspirations have been either promoted or subsequently enforced" (Clayden et al. 2010, 119; see also Rumble 2010) at natural burial grounds.

While many speak conceptually of natural burial in terms of what happens belowground, it is also what happens above-ground that frequently sets the image and popular perception of natural burial. What is absent above-ground (i.e., markers to the dead) facilitates natural burial grounds as serving more than a singular mortuary purpose by offering recreational opportunities as well. While a few natural burial grounds are consecrated,[3] with graves randomly placed in woodland glades with minimal memorialization, the majority of sites are not consecrated and may occupy a small area within an existing cemetery or crematorium's grounds, with graves in rows, and some memorialization may be permitted. Yet others may look to the casual observer like an overgrown meadow or field with little else to distract the eye or draw attention to the fact that people are buried there (figure 12.2).

The woodland burial ground that forms the basis for this chapter's discussion is Barton Glebe Woodland Burial Ground, inaugurated in 2000 by the Arbory Trust (a Christian charity that provides natural burial in affiliation with the Diocese of Ely under the auspices of the Church of England). The Arbory Trust (the Trust) calls its burial ground a woodland rather than a natural burial ground because one of the Trust's original aims was to establish "indigenous" woodland on the burial ground's site by planting thousands of young tree saplings. While the Trust wanted to provide a Church of England–endorsed woodland burial ground, it also aimed to provide a wooded area that attracted local flora and fauna, therefore allowing the woodland burial ground to be available to anyone to enjoy as a recreational space 365 days of the year. A few British natural burial grounds use a similar strategy of preserving or establishing local green spaces by creating a wildflower meadow or native woodland as a natural burial ground to subsequently be able to protect land from development and provide recreational places for the local community, in addition to serving a mortuary purpose.

RECREATIONAL USE OF CEMETERIES: HISTORICAL CONTINUITY AND CHANGE

Natural burial sites are qualitatively distinct from other burial places in contemporary Britain in two significant ways (Rumble 2010). First, they have an explicit dual purpose, both as a place to inter ashes or a corpse and as a place deemed to contribute to ecological preservation or improvement, which is subsequently to be enjoyed by the living. This makes a natural burial site "unlike a cemetery with its singular mortuary purpose" (Clayden et al. 2010, 135), and in Britain this is encapsulated in some providers' ambitions for making natural burial sites protected ecological places to be managed by environmental or wildlife trusts once burial sites become full and are no longer able to generate revenue through the sale of reservations for grave plots.

Second, beyond a place of interment and ecological conservation, natural burial sites may be identified as providing a contemporary therapeutic landscape for mourners. Contributing to this quality of place is the fact that there is often minimal visible presence of the dead when compared with a "traditional" cemetery. This fact provokes some criticism that natural burial is a recent cultural development indicative of death denial. For example, Fernwood's green cemetery in Mill Valley, California (USA), has been described as only a park. Such criticisms demonstrate that what is at stake is the perceived socio-cultural function and appearance of places of burial. Yet as Rugg (2000) and other historians of cemeteries have clearly demonstrated, the meanings and purposes of burial places are highly mutable because they are always subject to the sensibilities and tastes of the living.

The mutability of places for the dead has meant that over time some churchyards, once full or abandoned, are now retrospectively cultivated as public gardens and wildlife habitats for rare species. In spite of the enduring "landscape aesthetic of the churchyard" (Worpole 2003, 77), which is deeply embedded in British cultural landscapes for the dead, even churchyards are appropriated for other uses. Disused British cemeteries have also been shown to attract nature lovers, walkers, those with an interest in history, and educational visitors (Deering 2010; Dunk and Rugg 1994). Those interviewed in Deering's qualitative study identified engaging in these recreational activities in cemeteries: reading, picnicking, jogging, sunbathing, conducting historical/genealogy studies, nature watching, dog walking, taking photographs, drinking, and taking drugs (Deering 2010, 80). These are all recreational activities that indicate how disused cemeteries among other traditionally sequestered places for the dead have been appropriated for recreational uses, in addition to their original mortuary purpose. Nevertheless, there is an enduring association of cemeteries with death, as a man who pre-registered for a grave plot at Barton Glebe Woodland Burial Ground indicated in an interview when articulating what natural burial means to him:

> There's a sense of walking in a meadow among the trees and the sun's shining—a pleasantness of a place rather than lines of hard rock and stone with different names etched in them. It's just a softer picture to me than a cemetery... If you go to a graveyard there is only one purpose for you going to a graveyard, but if you go to a woodland burial site you can walk 'round and enjoy the flowers, the trees, and the birds, and you can go for a walk and you can remember and mull over without necessarily thinking: I'm going to visit the grave of so and so... The focus is very much different... just going to a place and walking around it, which you do when you go on country walks and enjoy the surroundings.

While some disused cemeteries have acquired the characteristics of local parks over time (Rugg 2000), this man aligns visiting a natural burial ground with recreational country walks. This is in part because of the lack of visible markers associated with death in a natural burial ground but also because a number of natural burial providers—whether individuals, trusts, charities, or private companies—simultaneously use their natural burial provision to facilitate habitat preservation or reinstatement (e.g., establishment of woodland or wildflower meadows).

CREATING THE NATURAL AND CONSERVATION BURIAL GROUNDS

The Arbory Trust, like a number of other natural burial providers, quickly recognized and harnessed the potential of achieving "wider environmental and community

FIGURE 12.3. The Lodge at Barton Glebe Woodland Burial Ground. Author photo.

goals" (Clayden et al. 2015, 62) beyond simply providing a place to inter human remains. The Trust consciously created Barton Glebe Woodland Burial Ground to look like a nature reserve (Rumble 2010), with aesthetic integrity enshrined in the Trust's decision to create deciduous woodland using trees native to Cambridgeshire, thus gaining significant financial support and professional expertise provided by the Forestry Commission.[4] The Lodge, which is used as a covered space for funerals and memorial services, as well as housing catering and toilet facilities and a small office for site staff, was deliberately chosen by the Trust because of its natural materials and rustic look—which were felt to be in keeping with the woodland burial concept the Trust was consciously creating (see figure 12.3). The use of wood is deliberate in the Lodge's design and that of the chosen signage about the woodland burial ground. Meanwhile, a large window in the Lodge provides a panorama of the woodland burial ground that draws mourners' gaze beyond the funeral gathering to what is present outside the building. Connections between buildings and the landscape they inhabit are often consciously created at natural burial grounds that have buildings, signage, or boundary markers (see Clayden et al. 2015), although farmers' meadow burial grounds typically have no signage or structures of any kind.

Rather than providing a shelter and ritual space deemed to be aesthetically more modern, utilitarian, or urban, the rustic Lodge was understood by the Arbory Trust to be more in keeping with the cultivated but naturalized landscape it was creating at Barton Glebe Woodland Burial Ground. This focus on aesthetic integrity in designing Barton Glebe mimics British "national park regulations... [that] confine the use of building materials to those available, and long used, locally" (Porteous 1996, 102). Furthermore, like National Park Rangers, Arbory Trust ground staff wear a uniform that identifies them as custodians of the designated area of land visited; in this case green jumpers that display the Trust's logo of a tree. Again, this uniform that distinguishes ground staff from visitors at the woodland burial ground mimics the type of practical outdoor uniforms British people have come to expect from National Park Rangers and employees of the National Trust and other conservation organizations. Furthermore, visitors are kept informed of the wildflower and bird species found within the woodland burial ground by leaflets distributed in the Lodge and available to download from the Trust's website. Dog walkers and bird watchers in particular are encouraged to utilize the woodland burial ground, and wooden stakes bearing the logo of the Forestry Commission help identify paths through the establishing woodland and burial glades for visitors. It is through the mimicry of practices more often associated with national parks and nature trails—such as the wooden path markers and Lodge, staff in green-colored outdoor clothing, free leaflets on the wildflowers and native plant and animal species found in the natural burial ground—that first-time visitors can be forgiven for not immediately associating Barton Glebe Woodland Burial Ground with precisely that: a burial ground.

Nevertheless, a paradox remains that neither Barton Glebe's landscape nor the rustic wooden lodge is naturally occurring; both have been created to form something that is of utility to the living. Thus, natural burial grounds inherently epitomize a natural-but-not-quite landscape. To a certain extent, the illusion of the natural is an integral part of creating a natural burial ground. Those natural burial grounds that secure regular media coverage are often those that have been most successful at illusion making and "theme parking" (Davies and Rumble 2012; Slater 2007) in fulfilling people's culturally informed expectations of woodland or nature. By commodifying woodland, these companies can charge high fees for their natural burial provision.[5]

In addition, some natural burial providers go so far as to grade the quality of their theme-park experience by charging different fees for burial plot reservations depending on where the plot is located in the forest or woodland and the views one is privy to from the chosen grave location in the woodland. Location and nature are very much a commodity in natural burial, so much so that the extent and success of commodifying woodland or a woodland experience by "judicious landscape planning" (Worpole 2003, 191) is evident in the fact that a number of natural burial

FIGURE 12.4. Signage at Barton Glebe Woodland Burial Ground attached to the boundary fence. Author photo.

grounds host events to attract visitors, in addition to mourners and the bereaved: "You know, I went to [named natural burial ground] and I thought, this is perfect: bluebell woods, the RSPB[6] are there, and there were kids racing about looking for Easter eggs. You know, it's a place you want to go" (founder of an eco-coffin company, interview with the author).

As this comment indicates, some natural burial grounds are hosting seasonal events (in this case, Easter egg hunts for children) to utilize the woodland setting and generate alternative sources of income. A number of natural burial grounds have also teamed up with conservation or ecological charities to enhance their appeal to potential customers who could be motivated to invest in natural burial because of its association with what is perceived as representing good ecological practice and sustainability.[7] However, natural burial grounds owned by charities or private commercial enterprises tend to be more commercially successful here because they have the resources to systematically target visitors other than the bereaved to classes and events in conjunction with hosting funerals and providing burial space, unlike natural burial grounds owned by a local government authority.

Resonating with Iitaka's contribution to this volume, encounters between visitors' leisure and relaxation and death/memorializing need not be separated and kept as discreet activities. Moreover, as Iitaka found with Japanese commemorative tours, nature often becomes the focus in these encounters and entanglements, more highly regarded and keenly observed. For example, in conjunction with natural burial provision, some of the activities advertised by providers include guided walks that focus on specific local flora and fauna—such as fungi or particular species of birds—and events for children, such as the "Animal Man—Live Animal Display and Lecture" aimed at educating children about natural history. One natural burial ground hosts a children's safari where "mini zoologists" can explore bugs and reptiles found in the burial grounds for the day. According to the websites for these natural burial grounds, these events aimed at children sell out.[8]

At specific times of year, natural burial grounds have sought extra income from visitors who attend an Easter egg hunt or a Christmas carol service, alongside annual open days and children's memorial or baby-loss services hosted by the owners or management at the natural burial ground. This effectively creates a community of bereaved linked to a particular natural burial ground. As with some cemeteries, certain natural burial ground providers have sought to diversify their sources of income by using the indoor facilities available at the natural burial ground, such as offering yoga and art classes. Similarly, a very successful company that has several woodland burial grounds in Britain recently ran a coloring competition for one- to eleven-year-olds using the company's endorsed book about bereavement aimed at children called *The Lonely Tree*. What these staged events, classes, and competitions at natural burial grounds highlight is that natural burial grounds are not necessarily just for funerals and are not just places of death and mourning. Indeed, a few natural burial grounds with ecologically designed or historical listed buildings on their premises, which are used for hosting funerals, have extended their repertoire by offering these facilities for weddings and other celebrations in addition to funerals; for example, Memorial Woodlands near Bristol offers its Georgian buildings and chapel for hire as a wedding venue. Thus, natural burial appears to be facilitating a "return to a time when the burial ground was a familiar landscape in which other significant celebrations, including weddings, took place" (Clayden et al. 2015, 93). The main reason this has become possible is because the "eco" buildings and landscape often found at natural burial grounds are not customarily associated with British burial grounds, and there are fewer visible reminders of the dead buried beneath one's feet because of the absence of headstones and grave markers. Perhaps unsurprisingly, then, natural burial grounds are having an impact on the rites and attitudes associated with funerals and grave visiting. As one administrator of a natural burial ground explained in an interview:

I have had people come to me and say: "Well, they won't let us do that, or we can't do that somewhere. We wanted to go into our local church, but there's not room for me or my husband." That's very often one of the things. "They won't let us have music by the grave. They won't let us do this. We can't reserve next to each other" . . . I've been to friends' funerals and they're just so soulless and morose and awful, and I'm not exaggerating this, but a burial up there [in the woodland burial ground] isn't. It isn't, and I can't put my finger on why it isn't. I think it's because people are having what they want. I think that's what it is. People are able to do what they want to do. And they don't feel inhibited there, whereas in a graveyard they can. Certainly, "Oh, I can't walk on that grave there." Those taboos, whereas walking through there [the natural burial ground] you don't actually feel like you're walking through a graveyard, you're walking through a forest or a wood. A wood. And I think it's all those little things that put people more at ease . . . they go back and have picnics up there. On people's birthdays families have gone up there and had a picnic with the children in the summer, and [slight pause] would you do that in a graveyard or in a cemetery? Probably not, but you can up there.

INFORMALITY AND LEISURE

The administrator quoted above mentions "those taboos" and people feeling "inhibited" in relation to graveyards; both comments are indicative of culturally received ideas and socially sanctioned behaviors regarding death and mourning and, to a certain extent, are implicitly expressed in the assumption that the relationship between leisure and death is tense. But for those who support natural burial, it is a burial innovation that encapsulates the opposite of taboo and inhibition; rather, for them, natural burial facilitates bringing the recreational activities of the living closer to places occupied by the dead in an informal manner free of "those taboos," as this civil celebrant attested in an interview: "I've also been up to [named natural burial ground] with my husband on a day I wasn't working and just walked around the grounds because they're so beautiful, and I've seen families sitting at graves having a picnic. And I think there's something very special about that. You know, that continuity of life and that people can feel comfortable to go into a cemetery and have a picnic with their relatives; how beautiful, and you never see that at municipal cemeteries." Bereaved visitors to Barton Glebe make similar comments, suggesting that there is less inhibition and greater latitude for individual expressions of grief, as the widow quoted at the beginning of this chapter illustrated when she said "I'd just go and sit and have my coffee and croissant next to [my husband's] grave. Or I'd take a sandwich out and just go and lie there and read."

Also, as another widow illustrates, children are not excluded from Barton Glebe Woodland Burial Ground: "I've taken my grandchildren over there and they just run around and create mayhem, and they don't know what it means but they talk about it and say 'this is Granddad's place,' and I think that's great. I mean, that was the whole idea of what it's all about" (author interview with the widow).

These comments emphasize that Barton Glebe Woodland Burial Ground is as much about informality as it is about environmentally sensitive practices and that people associate feeling less constrained by socially sanctioned behavior when visiting graves in a natural burial ground. With the absence of architectural and traditional constraints such as headstones and associated cultural ideas about decorum around the dead and solemnity, visitors to a natural burial ground perceive a less controlled environment that fosters informal, more leisurely behavior; a widow can take a sandwich and read or lie beside her husband's grave, and children can run around and "create mayhem." Natural burial grounds offer individuals in Britain "far greater choice, firstly about how they might deal with the deceased and secondly, about the style of burial landscape within which they and the deceased can be accommodated" (Powell et al. 2011, 2). Natural burial grounds allow for—indeed, facilitate—celebrations rather than restraint and somber funerals. Visitors to Barton Glebe Woodland Burial Ground perceive and experience greater freedom of expression in their behavior with the diminished visibility of graves, especially compared with the cultural image of municipal cemeteries: "In a cemetery you're invariably being buried so close to the next person that we're all standing on someone else's grave, and people find that quite difficult sometimes... I always think that cemeteries are made up of individual little beds, whereas in a green burial site there's so much room between them [the graves] and one could just go and sit on the grass next to Mum there and be able to feel close. And I actually think people go more to visit at a green burial site than they would do in a churchyard" (author interview with a funeral director).

So, here is an experienced funeral director stating anecdotally that the bereaved are more likely to visit a natural burial site than a cemetery because the diminished restrictions of the landscape and layout facilitate greater emotional and behavioral latitude. In other words, bereaved visitors and mourners have reported that they feel less obliged to conform to social norms and expectations; rather, they can simply "be" themselves. This is often commented upon in relation to the funeral ceremony because for those who have attended a funeral at a natural burial ground, one commonly voiced opinion is that the funeral is more relaxed for mourners:

> I think it [a woodland burial site] allows your emotions to be played out much more naturally than in a crematorium or in a church. [slight pause] I think there would

be less freedom for you to think and reflect at a crematorium and churchyard—it's a more controlling environment than I would imagine at a woodland burial site. I mean, some people like the control, as it helps them cope and get through it—from the moment they get there to the moment it's finished, everything is organized, and they have to do very little. And others might find the woodland burial approach—which I think does give you more freedom and flexibility and creativity—harder for some people. (Author interview with a local resident who attended a funeral at Barton Glebe Woodland Burial Ground)

In interviews, the bereaved and funeral professionals commonly spoke of crematoria and municipal cemeteries being "more controlling" than natural burial grounds. This perceived control is felt spatially, emotionally, and temporally. Spatially, in cemeteries and Gardens of Remembrance at crematoria, graves are laid out in designated rows and serried ranks, but in natural burial grounds such as Barton Glebe, the bereaved get to choose where the deceased is interred and dictate the orientation of the grave. Emotionally, funeral professionals manage transition rituals to help us "cope," and yet many natural burial grounds allow mourners to undertake a graveside funeral or memorial without a professional; this is commonly referred to as "DIY" or "home" funerals. The *Good Funeral Guide* (2015) is a book and online reference for those who want to organize and preside over a funeral with as little reliance on professionals as possible, and it states that a natural burial "rejects the so-called traditional funeral with its stuffy, Victorian, urban look, in favour of an outdoorsy, homespun, back-to-nature look. It prefers an unspoilt landscape to that of a regimented conventional cemetery."[9] This sentiment resonates with the current British appeal of "glamping" and the boom in organic products and green services, which is worthy of comment but beyond the remit here. Finally, there is a rejection not only of the spatial control encapsulated by the regimented conventional cemetery, but also of the temporal control of funerals, especially those held at crematoria. Crematoria have short allocated time slots for a funeral or memorial service, but this is not the case at a natural burial ground, where gatherings at the graveside can take all day. For those who preside over funerals at natural burial grounds, such as the independent funeral director and civil celebrant quoted below, it is commonly noted that the time keeping is more relaxed and that this temporal quality fosters a sense of leisure, celebration, and relaxation not commonly associated with Christian funerals and places inhabited by the dead:

> There was no hurry. 'Cause normally when you go to a crematorium you've only got half an hour ... but at [a natural burial site] nothing was hurried ... There was no hurry. We weren't timed or anything like that ... everyone just lingered on, you know. In fact, it took us a whole day and it was really, really lovely ... There wasn't any

hurry—there was no time factor coming into it, which was good . . . 'Cause as I say, if you go to the crematorium you can't always do what you want to do in half an hour. (Author interview with the funeral director)

While this independent funeral director reports that there "wasn't any hurry" at the natural burial ground, in an interview a civil funeral celebrant who regularly conducts funerals at natural burial grounds referred to the popular industrial, capitalist image of a crematorium: "People stay longer there than they do at a normal cemetery—well, obviously, at the crematorium you've got to get out because you're on a time limit; it's a sausage-making mentality. [giggles] You know, you're always watching the clock when you're in a crematorium, but I was amazed (it wasn't a particularly sunny day or hot, but it wasn't wet), we stood there absolutely for ages afterward. We stood there probably for half an hour talking and chatting." Similarly, in an interview an Anglican curate who conducts funerals at Barton Glebe Woodland Burial Ground commented on how mourners linger in a way they never could at a funeral held at a crematorium's chapel: "I think people felt a little more comfortable lingering afterward after I'd pronounced the blessings and the final words. Maybe because it's an open space; there's more of a chance to just pause and take [a] breath after the funeral has finished, but a churchyard is a bit crowded and [you're always] stepping on other people's graves. I mean, I think there was a slightly more relaxed atmosphere afterward at Barton."

TOWARD A LEISURELY FUNERAL AND RECREATIONAL BURIAL GROUND

Time is a crucial factor in enhancing support for natural burial precisely because a funeral held at a natural burial ground is deemed to be more relaxed in the absence of definitive time restraints for the mourners and professionals involved; consequently, funerals can take an entire day rather than the allocated time slot at a crematorium or church. Moreover, repeated observations that people "stay longer" or "linger" at the graveside in a natural burial ground suggest a relaxed atmosphere and a more positive mood than is customary at a funeral. This leisurely quality of funerals and grave visiting at natural burial grounds (i.e., no sense of time keeping and formality) is valued by those who support natural burial, as a woman who has preregistered for a grave space at Barton Glebe Woodland Burial Ground emphasizes by comparing crematoria and woodland burial sites: "I mean, it's a soulless place [a crematorium]. It's the sort of place where you feel you can't chat, you can't relax. Again, this difference: you know people are quiet, in the wrong sense of being quiet. Whereas I hope it would be very natural just to be yourself when you're going to a woodland burial and the funeral" (author interview with the woman).

For those who feel too constrained by what are perceived as "traditional" funerals, where one "can't chat" and "can't relax," funerals at natural burial grounds provide a welcome alternative. By creating a place for behavior that is sometimes far from somber, in which the geographical proximity of the dead is not discouraged by the living who often undertake activities such as dog walking, reading, picnics, and child's play in a landscape and soundscape that accentuate the natural world, the conceptual categories of life and death are brought closer together,[10] and in so doing, the distinction between them becomes more ambiguous. Subsequently, the designation and function of burial places are being gradually contested and redefined. For example, the Forestry Commission adviser to the Arbory Trust walked with me around the grounds of Barton Glebe Woodland Burial Ground one day. Stopping in his stride, he turned to me and said "you know, I like to think that my wife would come and walk the dog in here."

As this chapter has discussed, natural burial grounds often have a utility beyond that of burial and sequestering the dead from the living. For farmers who have set up a natural burial ground on their land to diversify income from their farm, it is not unusual to see grazing livestock in the natural burial ground in addition to bereaved visitors or mourners (with or without their dogs). Other natural burial grounds, like the one discussed in this chapter owned by the Arbory Trust, seek to generate future revenue from coppicing[11] trees growing in the burial ground. Moreover, the options for what can be done, said, and felt in natural burial grounds increase as the architectural constraints decrease, so that funerals and grave visiting become more aligned with celebrating a life and are therefore less restricted by or bounded to "duty" or formality. Rather, by aligning natural burial grounds with parks, nature reserves, and places of conservation or preservation, people perceive life affirmations arising from death and loss, as a woman who has pre-registered for a grave plot at Barton Glebe Woodland Burial Ground illustrated when she told me that a natural burial ground is "very much like any other quiet place where people can just sit, relax, and just be . . . the sort of place where somebody could take a book or their sandwiches and just sit down. Not radically different from another part of nature that you were comfortable to just sit and be in."

The temporal and spatial flexibility afforded to natural burial grounds has allowed them to become dynamic life-death environments, providing an alternative to sequestering the dead in a cemetery. Instead, the dead and death itself can become "a more overt dimension of everyday life" (Clayden et al. 2015, 200). Consequently, recreation, leisure, death, and mourning are no longer oddly aligned but rather inevitably so in this latest British deathscape.

NOTES

1. Japan, Taiwan, New Zealand, Australia, Canada, the United States, the Netherlands, Germany, Ireland, South Africa, and the Czech Republic.

2. These come in a variety of materials: cardboard, bamboo, seagrass, willow, wool, jute, or sustainably sourced pine, for example. See an extensive list of current coffin and shroud options in Britain in Cowling (2010, 164–69).

3. Consecration involves a legal change of status of land through a formal act by a legitimate ecclesiastical authority, in this case, the Church of England.

4. The Forestry Commission is the government department responsible for the protection and expansion of the woods and forests of England and Scotland.

5. See also Sanders (2009) for a discussion of commodifying funerals as "events" and "amusement."

6. The British-based charity, the Royal Society for the Protection of Birds.

7. In the quote above, it is the RSPB—a British bird protection charity—that is aligned with a natural burial ground.

8. It is worthy of future ethnographic research to find out why these children's events are so popular with both parents and children.

9. www.goodfuneralguide.co.uk/What-is-a-green-funeral/. Accessed January 22, 2017.

10. This stands in marked contrast to the popular and often-heard sociological narrative that in the West we have sequestered death from the rest of life by medicalizing it and relinquishing our contact with the dead to "experts" to foster a kind of "death denial" (Ariès 1981; Becker 1973; Gorer 1965; Kearl 1989; Mitford 1963; Walter 1994).

11. Derived from the French "couper," which means "to cut." Coppicing is the process of cutting trees down, allowing the stumps to regenerate for a number of years (usually 7–25), and then harvesting the resulting stems.

REFERENCES

Ariès, Philippe. 1981. *The Hour of Our Death*. Oxford: Oxford University Press.

Ariès, Philippe. 1994. *Western Attitudes toward Death from the Middle Ages to the Present*. London: Marion Boyars.

Becker, Ernest. 1973. *The Denial of Death*. New York: Free Press.

Clayden, Andy, Trish Green, Jenny Hockey, and Mark Powell. 2010. "From Cabbages to Cadavers: Natural Burial Down on the Farm." In *Deathscapes: Spaces for Death, Dying, Mourning, and Remembrance*, ed. Avril Maddrell and James Sidaway, 119–38. Farnham, Surrey: Ashgate.

Clayden, Andy, Trish Green, Jenny Hockey, and Mark Powell. 2015. *Natural Burial: Landscape, Practice, and Experience*. Abingdon, Oxon: Routledge.

Cowling, Charles. 2010. *The Good Funeral Guide*. London: Continuum.
Davies, Douglas J., and Lewis H. Mates, eds. 2005. *Encyclopedia of Cremation*. Aldershot: Ashgate.
Davies, Douglas J., and Hannah Rumble. 2012. *Natural Burial: Traditional-Secular Spiritualties and Funeral Innovation*. London: Continuum.
Deering, Bel. 2010. "From Anti-Social Behaviour to X-Rated: Exploring Social Diversity and Conflict in the Cemetery." In *Deathscapes: Spaces for Death, Dying, Mourning, and Remembrance*, ed. Avril Maddrell and James Sidaway, 75–93. Farnham, Surrey: Ashgate.
Dunk, Julie, and Julie Rugg. 1994. *The Management of Old Cemetery Land*. Crayford, Kent: Shaw and Sons.
Good Funeral Guide. 2015. "What Is a Green Funeral?" Accessed March 31, 2015. http://www.goodfuneralguide.co.uk/find-a-funeral-director/what-is-a-green-funeral.
Gorer, Geoffrey. 1965. *Death, Grief, and Mourning in Contemporary Britain*. London: Cresset.
Grainger, Hilary. 2005. "Architecture: Britain." In *Encyclopedia of Cremation*, ed. Douglas J. Davies and Lewis H. Mates, 19–21. Aldershot: Ashgate.
Green, James W. 2008. *Beyond the Good Death: The Anthropology of Modern Dying*. Philadelphia: University of Pennsylvania Press. https://doi.org/10.9783/9780812202076.
Harris, Marvin. 2007. *Grave Matters: A Journey through the Modern Funeral Industry to a Natural Way of Burial*. New York: Scribner.
Joyce, Kelly. 2009. "Green Burials." In *The Encyclopedia of Death and the Human Experience*, ed. Clifton Bryant and Dennis Peck, 527–29. Thousand Oaks, CA: Sage.
Jupp, Peter C. 2006. *From Dust to Ashes: Cremation and the British Way of Death*. New York: Palgrave Macmillan. https://doi.org/10.1057/9780230511088.
Kearl, Michael. 1989. *Endings: A Sociology of Death and Dying*. Oxford: Oxford University Press.
Lennon, John, and Malcolm Foley. 2000. *Dark Tourism: The Attraction of Death and Disaster*. London: Continuum.
Maddrell, Avril, and James D. Sidaway. 2010. *Deathscapes: Spaces for Death, Dying, Mourning, and Remembrance*. Farnham, Surrey: Ashgate.
Mitford, Jessica. 1963. *The American Way of Death*. New York: Simon and Schuster.
Porteous, J. Douglas. 1996. *Environmental Aesthetics: Ideas, Politics, and Planning*. London: Routledge.
Powell, Mark, Jenny Hockey, Trish Green, and Andy Clayden. 2011. "'I Bury Boxes, Not Bodies': Identity, Emotionality, and Natural Burial." *ASA Online*. Accessed March 5, 2011. http://www.theasa.org/publications/asaonline/articles/asaonline_0103.shtml.
Rugg, Julie. 2000. "Defining the Place of Burial: What Makes a Cemetery a Cemetery?" *Mortality* 5 (3): 259–75. https://doi.org/10.1080/713686011.

Rumble, Hannah. 2010. "Giving Something Back: A Case Study of Woodland Burial and Human Experience at Barton Glebe." PhD dissertation, Durham University, Durham, NC.

Rumble, Hannah, John Troyer, Tony Walter, and Kate Woodthorpe. 2014. "Disposal or Dispersal? Environmentalism and Final Treatment of the British Dead." *Mortality* 19 (3): 243–60. https://doi.org/10.1080/13576275.2014.920315.

Sanders, George. 2009. "Late Capital: Amusement and Contradiction in the Contemporary Funeral Industry." *Critical Sociology* 35 (4): 447–70. https://doi.org/10.1177/0896920509103978.

Slater, Eamonn. 2007. "Reconstructing 'Nature' as a Picturesque Theme Park: The Colonial Case of Ireland." *Early Popular Visual Culture* 5 (3): 231–45. https://doi.org/10.1080/17460650701633587.

Speyer, Josefine. 2006. "An Argument for Environmentally Friendly, Natural Burial." *Pharos International* 72 (2): 6–8.

Stone, Philip. 2011. "Dark Tourism Experiences: Mediating between Life and Death." In *Tourist Experience: Contemporary Perspectives*, ed. Richard Sharpley and Philip Stone, 21–27. Abington: Routledge.

Stone, Philip. 2012. "Dark Tourism and Significant Other Death: Towards a Model of Mortality Mediation." *Annals of Tourism Research* 39 (3): 1565–87. https://doi.org/10.1016/j.annals.2012.04.007.

Walter, Tony. 1994. *The Revival of Death*. London: Routledge. https://doi.org/10.4324/9780203220306.

West, Ken. 2008. "How Green Is My Funeral?" *Funeral Service Journal* 123 (1): 104–8.

Worpole, Ken. 2003. *Last Landscapes: The Architecture of the Cemetery in the West*. London: Reaktion.

Epilogue

Obituary Preparing Activity

JAMES FERNANDEZ

SOME GENERALITIES

Let us remind ourselves of several generalities. Mortality is without doubt, especially in a self-aware and complexly self-reflective and ultimately socially dependent animal like the human one, the great "inchoate" of our fleeting existence.[1] It carries with it suggestions not only of the ultimate dissolution of the self itself but the rending of the social fabric on which the self has been dependent and in which it has figured. Death is an inchoate upon which and into which we ceaselessly seek to predicate meaning. If nature, as it is said, abhors a vacuum, human nature, we might say, abhors the inchoate and seeks to give it cultural shape and enduring substance. The abhorrence of the inchoate is as much as anything perhaps the reason humans have cultures (Carrithers 1992).

These culture-creating predications are various in their configurations. The abhorrence of the "inchoate" of death has produced mighty works of the religious imagination in many cultures, none mightier, perhaps, than Dante's *Divine Comedy*. In that great work, it is interesting to remark, given the title of our collection, that while in the higher spheres of Paradise and particularly in the Seventh Heaven the blessed souls are engaged in leisurely contemplations and conversation, in the nine circles of the Inferno those guilty of the nine deadly sins have no leisure whatsoever but are endlessly tasked and tortured—condemned to an eternity of arduous, even devastatingly agonizing labor and suffering, totally unredeemed by the prospect, much less the presence, of leisure. The lower regions of Hell are a panorama of a variety of eternities of endless labor of which Sisyphus is the prototype. Other religions, less oppressed by the innate sinfulness of humankind, find it meaningful to predicate an eternity of dalliance for the faithful with undamaged damsels at one's beck and call, the ultimate leisure perhaps.

If we think of the philosophic rather than the religious imagination, in some modern philosophies of existence, particularly those that are phenomenological in nature, there can be no meaningful existence, no leisurely being or self-actualization that is free of the ever-presence and awareness of death, which is to say the ever-presence of being fated to finitude, ceaselessly facing the unconquerable fact of heedless and echoless infinitude. In such "existential" philosophies—philosophies in search of the *dassein* of "*existenz*"—no life, however leisurely, can escape the ever-presence of death and prevent life itself from being an "obituary preparing activity."[2] Leisure and death are co-occurrent and interactively co-informing. It is only through this constant apprehension of our mortality, this apprehension of the inevitable nonexistence of our existence bound up in the never-ending interweaving of leisure and death, that we can authentically be and become. Death here is the necessary accompaniment of the leisure that permits speculative, transcendent, intellectual activity. Though the title of our collection will suggest to many a quite unusual and stimulating conjunction of domains of experience, philosophically their conjunction has long been apprehended as the ultimate challenge to our understanding of our being and becoming.

It is also generally understood that the very rubric that has overseen these essays, the binary title *Leisure and Death,* has been in and of itself a signal stimulus to creative rethinking and re-figuration of our understanding of the meaning of leisure with death in mind. The various authors in their various chapters, as we see, have each taken fruitful but quite different advantage of a fundamental characteristic of human understanding. It is inevitably interstitial, inter-domainal in nature; and we have to, along with Polonius, not only by indirections but by conjunctions find directions or re-figurations out. By putting the endlessly open and unsettled domain of leisure, with its manifold iterations, into interactive relation with the most pronouncedly closed and settled of human experiences—death—we, that is to say our various chapter authors, are forced to figure things out. By exploiting the differential charges between the widespread popularity and pursuit in most modern societies of leisure activities, particularly tourism, on the one hand, and, to say the least, the unpopularity and aversion and revulsion of death, we get a sparking in our understanding that we might not otherwise achieve. This collection is impressively fertile in that regard.

Take, for example, the way Rachel Horner Brackett's chapter, on heritage hogs and agritourism in Tuscany, brings us to an understanding of how eating is, in civilized circumstances at least, a leisurely activity that is ultimately inseparable from the vegetarian or vegan realization of the deathly part of the meat eaters' nurturance—the slaughter of living beings. Or how, when reading Ray Casserly on Northern Ireland parades, we come to see that there are circumstances in a holiday activity such as parading that can, of a moment, suddenly evoke a long-existing, intractable, and murderous relationship between actors and onlookers, Protestants and Catholics, loyalists and republicans. Death and its minions of revengefulness take over the musical moment, and the happy high-flying flags are brought low.

Under the pressure of, or by the possibilities provoked in, this unusual rubric, leisure and death, understandings emerge that we might not otherwise obtain. There are many of these emergent moments of understanding in this volume. Many configurations of the inchoate emerge. As different domains of experience have different charges and produce different sparks of understanding, so every reader is differentially charged and subject to his or her particular readings, which is to say, sparkings of the imagination. What follows, therefore, is my particular fireworks. I could not, alas, in this final place, treat all the sparkings I have experienced in reading and rereading this work, by any means. Nor could I present the total experience in any reasonable compass. Onward, then, to only a few particularities of the many conjunctions and configurations that have been available here to a particular reader's reading. Onward, then, to some particular enrichments he has found in the collection at hand. An epilogue cannot be a plenitude but rather a brief account of how an attitude of appreciative apprehension has been formed of what has gone before.

SOME PARTICULARITIES

To be sure, we need not apologize for concluding with particularities in and of themselves. Certainly for ethnographers, particulars are famous for casting more light on generalities than vice versa. Since anthropology and ethnography and ethnographers are such a presence in this collection, it is hardly surprising that it is a collection especially charged for those of us with ethnographic experience and commitment. Let me begin with some evocations in my reading associated with or sparking out of my own ethnographic experiences.

ETHNOGRAPHIC EVOCATIONS

In Cyril Schäfer and Ruth McManus's discussion of tourist encounters with European ossuaries, for example, I could not help recalling ethnographic work conducted by my wife and myself on that end-of-October day Todos los Santos or El Día de los Muertos in the country villages of northern Spain. This holiday or fiesta day occurs in practically every Spanish-speaking country, where families make an almost obligatorily visit to the Campo Santo bringing flowers and other *obsequios* to their dead. It is the recent dead that are mainly attended and recollected, many in egalitarian deposits in *"los nichos"* but some in more elaborate and pretentious tombs that in the Campo Santo reflect an attempt by the *pudientes* of the village or town to perpetuate the social-economic hierarchy of which they were the exemplars and beneficiaries.

But one also notes that the presence of the dead is not permanent and that sooner or later even the *pudientes* will "die" a second time. Indeed, the chapter of our Asturian ethnography (in preparation) in which we discuss this phenomenon is tentatively titled "The Dead Die, Too." This occurs when they are no longer within the power of recollection of any living villager. At that judgment time they are at risk of being, or will be—to make room—carried away to be re-deposited in the ossuary in a second, usually offhanded interment. Only a few family *santos* will have any truly enduring presence in the sainted confines of the Campo Santo. Even they will eventually lose their status as recognizable social beings worthy of at least annual fiesta day interaction with the living. Schäfer and McManus indicate quite clearly how disappointing the bones alone can be to those engaged in the "dark tourism" of ossuary visitation. That is to say that the bones alone—those bones that have lost their "individuality and without some remnant of social being"—can have only limited interest, however artfully arranged in massive display.

In that regard, our experience in our Africa years with the Fang custom of keeping the skulls of important ancestors in bark reliquaries was also resonant in my reading of these chapters. These Fang skulls were, in annual celebration of the dead, removed from the reliquary to be dusted off, often enough washed with the animal blood of sacrifice, and placed upon a raffia platform. There they were danced to and lauded and in song beseeched for their benevolence and protection. But any skull might be replaced and returned finally to the earth. The bark reliquary was only so big, after all. In the event of the more recent death of an eminent elder now more vividly remembered and hence more potent in the affairs of his or her needy descendants, the older bones were replaced. Here, too, the dead have two lives. They die a second time when they lose the potency of their remembered individuality, that is, the effective benevolence or malevolence remembered in them and able to be resurrected by familiar supplication. In Kathleen Adams's chapter, it might be said that the dead occasionally have a third life as well via the grisly tourist consumption of someone else's ancestors.

I next turn to Shingo Iitaka's account of Japanese tourism to the bloody Pacific Island battlefields, the deathscapes of World War II. His account has been especially evocative for this reader, who has pursued an ethnographic comparison of visitations and "celebrations" of the "killing fields" of the Spanish and American Civil Wars.[3] There is, of course, an irony that these once again idyllic Pacific isles, which exemplary lifescapes for most tourists, can become once again deathscapes in such visitation. For these Japanese tourists, these often now idyllic islands are very surely "deathscapes." Iitaka's account will remind any American of an old tourism in the United States—even before tourism had a name, very probably: that of visiting on holiday one or several of the many battlefields of the Civil War, many set aside as national shrines and monuments. I can vividly recall visiting Gettysburg one hot late summer afternoon and in a leisurely manner following by foot Pickett's charge of July 3, 1863, across the wide and fertile farm fields leading up to Cemetery Ridge.

On that ridge there once lay the low stone wall from behind which General Meade's Federals mowed down the advancing Confederates like mowing grass on a hot summer day. As I slowly advanced across those once body-strewn but now pleasant and fertile fields, they became for me in the instance a deathscape if there ever was one. I calculated what my chances would have been of ever reaching that wall and jumping over it with a Rebel yell. I would have almost surely been a dead man halfway across the field. We are reminded here of the degree to which a "deathscape" may so often be a cultural construction, in this case constructed by informed ethnographic readings of the Civil War literature. And no doubt the deathscape of the island battlefield of Palau sprang to mind for the Japanese tourists, in important part because of their familiarity with the extensive literature on the War of the Pacific.

THE TRANSFORMATIVE INTERPLAY OF DEATHSCAPES AND LIFESCAPES

The deathscape/lifescape transformations we see here is a dynamic ambivalence that also emerges in Adam Kaul's and Patrick Laviolette's related studies of cliff jumping in the British Isles, in Ireland and Cornwall, respectively. These seaside precipices are variously construed. In the Irish case, the many suicides that have occurred at the Cliffs of Moher have made them predominantly a "deathscape" for many, despite the efforts of the Irish government to build an Interpretive Centre there. This centre features and seeks to emphasize and enhance the awesome natural beauty of these magnificent cliffs, to make of them a "metaphor for Irishness" and a source of national pride and wonder, a revitalizing lifescape for the Irish people to treasure and admire. One might conjecture, however, that the power of that metaphor, as in the case of many figurations, is that it is multivalent, possessing intimations of both life and death. And it is that multivalence, perhaps, that makes it and the site it is predicated upon powerful in the imagination.

In Laviolette's case, the Cornish cliffs seem to offer more of a natural lifescape, both because of their natural beauty and since it is also possible to skillfully take one's life in one's hands and manfully survive the tombstoning jump. The jump is breathtaking but not or very rarely suicidal, one understands. Still, the heights involved are daunting, provoking strong cautionary feelings of impending death in the balancing mechanisms of any human organism who surveys them. The tombstoning can thus be seen as a defiance of evident danger, a testimony to human pluck and daring-do and for that reason ultimately life-affirming.

The presence of possible death is more oppressive at Moher, we understand. Yet here too, as Kaul makes clear, one can still trick that feeling into life affirmation. Although any jump would be suicidal and death dealing, one can approach the "awful edge" and yet at the last minute or second turn away, making it thereby an emotionally powerful recommitment to life. One can just step away from death. One can contemplate it, experience its fatal attraction, feel its threatening power, and just step away in a signaly vital act of life affirmation. This "awful edging," we might call it, between deathscape and lifescape seems clearly revitalizing.

These two chapters are dealing with phenomenological complexities of human experience and human ambivalence and emotional volatility. This reader feels stimulated by the two pieces on cliff jumping because I think they address these complexities—really, issues of human revitalization and how humans obtain it—in a particularly stark and interesting way. In their way they also add complexity to our understanding of the volatility and transformational relation of the leisure/death connection.

At the least, we come to see that relation as a kind of emotional dialectic, a negotiation of vitalities and lethargies, ultimately revitalizing in its dynamic. I think these two chapters are instances of the various ways in this collection that the leisure/death conjunction becomes a kind of dialectic where death or the place of death is visited and contemplated and its argument is heard but ultimately turned away from and life is affirmed.

I ought to say, in clarification, that we are speaking here of a dynamic transformation or conversion in the human experience of life into death–death into life classically treated in Bloch and Perry's collection *Death and the Regeneration of Life* (Bloch and Perry 1982). The exception here is that, as regards such transformative processes, we are informed by revitalization theory in American anthropology anchored in the view of human life and culture as a continuing struggle to maintain vitality or a vital and flourishing balance against the various physical and cultural forces that induce or are subject to lethargy in both life and culture.

Two other chapters are of related interest here. They expand our sense of the revitalization and transformative dynamics to be found on the life/death interface of the funeral. Pipyrou's study of the often enough scurrilous, at least untoward, gossip concerning the dead that can occur at funerals shows how this rumormongering revitalizes the participants. That is, it "resurrects" the dead once again as the reprobates or scoundrels they once were to the considerable lively interest—even satisfaction—of the gossipers and enjoyment for them of rehearsing, one last time, long-felt resentments and judgmental feelings. In a way this gossip clears the air and rebalances the social order in a revitalizing way now that the miscreant has passed and can no longer be violating it. Adam's study of the Toraja walking dead of Indonesia evokes that fascinating archetypal yet awful embodiment of life/death transformation in and of itself, the zombie: here, miraculously, in lively motion there an obvious dead man still walking. And Adams shows just how attractive this transformative spectacle can be. Tourists flock to see it, and media people reclaim the presence of this double-valenced figure, refusing to accept that it is, in the end, only a tourist indulgence taking place in a largely Christian country whose inhabitants put little of their faith in zombies other than as entertainments to attract a tourist-overwhelmed third world.

PILGRIMAGE AND THE SEARCH FOR DISTINCTION

The concept of pilgrimage can apply to many of the chapters in this collection, not only and most obviously to Keith Egan's illuminating evocation of his deeply experienced pilgrimage to the tomb of Saint James in Compostela, northwestern Spain, but also to the Japanese journeys to the blood-soaked sands of Palau or costly American tours to the far reaches of Indonesia "in search of the Walking Dead," as well as the weekend visitations by Northerners and Southerners alike to the Civil War battlefields, many carrying still treasured remembrances of the now distant ancestors who died there.

One says "illuminating" about Egan's moving account of the pilgrimage to Compostela in Galicia, because he captures so well its ambiguities and ambivalences, the loneliness and sociality, the physicality and spirituality, the devotional and self-indulgent, the desolation and exaltation—in short, both the wine-imbibing part and the walking part of it, as he puts it. Egan's account is especially pertinent in raising the now long-treated issue in anthropology of authenticity in engaging with the challenges of life. This is especially the case when he addresses the in-authenticities of the surrounding commercialized and commodified world through which the pilgrim must make his or her way. The late capitalist world is everywhere pressing in upon and enticing the pilgrim. Finally, in Santiago itself, the bus and car tourist multitudes surround and commingle with the pilgrim in a merry lifescape, all too quickly absorbing him or her and bringing into question or at least minimizing the distinction achieved by his recent great effort of self-denial and expectation.

Etymologically, the pilgrim, as "peregrinus," is a foreigner, an alien wayfarer with the available leisure to wander in a foreign land from guide arrow to guide arrow, brass scallop shell to brass scallop shell embedded in the pavement, showing him or her the way to the far-off holy place and the blessings such pedestrian piety is sure to eventually bring. Only in the end, in Santiago itself, does the pilgrim, as Egan describes it, find herself swept along among the mass of tourists, many from her own part of the world, enjoying the same privileges and blessings and among them especially the privilege of escaping effort through various forms of mass transportation—as if to intrude upon, if not minimize, the distinction obtained through her many-week march. The overwhelmingly buoyant tourist presence can all too easily make the pilgrim feel, in a favorite put-down of the literati, all too pedestrian. The world culture of leisure and the hubbub that mass tourism fosters all too easily absorb her as they have absorbed the sainted sepulcher and the cathedral quietude of death itself. It is not too much to say, perhaps, that mass tourism puts at risk both the saintly aspect of the pilgrim's self-denial and commitment as well as the sacred atmosphere of the holy city and the sepulcher. Thus do the privileges of the leisure class put at risk the profound yet eventually revitalizing confrontation with death that the pilgrim deserves and may desire.

Still, Maribeth Erb's account of "Dying in a Strange Land" on Flores Island in eastern Indonesia does in its way bring home to the reader some of the underlying subtleties and authenticities of the cultural fact of foreignness. She shows the foreignness that lies in wait for anyone wandering in a foreign land and, unfortunately, dying there. In the case reported by Erb, in the absence of any effective contact with the dead person's family, an effort, if somewhat attenuated, is made by the locals—it is a human being, after all, who has died—to treat the unfortunate dead foreigner with the same attention and consideration that would be given to locals after their deaths, rites and attention that would be quite foreign in the dead man's homeland. In the last months of his life, the individual involved, a New Zealander, was pretty much subsumed into a very generalized, indeed global, tourist identity. But in death, in contrast to "in life," the lonely corpse without family or national directive, who had wandered so far from his homeland, is made into or given the respect and rites of local identity. He has at last, despite the globalized identity international tourism had originally assigned to him, gone native.

In this collection, in each chapter, in each author's exercise in conjoining the posited separate domains of experience, the reader finds stimulating understandings of the agentive exercise of the privileges of leisure and its limitations in the presence of death. But truly challenging and instructive are the three final chapters, in which all agency has been lost: the considerations of digital immortality, as raised by Tamara Kohn and colleagues in their study of Facebook, and reconsiderations of the funeral, that is, the final purpose and place of commemoration and other eternity preparing activity, as raised by Hannah Rumble in her discussion of natural—in her case, woodlands—burial. The agency of the dead is also called into question in Pipyrou's chapter, as rumors about the deceased keep him actively engaged as a character in the social world of gossiping mourners while the dead man is himself a passive bystander. In these three chapters, readers are truly challenged in their understanding of both agency and the afterlife.

ALTERNATE AFTERLIVES: VIRTUAL IMMORTALITY AND THE POLITICS OF COMMEMORATION

In Kohn and colleagues' chapter on Facebook, we confront the difference between physical and social being. The dead no longer possess physical being and lack their own agency, yet they can yet live on socially, at least digitally, and in often intimate contact with others (as far as the others are concerned). The absence of physicality is little impediment; indeed, it is readily overcome as one continues to be the passive object of recurrent affectionate or intimate postings, an object (if not a subject) of interest in the leisure-time internet lives of others with whom the deceased had once interacted. The deceased may no longer have agency of his or her own but can continue to "enjoy" patiency in the lives of others. Thus, does the digital enable the moving beyond of the final physicality of death's destruction of the physical?

This movement, this leisure practice of actively posting to the dead, can be more than a minor matter. It has the possibility of becoming a phenomenon of immense volume. As the authors point out, there are a billion and half active Facebook users. Already, Facebook has had to deal with over 30 million dead users, and an estimated 19,000 users with Facebook profiles are dying each day. One used to think of the funeral as the recognition of the ephemeral and a fashioning for finality. At the least, in social media the afterlife of the dead has become something much different and more enduring. At least this is true for those with the leisure to continue posting.

A rather different afterlife for the dead and a different politics of commemoration is offered in Rumble's study of British natural burial, where the dead are buried without the usual distinction of highly formal funerals, well-marked plots, and weighty headstones. They are buried "with much-reduced topographic visibility." Hence natural burial grounds are places where the living and the dead can continue to come together in myriad leisure and recreational activities. Children can play games over the decomposing and decomposed bodies of their ancestors. And the deathscape of the formal cemetery is made into much more of a lifescape for the truly recreational activity of the living undertaken in the subterranean presence of the dead. The dead are much less "sequestered" from the living but are found indiscriminately underfoot while in their imagined presence they are a continuing counterpart of the ongoing leisure life of the living.

It is true, of course, that integration of the dead with the recreational life of the living can happen and has happened in various ways elsewhere. It is well-known, if in a somewhat sotto voce way, that in America in most of the great beauty spots, the national parks, the scattering of the ashes of loved ones has been going on apace. It is actually allowed under permit in most national parks in out-of-the-way sites and at appropriate, less trafficked times of day. As in British natural park burial grounds, no markers, cairns, displays, signs, or plaques can be left. This means that, unlike the case in cemeteries, future memorializations or simple visitations of particular dead cannot be easily or exactly oriented. It is true that in some cases families preserve a record of the general site of the scattering in GPS coordinates. Muir Woods National Park north of San Francisco and its giant redwood trees has become one site of considerable attraction for veiled, out-of-the-way scatterings of ashes. It is not out of the question to suppose that the ashes of many thousands, including my parents, have been scattered there in anonymous deposition, making this magnificent park and its great trees a hallowed place beyond the splendor of its natural wonders.

The point is that in natural burial the individuality of the dead goes unremarked by the general public and is remembered in only general terms by relatives. The dead's personhood and family-hood, so often carefully distinguished in one way or another in cemeteries and carefully reiterated when returned to with flowers, are obviated. The dead do "enjoy" in natural burial, as Rumble indicates, an ecological and sustainable identification with the fate of all their fellow humans—"ashes to ashes, dust to dust." Cemetery burial and a cemetery, by definition, make a special and privileged claim on the use of space. Natural burial frees up space for a variety of recreational, leisure-time uses by succeeding generations of living humans and to a degree offers a different kind of communion with the dead than is characteristic of cemetery burial.

Anthropologists and the anthropological archives give ready evidence of native peoples who in thanatopic meditation showed reverence for the soil on which they trod as a composite of the remains of thousands of their ancestors. These meditations, no doubt, make the earth underfoot a respected repository resistant to crass material exploitation. These native natural burial grounds, moreover, coax humans away from preoccupation with their individuality and their accumulated distinctions and possessions, all very present in much of the obituary preparing activity of the modern life course. This contemplation of nature and the ground underfoot as a composite of mortal remains can suggest, it seems, an existential sense of common humanity, which is to say, a sense of our common mortality.

SOME "LAST WORDS" AND QUESTIONS

Perhaps as a ninth decade-er and one who at his back "doth hear time's swift chariot hurrying near,"[4] I may be permitted in this final place some final words more attuned to the moral than the empirical configurations and connections perceived and managed so skillfully by the contributors to this collection. To be sure, people my age can all too easily wax eloquent on the realities of the advancing years. When one lives beyond life expectancies, what can be and usually is distressing is the lamented loss of partners, friends, colleagues, and students to the Grim Reaper. Indeed, to live into old age is to experience the grievous impact of mortality on the social fabric in which one was nurtured and which one has endeavored to nurture.

In advancing age, one understands better, perhaps, Durkheim's argument that supernatural representations are in actuality substitute symbolisms for the once powerful and vital but now fraying fabric of society. They are a reformulation of that lost omnipotence of the social in the life cycle, in which spiritual beings replace social beings. One is tempted, therefore, in final place to discuss leisure and death in terms of the increasing impact of mortalities on the possibilities of meaningful "communicative interaction" with others. One is inclined to discuss the impact of the decimation of one's cohort on a meaningful social use of one's increased leisure. What would surely be worth discussing in this epilogue is the relevance for the advanced in age of the digitalization of social being through such platforms as Facebook.

But rather than trying to put a final finger on the sorrows of senectitude as a consequence of cohort death or examining cyber-world prospects for the alleviation of these sorrows, I would like to close by returning briefly to Rumble and to Thorstein Veblen—the latter of whom made pioneering though rather acerbic identification of the "leisure class" and its dedication to conspicuous consumption. It is fair to say, I think, that all of us who participated in this lively collection, most of us academics, are members of the leisure class. This is surely true as regards our relative freedom in choosing our work topic and scheduling, though perhaps not so true as regards our frequent workaholic ways or our lack of the available wherewithal for self- and project fulfillment.

It is true that the present leisure class is much expanded in numbers and more wide-embracing in income levels than the singular moneyed elite Veblen had in mind. For that reason—that it has become a much expanded class—and because it has taken a much increased advantage of the possibilities of tourism, the questions Veblen addressed to the leisure class of his day about their conspicuous consumption seem pertinent and might usefully be raised today to the modern leisure class and its heavy investments in tourism. That is to further say that in any discussion of leisure and death, the question of conspicuous consumption might usefully claim a presence.

We are now at too late a point in our reading of these fascinating chapters to enter into that leisure-class issue in any major way. But we can suggest something of its dimensions by highlighting two questions that emerge in this collection relevant to that discussion and relevant to the relation between death and leisure. In dealing with the dead, is there not a better, more ecological, and more sustainable way to deal with their demise than in contemporary forms of embalming, en-casketing, and tombstone memorialization? Above all, is there not a better way than burying the dead in the confines of somber, single-use cemeteries? These are, in fact, the questions Rumble puts to the reader: are contemporary death rituals and burial practices sustainable and ecological in the presence of a world population of soon enough 9 billion human beings? Do they actually take advantage of or invite leisure activities more integrative with the mortal condition and more communicative with those who have died? The natural burial movement Rumble discusses would seem to advocate burial without extravagant memorialization in natural burial grounds where the living can more easily visit with the dead and carry on more soulfully, even perhaps more joyfully, their leisure activities in proximity to their deceased loved ones.

At the same time, is there not some Veblen-esque question to be asked concerning conspicuous consumption to be put to "dark tourism," if not to tourism as a whole? Put simply, what part of the very large carbon footprint accumulated as this tourism vertiginously and massively circles the globe is aimed, as Veblen would argue, at status maintenance or enhancement and what part at deepening our adaptive knowledge of the world and mortality? With apologies to my leisure classmates, I will not attempt to answer that question or the question before it, answered anyway so well by Rumble, although I ask these questions of myself as well. But rather, let me conclude as I concluded my original discussion at the 2013 Chicago Anthropological Meeting about the session papers that were antecedent to these present chapters.

LEARNING TO DIE IN THE ANTHROPOCENE

Shortly before the 2013 Chicago meetings of the American Anthropological Association, I was pondering the challenge of my original comments to papers I had read in *The Stone*, the philosopher's blog of the *New York Times*, in particular a piece by a veteran of the Iraq wars, Roy Scranton, curiously titled "Learning How to Die in the Anthropocene" (Scranton 2013). Naturally, it peaked the interest of someone preparing comments to address the also curious conjunction between leisure and death. As a returned veteran, Scranton was reacting to what he was observing after returning home: a civilization in denial about climate change and living as if it was not facing an eventual threat from its consequences—indeed, as he put it, "the greatest threat the United States faces." For him, it was a threat "to our sense of what it is to be human."

Scranton recalled that during his several years in Iraq he had to learn to live under constant threat of being killed as a grunt or foot soldier in the Iraq War. To do so he had taken a leaf from the eighteenth-century Samurai manual *Hagakure*, which recommended beginning each day by meditating on inevitable death in the various forms of it that one faces. To live by Samurai standards in such a threatening environment under constant pressure from the Taliban, one must daily learn to die. By meditating each morning on the various deaths facing him, Scranton avers, "then before we rolled out through the gates I'd tell myself that I didn't need to worry because I was already dead." He gained freedom from incapacitating dread in this way, by learning to die. Hence the curious title of his essay.

He applies this learning to the disastrous situation he feels climate change poses for American civilization and American values, and he advocates that instead of mindlessly denying this threat, we meditate on it. We meditate on it and its various consequences every morning before we begin our day in the antropocene that surrounds us and which we humans, through our thoughtless activities, have created. I suppose I am suggesting that tourism and especially "dark tourism" is one of those activities to which we have not given sufficient thought, though I am a bit abashed about saying that in an epilogue to such a stimulating set of readings.

Beyond and behind that insufficiency, I suppose we have not given sufficient thought to the extraordinary growth of the carbon footprint of leisure activity and the tourism it enables and the threat it poses, the environmental cost we pay, the kind of death it augers. In any event, in my original comments in 2013 I ended the precis of my discussion by proposing, on Scranton's model, that instead of the covering rubric to our discussions being "Leisure *and* Death," it ought to be "The Death *in* Leisure." I return to that somewhat mischievous comment, then, as some kind of an answer, a revitalizing answer perhaps, suggested by Scranton, to the questions Rumble from within and Veblen from without pose to us at the end of our readings. In short, the various insightful efforts in this important collection might equally be entitled *The Death in Leisure*.

NOTES

1. The inchoate: those domains of experience or of all of life as a domain of experience, that are poorly understood, uncertain, or gnawingly incomplete in our understanding of them.

2. A phrase associated with the late Mary Douglas. The phrase is manifestly true in religions that posit a "final judgment" for which one must be prepared, but it is also true in

philosophies which argue that death is an essential, always present, and defining part of life. In "final judgment" religions, even one's use of leisure has moral implications and is to be finally taken into account. See the conclusion of this epilogue.

3. A comparison of the "celebrated," though highly politicized, excavation of the mass-execution graves of the Spanish Civil War with the celebration by both sides, North and South, of the battlegrounds, killing fields, really, of the American Civil War.

4. Along with Andrew Marvel.

REFERENCES

Bloch, Maurice, and Jonathan Perry. 1982. *Death and the Regeneration of Life*. New York: Cambridge University Press.

Carrithers, Michael. 1992. *Why Humans Have Cultures*. Oxford: Oxford University Press.

Scranton, Roy. 2013. "Learning How to Die in the Anthropocene." *The Stone, New York Times Digital*. November 10, 2013. https://opinionator.blogs.nytimes.com/2013/11/10/learning-how-to-die-in-the-anthropocene/.

Contributors

KATHLEEN M. ADAMS is professor of anthropology at Loyola University Chicago and adjunct curator of Southeast Asian Ethnology at the Field Museum of Natural History. She is the author of the award-winning book *Art as Politics: Re-crafting Identities, Tourism, and Power in Tana Toraja, Indonesia* and coeditor of *Everyday Life in Southeast Asia* and *Home and Hegemony: Domestic Work and Identity Politics in South and Southeast Asia* and has authored numerous journal articles and book chapters. She has conducted long-term ethnographic research in Indonesia and California, and her research on tourism, heritage, identity politics, museums, and the arts has been funded by Fulbright, the American Philosophical Society, and other foundations.

MICHAEL ARNOLD is associate professor and head of discipline in the History and Philosophy of Science Programme at the University of Melbourne. His ongoing research activities lie at the intersection of contemporary technologies and daily life: for example, studies of online memorials, body disposal, and other technologies associated with death; the phenomenology of robot surgery; the implications of digital technologies for domestic life; and social networking technologies and community informatics. Michael is also interested in ethical and normative assessments of technologies and philosophical approaches to technologies, in particular, Heidegger, actor-network theory, and object-oriented ontology. Michael has been chief investigator on many research projects and has coauthored three research books and over 100 peer-reviewed papers, including the recently published book *Death and Digital Media*.

RAY CASSERLY is academic director for the Council on International Educational Exchange's Global Institutes, overseeing the academic quality and development assurance processes for the several hundred courses offered and delivered in ten Global Institutes (Buenos Aires, Berlin, Cape Town, Copenhagen, London, Madrid, Paris, Rio, Rome, Santiago). He is experienced in the organization and delivery of numerous cross-community and cross-border initiatives with various music groups in Northern Ireland. Ray continues to incorporate his musical interests into his research on the highly sensitive political issue of parades in Northern Ireland. His academic interests include music and conflict, communal memory, and identity in the United Kingdom and Ireland.

JANE C. DESMOND is professor of anthropology and of Gender/Women's Studies at the University of Illinois at Urbana-Champaign, where she also directs The International Forum for U.S. Studies: A Center for the Transnational Study of the United States, which she cofounded with Virginia Dominguez. Desmond's scholarly work focuses broadly on issues of embodiment and social identity, grounding her work in tourism, cultural studies, performance, visual studies, and animal studies. Her books include *Staging Tourism: Bodies on Display from Waikiki to Sea World* (1999) and *Displaying Death and Animating Life: Human-Animal Relations in Art, Science, and Everyday Life* (2016).

KEITH EGAN is an independent scholar whose work has focused on describing vulnerability, resilience, and life transitions by using existential and phenomenological approaches to freedom in lived experience. The nurturance and preservation of meaning in lives experienced as precarious has been a central preoccupation in his writing and research. He has published widely on the topics of pilgrimage, tourism, and ethnography in *American Anthropologist*, *The Journal of Contemporary Religion*, *Journeys*, and beyond.

MARIBETH ERB is an associate professor in the Department of Sociology, National University of Singapore. She is the author of *The Manggaraians* (1999) and the coeditor of *Regionalism in Post-Suharto Indonesia* (2005), *Biodiversity and Human Livelihoods in Protected Areas* (Cambridge, 2007), and *Deepening Democracy in Indonesia? Direct Elections for Local Leaders* (2009). She has also written many articles on among other topics—tourism, political change, ritual, and history—in journals such as *Annals of Tourism Research*, *Journal of Southeast Asian Studies*, *Oceania*,

Pacific Affairs, *Indonesia and the Malay World*, *Asian Journal of Social Science*, and *Tourism Geographies* and various edited collections.

JAMES FERNANDEZ is a professor emeritus of anthropology at the University of Chicago, where he still teaches. He has spent a quarter century career as an Africanist working on religious movements in three parts of Africa: Gabon, Natal, and Ghana-Togo-Benin. Lately, he has been working on ethnic revitalization in Asturias (Spain) and Colorado.

MARTIN GIBBS is associate professor in the School of Computing and Information Systems at the University of Melbourne. His research interests lie at the intersection of science technology studies (STS) and human computer interaction (HCI). Current projects include media ecologies of the home, digital commemoration, and tabletop gaming. He was program co-chair for the Digital Games Research Association (DIGRA) 2017 conference and will repeat the role in 2018. His recent coauthored book, *Death and Digital Media*, was published by Routledge in 2018. He is currently working on an edited collection for Routledge, *Residues of Death*, and a coauthored book for Oxford University Press, *Digital Domesticities*.

RACHEL A. HORNER BRACKETT grew up on a family hog farm in northwestern Illinois. She holds a joint MPH/PhD from the University of Iowa and currently teaches across the four fields of anthropology at Black Hawk College in Moline, Illinois. Her research interests focus on the intersections of global/local identity, food, environment, and consumerism. Dr. Horner Brackett's most recent work examines the construction of Etruscan heritage among modern Italians, particularly as it relates to cuisine and the marketing of heritage food products. If you find yourself in Tuscany, Dr. Horner Brackett highly recommends taking a trip to her field site at Spannocchia, where you can experience some of the culinary treats mentioned her chapter. (www.spannocchia.com.)

SHINGO IITAKA is an associate professor of cultural anthropology at University of Kochi, Japan. Since 2002 he has conducted field research in the Pacific Island nation of Palau and in Okinawa, Japan. His research interests include Micronesians' colonial experiences and memories of the Pacific War in Micronesia. He investigates the way Palauan society was reorganized by colonial policies of the Great Empire of Japan, such as cultural assimilation of the indigenous and economic development through Japanese settlement. Currently he is investigating Micronesians' responses to battlefield tourism developed by various agencies from the United States and Japan. His publications include "Remembering Nan'yō from Okinawa:

Deconstructing the Former Empire of Japan through Memorial Practices" in *History and Memory* (2015).

ADAM KAUL is associate professor of anthropology at Augustana College in Rock Island, Illinois. He is the author of *Turning the Tune: Traditional Music, Tourism, and Social Change in an Irish Village* (2009) and coeditor, with Sharon Gmelch, of the third edition of *Tourists and Tourism* (2018). He has written numerous articles and book chapters on traditional music, busking, commodification, and tourism in Ireland. He is currently writing about Swedish-American heritage tourism and the emergence of the clean energy economy in the American Midwest.

TAMARA KOHN is associate professor of anthropology in the School of Social and Political Sciences at the University of Melbourne. Her current research interests include death studies, transcultural communities of practice, prison lives and personhood, body and senses, and research methods and ethics. Her publications that intersect around death and leisure include the new coauthored book *Death and Digital Media* (2018), the coedited book *The Discipline of Leisure: Embodying Cultures of "Recreation"* (with Simon Coleman, 2008/2010), the chapter "Crafting Selves on Death Row" in *Emotion, Identity, and Death: Mortality across Disciplines* (edited by Douglas Davies and Chang-Won Park, 2012); and the forthcoming coedited book *Residues of Death*.

PATRICK LAVIOLETTE is professor of anthropology at Tallinn University. He is the co-chief editor of EASA's journal *Social Anthropology/Anthropologie Sociale* (2015–19) and the incoming editor of the *Anthropological Journal of European Cultures* (2018–22). He is also the author of two monographs published in 2011: *The Landscaping of Metaphor and Cultural Identity* and *Extreme Landscapes of Leisure: Not a Hap-Hazardous Sport* (republished in 2016). In 2013 he coedited, with Anu Kannike, the volume *Things in Culture, Culture in Things*. He has an interdisciplinary background in the subfields of material and visual culture studies as well as medical and environmental anthropology, and much of his research deals with the formulation of British and European identities. He has spent four years working in New Zealand and seven in Estonia. He is currently completing a monograph on hitchhiking.

RUTH MCMANUS is associate professor of sociology at the University of Canterbury in Christchurch, New Zealand. Her research and teaching interests in the sociology of death and dying span from the cost of funerals to disaster memorialization. Ruth is a cofounder and inaugural president of the Society for Death Studies (http://societyfordeathstudies.org; set up in 2014 in New Zealand), which aims to aims to promote research and understanding across all areas of death studies with particular reference to New Zealand academic, professional, artistic, and practitioner communities.

JAMES MEESE is a lecturer at the University of Technology Sydney. He has recently published the coauthored book *Death and Digital Media*. Other work on death and digital media has been published in *Mortality, the International Journal of Communication*, and various edited collections. He also studies media law and regulation and is currently leading a research project on consumer rights to personal data. Research in this area has been published in *Television and New Media and Mobile Media and Communication*, and his monograph *Authors, Users, Pirates: Subjectivity and Copyright Law* is currently in press.

BJORN NANSEN is a senior lecturer in media and communications in the School of Culture and Communications at the University of Melbourne. He researches digital media and communications technologies, computer interaction, and network culture in the contexts of household, family, and everyday life. Utilizing a range of ethnographic, online, and visual research methods, he has interests that include technology adoption and use/non-use, home media environments, young children's digital culture, mobile and tangible media, material culture studies, and critical theory of technology. He is coauthor of *Death and Digital Media* (2018).

STAVROULA PIPYROU is lecturer in social anthropology and founding director of the Centre for Minorities Research at the University of St Andrews. She has conducted long-term research in Italy on minority governance, displacement, and silence and in Greece on death, performance, and nationalism. She is author of *The Grecanici of Southern Italy: Governance, Violence, and Minority Politics* (2016).

HANNAH RUMBLE is a research fellow at the Centre for Death and Society at the University of Bath, UK. She also sits on the editorial board of the journal *Mortality* and is the early career researcher's representative on the General Council for the Association for the Study of Death and Society (ASDS). Her ethnographic and qualitative research has focused on contemporary British funeral and deathcare innovations and their sociocultural impact, as well as researching funeral poverty and young people's attitudes toward death and contemporary deathscapes. Dr. Rumble has also produced a public art exhibition and two short films and performed stand-up comedy in order to informally develop death education.

CYRIL SCHÄFER was a senior lecturer in social anthropology at the University of Otago, Dunedin, New Zealand. He died suddenly as his chapter for this collection was underway. His research and teaching interests included death and dying, ritual, religion, evil, and human cruelty. His previous research examined the professionalization of funeral directing, the personalization of postmortem practices, and the emergence of funeral celebrants in Australasia. He was a cofounder of the Society for Death Studies (NZ). He is greatly missed.

JONATHAN SKINNER is reader in anthropology in the Department of Life Sciences at the University of Roehampton. He researches leisure practices (tourism and dance) and has worked on Montserrat in the Caribbean and in the United States and Northern Ireland. He is author of *Before the Volcano* (2004) and editor of a number of volumes including *Writing the Dark Side of Travel* (2012) and *The Interview: An Ethnographic Approach* (2012).

Index

Page numbers in italic indicate illustrations.

ABOD. *See* Apprentice Boys of Derry
accidents, 125, 134
adventurer, as artist, 79–80
aesthetics, of natural burial grounds, 269–70
affect, 80
agriculture, artisanal, 208–9, 210
agritourism, 217
Ahern, Bertie, 123
Aichl, Jan Santini, 167
Airplanes' Graveyard (Angaur Island), 151, *152*
Alaturbi jump, 91
Alfonso III, 60
ambivalence, of ossuarial displays, 173
American Civil War, 285, 294(n3)
ancestors, treatment of, 22, 100, 284; Torajan, 101, 106–7, 108, 114
Angaur Island, 144; heritage tourism on, 150–53, 154; memorials on, 145, 156(n13)
Angaur State Nature Park Project, 151, 152–53
animals, 7; sacrificed, 101, *102*, 104–5, 113
animism, 12–13
Annee Sociologique, L', 233
anthropocene, 293
Aokigahara Forest, 88
Apprentice Boys of Derry (ABOD), 202, 203(n3)

Aran Islands, 128
Arbory Trust, 267; and Barton Glebe, 268–70
archaeology, 164, 173
Ardoyne (Belfast), 194, 199
Ariès, Philippe, *Western Attitudes towards Death*, 7
Ark of Taste, 217–18
art theory, 21–22
artist, adventurer as, 79–80
astrology, Renaissance, 4
Asturia, 284
Australia, V. Gordon Childe in, 87
authenticity, 23, 41, 152, 287; of Camino de Santiago pilgrimage, 58, 62, 67–69; in encountering death, 176–82; of gastronomic tourism, 207–8; of ossuaries, 166–71, 182–84

Babeldaob Island, 144, 145, 156(n11)
baby-jumping festival, 91
Bali, 44
Barley, Nigel, 8
barriers, at Cliffs of Moher, 130–32
Barry, Vincent, 7
Barton Glebe Woodland Burial Ground, 263–64, 267, 268–70, *271*, 276; informality of, 273–74

301

INDEX

Basso, Keith, on place-making, 126
battlefield tours, 284–85; on Palau Islands, 150, 151
Battle of the Boyne, 24, 193, 196, 197
Battle of the Somme, 25, 197, 198, 201
battles, observing live, 7. *See also by name*; Pacific War; Spanish Civil War
Baudrillard, Jean, *Symbolic Exchange and Death*, 8
Beachy Head, suicides at, 20, 21, 88
Beauvoir, Simone de, *La force d'lâge* (*The Prime of Life*), 84–85
Becker, Ernest, 246
beheadings, xvi, 10
being, digitalization of, 291
Belfast, 191, 202; Twelfth of July parade, 192–96, 197–201
Bender, Barbara, 126
Benedict, Ruth, *Patterns of Culture*, 14
Berg, Evan "Nick," 10
biopolitics, 17
black magic, 111
Black Sea, 91
Bloch, Maurice, *Death and the Regeneration of Life*, 14–15, 286
blogs, 237; on Torajan funeral rites, 102–3, 104–6, 109, 116(n13)
blood sausage (*buristo*), 214–16
Bloody Sunday (Londonderry), 192
Bob: burial and grave of, 52–53; death in Indonesia, 20, 27, 45–46, 47
body, bodies, xiv–xv, xvi, 50, 79, 80, 234. *See also* corpses; skeletal remains
Body Worlds exhibition, 7, 164, 177
bombings, 7, 44, 54, 191
bones, 6, 101, 103; as displays of death, 172–73; in ossuaries, 165, 167–69, 175–76, 177
borderland, death as, 262
borders, life and death, 233–34
BoredBug–cure your boredom, 238
boundaries, between private and public life, 254
Bourdieu, Pierre, 209
Bourgois, Philippe, 99
Bowman, Michael, 153
brain death, 18
Bridge, The (documentary; Steel), 88
Bristol, Memorial Woodlands at, 272
Bristol Museum, *Death: The Human Experience*, 28–30

Britain. *See* Great Britain
British, as culinary tourists, 207
brochures, on ossuaries, 174
Bruner, Ed, 18
bull jumping, 91
Bundy, Ted, 5, 10
bungee jumping, 87
burials, burial grounds, 24, 26, 278(n2), 290; in Church of All Saints cemetery, 166–67; natural, 261–62, 263–67, 270, 271; visiting, 272–75
buristo, 214–16
Burke, William, 9
butchering, butchery, 219–20; at Spannocchia, 213–15

cadavers, 9. *See also* corpses
California, 267, 290
Callaway, Helen, 85
Cambodia, 178
Cambridgeshire, natural burial ground in, 261–62, 269
Camino de Santiago, xii, 58–59, 60, 74(n5), 288; experience of, 72–73; memoirs of, 67–69; pilgrims on, 62–67, 70–71, 287–88; as recreation of self, 61–62; walking, xiv, xv, 20–21
Campbell, John, 254
Campo Santo, 284
Camus, Alfred, 88
Carlisle Cemetery, 264
Carrickhill (Belfast), 194, 195, 199
casualties, Pacific War, 144
Catholicism. *See* Roman Catholics, Catholicism
Cebrero, O, 69
cell death, 18
cell-phones, in Indonesia, 107, 108
cemeteries: activities in, 268, 275; behavioral control in, 272–73; and ossuaries, 165, 167; visiting, 273–74
Chammünster ossuary (Germany), 168
charity campaigns, 90
Charles, responsibilities of, 52–53
charnel houses, 24. *See also* ossuaries
Childe, Vere Gordon, death of, 87–88
Christianity, Christians, 73(n1), 184(n2); death cult in, 21, 164; and skeletal remains, 174–75; Torajan, 100, 101, 108, 115
Chrzan, Janet, 211
churches, on Camino de Santiago, 61. *See also by name*

Church of All Saints cemetery (Sedlec), burial in, 166–67
Cinta Senese pigs, 25, 206, 207; on Ark of Taste, 217–18; butchering of, 213–15; as heritage breed, 216–17; product availability, 218–19; at Spannocchia tours, 211–13
civil rights and liberties, in Northern Ireland, 198
Civil War battlefields, 285, 294(n3)
Clare, County, 128
Clavijo, battle of, 60
cleansing, corpse- and grave-, 107, 108, 114
click bate, selfies-before-death as, 238
cliff-jumping, xii, 77, 87–88, 285–86; at Devil's Frying Pan, 81–84
Cliffs of Moher, xiv, 22–23, 122, 125; deaths at, 123–24, 136; interpretive center at, 126–30; jumping or falling at, 134–35, 286; risk-taking at, 132–34; stone walls at, 130–32
Clifton Suspension Bridge, 88
climate change, 293
climbing, free, 84–85, 86
Closing of the Gates parade, 202
coat of arms, Schwarzenberg, 167
Codex Calixtinus, 68, 69
Coehlo, Paulo, 67
Cohen, Anthony, 255
Cohen, Erik, 41, 42, 43
Colacho, El, 91
commemoration, 27; in natural burial grounds, 289–90; Northern Ireland parades as, 193, 197–200, 201. *See also* memorialization
commodification: of death, 178; in natural burial grounds, 270–71; of Tuscany, 208
communism, in Greece, 248
conflict, Catholic-Protestant, 197–98
confrontation, with mortality, 163–64
conservation areas, burial grounds in, 262
consumerism, virtuous, 218
consumption, 10, 284
context collapse, 229
Cook, Thomas, 29
Co-operative Funeralcare, 29
Co-operative Group, 29
Copeland, Paul, 196
coral reefs, bombing of, 54
Cornwall, 77, 78; cliff jumping in, 81–83, 285–86
corpses, 7, 9, 10, 22; guarding, 20, 46, 50–51; reanimation of, 98–99; in Torajan rituals, 101, 106–7, 108, 112, 114

Costa Rica, murders in, 41, 54, 55(n2)
Counter-Reformation, and ossuaries, 166
Coville, Elizabeth, 108
cremations, 265–66, 290
crematoria, 264, 275, 276
criminals, criminality, 9, 10
crusade, Santiago de Compostela, 60
Cruz de Ferro, 68, 74(n10)
CSI (television series), 6, 10
culinary tourism, 207, 208
cultural capital, 113
cultural content, of ossuaries, 175
cultural omnivores, 210, 211
Culture War, in Northern Ireland, 190, 203(n1)
Czech Republic (Czechoslovakia), ossuaries in, 24, 164, 166

Danforth, Loring, 246
danger, 50, 78. *See also* risk, risk taking
Dangerous Sports Club, 87, 88
danse macabre, as *memento mori*, 171
Dante Alighieri, *Divine Comedy*, 281–82
dark tourism, xi–xii, 4, 19, 27, 41, 153
Dark Tourism (Lennon and Foley), 27, 135
dead, the, 48, 50, 164, 240; on Facebook, 227–28, 229–33; online personas of, 235–36; re-clothing of, 107, 108. *See also* body, bodies; corpses; skeletal remains
death(s), 5, 6, 9, 11, 12, 14, 18, 25, 98, 116(n11), 144, 184(n2), 212; attitudes toward, 3–4; authenticity of, 182–83; Christian cult of, 21, 164; at Cliffs of Moher, 123–24; as commodity, 31, 154; confronting, 163–64; defining, 7–8; encountering, xv–xvi, 176–82; jumping to, 87–88; narratives of, 124–25; as process, 15–16; rituals of, 234–35; selfies before, 238–40; of tourists, 43–44, 288; transparency of, 172–73
Death, Mourning, and Burial (Robben), 19
Death, Property, and the Ancestors (Goody), 15
Death: The Human Experience (Bristol Museum), 28–30
Death and Disaster series (Warhol), 88
Death and the Regeneration of Life (Block and Parry), 14–15, 286
deathscapes, battlefields as, 284–85
decay, xvi, 176
decomposition, xvi, 176, 182
Dee, John, 4

Democratic Unionist Party (DUP), 202, 203(n1)
de-personalization, of ossuarial remains, 177
Derrida, Jacques, 43
Devil's Frying Pan (Cornwall), xii; tombstoning in, 81–83
Día de los Muertos, El, 283–84
Digital Commemoration, 237
Dignitas Room, *29–30*
discipline, public execution as, 5
dissection, 9
dive shops, in Labuan Bajo, 54
Divine Comedy (Dante), 281–82
diving, 54; in Palau, 141, 147, 148
domesticity, vs. consumerism, 218
Douglas, Mary, 14
Down, County, bombings in, 191
dry funerals, 16
DUP. *See* Democratic Unionist Party
Durkheim, Émile, 15, 125, 291; *Le Suicide*, 13
dying, xv, xvi, 7, 12

earth dive ritual, 87
eating, 206, 212, 282–83
Ebert, Chaz, 236
Ebert, Roger, 236
eco burial, 264. *See also* natural burial grounds
ecological principles/preservation, 267; of natural burial, 265–66
Edensor, Tim, 127
edgework, xiv, 4, 123, 132
Edinburgh Medical College, 9
effigies, 100, 108
Egan, Kerry, Camino de Santiago memoir, 68–69
Eiffel Tower, 88
Ely, Diocese of, Arbory Trust, 267
embodiment, 18–19
emotion, xiv, 14, 114
Enlightenment, 166
enslavement, zombies and, 99
entertainment, 5, 9, 10, 191
entrepreneurship, zombie, 111
environmental protection, 262, 267, 274
Errington, Frederick, 209
Estonia, 77
Ethiopia, bull jumping in, 91
ethnic tourism, 22, 113
Europe, 5, 217; charnel houses in, 165–66. *See also various countries*

European City of Culture, Santiago de Compostela as, 61
European Premier Cultural Itinerary, 61
European Union (EU), 61, 251
euthanasia rollercoaster, 12
Evans-Pritchard, Edward E., 16
events, attention to, 239–40
Evers, Clifton, 80
executions, xvi, 5, 6, 9, 10
exploitation, in ethnic tourism, 22
extreme sports, 90. *See also* cliff-jumping
extremists, Islamic, 10

Facebook, xv, 25, 27, 291; dead users on, 227–28, 229–31; digital immortality, 288–89; memorialization on, 231–33; online performance of, 235–36
Falling Blossoms (Funasaka), 144, 155(n4)
Falling Man, 88, 89
"Famine Hill," symbolism of, 195–96
Fang, 284
fantastic realism, 105, 113–14
fear, 50, 91; encountering, 84–85, 86
feminist studies, 17
femurs, in ossuaries, 165, *169*
Fernwood, green cemetery in, 267
Festival of Pacific Arts, 148, 156(n9)
"Fields of Athenry, The," 191
Finisterre, Camino de Santiago pilgrims at, 71–72
Fish 'n Fins, 147, 148
Flaherty, Robert, *Man of Aran*, 128
Flores Island, 20, 43, 47, 288; rituals for the dead in, 49–51; value and worth in, 48–49
Foley, Malcolm, *Dark Tourism*, 27, 135
food, culture of, 208, 219
foodies, food cycle and, 219, 220
force d'lâge, La (*The Prime of Life;* Beauvoir), 84–85
Forestry Commission (Great Britain), 269, 278(n4)
Foucault, Michel, 79
free climbing, 21, 84–85, 86
free falling, 90–91
French Way, 61
Funasaka, Hiroshi, 144, 155(n3)
functionalism, 13
funerals, xvi, 14–15, 16, 29; gossiping at, xiv, 25–26; in Greece, 252, 256; mourning at,

246–47; rumormongering at, 286–87; selfies at, xi, 228, 237–38, 240–41; social role of, 254–55; time and, 275–76; Torajan, 101–3
Funeral Services Limited, 29
funerary archaeology, 164

games, hazardous, 78
gaming, zombie-themed, 110
Gardens of Remembrance, structure of, 275
gastronomic tourism, xiv, 206, 209, 210; authenticity, 207–8; at Spannocchia, 211–13
Gaza, bombing of, 7
Gelmirez, Diego, 60, 74(n10)
Germany, 151; ossuaries in, 24, 164, 167–69, 178
Gettysburg, 285
Gewertz, Deborah, 209
glamping, 275
Golden Gate Bridge, 88
Golgotha soil, and Church of All Saints cemetery, 166
Good Funeral Guide, The, 275
Goody, Jack, *Death, Property, and the Ancestors*, 15
Gorer, Geoffrey, xvi; on pornography of death, 6, 99
gossip, gossiping: in Greece, xiv, xvi, 25–26, 124, 246; as narrative, 255–56; social role of, 254–55, 256–57
Government Tourism Board of Western Manggarai Regency, 44
Govett's Leap, 87, 88
Grafton Bridge, 88
Grand Orange Lodge of Ireland. *See* Orange Order
Grand Tour, 6, 207
graves, along Camino de Santiago, 69–70
gravestones, in Labuan Bajo, 48, 52–53
graveyards, 5; behavior expected at, 272–73, 273, 274
Great Britain, 77, 87, 207, 285; natural burial grounds, 264, 289–90; and Northern Ireland, 192, 197
Greding, St. Martin's Basilica charnel in, 167, 173, 176
Greece: funerals in, 246, 247, 252, 256; gossiping in, xiv, xvi, 25–26, 124; relocations in, 248–49
green burials, xiv, 264, *266*, 278(n2). *See also* burials, burial grounds
green funerals, 16

Griaule, Marcel, 80
grief, grieving, 252; on social media, 228, 233
grief tourism, 238
Grimes, W. F., 87
Ground Zero, 27
guarding, corpse, 20, 47, 50–51
guides: corpse guarding by, 47, 50; at ossuaries, 171, 173, 174–75

Hagen, Gunther von, *Body Worlds* exhibition, 7, 164
Hamar, bull jumping, 91
hanging, 134
Harney, Nicholas, 257
hazards, 77–78, 79
head cheese (*sopressata*), 214–16
headhunting, Illongot, 17
Hell in the Pacific (film), 145, 155(n6), 156(n14)
heritage breeds, Cinta Senese pigs as, xiv, xvi, 25, 206, 216–17
heritage tourism: Camino de Santiago as, 58; Pacific War, 142–43, 150–54
Hertz, Robert, 17, 18, 233; on death as process, 15–16
Herzfeld, Michael, 246, 254
hiking, xiv, 84–85
Historic Preservation Office (Palau), 150, 151
hogs. *See* pigs
Home Rule movement, 197, 198, 199
homestays, 46, 111
Homo Ludens (Huizinga), 91–92
hospitality, 20, 43; and responsibility, 47, 52–55
Hospitallers, and Camino de Santiago, 60
hosts, 43
hotels, bombings, 44
Huizinga, Johan, 87; *Homo Ludens*, 91–92; on play, xii, 22, 30, 78
Humans versus Zombies, 110
humor, 5; dark, 126–27, 133–34
Hussein, Saddam, execution of, 6, 10
Hutchinson, Billy, 199
hyper-tourism, 78

identities, 236, 248; digitally mediated, 228–29
illness, death as, 8
Ilongot, 17
imagination, philosophic, 282
immigrants: Japanese, 141–42, 143–44, 145, 156(n7)

immortality, digital, 288–89
indigenous peoples, and zombies, 109–10
individuality, individualism, 290; and ossuary displays, 177, 180, 182
Indonesia, 22, 46, 110, 116(n8), 288; death rituals in, 49–50; social media in, 107–8, 115, 118(n29); tourist deaths in, xvi, 20, 44; zombies in, 4, 97, 105–6
industry of death, 4
infant mortality, in Nusa Tenggara Timur, 48, 49
Infinity Cascade, The, 130
Institute for Dark Tourism Research, 27
institutionalization, and risk taking, 90
internet: and cultural capital, 112–13; mortuary tourism, 98, 102–7
interpretive center, at Cliffs of Moher, 125, 126–30
inter-subjectivity, on social networks, 236–37
intimacy, 179
Iphofen, St. Michael church ossuary at, 167, *168*
Iraq veterans, 292–93
ireidan. See memorial tours
Ireland, 124, 128, 285. See also Cliffs of Moher
Israel, battle watching, 7
Italy, xiv, 206. See also Tuscany

Jakarta, bombings in, 44
James the Greater, St. (Santiago), 58, 59, 60, 71, 72, 73(n2) 288
Japan, and Micronesia, 141–42
Japanese, xiv, 155(n3); memorial tours, 23, 144–47; in Micronesia, 141–42, 143–44, 153–55, 156(nn7, 13); and Pacific War tourism, 148, 149, 150
Jim, on Facebook, 227–28
Jimbaran, bombings, 44
John, Augustus, 128
joking, jokes, at Cliffs of Moher, *133–34*, 135
Jolly Judge Bar, bombing of, 191
Josef II, 167
jumping, 28; liminality of, 90–91; suicide by, 87–88, 89–90, 134; from World Trade Center, 88–89

Kapferer, Jean-Noel, 254–55
Kaplica Czazek ossuary (Poland), 174
Kern, Roger, 210
Kincaid, Jamaica, *A Small Place*, 43
kinship, 255
Knight, Daniel, 251
Komodo National Park, 44
Koror, 141, 145, 146, 147
Kota, funerary rituals, 16
Kurara, Yōji, 151

Labuan Bajo, 20, 44, 48; burial responsibilities in, 52–53; rituals for the dead, 49–51; tourist death in, 45–47; treatment of tourists in, 51–52, 53–55
landowners, Tuscan, 209
landscape, 79, 126, 128; of natural burial grounds, 270–71; symbolic, 179–80
Lane, Nick, 18
Lange, Dorothea, 128
lardo, 209, 215
Lardo di Colonnata, 209
Larisa, 249
leaps of faith, 82, 83, 88
"Learning How to Die in the Anthropocene" (Scranton), 292–93
Ledge, The (film), 128–30
Legacy Contact, 230–31
Legian, bombings in, 44
leisure, xii, xiii, xiv, 28–29, 30, 191, 247; digitally mediated, 228–29
leisure class, 28, 291
Lennon, John, *Dark Tourism*, 27
Lévi-Strauss, Claude: *The Savage Mind*, 14; *Tristes Tropiques*, 14, 78–79
liminality, xiii; of jumping, 90–91
Lindemann, Klaus, 148
livestock breeds, 207; heritage, 216–17
livestock production, 212–13
LoDaaga people, 15
Logroño, 60
Londonderry, 192, 202
Lonely Tree, The, 272
Luchetti Lookout, 87
Lyng, Stephen, 90, 123

Macedonia, migrants from, 249
MacLaine, Shirley, 67
Malinowski, Bronislaw, on functionalism, 13
Mamasa Toraja, 111–12
Mandelbaum, David G., *The Meaning of Death*, 16
ma'nene' ritual, *107*, 108

Manggaraians, 46, 48; rituals, 49–50, 52; treatment of tourists, 53–55
Man of Aran (film; Flaherty), 128
marching music, 191
marginality, marginalization, 54, 113, 118(n34)
Mariana Islands, 144; Okinawans in, 141–42
martyrs, relics of, 6
Marville (France), St. Hillaire Cemetery, 166
massacres, in Northern Ireland, 192
mass leisure, 28
mate, 234
maternal mortality, in Nusa Tenggara Timur, 48, 49
Mauss, Marcel, 17, 79
May, Elaine Tyler, 218
Mayes, Frances, *Under the Tuscan Sun*, 208
McCausland, Nelson, 202–3
meadows, as burial grounds, 26
Meaning of Death, The (Mandelbaum), 16
Meat Camp, 220
meat production, 25, 206; at Spannocchia, 213–16
media, zombie tourism, 98
medical anthropology, 12
medieval period, 60, 184(n2); at Church of All Saints cemetery, 166–67
memento mori, 23, 27, 42, 63; ossuaries as, 165, 171–73, 183
memoirs, of Camino de Santiago, 67–69
memorialization, 27, 272; on Facebook, 25, 228, 231–33, 288–89
memorials, 69; Camino de Santiago, 63, *64*, *65*, 74(n4); in Palau Islands, 144–46, 150, 156(n13)
memorial services, on Peleleiu, *147*
memorial tours, 23; Palau, 142–43, 144–*47*, 148, 153–54, 155(n3)
Memorial Woodlands (Bristol), 272
memory, 23, 84, 150
Meneley, Anne, 208
meta-narrative, Cliffs of Moher Experience as, 128
metaphors, life and death, 263
mete, 46, 47, 51
mezzadria, 208–9
Michaelskappelle ossuary (Oppenheim), *169*
Micronesia: Japanese administration of, 141–42; memorial tours to, 144–45
Mifune, Toshirō, 145, 155(n6)

militancy, of tourists, 42
militants, Pakistani, 10
Miller, Daniel, 236
Mill Valley (Calif.), Fernwood green cemetery in, 267
"Minstrel Boy, The," 191
misinformation, in Labuan Bajo deaths, 46–47
mnemonic devices, bodies as, 80
mock funerals, 11
mock-suicides, YouTube videos of, 133
modernity, 91; in Toraja, 108–9
Moher. *See* Cliffs of Moher
Monaco, 85–86
monastery, at Church of All Saints, Sedlec, 166–67
money, Manggaraians and, 50, 51–52
monuments, on Camino de Santiago, 58, *64*, *65*
Moore, Billy, 202
moral entrepreneurs, 69
mortality, 281, 291; confronting, 163–64, 177; eating and, 212
morality, consumerism and, 218
mortality rates, in Nusa Tenggara Timur, 48–49
moral superiority, gossip and, 254
mortuary tourism, tourists, 22; behavior of, 103–4; among Toraja, 100–103, 104–5, 116(n13)
mortuary traditions, Torajan, 98, 99, 100–101, 102–5
mourning, 15; rumors and, 246–47
Muir Woods National Park, 290
murders, of tourists, 41, 54, 55(n2)
Murphy, Eileen, 123
Murphy, Greg, 235–36
Murphy, Natalie, 235–36
music, in Northern Ireland, 190–91, 195–96
Muslims, 60
mutual aid societies, Palau, 145

Nan'yō (South Sea), 143
Nan'yō Guntō (South Seas Islands), 141
narrative, gossip as, 255–56
nationalism, sectarian, 60
natural burial grounds, 261, 263–67; activities in, 262, 270, 271, 272–73, 277; commemoration in, 289–90; visiting, 274–75
natural environment tours, 151
nature, and death/memorializing, 272
nature reserve, Barton Glebe as, 169–70
Nenedakis, Andreas, 254

Newtownards (County Down), bombing in, 191
New Zealand, 77, 89
Ngerekebesang Island, 141, 142, 156(n11)
Niagara Falls, 88
niche tourism, 4
9/11: The Falling Man (documentary), 89
Nooteboom, Cees, 67
Northern Ireland: music in, 190–91; parading in, xiv, 24, 203(n2), 283; politics and violence in, 197–98, 202–3; Twelfth of July parade in, 192–96, 200–202
nostalgia, Japanese tourism, 143, 145, 146–47, 153–54
Nusa Tenggara Timur (NTT), living and dead in, 48–49

O'Brien, Cornelius, 123, 137(n3)
obsidian, 4
Oca, Montes de, 69
Oceanic Wildlife Society (OWS), 151, 156(n12)
offerings, tourist, 51–52
Okely, Judith, 85
Okinawa no Tou, 146
Okinawans, 156(n7); memorial tours, 145–47; in Palau, 141–42
Operation Desecrate I, 148
Oppenheim (Germany), ossuary in, xiii, 168, *169*, 173, 174–75
Orangefest, 193
Orange Order (Grand Orange Lodge of Ireland), 197, 203(n3); Twelfth of July parade, 193–96, 198
organ trafficking, 10, 18
ossuaries, xiii, 23, 24, 164, 284; authenticity of, 170–71, 182–84; in Czech Republic, 166–67; displays in, 175–76; encountering death in, 176–82; in Europe, 165–66; in Germany, 167–69; *memento mori* inscriptions in, 171–73; photography in, 173–74
Other, xv, 22; death of, 239, 246
Othering, ethnic tourism as, 113
O'Toole, Fintan, 130
OWS. *See* Oceanic Wildlife Society
Oxford University, Dangerous Sports Club, 87

Pacific War: in Micronesia, 143–44; tourist development and, 142–43, 148–55, 156(nn11, 14, 15)
Palasia Hotel, 146

Palau, xii, xiv, 23; Japanese immigrants in, 141–42; mass tourism in, 147–50; memorial tours to, 144–47; Pacific War in, 143–44; war-oriented tourism on, 150–55, 156(n11)
Palau Battle, 144, 148
Palau Cherry Blossom Association (Palau Sakura Kai), 145, 146
Palau Pacific Resort, 141, 143, 147, 155(n1)
palimpsest, Camino de Santiago as, 67
panic, encountering fear, 86
Panos the Vlach: funeral of, 26, 27; rumors about, 251–52, 256, 257; in Trikala, 248–49, 250–51; wake for, 252–53
Panourgia, Neni, 246
Parades Commission for Northern Ireland, 194–95, 200, 202
parading, parades, xiv, 24, 191, 283; Twelfth of July, 192–96, 197–202; violence at, 202–3
paramilitary groups, Northern Ireland, 191
Paris Morgue, 7
Parry, Jonathan, *Death and the Regeneration of Life*, 14–15, 286
Parsons, Talcott, 125
passports, for Camino de Santiago, 62
Patterns of Culture (Benedict), 14
peace process, Northern Ireland, 200, 202
Pearl, Daniel, 10
peasants, 208, 209
Peleliu Island, 144, 145, *147*, 150
Peleliu War Museum, 150, 154
Pentecost Island, earth diving ritual, 87
Perec, Georges, on attention to big events, 239–40
performance xiv; of music, 190–91; parading and, 195–96
personhood, 17, 176, 228
Peterson, Richard, 210
Pezzullo, Phaedra 153
Phipps, Peter, 135–36, 247
photographs, 42; of ossuaries, 173–74, 176, 178
Phuket, Vegetarian Festival, 114
physical suffering, osteological displays of, 177
Pickett's charge, 285
piety, and ossuaries, 174
pigs: Cinta Senese, 25, 206, *207*, 211–13; heritage breeds, 216–17, 282–83; in Toraja funeral rites, 104, 105
pilgrimages, xii, 6, 287–88; authenticity of, 67–69; Camino de Santiago, 20–21, 58–59,

60; end of, 71–72; experience of, 72–73; motives for, 62–66, 68–69; as self re-creation, 61–62
pilgrim-promoters, 67
pilgrims, 74(n11); on Camino de Santiago, 62–66; at Finisterre, 71–72; as tourists, 70–71; transformation of, 66–67, 72–73, 74(n7)
Pindos Mountains, 248
Piskie Cove (UK), *92*
place making, Cliffs of Moher, 126
play, xii, 22, 30, 78; mortuary-themed, 103–4
polenta, 209
Police Service of Northern Ireland (PSNI), 190, 192, 195, 200–201, 202
politics, xiv; Northern Ireland, 190, 196, 197–98, 200, 202
pollution, death as, 14
Polonius, 282
Pompeii, 6
pop culture, zombies in, 98, 99
pork, pork products, Cinta Senese, 206, 207, 209, 214–16, 218–19
pornography of death, 6, 99
pornography of the macabre, xvi, 11, 99
pornography of violence, 99
postmodernism, xiii; death and, 8–9
Potamia, 246
poverty, in Tuscany, 209
Praa Sands, jumping at, *92*
pregnancy, of Kota widows, 16
Primitive Culture (Tylor), 13
primitivity, zombies and, 109–10
process, death as, 8, 15–16
prosciutto, *215*
prosthesis (*prosthéto*), 255
Protestants: in Northern Ireland, 24, 283; parading, 191–96, 203(n3); Ulster Volunteer Force, 197–98
provocation, by YCV band, 195–96
proximity, in ossuaries, 178–79
pseudo-social engagement, with dead users, 235
PSNI. *See* Police Service of Northern Ireland
public gardens, natural burial grounds as, 268
public houses, music in, 191
public performance, of music, 190

rapes, attempted, 54
Rapport, Nigel, 255
rare breeds program, Spannocchia, 211–13
reanimated corpses, 98–99, 111
re-clothing, of Torajan corpses, 107, 108
recreation, high-risk, 90
Red Hand Commando, 191
reformation, and ossuaries, 166
refuges, on Camino de Santiago, 62
relics: Catholic, xiii, 6, 169; Pacific War, 151–*52*
religion, animism and, 13
relocation, of Vlach, 248–49
remembrance(s), xiv, 42
Renaissance, 4
Republicans, in Northern Ireland, 25
resorts, symbolic death in, 5
respect, for dead, 48, 50
responsibility, 47; for the dead, 50–51; for tourists, 20, 52–55
resting, death as, 5
Resurrection, 165, 169
reverence, of ossuaries, 178, 179
Rint, Frantisek, 167
rioting, xiv, 24, 202; at Twelfth of July parade, 194–95, 196
risings, Irish, 191
risk, risk taking, 77, 78, 79, 81, 87; at Cliffs of Moher, 130–34; death-defying, xi, 22–23, 84–86, 88; in free falling, 90–91
risk society, 91
rites of passage, 24, 42, 91
Ritual Process, The (Turner), 14
rituals, 7, 15, 16, 99; death, 234, 292; in Labuan Bajo, 48, 49–51; memorial, *147*, 155(n3); risk, 81; Torajan, 101, 106–7, 108, 114
Rivers, William H. R., 234
Robben, Antonio C. G. M., *Death, Mourning, and Burial*, 19
Rock Islands, 141, 148; World War II remnants, 149–50
Rock Islands Southern Lagoon, 148, 150
Rojek, Chris, *Ways of Escape*, 28
Roman Catholics, Catholicism, 124; and Camino de Santiago, 61, 67, 74(n11); in Northern Ireland, 24, 191, 195, 196, 197–98, 199, 200, 283; Resurrection and, 165, 169
Rosaldo, Michelle, 88
Rosaldo, Renato, 14, 15, 16–17
rumors, 257; about Panos the Vlach, 251–52, 253; as part of funeral mourning, 246–47, 286–87; social role of, 254–55
Runt of the Web, 238

rural culture, 208
rural areas, 113
Russell, Nicole, 235–36

Sa'adan Toraja, 97, 100; on Mamasa Torajans, 111–12. *See also* Toraja
sacrifices, animal, 101, 104, 113
St. Catherine church (Oppenheim), Michaelskapelle ossuary at, *169*, 174–75
St. Hilaire Cemetery (France), boxed skulls in, 166
St. Martin's Basilica ossuary (Greding), 167
St. Mary's church ossuary (Chammünster), 168
St. Michael church ossuary (Iphofen), 167, *168*
St. Patrick's Church (Carrickhill), Twelfth of July parade and, 195, 196
saints, relics of, xiii, 6
Santiago de Compostela, *59*, 61, 74(n11); pilgrimage to, xii, 20–21, 60, 287; pilgrims as tourists in, 70–71, 73
Santiago de Real (Logroño), 60
Santiago Matamoros, 60, 73(n2)
Santiago Peregrino, 60, 70, 73(n2), 288
Sartre, Jean-Paul, 88
"Sash My Father Wore, The," 196
Savage Mind, The (Lévi-Strauss), 14
scallop shell, as symbol of Santiago, 60, 74(n3), 288
Scarpato, Rosario, 208
Scheper-Hughes, Nancy, 10, 18–19, 99
Schwarzenberg family, 167
Scott, David, 197; on commemoration, 198–99
Scranton, Roy, "Learning How to Die in the Anthropocene," 292–93
scrying, 4
Seaton, Anthony V., 135, 212
second burial, 24
secularization, of ossuaries, 167
security, and violence, 42
Sedlec (Czechoslovakia), ossuary in, 166–67, 173, 174, 175
segregation, in Northern Ireland, 191
self, 17, 246
selfies, 22; at funerals, xi, 237–38, 240–41; in Indonesia, 4, 108; just before death, 228, 238–40; at ossuaries, 173–74
Selfies at Funerals blog, 237
senses, sensuality, and authentic experience, 180–81

sensual heritage, 25
September 11, 2001, World Trade Center jumpers, 88–89
Seremetakis, Nadia, 256
services, overcharging for, 46–47
sex tourism, 41
Shankill Protestant Boys, 201
sharecropping, in Tuscany, 208–9
Shewstone, 4
shipwreck diving, 148
shock sites, 10
shrines, on Camino de Santiago, 62
Siderot, on battle watching, 7
silence, of suicide, 124
Simmel, George, on adventurer as artist, 79–80
Sinn Féin, 200, 202
site managers/administrators, of ossuaries, 175–76, 182–83
skeletal remains, 180; Christian doctrine and, 174–75; display of, 175–76
skull and crossbones, 165
skulls (crania), 166, 284; in ossuaries, *168*, *169*, 175–76, 177; symbolism of, 165, 181
skydiving, 5
"slasher" movies, 6
slaughtering, pig, 213–14
slavery, 27
Sliptalk, 239
Slow Food Foundation for Biodiversity, Ark of Taste, 217–18
Slow Food Movement, 217
Small Place, A (Kincaid), 43
smell, skeletal remains and, 180, 181, 182
smoke mirrors, Aztec, 4
Snopes, on Torajan zombies, 106–7
social consciousness, 15–16
social hierarchy, in Trikala, 251
social inequality, reproducing, 209
sociality, and social media, 228
social media, 22; dead on, 25, 227–28, 233; immortality in, 288–89; in Indonesia, *107–9*, 115, 118(n29); online *persona* of, 235–36; posting and reposting on, 5–6; selfies before death, 239–40
social network, 228; of dead users, 231, 235–37; inter-subjectivity of, 236–37
social spaces, 43; of death, 8, 233–37
social status, 255, 290
Solomon Islands, death rituals in, 234

songs: Irish, 191, 195–96, 198–99, 201
sopressata, 214–16
South Korea, mock funerals, 11
South Seas Bureau (Nan'yō-chō), 141
South Seas Development Company, 142
Southwest Seaplane Base Arakabesan Island, 141, 142
souvenirs, 6–7, 42, 70
Spain, 74(n5), 91, 283–84. *See also* Camino de Santiago; Santiago de Compostela
Spanish Civil War, 69, 285, 294(n3)
Spannocchia, Tenuta di, 206; butchering at, 213–15; gastronomic tourism at, 210–13; pork products from, 215–16
Spannocchia Foundation, 211
Spellissy, Sean, *Suicide: The Irish Experience*, 124
Spence, Gusty, 197
spirits, respect for, 50
spirituality, xiii, 21; and ossuaries, 174, 179–80, 183
sport(s), 80, 191
Starkie, Walter, 68
stars, posthumous, 7
Steel, Eric, *The Bridge*, 88
stereotypes, stereotyping, 110, 208; of Vlach, 249–50, 256
stigma, of suicide, 124, 125
Stokes, Martin, 201
Stone, Philip, 27, 153
students, and zombies, 109–10
stunts, risky, 88
Suicide, Le (Durkheim), 13
Suicide: Purple Falling Man (Warhol), 88
suicide(s), 13, 136–37(n2); at Beachy Head, 20, 21; at Cliffs of Moher, xiv, 22, 123–24, 126, 134–35; jumping as, 87–90; narratives at, 124–25; tourism, 19, 29
Suicide: The Irish Experience (Spellissy), 124
suicide counselors, 28
Sukōjyō, 142
Sulawesi, 92, 100, 110. *See also* Toraja
sword, as Santiago Matamoros, 60
Symbolic Exchange and Death (Baudrillard), 8
symbolism: of Cinta Senese pigs, 219; of "Famine Song," 195–96; of Irishness, 128; of ossuaries, 179–80; of risk taking, 91; of skull and cross bones, 165; of skulls, 181; of Union flag, 192
Synge, John Milton, 128

Tana Toraja, 17, 22; mortuary ceremonies, 100–101
taxidermy, 7
teleology, of selfies-before-death, 239
Templars, 60
territory, 91
terrorists, execution videos, 10
Texas Book Depository, xii, 28
Thailand, 41, 43, 114
thanatopsis, 135, 164
thanatourism, 27, 135
therapeutic tourism, 59
Thessaloniki, 249
36th Ulster Division, 197
Three Living and Three Dead motif, as *memento mori*, 171
thrill seeking, 22, 78
Todos los Santos, 283–84
tombs, 58, 102
tombstoning, 21, 77, 91; in Cornwall, 81–83, 285–86
Tomlinson, John, 91
Toraja, 116(nn11, 13), 117(n21); fieldwork among, 99–100; funerals, 101–3; modernity in, 108–9; mortuary practices, 100–101, 104–5, 114–15; social media use, 107–8; "zombies," in, 97–98, 105–7, 110–11, 287
Toribiong, Francis, 147, 148
tour guides: corpse guarding by, 47, 50; at ossuaries, 171, 173, 174–75, 176; on respect for dead, 177–78, 179
tourism, 19, 30, 42; at Cliffs of Moher, 122–23; Micronesia, 144–45; ossuaries and, 166–71; Pacific War, 148–52, 154–55, 156(nn11, 14, 15); on Palau, 142–43, 147–48. *See also by type*
tourism industry, in Ireland, 125–26
tourist enclave, Cliffs of Moher as, 127
tourist gaze, at ossuaries, 173–74
tourists, 66, 284; authentic encounters for, 170–71; behavior of, 173–74; Cinta Senese meat products, 215–16; at Cliffs of Moher, 130–32; dark humor of, *133*–34, 135; deaths of, xvi, 20, 41–42, 43–44, 45–47; gastronomic, 208–9; guarding dead, 50–51; hospitality and responsibility for, 52–55; money from, 51–52; at ossuaries, 176–82; in Palau, 146–50; pilgrims as, 70–71, 73; at Spannocchia, 210–11; symbolic landscape of, 179–80; in Torajan highlands, 102–6, 19, 116(n3), 117(nn21, 26)
Tower Bridge, 88

tradition, landscape and, 128
transformation, 286; of pilgrims, 66–67
transformation kitchen, at Spannocchia, 212, 213
transplant tourism, 19
Transylvania, 113
tree graves, Torajan, 102
trekking, Mamasa Toraja, 112
trephination, 177
tribalism, zombies and, 109–10
Trikala, 246; Panos the Vlach in, 250–51; Vlach in, 248, 249–50, 254, 258(n1)
Tristes Tropiques (Lévi-Strauss), 14, 78–79
Troubles, 198
tsunami, in Thailand, 41, 43
Tumblr, *Selfies at Funerals* blog, 237
tunes, in Twelfth of July parade, 198–99
Turkey, Alaturbi, 91
Turner, Victor, xiii, 30, 66; *The Ritual Process*, 14
Tuscany, 206, 207; agriculture in, 208–9; Cinta Senese pigs in, 216–17; heritage breeds in, 282–83
Twain, Mark, 7
Twelfth of July parade, 197, 202; in Belfast, 192–96; music, 198–99; PSNI and, 200-201
Twitter, 236
Tylor, Edward B., 12; *Primitive Culture*, 13

UDA. *See* Ulster Defense Association
Ueki, Minoru, 145
Ulster Covenant, 197
Ulster Defense Association (UDA), 199, 200
Ulster Volunteer Force (UVF), 197–98, 199, 200, 201
Under the Tuscan Sun (Mayes), 208
Union flag, symbolism of, 192
Unionists, 24
United Irishman rebellion, 191
United Kingdom, xiv, 29, 92, 192. *See also* Cornwall; Great Britain; Northern Ireland
United Nations Educational, Scientific, and Cultural Organization (UNESCO), 60
United States: and Micronesia, 144–45; and Pacific war, 142, 148, 150–51
US National Park Service, and Peleliu Island, 150
University of Lancashire, Institute for Dark Tourism Research, 27
Urbain, Didier, 5
Urry, John, 105
UVF. *See* Ulster Volunteer Force

Valiña Sampedro, Elias, 69
value: of dead and living, 48–49; of dead tourists, 53–55
Vanuatu, 87
Vegetarian Festival, 114
videos: execution, 10; mock-suicide, 133
violence, 91; in Northern Ireland, 190, 194–95, 196, 197–98, 199–200, 202–3; recreational, 24–25; and tourism, 41, 42, 43, 54–55
Viralnova, 238
Virilio, Paul, 91
virtual reality, xv; *The Ledge*, 128–30
virtuous consumerism, 218
Visitor Center, at Cliffs of Moher, 125, 126–30
Vlach, Vlaches, 254; relocation of, 248–49; in Trikala, 249–50, 258
voyeurism, 99, 238

wae luqu, 50
wakes, 233, 252–53
walkers, walking, 28, 73(n1); Camino de Santiago, 21, 62–67, 70–71
walking dead, xv; Torajan, 105–7, 112, 287
walls, stone, at Cliffs of Moher, 130–32
Wall Street Crash, 88
Warhol, Andy, 22; *Suicide: Purple Falling Man*, 88
war memory, 23
warning signs, at Cliffs of Moher, *131*, 132
water buffalos, *102*, 104
Waterloo, souvenirs from, 6–7
Ways of Escape (Rojek), 28
wealth, displaying, 48
web sites: mortuary tourism, 102–5; on Zombie tourism, 98, 105–7
Welcome Trust, 29
Werther Effect, 134
West, Ken, 264
Western Attitudes towards Death (Ariès), 7
widows, Kota, 16
wildlife habitats, natural burial grounds as, 264, 268, 270
wildlife trusts, 267
Woking Crematorium, 264
woodland burial grounds, 26, 264, *265*, 267, 272, 273. *See also* natural burial grounds
World Heritage Sites: Rock Islands Southern Lagoon, 141, 148, 150; Santiago de Compostela as, 60
World Trade Center, jumpers from, 88–89

World War I, Ulster Volunteer Force, 197, 199
World War II: in Palau, 23, 141, 142, 143–44; tourism focused on, 148–52, 154–55, 156(nn11, 14, 15), 284–85
Wreck diving, 148
Wrexpedition, 148

Yamashita, Shinji, 143
Young Conway Volunteers; Young Citizen Volunteers (YCV), 195–96

YouTube, 133
Yugoslavia, 248

Zero fighter plane, in Palau, 148–*49*, 153–54
Zinovieff, Sofka, 254
Zombie Research Society, 106–7
"zombies," xv; on Internet, 112–13; Torajan, 4, 22, 97–98, 105–7, 110–11; western concepts of, 109–10

www.ingramcontent.com/pod-product-compliance
Ingram Content Group UK Ltd.
Pitfield, Milton Keynes, MK11 3LW, UK
UKHW042122200326
4879IPUK00002B/26